REGICIDE OR REVOLUTION?

Norah Carlin

Regicide or Revolution?

*What Petitioners Wanted,
September 1648 - February 1649*

BREVIARY STUFF PUBLICATIONS
2020

First published in 2020 by Breviary Stuff Publications,
BCM Breviary Stuff, London WC1N 3XX
breviarystuff.org.uk
Copyright © Norah Carlin, 2020
The centipede device copyright © Breviary Stuff Publications

All rights reserved. No part of this publication may be reproduced, stored in a retrieval system, or transmitted, in any form or by any means, electronic, mechanical, photocopying, scanning, recording, or otherwise, without the prior permission of Breviary Stuff Publications

A CIP record for this book is available from
The British Library

ISBN: 978-1-9161586-0-3

Contents

About the author	*vii*
Abbreviations	*viii*
Acknowledgements	*x*
Introduction	1

1 Petitions To Parliament, September - November 1648
1. London Levellers' Large Petition — 13
2. Oxfordshire — 22
3. Leicestershire — 27
4. Newcastle-Upon-Tyne — 33
5. Yorkshire — 37
6. Fleetwood's Regiment — 42
7. Four Northern Counties — 46
8. Wiltshire — 50
9. Berkshire — 56

2 Genesis Of The Army Remonstrance, September - November 1648
10. Northern Army Letters to Fairfax — 63
11. Ireton's Regiment — 70
12. Ingoldsby's Regiment — 75
13. Fleetwood's Regiment — 78
14. 'Several Regiments' — 79
15. Fleetwood's, Whalley's and Barkstead's Regiments — 82
16. Rainborowe's Regiment — 87
17. Overton's Regiment — 91
18. The Remonstrance of the Army — 94

3 Army Petitions, From The Remonstrance To Pride's Purge, November - December 1648
19. Harrison's Regiment — 109
20. Cromwell's Regiment — 114
21. Pride's and Deane's Regiments — 118
22. Pride's Regiment — 123
23. North-East Garrisons — 128
24. Hewson's Regiment — 132
25. Horton's Regiment and South Wales Garrisons — 137
26. Northumberland Horse Regiment — 141
27. Sir Hardress Waller's Brigade — 149
28. Regiments of Scroop And Saunders — 153
29. Walton's Regiment — 157
30. Sussex Garrisons — 162
31. Nottingham Castle Garrison — 165

4 Army Petitions, From Pride's Purge To The King's Trial, December 1648 - January 1649

32. General Council of Officers — 171
33. Lambert's Brigade — 176
34. Regiment of John Reynolds — 183
35. Dover Castle Garrison — 187
36. Boston Garrison — 190
37. Garrisons Of Shrewsbury and Ludlow — 192
38. Lancashire Officers — 196
39. Four Ships In The Downs — 199
40. Livesay's Regiment — 204
41. Denbigh Castle Garrison and Local Supporters — 207
42. Oxfordshire County Troop — 211
43. Portsmouth, Isle of Wight and Hurst Castle Garrisons — 214
44. Garrison of Hull — 218
45. Regiments Besieging Pontefract — 232

5 Local Petitions To The Army, From The Remonstrance To The King's Trial, November 1648 - January 1649

46. Rutland — 239
47. Berkshire — 244
48. Surrey — 247
49. 'County Of Ware' — 252
50. Bristol — 254
51. Kent — 258
52. Glamorgan — 262
53. Newport Pagnell — 266
54. Hertfordshire — 271
55. Worcestershire — 276

6 Petitions To Parliament, From Pride's Purge To The King's Execution, December 1648 - February 1649

56. Somerset — 283
57. Kent — 288
58. Garrison of Hull — 290
59. Norfolk — 292
60. Herefordshire — 296
61. Common Council of The City Of London — 303
62. South Coast and Malmesbury — 309
63. Nottinghamshire — 317
64. Surrey — 323
65. Kent — 326
66. Buckinghamshire — 331

Index — 337

About the author

Before retirement Norah Carlin was a Principal Lecturer in History at Middlesex University (London). She is also the author of *The Causes of the English Revolution* (Oxford, Blackwell for the Historical Association, 1999) and a number of articles on aspects of the seventeenth-century English revolution. Having moved back to her native Edinburgh some years ago, she is currently pursuing research on the kirk and rural society in Scotland in the century after the Reformation.

Abbreviations

(i) ACRONYMS

BL: British Library
CSPD: *Calendar of State Papers, Domestic: Charles I*, 1654-47 and 1648-49 (London, 1891-93)
EEBO: Early English Books Online (eebo.chadwyck.com).
ODNB: *Oxford Dictionary of National Biography* (Oxford University Press, 2004, as revised at www.oxforddnb.com to October 2018).
VCH: *Victoria History of the Counties of England* (published under various forms of title and specific to each county).

Note: the form BL/EEBO indicates references to the Thomason tracts in the British Library in the format required by EEBO for search by bibliographical number.

(ii) PRINTED SOURCES AND CALENDARS

Commons Journal: *Journal of the House of Commons*, vols 4-6 (London, 1802).
Clarke Papers: William Clarke (ed. C.H. Firth), *Clarke Papers: Selections from the papers of William Clarke, Secretary to the Council of the army, 1647-1649, and to General Mock and the commanders of the army in Scotland, 1651-1660* (London, Camden Society, 1891-1901).
Hamilton Papers: Samuel Rawson Gardiner (ed.), *The Hamilton Papers* (Camden Society vol.27, 1880).
Firth & Rait: *Acts and Ordinances*: C.H. Firth and R.S. Rait, *Acts and Ordinances of the Interregnum, 1642-1660* (London, 1911).
Rushworth, *Historical Collections*: John Rushworth, *Historical Collections of Private Passages of State* (London, 1721).

Note: in referring to major sources available online, page numbers have been ignored in favour of dates (calendars) or names (where published in alphabetical order).

(iii) SECONDARY SOURCES

Ashton, *Counter-Revolution*: Robert Ashton, *Counter-Revolution, The Second Civil War and its Origins, 1646-8* (New Haven, CT and London, Yale University Press, 1994).
Firth & Davies, *Regimental History*: Charles Harding Firth and Godfrey Davies, *The Regimental History of Cromwell's Army* (Oxford, Clarendon, 1940).

Gardiner, *Great Civil War*: Samuel Rawson Gardiner, *History of the Great Civil War* (London, Windrush Press, 1987 edition).

Gentles, *New Model Army*: Ian Gentles, *The New Model Army in England, Scotland and Ireland, 1645-1653* (Oxford, Blackwell, 1992).

Rees, *Leveller Revolution*: John Rees, *The Leveller Revolution* (London, Verso, 2017).

Underdown, *Pride's Purge*: David Underdown, *Pride's Purge, Politics in the Puritan Revolution* (paperback edition, London, Allen and Unwin, 1985).

Wanklyn, *Reconstructing the New Model*: Malcolm Wanklyn, *Reconstructing the New Model Army, vol. 1: Regimental Lists April 1645 to May 1649* (Solihull, Helion, 2015).

Woolrych, *Soldiers and Statesmen*: Austin Woolrych, *Soldiers and Statesmen, The General Council of the Army and its Debates, 1647-1648* (Oxford, Clarendon, 1987).

Acknowledgements

Over two decades of intermittent research and writing about these texts (beginning after a conference on the 350th anniversary of the regicide) I have benefited from the help and advice of too many people to remember, and must apologise for any culpable omissions. Prominent among them have been Ariel Hessayon, Sean Kelsey, Joyce Macadam, Jason Peacey, Stephen Roberts, the late Ian Roy, and other members of the seventeenth-century British political history seminar at the Institute of Historical Research in London 2002-06. Jacqueline Eales, Peter Seddon, Alan Thomson and Edward Vallance have commented on my research and kindly shared their own with me. Any errors are my own responsibility. Above all, I have to thank Paul Mangan for taking an interest and encouraging me to complete the work when I had put it aside for several years.

Introduction

To tell the whole story of the English Civil War from its origins, or even from its outbreak in 1642, would require a far longer introduction than is possible here. Readers interested in a longer-term perspective on the revolutionary events of 1648-9 may care to read some of the general works suggested below. The focus here will be on the developments that in the shorter term led up to the purging of Parliament, the trial and execution of King Charles I, the abolition of the monarchy and House of Lords, and the declaration of the English republic or Commonwealth. All the documents included in this study, except the last, were composed and subscribed over a period of five months, between the opening of Parliament's negotiations with the king on the Isle of Wight in September 1648 and his execution at Whitehall on 30 January 1649; though a handful did not reach their intended recipients, or were not printed, until after the king's death. Petitions are widely recognised as having played a part in these developments by influencing the political and military leaders who took action at the time.

There has never been a comprehensive examination of the content and background of these petitions, though isolated quotations have often been used to dramatic effect. Some historians have little interest in the texts, maintaining that they represent no more than a propaganda campaign engineered by a few individuals to justify their own actions. Specific petitions are sometimes attributed to individual leaders without examining their actual content and circumstances. Only presenting the whole body of surviving petitions in all their diversity, together with as much information as can be found about the background and circumstances of each, can offer a real prospect of assessing their contribution to the revolutionary situation. We must start by recognising that they were responding to events as they occurred, and resist the temptation to see them as causing the events which we know followed. The execution of King Charles I is an especially tempting focus of hindsight. The place of each petition in the sequence of events will be made clear wherever possible, but an outline of the most important issues as they stood in late 1648 may be helpful here.

The crisis resulting from several years of civil war in England, Scotland and Ireland was still dangerously unresolved, despite the fact that the king had been defeated by the armies of his English and Scottish parliaments. Militarily, the royalist cause had never recovered from its defeat by the New Model Army at Naseby in June 1645. Eleven months later, Charles had turned himself in at the Scottish army headquarters in Nottinghamshire after a bizarre journey in disguise from Oxford via Norfolk. Over two years had passed since then with no political or constitutional settlement, the three kingdoms hanging in the balance between war and peace. Meanwhile divisions grew within Parliament and among its supporters. Presbyterians and Independents (named after religious affiliations but not narrowly defined by them) disagreed over what kind of settlement they wanted in church and state, and how to achieve it. Localised risings against Parliament's rule broke out again in England and Wales from April 1648, and a new Scottish army crossed the border in July, this time to fight for the king.

The New Model Army had been raised by the English parliament in 1645, to reform and unify its forces after more than two years of inconclusive civil war. It was commanded by Sir Thomas Fairfax, with Oliver Cromwell as his lieutenant-general, and promotion was by merit rather than birth or patronage. Though triumphant in battle, the New Model's dramatic and unprecedented interventions on the political scene had so far failed to settle anything. An alliance between the common soldiers and the more radical of their officers had averted a threat of disbandment in early 1647, and after a detachment of troopers seized the king from Parliament's custody, the army leaders took the political initiative. In July 1647 they offered the king a prospect of early restoration, conditional on concessions regarding religious freedom and the reform of Parliament that he found unacceptable. Playing for time in the hope of reviving his cause, Charles accepted neither these proposals nor the English and Scottish parliaments' terms, which were considerably harsher and insisted on a Presbyterian church settlement.

In October 1647 the New Model Army turned to discussing more radical schemes, which would have re-shaped parliamentary constituencies and extended the right to vote, as well as stripping the monarchy of all its legislative and much of its executive power. At Putney a General Council of the army, including representatives of the common soldiers as well as officers, debated a proposed new constitution, *An Agreement of the People*, put forward by radicalised soldiers and their civilian allies. But the discussions proved divisive. The army commanders brought the meetings to an inconclusive end, and the political situation was soon transformed by the king's escape from custody at Hampton Court. Charles got only as far as the Isle of Wight, however. He was stopped and imprisoned there by the military governor of the island, Colonel Robert Hammond, but from his captivity at Carisbrooke Castle he plotted to re-open the civil war. By a secret pact called the Engagement, the Scottish parliamentary leaders undertook to raise a new army for him; and he did not give up hope of escaping from Carisbrooke, or of renewing the military struggle with help from Europe and Ireland.

The English parliament, frustrated by the king's persistent rejection of its demands, suspended all negotiations by a 'Vote of No Addresses' in January 1648. The army's Council of Officers, now meeting without the common soldiers' representatives, declared their support for this resolution, and for 'the settling and securing of the Parliament and kingdom without the king, and against him' if he remained obstinate. In an official declaration justifying their own resolution, Parliament published a wide range of charges against Charles: practising arbitrary rule, raising unconstitutional and oppressive taxes, secretly inciting the Catholic Irish to rebellion in 1641, inviting his Danish relatives to invade his kingdom, and even colluding in the alleged poisoning of his own father, as well as making war on his own people. At the end of April a large body of army officers, meeting for a prayer session at Windsor before setting out to suppress a new royalist rising in Wales, bitterly repented of their own past approaches to the king and resolved, according to a later account, to have no more dealings with 'Charles Stuart, that man of blood'.

The English parliamentary forces were successful again in this second civil war. The regional risings were suppressed, the parliamentary hold on London was maintained, and the Scots were defeated at Preston in late August. The royalist stronghold of Colchester (Essex) fell in August after a bitter siege, though Pontefract castle in Yorkshire would not surrender until March 1649. Yet the captive king still showed no sign of coming to terms with the victors. Parliament and the army faced increasing unpopularity due to the costs and hardship of the military and political stand-off; while a dismally wet summer in 1648 raised the prospect of a bad harvest, with the possibility of food riots. Many parliamentarians began to fear popular disturbances more than they feared compromising with the king. In response to pressure to bring Charles to London and make peace, the Vote of No Addresses was repealed. The king agreed to new talks at Newport on the Isle of Wight, Parliament still fearing that bringing him to London would trigger an uncontrollable royalist revival and orgy of revenge.

The Newport 'treaty', or negotiations as the word meant at the time, opened on 18 September 1648. Parliament's first condition for restoring Charles to a modified role in government was his acknowledgement that Parliament had fought a just war in its own defence, exonerating all who had taken up arms against him. The king's provisional acceptance of this clause was believed by many of his opponents to be an admission of his own responsibility for the conflict. Charles was playing for time, and is now known to have instructed his chief lieutenant in Ireland to ignore reports of royal concessions. The talks continued until late November, and after Parliament ignored the *Remonstrance* addressed to them by the Council of Officers, the New Model Army leaders resolved to intervene. Soldiers removed the king from the Isle of Wight to the more isolated fortress of Hurst Castle, and the army moved towards London. On 6 December, the day after the House of Commons voted to proceed to a settlement falling short of their own previous demands, Colonel Pride and his men were sent to exclude those members who had voted in favour. These were the actions that led up to the trial and execution of the king.

The events that stimulated the largest numbers of petitions were the negotiations at Newport, the Council of Officers' meeting that produced the *Remonstrance*, and Pride's Purge. The proportion that directly influenced this course of events may be rather small, but their very existence, along with exaggerated reports of their numbers and content, fuelled the fears of some and the confidence of others at the forefront of the political crisis. The petitioners' declared intentions progressed from stopping the Newport peace talks and bringing the king and his supporters to justice, to supporting the army's intervention and Pride's Purge, welcoming the setting up of a court to try the king and — in the last few only — showing their support for his condemnation and execution. Their evolving aims reflect the shrinking range of possible outcomes as the crisis mounted. They also show a narrowing and hardening of radical support for unprecedented and controversial actions such as purging Parliament and trying the king. Read as a whole and in context, these documents seem to have amounted to sufficient evidence of support in the provinces to encourage those who took action to go ahead. Their belief that the new regime could run the country without the previously entrenched layers of landowning gentry, regarded by many as the natural rulers of provincial England, was largely justified in eleven years of republican rule.

Royalists claimed that these were all fake petitions, written by a few individuals. Their usual suspects were Oliver Cromwell, his son-in-law Henry Ireton, the republican MP Henry Marten, and the Baptist preacher Paul Hobson. Members of Parliament alarmed by their radical content saw them as a single campaign orchestrated on a national scale by the London group known as the Levellers. Many petitions were influenced by the 'Large Petition' presented to Parliament by the Levellers in London on 11 September 1648, which stands at the head of this collection; but those that followed it are too diverse to be the work of this group alone. Although the Levellers did have circles of sympathisers outside London and the army, the reach of their ideas was longer than that of their known organisational networks.

The Levellers grew from a group of London activists and pamphleteers, who came together in 1645-6 to advocate toleration for the religious sects and Independent congregations that had multiplied during the civil war. From Parliament's claims and their own experience of London's city politics, they had also come to attach a central importance to representative government. Their coming together produced a twofold concept of liberty: on the one hand personal freedom from arbitrary rule and individual oppression, such as arrest and imprisonment without trial; and on the other, the 'liberties' enjoyed by English people as a whole, such as constitutional government through Parliament, the common law, and trial by jury. Their leaders disliked the nickname of Levellers, because it implied a redistribution of property, and a more radical belief in equality than most of them actually held. But they frequently challenged the inequality of rich and poor, and firmly held to the belief that the common people in general, not property owners alone, had a direct interest in the personal and constitutional liberties for which Parliament had fought the civil war

The Texts

All but two of the texts below appeared in print between September 1648 and 14 February 1649; Nottinghamshire's (63 below) does not appear ever to have been printed, and the revolutionary programme from the Hull garrison (44 below) was not published until six weeks after the king's death. In the seven cases where both manuscript and printed copies survive, the printed versions have been selected here for their comparative ease of reading, with the very few significant variations from the corresponding manuscripts duly indicated. Twenty-three were recorded in the official journal of the House of Commons as having been presented, read, and in some cases debated there. Eighteen of these came from named counties or cities, four from bodies of soldiers, and one from a mixed body of soldiers and others. The content of these petitions was not included in the parliamentary record, but full texts survive in print among the cheap pamphlets, broadsheets and weekly newsbooks that had multiplied many thousandfold since 1641. Through them news, political ideas and competing points of view reached a wide audience both geographically and socially, enabling and feeding an unprecedented expansion of public interest and participation in politics. Since parliamentary proceedings were an essential component of news reporting, the promoters of a petition that had been read in Parliament were naturally keen to supply their text to the press, and editors keen to procure it. The newsbook editor who claimed in late December that nearly a hundred petitions had already been published was exaggerating, but news of the petitions had certainly spread far and wide.

Meanwhile, thirty-four were addressed by units of the army to Fairfax, as commander of all the parliamentarian forces, and his Council of Officers. The earliest appear to have been spontaneous responses to news of the London Levellers' 11 September petition, but petitioning the general was soon actively encouraged by the army leadership. Some of the resulting texts were printed in batches by the army's regular printers; while a larger number were copied into weekly newsbooks. Ten more were addressed to Fairfax by groups of civilians in support of the army's intervention, following the Council of Officers' *Remonstrance* of 18 November. The closing sections of the *Remonstrance* itself are included here (at 18 below) in order to clarify what the petitions that mention it were supporting. The list of demands sent to Parliament by the leading army officers on the morning of Pride's Purge (32 below), though strictly speaking not a petition, is also included, to reinforce the point that they expected Parliament, rather than military force, to determine the consequences. By the end of December it was clear that the trial of the king would take place, though it was still uncertain whether it would end in his death, and what constitutional changes might follow.

The origins, organisation and content of each petition will be discussed in detail below, but a number of issues can be signalled here. All the texts claim to have been organised and subscribed by groups of people rather than individuals. They may show individual eccentricities or unusual turns of phrase that suggest a document drafted by one person before being agreed, with or without amendments, by a group. Inconsistencies and even incompatible demands in a petition — features that to this day would invite the comment 'composed by a committee' — are more likely to reflect traces of argument and compromise than the indecision of a single author. Since the early 1640s some petitioning campaigns had been launched by publishing an exemplary text to be shared or adapted by groups in other localities, but there is little evidence of this here, with the exception of the near-identical demands of Harrison's and Cromwell's regiments (19 and 20 below). A few petitions were agreed in the name of two or more regiments who happened to be in the same place or in close contact at the time, but each text is unique. Even those which incorporate a selection of demands from the Levellers' Large Petition make adjustments or additions to them.

The Petitioners

Although the petitions that came from outside the army were identified by their county or city of origin, most claimed to represent not an entire community, but members of it sharing a particular political allegiance, those 'well affected' to Parliament's cause. While royalist newsbooks assert, for example, that the petition from Oxfordshire is false because 'the generality' of that county are royalist, the petition claims to represent specifically the 'many well-affected' among the inhabitants. Petitions from 'divers' (some) of a county's inhabitants, its ministers or gentry, or the 'honest inhabitants', indicate a realistic awareness that in a divided nation, supporters of a cause had to stand up and be counted, despite the traditional aversion to party divisions. Bodies such as the grand jury of a county or the corporation of a city could, however, traditionally claim to represent their whole community. In Newcastle (4), London (61) Somerset (56) and Herefordshire (60), local government being in the hands of parliamentarian supporters enabled such claims to be made.

Information about the number of subscribers is unfortunately thin. All the surviving lists, whether in print or a single hand, are copies. Signatures collected on separate sheets would probably be engrossed (copied on to continuous sheets), as they were for the nation-wide Protestation of 1642. A few petitions claim the support of hundreds or thousands. The Levellers' organisation in London was probably capable of collecting large numbers of signatures in the Independent congregations and other meeting-places they frequented; though John Lilburne is known to have said that the point of collecting signatures was not the number but the process of 'informing the people of their liberties and privileges'. The two manuscript copies of the January 1649 petition from Kent (65) each list 1135 names; while the Nottinghamshire men who sent Colonel John Hutchinson their petition with 309 (63) apologised for the number subscribing being 'but few', suggesting higher expectations were normal. The manuscript version of the Herefordshire petition bears twenty-seven names and the printed one (60) fifty-nine.

The soldiers' petitions are addressed to Fairfax in the names of sixteen regiments of the New Model Army, four additional forces raised in the second civil war, twenty-six garrisons, three mixed bodies of soldiers and others, and four ships of the navy. Officers may have considered themselves entitled to represent the men under their command with or without consultation, but some are more specific. The north-east garrisons' petition (23), for example, claims to be signed 'by us the Officers of the said Garrisons with the joynt consent of the Soldiers, &c'. The names of six officers of Ireton's regiment were printed with their petition (11), while seventeen autograph signatures survive on a letter to Cromwell from his own officers (20), and a list of eighteen of Overton's in a single hand (17). The minutes of the council of northern army officers held at Pontefract on 12 December (33) give the fullest account of discussions leading to a petition. It should not be assumed that officers were less radical than the men they commanded, as some of the rank and file agitators of 1647 had since been promoted. Literacy rates in the army were high for their time, and reading aloud from the latest publications could carry the latest news to a wider audience.

The Contents

Though readers must assess the contents of the petitions for themselves, some pointers can be offered here to the most important issues. The first — foremost in historians' minds though not in every petition text — is the demand that the king must be 'brought to justice'. This phrase is still familiar to us in the context of war crimes and terrorism, while the possibility of a civil war being followed by reconciliation without trials and retribution was rare indeed before the late twentieth century. Whether 'justice' implies capital punishment nowadays depends largely on which side of the Atlantic the word is used, and we should not assume too readily that those who made this call in 1648-9 were demanding the king's death. The biblical command justifying capital punishment for killing, 'Whoever sheds man's blood, by man shall his blood be shed' (Genesis: 9,6) is cited in only two of the petition texts, one of them composed after the king's trial had already begun and published after his execution (28, 65). Old Testament stories of leaders punished by god for failing to kill tyrants and oppressors appeared in many pamphlets and sermons at the time; there are, however, only a few references to these biblical precedents in the petitions. As Charles continued to evade a settlement, and was believed to be planning a new civil war even from his prison, bringing him to justice did move to the forefront of petitioners' concerns; but several envisage the possibility that he might not be found guilty of all those charges of which he was being accused.

Eighteen texts cite the belief that a land which has been polluted by bloodshed must be purged by the blood of those responsible, in order to appease god's anger. Fewer than half of these single out the king, even when insisting that the justice they demand must be 'impartial' or equal, the same for all the guilty men from the highest to the lowest. Logically, 'the highest to the lowest' of the guilty parties need not include the king if he is not specifically mentioned; alternative candidates for 'highest' could include, for example, the king's cousin and leader of the Engagement army, the Duke of Hamilton. Several petitions that do mention the king refer to him only as 'the capital offender' among many who must be brought to justice. Readers may search the texts below in vain, however, for the words said to have been used at the officers' prayer meeting in the spring of 1648, 'Charles Stuart, that Man of Blood'. This phrase has been given a crucial importance by historians since Patricia Crawford suggested, in 1977, that belief in Charles's personal blood guilt provided the logic that justified the army's intervention in later events. 'Regiments petitioned for the prosecution of the Man of Blood', wrote Marxist Christopher Hill, and a more radical revolution failed because 'the Bible was primarily responsible for the execution of Charles I'. Though the phrase was undoubtedly current among pamphleteers and preachers, army leaders and indeed Levellers at the time, it evidently failed to resonate with petitioners.

References to bloodshed appear more frequently in the context of suffering than that of guilt. Several petitions lament the expense of 'blood and treasure' — another phrase that has curiously survived into present-day parliamentary language. They dwell on the costs of civil war, the loss of life and livelihoods, afflicting innocent civilians as well as combatants, and fear that all this bloodshed and misery may have been in vain. The soldiers' anger and frustration were sharpened by the belief that the king was stubbornly refusing to accept the judgement of god, who had repeatedly brought his armies to defeat. Many of their petitions condemn the second civil war, which although short was bloody and bitter, as an unnecessary prolongation of the misery by the royalists' refusal to accept the divine judgement manifested in the result of the first.

This was not the last war to be followed by military men lambasting politicians for failing to bring their victories in battle to fruition in the political field, nor the last body of combatants to believe that their god had a decisive hand in the outcome. Considering that the language of Christianity was commonplace in political discourse in seventeenth-century England, it is more surprising that one or two petitions do not mention god at all. Most do use religious language, some superabundantly, and characterise their subscribers' participation in civil war and national politics as a religious and moral commitment. But demands relating exclusively to religion, such as the abolition of tithes or freedom of worship, appear in only a few.

All the petitioners agree, explicitly or implicitly, that Parliament had fought a just war as the English people's representative, defending the liberties, laws, freedom, 'common right' or birthrights of the whole nation. If these liberties were not secured, the war would have been fought in vain, which appeared only too possible if the Newport Treaty were to be successful and the king brought back to London. Several demand the abolition of the 'negative voices' or veto over legislation enjoyed by the king and House of Lords; or agree with the Levellers that the House of Commons should simply declare itself the supreme authority in the nation. A significant re-definition of England's ancient constitution was needed, they believed, to secure a lasting settlement.

The Levellers' Large Petition (1 below) also puts forward a list of over thirty desirable reforms in government, law and society: from annual elections, non-interference by government in religious belief and worship; and the abolition of tithes, conscription and imprisonment for debt; to reforms in public finance, taxation, and trade. Many subsequent petitions show knowledge of and support for these reforms, and half a dozen include a selection, or their own similar proposals. Free quarter — the requisitioning of lodgings and supplies for the army without payment — is a common theme, complained of not only by local and regional petitioners, but by soldiers themselves, who knew how unpopular it made them. Some saw it as a deliberate conspiracy to withhold payment from the army in order to stir up people against them. Many petitions plead for additional resources for their own county, locality, regiment or garrison; but no petition is devoted only to bread-and-butter issues. The public debt incurred by Parliament during the wars is frequently mentioned, and many proposals for the reform of public finances are offered, usually through some form of decentralisation: local taxes to be spent on local needs.

There are many reasons for reading the petitions as a whole. The texts show that not even the soldiers' petitions were dominated by the 'vicious regicidal attack, homing in on Charles as an individual' (Sarah Barber) alleged by many historians in recent times, with or without the most lurid quotations from one or two texts. A more difficult issue is the assertion that the petitioners were motivated chiefly by religious zeal rather than political consciousness. This is in seventeenth-century terms a false dichotomy: religion, especially in the Calvinist traditions of England and Scotland, was widely regarded as an integral part of politics, and vice versa. The petition texts occasionally juxtapose them in terms such as 'zeal to the glory of god and affection to the good of the kingdom' (5). The insistence of some historians on seeing any text that uses religious language as essentially religious may be as distorting as some early Marxist historians' reduction of everything to the economic dimension.

The language of politics rooted in classical republicanism also has a place in our texts: the public good or public interest, the safety of the state, liberty (or liberties), equity, and rights. Petitioners can appeal to nature and reason as well as conscience, cite classical maxims alongside Old Testament references, and address the army favoured by god as 'blessed patriots' (55), hailing Fairfax as god's instrument but also *Pater Patriae*, father of the fatherland (54). Ideas about England's history and constitution had spread well beyond the educated elite, through the politicisation and participation of local communities in national affairs, not to mention the experience of the New Model Army. Though these petitions were in some cases prompted from above, the evidence suggests that they were actually produced by groups of activists in meetings and discussion, and gained the support of many more in subscriptions. What they chose to say and support is worthy of our attention for their own sake, and may serve to put the actions of the leaders of the English revolution in a new perspective.

A Note On Language

To avoid distortions of meaning, the texts are presented with the original spelling and punctuation. Where words still in common use have changed their meaning drastically (e.g. 'resentment' meaning a feeling but not necessarily a negative one), the contemporary meaning has been indicated in the square brackets [ ] that signal editorial intervention, which has been kept to a minimum.

Further Reading

Austin Woolrych, *Britain in Revolution* (Oxford University Press, 2002)
Jason Peacey, *Print and Public Politics in the English Revolution* (Cambridge University Press, 2013)
David Underdown, *Pride's Purge, Politics in the Puritan Revolution* (London, Allen and Unwin, 1985)
John Rees, *The Leveller Revolution* (London, Verso, 2017)
Robert Ashton, *Counter-Revolution, The Second Civil War and its Origins, 1646-8* (New Haven, CT and London, Yale University Press, 1994)
Patricia Crawford, '"Charles Stuart, that man of blood"', *Journal of British Studies*, vol. 16 (1977), pp. 41-61.
Sarah Barber, *Regicide and Republicanism, Politics and Ethics in the English Revolution, 1646-1659* (Edinburgh University Press, 1998). Quotation above, p. 112.
Christopher Hill, *The English Bible and the English Revolution* (London, Allen Lane, 1993). Quotation above, p. 329.

PART ONE

PETITIONS TO PARLIAMENT

SEPTEMBER - NOVEMBER 1648

1: LONDON LEVELLERS' LARGE PETITION
11 September 1648

Context

The principal aim of this petition was to stop the planned treaty negotiations about to begin between Parliament and King Charles I. Often referred to in the texts below as 'the Large Petition', it is large in scope as well as length. After a long preamble setting out the Levellers' analysis of the causes and outcome of the civil wars, their list of so far unfulfilled desires begins with a constitutional programme aimed at clarifying and strengthening the principle of representative government. In their view, such a settlement would justify all the actions of the House of Commons since 1641. If this is not achieved, the guilt for all the blood that has been shed will fall on Parliament and all who fought for it. Wide-ranging legal, social and economic reforms are also envisaged here, including religious freedom without any of the qualifications or reservations proposed by the Levellers at other times.

The petition's call for justice against those who had caused and protracted the civil wars appears only near the end, though hindsight has awarded these two clauses (25 and 27) more attention than all the rest. Nevertheless, this cannot be seen as a call for the king's death, despite previous discussion of this possible outcome among the Levellers, army radicals and Independent preachers. The focus of concern was still on Parliament's demand for the exemption of named royalist 'delinquents' from any general pardon or Act of Oblivion. The English and Scottish parliaments had proposed in 1646 that an Act of Oblivion or general pardon for wartime acts should be passed, but with a long list of individuals to be excepted from it. The army's *Heads of the Proposals* in 1647 had offered that only five should be 'reserved to the further judgement of the Parliament', and haggling at Westminster over the numbers and names continued throughout the Newport negotiations. As Charles steadfastly refused to sacrifice any of his friends, the frustration of the expectation that at least a few royalists' heads would roll led, perhaps inevitably, to a focus on the king himself.

Text

To the Right Honorable, The Commons of England, In Parliament Assembled.

The humble Petition of divers wel affected Persons inhabiting the City of London, Westminster, the Borough of Southwark, Hamblets, and places adjacent. With the Parliaments Answer thereunto. BL/EEBO: E.464[5]

[The binding of pages in the wrong order has been rectified here, and some obvious misprints corrected in the light of the other surviving texts listed below.]

Sheweth, That although we are as earnestly desirous of a safe and wel-grounded Peace, and that a finall end were put to all the troubles and miseries of the Common-wealth, as any sort of men whatsoever: Yet considering upon what grounds we engaged on your part in the late and present Wars, and how far (by our so doing) we apprehend ourselves concerned, Give us leave (before you conclude us by the Treaty in hand) to acquaint you first with the ground and reason which induced us to aid you against the King and his Adherents. Secondly, What our Apprehensions are of this Treaty. Thirdly, What we expected from you, and do still most earnestly desire.

Be pleased therefore to understand, that we had not engaged on your part, but that we judged this honourable House to be the supream Authority of England, as chosen by, and representing the People; and entrusted with absolute power for redresse of Grievances, and provision for Safety: and that the King was but at the most the chief publike Officer of this Kingdom, and accomptable to this House (the Representative of the People, from whom all just Authority is, or ought to be derived) for discharge of his Office: And if we had not bin confident hereof, we had bin desperately mad to have taken up Armes or to have bin aiding and assisting in maintaining a War against Him; The Lawes of the Land making it expresly a crime no lesse than Treason for any to raise War against the King.

But when we considered the manifold oppressions brought upon the Nation, by the King, His Lords, and Bishops; and that this Honourable House declared their deep sence thereof; and that (for continuance of that power which had so opprest us) it was evident the King intended to raise Forces, and to make War; and that if he did set up his Standard, it tended to the dissolution of the Government: upon this, knowing the safety of the People to be above Law, and that to judge thereof appertained to the Supream Authority, and not to the Supream Magistrate, and being satisfyed in our Consciences, that the publike safety and freedom was in imminent danger, we concluded we had not only a just cause to maintain; but the supream Authority of the Nation, to justifie, defend, and indempnifie us in time to come, in what we should perform by direction thereof; though against the known Law of the Land, or any inferiour Authority, though the highest.

And as this our understanding was begotten in us by principles of right reason, so were we confirmed therein by your own proceedings, as by your condemning those Judges who in the case of Ship-money had declared the King to be Judge of safety; and by your denying Him to have a Negative voice [veto] in the making of Laws; where you wholly exclude the King from having any share in the supream Authority: Then by your casting the Bishops out of the House of Lords, who by tradition also, had bin accounted an essential part of the supream Authority; And by your declaring to the Lords, That if they would not joyn with you in setling the Militia, (which they long refused) you would settle it without them, which you could not justly have done, and [if] they had any real share in the supream Authority.

These things we took for real Demonstrations, that you undoubtedly knew your selves to be the supream Authority; ever weighing down in us all other your indulgent expressions concerning the King or Lords. It being indeed impossible for us to believe that it can consist either with the safety or freedom of the Nation, to be governed either by 3. or 2. Supreams, especially where experience hath proved them so apt to differ in their Judgements concerning Freedom or Safety, that the one hath been known to punish what the other hath judged worthy of reward; when not only the freedom of the people is directly opposite to the Prerogatives of the King and Lords, but the open enemies of the one, have been declared friends by the other, as the Scots were [in July 1648] by the House of Lords.

And when as most of the oppressions of the Common-wealth have in all times bin brought upon the people by the King and Lords, who nevertheless would be so equal in the supream Authority, as that there should be no redress of Grievances, no provision for safety, but at their pleasure. For our parts, we profess our selves so far from judging this to be consistent with Freedom or Safety, that we know no great cause Wherefore we assisted you in the late Wars, but in hope to be delivered by you from so intollerable, so destructive a bondage, so soon as you should (through Gods blessing upon the Armies raised by you) be enabled.

But to our exceeding grief, we have observed that no sooner God vouchsafeth you victory, and blesseth you with success, and thereby enableth you to put us and the whole Nation, into an absolute condition of freedom and safety: but according as ye have bin accustomed, passing by the ruine of a Nation, and all the bloud that hath bin spilt by the King and his Party, ye betake your selvs to a Treaty with him, thereby puting him that is but one single person, and a publike Officer of the Common-wealth, in competition with the whole body of the people, whom ye represent; not considering that it is impossible for you to erect any authority equall to your selves; and declared to all the world that you will not alter the ancient Government, from that of King, Lords, and Commons: not once mentioning (in case of difference) which of them is supream, but leaving that point (which was the chiefest cause of all our publike differences, disturbances Wars and miseries) as uncertain as ever.

In so much as we who upon these grounds have laid out our selves every way to the uttermost of our abilities: and all others throughout the land, Souldiers and others who have done the like in defence of our supream authority, and in opposition to the King, cannot but deem our selves in the most dangerous condition of all others, left without all plea of indemnity, for what we have done; as already many have found by losse of their lives & liberties, either for things done or said against the King; the law of the land frequently taking place, and precedency against and before your authority, which we esteemed supreame, and against which no law ought to be pleaded. Nor can we possibly conceive how any that have any waies assisted you, can be exempt from the guilt of murders and robbers, by the present laws in force, if you persist to disclaime the Supreame Authority, though their owne conscience do acquit them, as having opposed none but manifest Tyrants, Oppressors and their adherents.

And whereas a Personall Treaty, or any Treaty with the King, hath been long time held forth as the only means of a safe & wel-grounded peace; it is well known to have been cryed up principally by such as have been dis-affected unto you; and though you have contradicted it: yet it is believed that you much fear the issue; as you have cause sufficient, except you see greater alteration in the King and his party then is generally observed, there having never yet been any Treaty [negotiation] with him, but was accompanied with some underhand dealing; and whilst the present force upon him (though seeming liberty) will in time to come be certainly pleaded, against all that shall or can be agreed upon: nay, what can you confide in if you consider how he hath been provoked; and what former Kings upon lesse provocations have done, after Oaths, Laws, Charters, Bonds, Excommunications, and all ties of Reconsilliations, to the destruction of all those that had provoked and opposed them: yea, when your selves so soone as he had signed those bils in the beginning of this Parliament, saw cause to tell him, That even about the time of passing those bills, some design or other was one fact which if it had taken effect would not only have rendred those bills fruitlesse, but have reduced you a worse condition of confusion than that wherein the Parliament found you.

And if you consider what new wars, risings, revolting invasions, and plottings have been since this last cry for a Personall Treaty, you will not blame us if we wonder at your hasty proceedings thereunto: especially considering the wonderfull victories which God hath blessed the Army withall.

We professe we cannot chuse but stand amazed to consider the inevitable danger we shall be in, though all things in the Propositions were agreed unto, the Resolutions of the King and his party have been perpetually violently and implacably prosecuted & manifested against us; and that with such scorn and indignation, that it must be more than such ordinary bonds that must hold them.

And it is no lesse a wonder to us, that you can place your own security therein, or that you can ever imagine to see a free Parliament any more in England.

The truth is (and we see we must either now speak it or for ever be silent,) We have long expected things of an other nature from you, and such as we are confident would have given satisfaction to all serious people of all Parties.

1. That you would have made good the supreme of the people, in this Honourable House, from all pretences of Negative Voices, either in King or Lords.
2. That you would have made laws for election of representatives yearly and of course without writ or summons.
3. That you would have set expresse times for their meeting Continuance and Dissolution: as not to exceed 40 or 50 daies at the most, and to have fixed an expressed time for the ending of this present Parliament.

4. That you would have exempted matters of Religion and Gods worship from the compulsive or restrictive power of any Authoritie upon earth, and reserved to the supreme authoritie an uncompulsive power only of appointing a way for the publick, whereby abundance of misery, prosecution, and hart-burning would for ever be avoyded.
5. That you would have disclaimed in your selvs and all future Representatives, a power of Pressing and forcing any sort of men to serve in warrs, there being nothing more opposite to freedom, nor more unreasonable in an authoritie impowered for raising monies in all occasions, for which, and a just cause, assistants need not be doubted: the other way serving rather to maintain in justice and corrupt parties.
6. That you would have made both Kings, Queens, Princes, Dukes, Earls, Lords, and all Persons, alike liable to every Law of the Land, made or to be made; that so all persons even the Highest might fear & stand in aw and neither violate the publick peace, nor private right of person or estate, (as hath been frequent) without being lyable to accompt as other men.
7. That you would have freed all Commoners from the jurisdiction of the Lords in all cases: and to have taken care that all tryalls should be only of twelve sworn men, and no conviction but upon two or more sufficient known witnesses.
8. That you would have freed all men from being examined against themselves, and from being questioned or punished for doing of that against which no Law hath bin provided.
9. That you would have abbreviated the proceedings in Law, mitigated and made certain the charge thereof in all particulars.
10. That you would have freed all Trade and Marchandising from all Monopolizing and Engrossing, by Companies or otherwise.
11. That you would have abolished Excise, and all kind of taxes, except subsidies, the old and onely just way of England.
12. That you would have laid open all late Inclosures of Fens, and other Commons, or have enclosed them onely or chiefly to the benefit of the poor.
13. That you would have considered the many thousands that are ruined by perpetual imprisonment for debt, and provided to their enlargement.
14. That you would have ordered some effectual course to keep people from begging and beggery, in so fruitful a Nation as through Gods blessing this is.
15. That you would have proportioned Punishments more equal to offences; that so mens Lives and Estates might not be forfeited upon trivial and slight occasions.
16. That you would have removed the tedious burthen of Tythes, satisfying all Impropriators, and providing a more equal way of maintenance for the publike Ministers.
17. That you would have raised a stock of Money of those many confiscated

Estates you have had, for payment of those who contributed voluntarily above their abilities, before you had provided for those that disbursed out of their superfluities.

18. That you would have bound your selves and all future Parliaments from abolishing propriety [property], levelling mens Estats, or making all things common.

19. That you would have declared what the duty or busines of the Kingly office is, and what not, and ascertained the Revenue, past increase or diminution, that so there might never be more quarrels about the same.

20. That you would have rectified the election of publike Officers for the Citie of London, of every particular Company therin, restoring the Comunalty thereof to their just Rights, most unjustly withheld from them, to the producing and maintaining of corrupt interest, opposite to common Freedom, and exceedingly prejudecal to the trade and manufactures of this Nation.

21. That you would have made full and ample reparations to all persons that had bin oppressed by sentences in high Commission, Star-Chamber, and Council Board, or by any kind of Monopolizers, or projectors, and that out of the estates of those that were authors, actors or promoters of so intollerable mischiefs, and that without much attendance.

22. That you would have abolished all Committees, and have conveyed all businesses into the true method of the usuall Tryalls of the Commonwealth.

23. That you would not have followed the example of former tyrannous and superstitious Parliaments, in making Orders, Ordinances or lawes, or in appointing punishments concerning opinions or things super-naturall stiling some blasphemies others heresies; when as you know your selves easily mistaken and that divine truths need no human helps to support them: such proceedings having bin generally invented to divide the people amongst themselves, and to affright men from that liberty of discourse by which Corruption & tyranny would be soon discovered.

24. That you would have declared what the businesse of the Lords is, and ascertain their condition, not derogating them the Liberties of other men, that so there might be an end of striving about the same.

25. That you would have done Justice upon the Capitall Authors and Promoters of the former or late Wars, many of them being under your power: Considering that mercy to the wicked, is cruelty to the innocent: and that all your lenity doth but make them the more insolent and presumptuous.

26. That you would have provided constant pay for the Army, now under the Command of the Lord Gen. Fairfax, and given rules to all Judges, and all other publike Officers throughout the Land for their indempnity, and for the saving harmlesse all that have any wayes assisted you, or that have said or done any thing against the King, Queen, or any of his party since the begining of this Parl. without which any of his party are in a better

condition then those who have served you; nothing being more frequent with them, then their reviling of you and your friends.

The things and worthy Acts which have bin done and atchived by this Army and their Adherents (how ever ingratefully suffered to be scandalized as Sectaries and men of corrupt Judgements) in defence of the just authority of this honourable House, and of the common liberties of the Nation, and in opposition to all kind of Tyranny and oppression, being so far from meriting an odious Act of Oblivion, that they rather deserve a most honourable Act of perpetual remembrance, to be as a patern of publike vertue, fidelity, and resolution to all posterity.

27. That you would have laid to heart all the abundance of innocent bloud that hath bin spilt, and the infinite spoil and havock that hath been made of peaceable harmlesse people, by express Commissions from the King; and seriously to have considered whether the justice of God be likely to be satisfyed, or his yet continuing wrath appeased, by an Act of Oblivion.

These and the like we have long time hoped you would have minded, and have made such an establishment for the Generall peace and contentfull satisfaction of all sorts of people, as should have bin to the happines of all future generations, and which we most earnestly desire you would set your selves speedily to effect; whereby the almost dying honour of this most honourable House, would be again revived, and the hearts of your Petitioners and all other well affected people, be a fresh renewed unto you, the Freedom of the Nation (now in perpetuall hazard) would be firmly established, for which you would once more be so strengthened with the love of the people, that you should not need to cast your eyes any other wayes (under God) for your security: but if all this availeth nothing, God be our Guide, for men sheweth us not a way for our preservation.

The house received this Petition, and returned answer thereunto which was to this effect, viz That the house gave them thanks for their great paines, and care to the publike good of the Kingdom, and would speedily take their humble desires into their serious consideration.

Other editions

To the right honourable the Commons of England, in Parliament assembled...
    BL/EEBO: 669.f.13[16].
The Moderate, No. 9, (5-12 September 1648), BL/EEBO: E.462[32].
A. L. Morton (ed.), *Freedom in Arms, A Selection of Leveller Writings* (London, Lawrence and Wishart, 1975), pp. 181-94.
Andrew Sharp (ed.), *The English Levellers* (Cambridge University Press, 1998), pp. 131-9.

Background

The composition and organisation of this petition was undoubtedly one of the greatest achievements of the Leveller activists' organisation in and around London. Parliament had rejected their first major petition, in March 1647, and ordered it to be burned by the common hangman. In the months that followed, their organisational efforts had been directed mainly at a united front with radicalised soldiers in the New Model Army. This alliance came to a peak at Putney in late October with the introduction of a programme for radical constitutional reform, *An Agreement of the People*, into the debates of the General Council of the New Model Army, which included representatives of the common soldiers as well as the officers. The army leadership, fearful of a more radical outcome than they wished, closed down the debates, dispersed the army, and took disciplinary action against the regiments who challenged the crackdown by appearing against orders at Ware on 15 November. The Levellers and their friends among the soldiers were far from crushed, however. By January 1648 the London leaders were planning another major petitioning campaign. At a meeting in Wapping, when the usefulness of addressing Parliament again was called in question because it had 'never done us any Right', John Lilburne replied that Parliament was the only visible authority for the time being.

At the same time, the Leveller leaders had not given up on the idea of a general agreement for the reform or redefinition of the constitution, to be legislated by Parliament, adopted by mass popular subscription, or contracted between electors and their representatives. Several further versions surfaced in print during 1648, and the London Levellers would be quick to seize the opportunity to revive the project in the Council of Officers the following December. But because the disturbing events of the summer of 1648 had begun with anti-parliamentary petitions, followed by the Presbyterian-led surge demanding a personal treaty with the king, counter-petitioning against these movements took priority. The Large Petition became an extension and amalgamation of the Levellers' political ideas, together with the constitutional and legal proposals previously framed in *An Agreement of the People* (though omitting the contentious question of the electoral franchise), and the legal and social reforms they had most frequently advocated. Nor did they forget to include a repudiation of any intention to destroy private property, as they had frequently been accused of having. John Rees has aptly called it 'as comprehensive an account of what the Levellers stood for as anything they ever wrote'. Many of the petitions that follow in this collection bear witness to its effects in stimulating awareness and debate, despite its lack of impact on Parliament itself.

Though the *Commons Journal* records the reading of the petition on 11 September 1648, there is no confirmation there of the positive response printed above, and some London newsbooks say no answer was given. Two days later, a group of supporters appeared at the Parliament door protesting that their petition had been laid aside and tried to present a 'humble and speedy re-adresse', protesting at the House's 'unaccustomed bearing towards Wel-affected Petitioners … earnestly praying, that you will be pleased to reassume the consideration of the whole and every part of the said Petition, before you proceed with the Treaty intended'. This was not accepted by the house, but the royalist *Mercurius Pragmaticus* obtained the text, and published it with an account of how its supporters clamouring at the doors cried out that 'they had no use for a King, or Lords any longer' — a typical accusation from this source, which may nevertheless be true. Several Independent MPs came out to speak with them, and another was reported to have said, 'to his knowledge there were 40,000 hands to the Petition, and that the House must yield to them, or else it may be too hot to hold those that oppose it'. By this time, however, plans for the Newport Treaty were well advanced: on 13 September, as the petitioners congregated at the doors, the commissioners appointed by the Commons to negotiate for Parliament received their formal instructions.

Related sources

Commons Journal, vol. 6, 11 and 13 September 1648.
The Perfect Weekly Account, No. 26 (6-13 September 1648), BL/EEBO: E.436[5].
Perfect Occurrences, No. 89 (8-15 September 1648), BL/EEBO: E.526[5].
A Perfect Diurnall, No. 288 (11-18 September 1648), BL/EEBO: E.526[6].
Mercurius Pragmaticus, No. 25, (12-19 September 1648), BL/EEBO: E.464[12].
H. N. Brailsford, *The Levellers and the English Revolution*, ed. Christopher Hill (Manchester, Nicolls, 1961).
John Rees, *The Leveller Revolution* (London, Verso, 2017), Quotation above, p. 253.
A. L. Morton (ed.), *Freedom in Arms, A Selection of Leveller Writings* (London, Lawrence & Wishart, 1975).
Andrew Sharp (ed.), *The English Levellers* (Cambridge University Press, 1998).
Michael Mendle (ed.), *The Putney Debates of 1647: the Army, the Levellers and the English State* (Cambridge University Press, 2001).
Philip Baker and Elliot Vernon (eds.), *Agreements of the People, the Levellers, and the Constitutional Crisis of the English Revolution* (Basingstoke, Palgrave Macmillan, 2012).

2: OXFORDSHIRE

30 September 1648

Context

This petition explicitly supports the one above, selecting a few of its main points for special mention, and hints at the King's guilt while not targeting him specially for trial. It introduces a theme to be found in many of the petitions that follow: Parliament's resolution of the previous January that 'No Further Addresses' should be made to the king, after he had rejected the conditions put to him for a settlement. That resolution had been revoked in August 1648, to enable the Newport negotiations to take place. These were now proceeding rather slowly, on the basis of the propositions that Charles had rejected at Newcastle in 1646 and again at Hampton Court in August 1647, modified by the removal of matters relating to Scotland. The Scots, being still in arms against England's parliamentary forces, were not invited to the peace talks. As the time initially agreed for the treaty was forty days, opponents hoped to stop it by further mass petitioning. Meanwhile, the written answers that passed between the two sides at the treaty were read in both Houses of Parliament and openly reported in the press.

The king had agreed to recognise that Parliament fought the wars in self-defence; but only on the basis that nothing was finally agreed until the whole treaty was concluded. Other matters, such as control of the militia, were at least partly agreed; but on 25 September the subject of a church settlement was raised — the business that would draw out the negotiations to breaking point and beyond. Charles would never agree to Parliament's unqualified demand that he should accept the 1643 Covenant with the Scots and agree to Presbyterian church government and worship.

Text

The Moderate, No. 12, 26 September – 6 October 1648. BL/EEBO: E.465[25]

Dateline 30 September

A petition from the County of Oxon, subscribed by many thousands, read in the House, and no Answer given to it at present, and because of concernment, take it at large:

To the Right Honourable the House of Commons, Assembled in Parliament at Westminster.
The Humble Petition of Many well-affected in the County of Oxon.

Humbly sheweth, How well our desires are exprest in the late humble petition, presented by so many Well-affected in the City of London, Westminster and places adjacent to this Honourable House acquainting you therein with our earnest desires after a well-grounded peace, giving you the ground and reason which first moved us to engage with you against the King and all his adherents. Judging you then to be the supreame Authority of this kingdome, whom we expected to redresse all our grievances, and provide for our safety, though now of late you give as much cause to fear the contrarie. Secondly, for our apprehensions of this Treaty to be that, from which we can expect no blessing, but a Curse, as experience hath taught you in the former; therefore we humbly conceive you once Voted and Declared highly against it, but now you are turned back again to the same things; seemes strange to your friends with us, it being that your enemies so laugh at, your friends mourne for, your selves feare, and we desire you may be delivered from. Thirdly, what we long before this expected from you, and do still most earnestly desire, were then expressed in many particulars, these three especially we supplicate for at this time. Firstly, that Justice may be executed upon the Capitall Offenders in the first and this last Rebellion. Secondly that your gallant Army under the Lord Fairfax, may be more carefully preserved, and better maintained then formerly it hath been or now is, having under God, as you well know, so often redeemed you, and the whole kingdome from most apparent ruine. Lastly, that the cry of so much innocent blood as hath been shed in this kingdome first and last, in which the City of London hath not had a little share, & all by Commissions from the King, may be better sought into, and avenged without partiality, and not passed over with an act of Oblivion, lest it fall heavily on you, your Children and Kingdome.

May it therefore please you to take these our earnest desires into your serious consideration, that we perish not suddenly, while we cry peace, peace, but returne again to the good work from whence you are fallen, that Gods wrath may be appeased, your enemies subdued, your friends reconciled, and all good men satisfied, which will be like life from the dead, to this poore dying kingdome, and so by this meanes a well grounded peace better established.

And your petitioners shall ever pray, &c

Background

This petition follows closely behind the Leveller one of 11 September, selecting and expanding some of its points — notably the need to appease God's anger at the bloodshed of civil war, so that it does not fall on Parliament itself. Its authors and supporters are unknown, however. The *Commons Journal* records only that it was brought to their door by 'divers inhabitants' of Oxfordshire and presented by 'one Mr Butler'. According to the royalist newsbook *Mercurius Elencticus*, it was 'contrived by the Independents in the House, and put into the hands of a few, (perhaps half a Dozen) beggarly Mechaniques of that County to clamour with against the Treaty'. No gentlemen could be supporting it, and 'we know the Generality of Oxfordshire, to be as great Lovers of Monarchy as any County of England.' These were typical royalist reactions. Where evidence survives — mainly for

Oxford and other sizeable towns such as Banbury, Witney and Henley — it suggests that at least the urban population was more parliamentarian than royalist. Though the king had been first to raise forces in the county at the start of the civil war and the major strong points were occupied by royalist troops for most of its course, the armies of both sides fought back and forward across Oxfordshire and some places changed hands more than once. A new cavalry troop was readily raised for Parliament at the start of the second civil war, but there was no royalist mobilisation in the county this time round.

This was not the first petition from Oxfordshire to address radical demands to Parliament. A year earlier, certain inhabitants of the county — 'many of us being men of mean estates, in Tillage, and almost swallowed up in our Estates, by Taxations, Plundering, Quartering of Souldiers in the time of war, and now also Free quarter' — had petitioned for the abolition of tithes, demanding 'liberty in our owne [property] ... and to refuse thraldom and bondage'. The evidence for widespread resistance to tithes in the area of the Chiltern Hills (see 54 and 66 below) suggests that this came from the south-eastern part of Oxfordshire. A joint petition with neighbouring Berkshire and Buckinghamshire inhabitants, published simultaneously, added a further political dimension by demanding the removal of eleven Presbyterian MPs already singled out by the New Model Army, in order that 'justice may bee executed on offenders'.

In Oxford itself, where the city was predominantly parliamentarian in opposition to the university's royalism, the mayor and some of the corporation had to flee when the king's forces occupied it in late 1642. While it functioned as Charles's capital from 1643 to 1646, conditions in the overcrowded, insanitary city scarcely endeared the king's cause to the inhabitants. Forced loans were demanded of the council, and the inhabitants were heavily taxed. They suffered repeated outbreaks of disease and extensive damage by an accidental fire in 1644, as well as the deliberate destruction of suburban houses by the defending force; and those councillors who petitioned for relief from taxation were thrown in prison. The old regime that returned after the royalists' surrender in June 1646 was reinforced by Parliament's overturning of the mayoral election in September 1647 and adding a few army officers to the city council, but it was not essentially imposed from outside. The city was occupied by soldiers from Ingoldsby's regiment under Lieutenant-Colonel Thomas Kelsey (see 12 below); and it was there that the printer Henry Hills, in partnership with John Harris the Leveller, set up a press to publicise the New Model Army's resistance to disbandment in 1647. We do not know how much of the soldiers' politics rubbed off on Oxford's citizens; but a petition from the mayor and corporation to Parliament in 1649, opening with congratulations to the republican regime for freeing the people from tyranny, would be printed in London in April 1649 for Giles Calvert, who published many works by political and religious radicals.

On the county's boundary with Northamptonshire, Banbury had been notable for puritan ministers for some time before the civil war. Its castle was occupied by the king's forces in October 1642, and remained a royalist stronghold in an area of predominantly parliamentarian sympathies. At the time of this petition the town's preachers leaned towards Presbyterianism, and along with seventeen other ministers from the area they would petition Fairfax in January 1649 to act to reverse Pride's Purge and suspend the king's trial. A few months later, however, William Thompson would raise the standard of his Leveller-inspired rising in Banbury. He may have gained support from some of the inhabitants of that area, though contemporary narratives focus chiefly on the soldiers who joined him from part of Colonel Reynolds's regiment, who were stationed there (see 34 below), and the county cavalry troop. It is possible that this county troop, as inhabitants of Oxfordshire spurred into action by the crisis of the second civil war, also played a part in promoting the petition above; but their own petition, addressed to Fairfax and the army council in late December or early January 1649, is very different in tone and emphasis (42 below).

It is highly unlikely that the petition originated with the county's Independent members at Westminster. The dominant political influence in the county after the first civil war was that of William Fiennes of Broughton, Viscount Saye and Sele, known as 'Old Subtlety' for his political manoeuvring. Though he had been an early patron of Oliver Cromwell, Saye had parted company with the Independents over the treaty negotiations, along with others branded by pamphleteers as 'Royal Independents' rather than real ones. Saye's son Nathaniel Fiennes — MP for Banbury since 1640 — was now on the Commons' team at the Newport treaty negotiations, along with Viscount Wenman, one of the knights of the shire. In December 1648 all the county's MPs would be excluded at Pride's Purge (see 56 below) except for William Lenthall, Speaker of the Commons, and John Nixon (Mayor of Oxford 1647-9) who absented himself.

As Oxfordshire was one of the counties where the Levellers intended to raise support for their new petition in January 1648 (p. 19 above), we can assume that they expected to find supporters there, perhaps through radical soldiers. Though Independent, separatist and sectarian congregations were also frequently a source of Leveller support, the evidence for these in Oxfordshire is tantalisingly out of reach for this period. The volumes of the Victoria County History for the shire note the evidence for dissenting churches in towns such as Bicester, Henley, Watlington, Witney, and even some villages — but only from the 1650s, when the Baptists formed regional associations and the Quakers added a new dimension to the picture; or from the 1660s when these sects were subject to persecution. It is unlikely that such groups were unknown in Oxfordshire in 1648-9, but without further local research their existence cannot be confirmed.

Related sources

Commons Journal, vol. 6, 30 September 1648.

Mercurius Elencticus, No. 45 (27 September – 4 October 1648) BL/EEBO: E.465[33].

The copie of three petitions as they were presented to the Honourable, the Commons assembled in Parliament, September 14th. and 15th. 1647. BL/EEBO: E.407[29].

The humble advice and earnest desires of certain well-affected ministers, lecturers of Banbury in the county of Oxon ... to his Excellency Thomas Lord Fairfax. 1649. BL/EEBO: E.540[12].

The Humble petition of the major, aldermen, bayliffs, and commonalty of the city of Oxon, in the county of Oxon to the supreame authority of the nation, the Commons in Parliament assembled ... London. Printed for Giles Calvert, 1649. BL: c.114.b.29.

David Eddershaw with Eleanor Roberts, *The Civil War in Oxfordshire* (Stroud, Sutton 1995).

Alfred Beesley, *The History of Banbury* (London, Nichols, 1841).

H. E. Bannard, 'The Berkshire, Buckinghamshire and Oxfordshire Committees of 1642-1646', *Berks, Bucks & Oxon Archaeological Journal*, 31 (1927), pp. 173-92. (Online access via Archaeological Data Service).

David Eddershaw, *Chipping Norton, The Story of a Market Town* (Chipping Norton, Poundstone, 2006).

VCH: *Oxfordshire*, vols 4 (Oxford), 6 (Bicester), 8 (Watlington), 12 (Witney, Cogges), 16 (Henley), 13 (Aston and Cote).

Rosemary Kelly, 'A City Parish in the English Civil War: St Aldate's, Oxford, 1642-46', *Oxoniensia*, vol. 76 (2011).

Stephen Porter, 'The Oxford Fire of 1644', *Oxoniensia*, vol. 44 (1984).

Valerie Pearl, 'The "Royal Independents" in the English Civil War', *Transactions of the Royal Historical Society*, 5th Ser. vol. 18 (1968).

3: LEICESTERSHIRE

2 October 1648

Context

Charles I is the sole focus of this petition. Its authors' willingness to consider the possibility that a trial could lead to his acquittal must be seen in the context of the charges against him published by the House of Commons the previous February in defence of the Vote of No Addresses. A note on the manuscript copy observes that several additional charges — presented in { } brackets below — were added to the printed version of the petition; but as they had appeared in the Commons' official publication, their insertion seems to be consistent with the authors' intentions. When it came to the king's trial in January 1649, the actual charge — agreed only a few days before the proceedings opened — would be more limited but concentrated: deliberately breaking his coronation oath with the intention of making his own power absolute, and making war on his people to achieve that end. The Leicestershire petitioners take most seriously the allegation that the king is responsible for all the bloodshed of the civil wars, whatever the truth about the other charges.

Text

The Humble Petition of the Committee, Gentry, Ministry, and other the inhabitants of the County of Leicester, as it was presented to the right honorable The Commons Assembled in Parliament, October 2. 1648. With the Parliaments Answer thereunto. London, Printed for G. Calvert. 1648. BL/EEBO: E.465[34]

Humbly sheweth, That whereas Your Petitioners have long lien under the burthen of these intestine and devouring Wars, and are now lifted up with the hopes of a blessed Sunshine of Peace breaking forth upon us for the dispelling of all those mists that have wrapt us up in this long Misery: In which Peace well setled, none shall more rejoyce then your Petitioners, being ready to accept it as the fruit of all our labors, losses, crosses, yea all our hazards in this great adventure: Heartily praising the Lord for all your faithful endeavors to extricate us, and our afflicted Friends of these three Kingdoms out of our deep and unparaleled miseries: And perceiving the present Treaty to be looked on by you as the great and last way for you to bring over unto us this so much beloved and longed for Peace, in which (seeing our concernment is so eminent, and our posterity gasping to receive the fruits of what we have sowen in tears and blood) we humbly crave leave to mind you of two Declarations, the one from the Assembly of the Church of Scotland, dated July the 5. 1645 charging his Majesty with spilling the blood of many Thousands of his best Subjects in the three Kingdoms: and the other of your own, Febr. the 15. 1647[8]. wherein you give Reasons for no further Addresses, and speak as high as that of Scotland. We might add thereunto that also in answer to the Scottish Commissioners Papers, dated the 4th of March 1647[8]. All which have made our ears to tingle and our hearts to tremble, expecting with amazement what satisfaction you might have to these loud-crying and Heaven-provoking Crimes: viz. That about the death of his Royal Father: The betraying of Rochel; {The Spanish Fleet with an Army in it: His Proclamation to cry down Parliaments}: His correspondency with Rome: The private Articles of his Marriage: {His Commissions to the Rebels in Ireland: His violent attempt upon the House of Commons: The inviting of Forreigners to inslave the three Nations: His proclaiming the Parliament of England Rebels: The designed bloody Massacre in London by his Commission}: His destructive principle of yeelding an Account to none but God: His inviting over the Irish Rebels to subdue this Parliament: His backwardness to declare against them: Together with the eight years Misery of the three Kingdoms; *Cum multis aliis* [with many other things]. And yet your selves say these are but some few of the many Reasons why you cannot repose any more trust in him.

The Premises considered, we desire, for our selves and the whole Nation, we may not be left in the dark concerning these Suggestions and Charges; which if true, that proceedings may be accordingly, that we may not build our Peace upon such ruining foundations: but if otherwise, that his Majesty may be cleared so fully, that we may neither fear your Treating with him nor Trusting him in the great and weighty affairs of the three Kingdoms. And we most earnestly beg, that since Your God and ours hath put so many principal Enemies into Your hands, even to wonder, that impartial and personal Justice may equally and speedily be administred, which we look at as the undoubted Remedy of all our Maladies; for Justice exalteth a Nation and establisheth a Throne. In the obtaining of these (we suppose) but just Requests, we are ready to adventure our All with You and for You.

And shall dayly pray, &c.

The said Petition was by twenty Gentlemen, Ministers and others of the said County delivered at the Bar, which was acceptably received, read and debated; the *Petitioners* being withdrawn, were again called in, & had this Answer by Mr *Speaker* returned.

The Answer of the House to the Petitioners, by Mr. Speaker.

Gentlemen of the County of Leicester, The House hath read your Petition and hath considered of your desires and hath commanded me to give you this Answer, That they are engaged in a Treaty with the King, wherein they will take care for the preservation of Religion, Laws, Liberties, and Protection of those that have engaged with them: and so far I am commanded to acquaint you.

FINIS.

Imprimatur, G.M. [Gilbert Mabbott, licenser of publications]

Manuscript

Bodleian Library: 'To the Right Honorable the House of Commons Assembled in Parlament. The humble Petition of the Committee Gentrie Minestrie & others Inhabitaunts of the Towne and Countie of Leicester', Nalson Ms 22, fo. 369.

Another edition

A Perfect Diurnall, No. 271, 2-9 October 1648. BL/EEBO: E.526[14].

Background

The manuscript of this petition in the Bodleian Library adds, after the text of the petition but before the account of its presentation: 'Tho. Hasillrige, Fr. Smalley, Sa. Blackerby, Minister of Langton & William Smith & others.' The first two of these names are directly linked to the Commons' declaration in support of the Vote of No Addresses, which features prominently above. On 24 February 1648 Thomas Hesilrige, brother of the Leicestershire MP Sir Arthur Hesilrige and a member of the County Committee, was ordered to bring before the House of Commons Mr Francis Smalley, another committee member. Smalley claimed some knowledge of the Star Chamber case of 1626 in which the Duke of Buckingham had faced accusations 'touching the Death of King James', namely of hastening the old king's death by administering poison in the guise of medicine. When Smalley appeared on 13 March all he could show was Charles I's warrant ordering the case file to be removed from the court records — which many people at the time thought to be a cover-up. Though the charge that Buckingham had murdered King James I is now held to be groundless, it was much discussed at this time. Alastair Bellany and Thomas Cogswell have recently argued that it is an important part of the background to Charles's bad relations with his Parliaments.

Smalley's information was referred to the committee of nine MPs who had supervised the Commons' declaration justifying the Vote of No Addresses. This *Declaration of the Commons of England*, published on 15 February, had included all the accusations in the printed version of this petition except 'the private articles of his marriage', by which Charles was believed to have agreed to toleration for Catholics. Some of these charges hark back to Charles's foreign policy in the 1620s: the failure of English attempts to assist the French Protestants of La Rochelle, the collusion with Spanish suppression of the Protestant Dutch revolt by allowing their fleet to pass through the Channel in 1639, the hiring of mercenary cavalry (for war on the Continent), and his diplomatic relations with the papacy. Others recall more recent events: the Irish rebellion of 1641 which Charles was believed to have encouraged, his proclamation against Parliament when it took control of the militia in 1642, and his seeking military aid from his mother's

Danish relatives and the Dutch. The fact that Thomas Lord Grey of Groby, one of the borough of Leicester's two MPs, was a member of the committee for the *Declaration* also links the content to this county.

The petition avoids all reference to the Levellers' Large Petition or any of its specific demands, but not because there were no political or religious radicals in Leicestershire. Robert Everard and Samuel Oates had recently been preaching radical religion and publicising *An Agreement of the People* there. Baptists who refused to bring their children to church to be christened were being punished by local magistrates including Peter Temple, Grey's fellow MP for Leicester since 1645, when he was high sheriff in 1644. Grey himself, recruiting forces to fight the Scots invasion in the summer of 1648, had written a call to arms, *Old English Blood Boyling Afresh in Leicestershire Men*, which appealed to the godly 'to preserve a Kingdome, that must be saved against its will, for which God hath so immediately and even miraculously spoken from Heaven'. This sentiment relates more strongly to the idea of 'godly rule' — whereby a dedicated band of god's elect would seize power and bring in a new millennium — than to the belief in popular sovereignty espoused by the Levellers, a distinction important to any assessment of the petitions in this volume.

Grey would go onto assist Colonel Pride at the army's purge of the House of Commons on 6 December 1648, to attend the king's trial regularly, and to sign his death warrant; but this petition is still a long way from those events. It calls for the king to face trial, but suggests that he could be acquitted so fully as to be trusted again; yet it unambiguously lays on him the guilt of the blood shed in the civil wars. Such apparent contradictions in the content of several petitions at this time may be the result of compromises between different sets of people. The references here to the Scottish declaration in 1645 and the more recent reply by both houses of the English parliament to the Scots commissioners' demand for a personal treaty, together with Grey's assertion in *Old English Blood* that the Scots would be welcome 'did they not undermine that Gospel, that they say they come to serve', point to Leicestershire's Presbyterians. These may not have been as narrow in their political views as the party at Westminster that had now appropriated their name. The key person may have been Samuel Blackersby, who had replaced the previous rector of Langton, deprived by Parliament's commissioners for the rooting out of 'scandalous' ministers, though there is no positive evidence that he was a Presbyterian. A letter published in late June 1648, reporting the raising of forces in Leicestershire and neighbouring counties, claimed that in Northamptonshire, where similar efforts were being made, 'both Presbyter and Independent joyne now cordially in that County, and indeed it is so in every place where I come.' This may not have been literally true, but it suggests that such a united front against regional royalists and Scots invaders was some participants' ideal.

In March 1649, after the King's death, Leicestershire produced two further petitions. One was addressed to Parliament, urging a list of radical reforms, including freedom of religion and the abolition of tithes, that suggest sympathy with the Levellers. The other, however, called on Fairfax as head of the army — assuring him that 'we are of them, that have loved and honoured you' — to prevent religious toleration, which would open the floodgates to impiety and blasphemy and encourage 'Idolaters [Catholics], Turks [Muslims] and Heathens'; and condemned the Levellers' current plan to promote *An Agreement of the People* by mass subscription. These were the attitudes of the more conservative leaders among religious Independents, who were moving rapidly away from the Levellers towards acceptance of a more authoritarian 'godly rule', and their petition was published in London by Henry Hood, who also published Independent sermons.

William Smith, named fourth above, has not been identified, though he may have been related to Henry Smith of Withcote, Sir Arthur Haselrige's fellow MP for Leicestershire since 1645. Henry Smith, along with Grey of Groby and Peter Temple, all took part in the king's trial and signed his death warrant. So also did Thomas Waite or Wayte, who had held a seat for Rutland since 1646 but was appointed to several committees in his native Leicestershire.

Related sources

Commons Journal, vol. 5 (24 February and 13 March 1648) and vol. 6 (2 October 1648).

A declaration of the Commons of England in Parliament assembled. Printed for Edward Husband, Printer to the Honorable House of Commons, Feb. 15. 1647[48]. BL/EEBO: E.427[9].

Thomas Grey, Lord Groby, *Old English Blood Boyling Afresh in Leicestershire Men*. London, Printed for Giles Calvert, 1648. BL/EEBO: E.461[7].

The Humble Representation of the Committee, Gentry, Ministry and other well-affected Persons in the County of Leicester. Printed for Henry Hood, 1648. BL/EEBO E.545[22].

*To the supreme authority, the Commons of England assembled in Parliament, The humble Petition of divers well-affected of the County of Leicester.*1648[49]. Published by Giles Calvert, 1648[49]. BL/EEBO: 669.f.14[6].

Jeff Richards, *Aristocrat and Rebel, The Life of Thomas, Lord Grey of Groby* (Wotton-under-Edge, New Millennium, 2000).

John Nichols, *The History and Antiquities of the County of Leicester*, vol. 3, part 4, Appendix: 'The Civil War in Leicestershire' (London, Nichols and Son, 1804; facsimile edition Wakefield, SR Publishers, 1971).

Alastair Bellany and Thomas Cogswell, *The Murder of King James I* (London and New Haven, CT, Yale University Press, 2015).

VCH: *Leicestershire*: vols 2 (Political History) and 5 (Church Langton).

Alan Betteridge, 'Early Baptists in Leicestershire and Rutland', *Baptist Quarterly*, vol. 25(8), 1974-5. https://biblicalstudies.org.uk/pdf/bq/25-8_354.pdf.

D. Fleming, 'Faction and Civil War in Leicestershire', *Transactions of the Leicestershire Archaeological and Historical Society*, vol. 57 (1981-2).

ODNB: E. T Bradley, rev. Sean Kelsey, 'Grey, Thomas, Baron Grey of Groby (1622-1657), regicide'.

ODNB: Sarah Barber, 'Temple, Peter (bap. 1599, d. 1663), regicide'.

ODNB: K. R. Gardiner & D. L. Gardiner, 'Smith [Smyth], Henry (b. 1619/20, d. in or after 1668), politician and regicide'.

4: NEWCASTLE-UPON-TYNE

10 October 1648

Context

The *Commons Journal* records the reception of this petition and the next on 10 October 1648. Both appealed to Parliament to stop the Newport negotiations and bring to justice those believed guilty of starting and prolonging the civil wars. The two petitions were followed by a 'presentment' (described in some reports as a third petition) from the Grand Jury at the Somerset assizes held in Taunton a few weeks earlier, for which no text survives (see 56 below). A brief account of the debate on these, evidently written by someone who was present though perhaps not for all of it, was published two days later in *Mercurio Volpone, or The Fox*, a short-lived royalist weekly appearing on Thursdays. *The Fox*'s promise of more to follow next Tuesday was was amply and sensationally fulfilled by the most notorious of royalist newsbooks, Marchamont Nedham's *Mercurius Pragmaticus*, on 17 October.

Despite *Pragmaticus*'s many passages purporting to be direct quotations, his unknown reporter's account of it does not justify the editor's accusation that 'they stick not to shoot their bitter Arrowes at the sacred person of his Majesty'. The debate was undoubtedly emotional, and the subject of blood guilt played a part in it; but the only hint of regicide reported was in a speech by Dennis Bond, MP for Dorchester (Dorset) and an Independent, who argued that the Commons could and should have the power to try members of the House of Lords, such as the Earl of Norwich, directly without involving the peers. When Bond said that he hoped to see 'the day when we may have power to hang the greatest Lord of them all', the report indicates that he immediately added 'if he deserves it.' If this is an accurate account, it is incidentally interesting that Bond referred to a bloodless form of execution. Although he was nominated to the High Court of Justice that tried the king the following January, he did not attend any of its sessions and was in no way associated with the monarch's beheading. Freed from this allegedly regicidal context, the Newcastle petition can clearly be seen to call for the postponement of a final treaty with the King until after the trial and execution of some of the leading Royalists, a scenario that requires the king to survive the bloodletting.

Text

The Moderate, No. 14, 10-17 October 1648. BL/EEBO: E.468[2]

To the Honourable, The Knights, Citizens and Burgesses assembled in Parliament. The Humble Petition of the Maior, Aldermen, Sheriffs, Common-Counsell men, and other wel-affected of the Town of New-Castle upon Tine.

Humbly sheweth, That we cannot but deeply resent [feel], what hath been presented to you by the well-affected in the Southerne parts, as concerning this present Treaty; that if after all the experiences of the mischiefes which have happened to us from former Treaties, of all Gods wonderfull ownings of you, both formerly, and of late in midst of so many oppositions from all hands, and of all his gracious appearings, against the king and his party, you go on to Treat before full and exemplary Justice be done upon the great Incendiaries of the Kingdome the fomentors of, and actors in the first and second war, and the late bringing in of the Scots, we can expect nothing as the issue thereof but the sudden dissolution of the Parliament, and Army, the destruction of all the well-affected, the involving of this Nation in more blood, misery and slavery then ever.

May it therefore please you in this Juncture of time to hearken to your Petitioners, who have Constantly adhered to you, and before you conclude this Treaty, to execute Impartiall and speedy Justice (though upon the greatest offenders) wherein you cannot want assistance from God, and from man, to strengthen you in your endeavors, to settle this Kingdome in Peace and Righteousnes.

[Followed by the names of Mayor Thomas Ledger and 84 others.]

Background

A copy of the list of eighty-five signatories published in *The Moderate*, made and annotated after the Restoration, was examined in the 1960s by Roger Howell for his history of Newcastle during the civil wars. He found that it included many members of the ruling group installed in the city after the first civil war, including a significant number of merchants and lesser tradesmen who had not held power before. This post-war regime replaced one that had long been dominated by a small circle of coal shippers and mercers who were members of the Hostmen's coal shipping monopoly. Persistent opposition to this 'inner ring' overlapped to some extent with a well established puritan movement in the city. John Knox in his time at Berwick and Newcastle (1549-51) had a lasting influence, and several Presbyterian congregations in Newcastle had existed continuously since the 1580s. The Archbishop of York in the 1630s, Richard Neile, provoked increased opposition to the established church with his anti-Calvinist theology, Laudian church policies and high ceremonialism. There was therefore some sympathy among the citizens for the Scottish National Covenant (1638) and the Covenanters' invasion during the second Bishops' War (1640); while Scottish labourers employed in the coal mines outside the city resisted the royalist occupation of the area at the start of the civil war.

After a difficult period of Scottish occupation after the second Bishops War (1640), followed by Royalist occupation, parliamentarian blockade, and re-occupation by the Scots in 1644-6, most of the city's old leaders were removed because of their collaboration with the royalists — an exercise that owed as much to internal divisions in Newcastle as to intervention by Parliament.

Howell found that the new regime included fewer of the old oligarchs and more men from the lesser trades, dominated by the powerful Dawson family and their allies; but he believed there was no concern for national political issues in Newcastle in this period except for the above petition. The petition and its list of signatories (among whom Howell identified members of the Dawson circle) do seem to call this conclusion in question, as does Howell's research on the future regicide John Blakiston, one of the two MPs for the city elected in 1640. Blakiston returned to the city in 1645 and was elected mayor for the coming year, remaining in close contact with the corporation despite his duties in Parliament. His increasing involvement with the Independent party, particularly its most radical wing, may explain why it was Cornelius Holland, MP for Windsor (see 47 below), who presented this petition in the Commons, though he had no known connections with Tyneside.

The petition may also have been influenced by Newcastle's military governor, Sir Arthur Hesilrige, and his deputy Paul Hobson. Hesilrige was one of the MPs for Leicestershire, but had quarrelled with Lord Grey of Groby's family and was re-founding his fortune in the north-east. He was a long term enemy of Presbyterianism in politics, an Independent hard liner, and a friend of the army but not of the Levellers. As governor of Newcastle he lobbied successfully for money to relieve the city's burdens, and appears to have kept the peace between religious factions. According to visitors to the city, Independents and Presbyterians still prayed and fasted together there in the 1650s, when they maintained a united front in opposition to the more radical Baptists and Quakers. Hesilrige remained in the north throughout the dramatic events of December 1648 and January 1649, opposing Pride's Purge and taking no part in the king's trial or death.

Paul Hobson was a Baptist lay preacher who had been active in London before he was arrested by Sir Samuel Luke at Newport Pagnell for unlicensed preaching (see 53 below). Hobson continued to preach as a soldier in London, Bristol and Exeter; then left the army for a time, but returned in 1647 as a major in Colonel Robert Lilburne's regiment. By July 1648 he was with this regiment in Newcastle, and by September he was promoting a letter to Fairfax from regiments in the north-east supporting the Levellers' Large Petition (see 10 below). Shortly before that, John Lilburne (the colonel's brother) had passed through Newcastle on a visit to his home county of Durham; but as he had just launched a personal campaign against Hesilrige over individual grievances concerning money and property, he is unlikely to have had friendly contact with this circle.

The same issue of *The Moderate* includes a letter to the editor ('Sir') dated at Newcastle four days after the Commons debate. Given the distance of 247 miles that first the news and then the letter would have had to travel, it seems more likely to have been written in London by a correspondent known to the editor. Nevertheless, this letter has been mistaken by some historians for a second petition, in the name of the mayor and whole corporation. It seems to come from at least one member of the corporation, as it begins, 'The Maior

Aldermen and Commonalty of this Town did most freely and unanimously joyne in a Petition to the House of Commons, ... this we grounded upon our Solemne league and Covenant ...'

The letter may have been written by a member of the corporation who happened to be in London at the time, introducing sentiments and language that the subscribers had not put their hands to. In the face of betrayal by 'our Trustees' in Parliament, *The Moderate*'s correspondent says, 'we must still endeavour to keep our first integrity with out spot or blemish, for if we would never bow the knee to Baall at the Kings Command, we will never bow it at the Parliaments, and if they act against the truth [*sic*] reposed in them by the People, the people are bound in conscience and duty to act against them, *Salus populi* being *Suprema Lex*.' They pray to god to direct them for 'the good of the poor Comons of England who are like[ly] to be bought and sold, because they are ignorant of their owne freedoms and birth-rights, which they are willing to sell for a Messe of Pottage, so that they may enjoy a slavish Peace ...' The English translation of *salus populi suprema lex* — the safety of the people is the supreme law — appears in the Large Petition of 11 September; but the explicit intention expressed here, of a minority of activists saving the people from their own ignorant submissiveness, has more in common with Lord Grey of Groby's *Old English Blood* (see 3 above).

Related sources

Commons Journal, vol. 6, 10 October 1648.

Henry Bourne, *The History of Newcastle upon Tyne; or, the Ancient and Present State of that Town* (Newcastle-upon-Tyne, 1736), p. 237.

Roger Howell, *Newcastle-upon-Tyne and the Puritan Revolution, A Study of the Civil War in North England* (Oxford, Clarendon, 1967), pp. 169-217.

Roger Howell, 'Newcastle's regicide: The Parliamentary Career of John Blakiston', *Archaeologia Aeliana*, 4th series vol. 42 (1964).

ODNB: Richard L. Greaves, 'Hobson, Paul (d. 1666), Particular Baptist preacher'.

ODNB: Christopher Durston, 'Hesilrige [Haselrig], Sir Arthur, second Baronet (1601-1661)'.

ODNB: J. T. Peacey, 'Blakiston, John (bap. 1603, d. 1649), politician and regicide'.

5: YORKSHIRE

10 October 1648

Context

In the *Commons Journal* we read that second petition of 10 October 1648 was presented in the name of 'the Gentlemen, Ministers, Freeholders and other Inhabitants of the County and City of Yorke, well-affected to the Safety of the Kingdom, and the Honour of the Parliament'. Several newsbooks add that Alderman Thomas Hoyle, MP for York, presented it; though *Mercurius Pragmaticus* took it from his and *The Fox*'s source that the petition Hoyle drew from his pocket came from London. The account *Pragmaticus* gives of these petitions and the debate that followed is full of content that cannot be found in either this petition or the last above. All are said to have agreed on 'the Treaty as being the last Refuge of the King and his Party, for the ruine of Gods people', and to have called for 'Justice to be executed upon all Delinquents, from the highest to the lowest without exception, even in all that have had a hand in the precious blood of the Saints'. An alternative account published in the eighteenth century attributes some of these words to the Somerset Grand Jury's presentment on the same day, which will be considered below. (See 56.)

Both royalist newsbooks reported the moving of a resolution that a committee should be set up, 'to consider of a certain number of Persons to be selected out of the old and new Delinquents ... to except them out of mercy and order them to be proceeded against as capitall offenders'. This situates the debate in the context of ongoing arguments about excepting individual royalists from an Act of Oblivion, rather than a step along the road to regicide, which Nedham was constantly predicting in his publications at this time. It also shows, incidentally, that 'capital offenders' could be used in the plural and need not point to the king, as the singular would explicitly do in the army's *Remonstrance* the following month (18 below).

Nedham also reported a speech on blood guilt which is important here because he vaguely attributes it to Thomas Hoyle, together with John Weaver, MP for Stamford, 'and others':

> That the bloud of the People being shed, it would be required somewhere; and that if the House did not do justice now it is in their power, upon their capital enemies from the highest to the lowest, that had a hand in the former or later wars, there is no question but all the bloud would be required at their hands. And therefore to remove the guilt from our selves (Mr Speaker) we desire a Committee may be appointed to consider of a certain number of persons to be selected out of the old and new Delinquents, and propounded unto the House to exempt them out of mercy, and order them to be proceeded against, as capitall Offenders.

Many pamphleteers and preachers are known to have suggested that unless

37

Parliament shed the blood of those responsible for the wars, the guilt would fall on its own members and their army. None of the petitions found for this collection, from soldiers or civilians, use the idea of blood guilt falling on themselves to call for the death of the king in particular, and some of them do suggest that there are other ways of removing it than further bloodshed. Nedham's fudging of the speaker's identity, and his artful insertion of '(Mr Speaker)' for realistic effect, must throw some doubt on whether it is an accurate report, and distance the York petition from such a context.

Text

The Moderate, No. 14, 10-17 October 1648. BL/EEBO: E.468[2]

To the Honourable House of Commons, Assembled in Parliament.

The Petition of the Gentlemen, Ministers, Freeholders and other Inhabitants of the County and City of Yorke, of the County and Towne of Kingston Sup[er] Hull, well affected to the safety of the Kingdome, and the Honour of the Parliament.

Humbly sheweth, That as they cannot without admiration, consider those wonders of mercy which God hath lately vouchsafed to this distracted Kingdome, in disappoynting the desperate designs, and defeating the Numerous forces lately raised by the subtill and Malitious Enemies thereof, so neither can they without the staine of ingratitude, neglect to acknowledge the fidelity and stedfastness of this Honourable House, unto the Interest and welfare of this Nation, in the midst of all these insurrections and Invasions.

Yet together with their thankfulness, your Petitioners are Commanded by their zeale to glory of God and their affection to the good of this Kingdome, further to represent their humble thoughts and desires for the improvement of the great things which God hath done for us to a happy establishment of Peace and Truth, Religion and Reason have aboundantly convinced us that there is [no] more hopefull expedient to the settling or strengthening the tranquility of any State, then the Impartial and speedy execution of Justice upon offenders, especially such as are guilty of polluting a land with blood; and our own sad experience hath told us, that the neglect thereof hath had a special Influence into these late revived calamities, which hath befalln us; neither have we any ground to beleeve that the second indulgence towards such Delinquents, and Incendiaries should produce any better effect then the first, which appears to be nothing but distractions, and danger of ruine.

Your Petitioners therefore in Conscience to their duty, make it their earnest request unto this Honourable House, that seeing God hath delivered into your hands sundry treacherous and implacable enemies, guilty of much blood, and cruelty to this poor Kingdom, you would not endanger the forfeiture of all these great experiences of Gods goodness to us, by delivering these distroyers, but that according to the declarations of Parliament, our protestation, and

Solemne Covenant, with God and this Kingdome, daily expect the performance of exemplary Justice be executed upon them without delay, which in such cases is bound to be most pernicious. That God may be glorified, the Cause and honour of the Parliament asserted and vindicated, the land cleansed from blood and rendered Capable of some happie establishment.

And your petitioners take Freedome further to represent, that for the most part they finde things so ordered that the greatest weight of all burthens falls upon those who have adhered most stedfastly to the Parliament in this cause of God and the Kingdome, and therefore do offer this additionall desire, that this honourable House would not neglect this prize in their hands, of easing their friends and discharging the Arreares of souldiers, and other publike debts, out of the Estates of Delinquents, especially such who are, or shall be found guilty of this second mischiefe to the Kingdome.

Background

This text also was followed in *The Moderate* by a letter to the editor, dated at York on 14 October and claiming to be from the petitioners of Kingston upon Hull, the 'city and county' (insistently independent of the East Riding) singled out in *The Moderate*'s headline though not in the Commons' record. The letter complains about Parliament rejecting such loyal supporters as the petitioners have always been, and invokes the Solemn League and Covenant (twice), as well as the Protestation of 1641-2 and Parliament's own printed declarations, as their motivation for taking up arms. The editor of *Mercurius Pragmaticus* accused members of the anti-Presbyterian party in the Commons of hypocrisy when they invoked it, as some of them were known to regard it as worthless. Its inclusion here (as in 2 and 4) may be more meaningful, however. The Covenant contained both a resolution to preserve the person of the king and a commitment to bringing all 'incendiaries, malignants or evil instruments' involved in the civil war to 'public trial and condign punishment', which could be seen at this stage as calling for blood without targeting the king personally.

If Parliament's leaders had stuck to their principles, the letter says, instead of 'making our enemies, and Conquered slaves, to be our Masters, and Commanders … they might have still engaged our hearts from them, & not incline us to seek any otherwayes to prevent the miserable bondage and destruction that attends the Nation by this Treaty'. Now, however, the petitioners 'must look to, and depend upon the Law of nature for our preservation against these devilish and malignant principles.' This implied threat of popular action echoes the Levellers' habitual enlargement of the right of self-defence into a justification for resistance. It is more credible that this letter could have come from York within four days of the debate than the one from Newcastle (4 above). The radical MP and friend of the Levellers Henry Marten, who was reported by another royalist newsbook to have arrived in York by 4 October, could possibly have been involved, though not a member of the corporation, and indeed (as Nedham pointed out) one of those who held the Covenant in low regard. If it was written in London by a member of Hull's corporation close to *The Moderate*, the author could have been Hull's MP Peregrine Pelham, an Independent in politics and future regicide.

The corporation and people of Hull had stood by Parliament throughout the civil wars, despite suffering two sieges, losses at sea from pirates, and trading difficulties while York was occupied by the royalists (1642-44). They had strong puritan traditions: the dominant city preacher John Shaw was a Presbyterian, and an Independent congregation had been established in 1643. In York itself, the self-perpetuating oligarchy that dominated the corporation inclined, like many of the population, towards Parliament. Some corporation members simply stayed away from meetings during the royalist occupation; but a few, including Thomas Hoyle, took refuge in Hull and returned when the garrison surrendered in July 1644. According to Andrew Warmington, York's post-war regime did not usher in the rule of 'parvenu committee men', but restored the pre-war merchant oligarchy. All its members took the Covenant oath in 1644, in a demonstration of unity free from religious antagonisms. Hoyle's radical Independent views proved divisive when he urged Parliament to expel six aldermen from the corporation for their activities in support of the royalist regime in the city.

Thomas Hoyle had a long history of civic and religious leadership in York, defending ministers who refused to conform to the Laudian ceremonies in the 1630s, sponsoring charities to provide work in textile manufacturing, and replacing the corporation's traditional Christmas feast by a distribution of money to the poor. He was first elected to Parliament in 1628, served as lord mayor in 1632 and 1644, and represented the city in the Long Parliament alongside his fellow alderman William Allanson. The report of the 10 October debate includes him, along with MPs Weaver, Harvey 'and others', among those supposed to have said, 'That the bloud of the People being shed, it would be required some where; and if the House did not doe justice now it is in their power, upon their Capitall enemies from the highest to the lowest ... there is no question but all the bloud will be required at their hands.' Hoyle's suicide on the first anniversary of Charles I's execution was attributed by royalists to regicidal guilt, but he played no part in the king's trial or execution, and had ceased to attend the Commons regularly since November 1648. The death of his daughter triggered his 'melancholy', which we would call depression; but perhaps he was troubled also by the outcome of the revolution of 1648-9.

The Yorkshire gentry were deeply divided during the civil wars, and the majority known to have declared for one side or the other were royalists. Those who fought for Parliament included prominent army commanders Ferdinando Lord Fairfax, his son Sir Thomas, Sir William Constable and John Lambert. The strongholds of parliamentary support were the cities of York and Hull and the textile manufacturing districts of the West Riding, where the Bradford 'clubmen' had kept the king's army out of their town at the start of the civil war. Though eighteen of the thirty MPs elected in 1640-42 from the county and its many boroughs were later expelled as royalists, their 'recruiter' replacements elected in 1645 had credible local roots and mostly Independent politics. Only four were excluded at Pride's Purge, and thirteen were nominated to sit on the High Court of Justice to try the king, though only seven of these actually took part in the proceedings and six signed the king's death warrant.

Related sources

Commons Journal, vol. 6, 10 October 1648.
Mercurio Volpone, or the Fox, No. 2, 5-12 October 1648: BL/EEBO E.467[2].
Mercurius Pragmaticus, No. 29, 10-17 October 1648: BL/EEBO E.467[38].
Mercurius Elencticus, No. 45, 29 September – 4 October 1648: BL/EEBO E.465[33].
Old Parliamentary History, vol. 18 (pp. 30-32).
Andrew R. Warmington, 'The Corporation of York in Peace and War 1638-1645', *York Historian*, 9 (1990), pp.16-26.
Claire Cross, 'A man of conscience in seventeenth-century urban politics, Alderman Hoyle of York', in John Morrill, Paul Slack and Daniel Woolf (eds.), *Public Duty and Private Conscience in Seventeenth-Century England* (Oxford, Clarendon, 1993).
W. L. F. Nuttall, 'The Yorkshire commissioners for the trial of Charles I', *Yorkshire Archaeological Journal*, vol. 43 (1971), pp. 147-57.
Ronald A. Marchant, *The Puritans and the Church Courts in the Diocese of York, 1560-1642* (London, Longmans, 1960).
VCH: *Yorkshire*, City of York.
VCH: *Yorkshire, East Riding*, vol. 1: *The City of Hull*.
Andrew J. Hopper, 'A directory of parliamentarian allegiance in Yorkshire during the civil wars', *Yorkshire Archaeological Journal*, 73 (2001), pp. 84-122.
ODNB: Andrew J. Hopper, 'Pelham, Peregrine (bap. 1602, d. 1650), politician and regicide'.
Jack Binns, *Yorkshire in the Seventeenth Century* (Blackthorn Press, Pickering, 2007).

6: FLEETWOOD'S REGIMENT

18 October 1648

Context

This is the only petition addressed directly to Parliament by a regiment of the New Model Army before Pride's Purge, and the *Commons Journal* indicates that it was forwarded to them by Fairfax himself. The short petition in which they addressed the Lord General (13 below) was also read in the House, but neither of these gives any hint of the turmoil developing within the army that will become evident in the next section. These soldiers stress their loyalty to Parliament and avoid controversial political proposals. Both texts reflect the fear, evidently shared by the army leadership and many of their soldiers, that arrears of payment to Parliament's army were precipitating a crisis in relations between the troops and local communities.

Text

The Copies of Two Petitions From the Officers and Souldiers of Col. Charles Fleetwood's Regiment, concerning their severall Grievances, One of them presented to his Excellency the Lord Gen. Fairfax. The other to the Right Honourable the Commons of England in Parliament assembled. Signed by the Chief Officers present with the said Regiment.

With the Parliaments Answer touching their sending down Commissioners upon Tuesday 24. of Octob. to consult with his Excellency for redressing the said Grievances.

William Coleman Major.	*Robert Stanard Lieutenant.*
Richard Sankie Captain.	*William Bucke Cornet.*
Steven White Captain:	*William Williams Cornet.*

Printed by John Clowes, 1648. BL/EEBO: E.468[32]

To the Right Honorable the Commons of England in Parliament Assembled,

The humble Petition of the Officers and Souldiers of Colonell Charles Fleetwoods Regiment.

SHEWETH,
That your petitioners have even from the beginning of your sitting stood by you, using their utmost ability for you in the Kingdoms preservation, & when they saw you could no longer subsist without Jeaparding your lives, they did thereto shew much willingnesse, not making their own termes, but with all their strength did endeavour the pulling down of your and the Kingdoms enemies, which when they had (through the goodness of God crowning their endeavours) done, they did then expect some satisfaction for their services and former losses, and a settlement of the Kingdom in their Birth-rights and priviledges, as the purchase of so much Blood and Treasure, which, while they

looked for contrary to their expectation, they found a second Enemy let loose, not only on them, but on you, seeking to involve the Nation in slavery and ruine, and then again did your Petitioners (though formerly much discouraged and neglected) freely adventuring their lives in your defence, refusing no danger nor labour, nor in your low Condition troubled you with clamorous Petitions, or requests though they saw others game by runing that uncivill course, but wholly betook themselves to the work in hand, which they suddenly through Gods owning of them, brought to an hopefull Issue, forsing those that rose up against you to ly at their feet, though it was not gained without the losse of much blood, and the lives of our dear and faithfull friends, yet to their unspeakable grief, even in this time they found themselves neglected, and not paid; having received but one months pay since the 12 of May last, so that they are constrained to lye upon free quarter, although much mony hath been collected for them, which hath begotten in the Kingdom an evill opinion of them, though undescorned [*sic*], your Petitioners therefore for pervention [*sic*] of this insupportable burthen of free quarter humbly pray,

1. That you will please to assign each Regiment of the Army, the particular County out of which they are immediately to receive their pay, whereby not only the great Fees to Treasurers at Warre, amounting to near Ten thousand pounds, per Annum, besides what Committees, Clarkes, and other attendants belonging to them may be cut off, and your Petitioners freed from tedious attending, and great expences, as usually they are exposed to. But the Countrey by the Souldiers receiving of constant pay, eased of this intolerable oppression of free quarter.
2. That you will under [*sic*] the pay of our Arrears from the 5. of Jan. last, according to your engagements to us, out of the money already paid in for that purpose, that so we may be inabled to cloth our selves, as the season of the year requires, and repair our losses in the late troubles.
3. That some course may be taken for recruiting the Regiment with Horses, having had none almost of [*sic*] three years, which we leave to your consideration, And pray, &c …

Answer was returned by Mr. Scowen, Esquire, and Chairman of the Committee of the Army to this effect, viz. That the House had taken their Petition into serious consideration. And for that purpose had thought upon a way to send down Commissioners of their own to consult with his Excellency the Lord Gen. Fairfax, whereby to take some speedy course for full satisfaction of their desires in their said Petition.

Background

Fleetwood's regiment had been involved in all the major political upheavals in the New Model Army in 1647, including the appointment of agitators to represent them in the Army Council, the seizing of the King at Holdenby, and the debates on the constitution at Putney. During the second civil war they had been on active service in East Anglia alongside Walton's and Whalley's troops. Here, Fairfax and his fellow leaders are perhaps anxious to show that they are under control and behaving according to their senior officers' wishes. Colonel Charles Fleetwood was to play no part in the regicide, though he took an active part in the Commonwealth and Protectorate regimes. He is not to be confused with George Fleetwood, also a colonel in the New Model Army, who sat on the High Court of Justice and signed the King's death warrant, but was no known relation of this colonel's. All the officers named above can be found in Malcolm Wanklyn's invaluable New Model Army listings.

This is the first in the current round of petitions to highlight the issue of 'free quarter'. Because many historians have discussed this practice without defining it, it is important to understand that it was not the same as plunder. Board and lodging for parliament's troops were requisitioned without payment when their pay had not arrived, and this was becoming a common situation. If properly implemented (which was not always the case) the householders or innkeepers on whom soldiers were billeted were given 'tickets' promising future reimbursement. Many files in the Commonwealth Exchequer archives at Kew contain claims for compensation, and records of when they were paid off (see 11 and 64 below).

As the quest for a settlement dragged on, and the programme of selective disbandment agreed by Fairfax in December 1647 was reversed in the second civil war, the state's creditors had less and less faith that they would get their money. Some commanders or governors attempted to target those inhabitants who had not paid their taxes, which looked like blackmail; though imposing free quarter on those who had paid up seemed unfair. This could become a vicious spiral in which it became increasingly difficult to raise the taxes to pay the army, while taking free quarter made taxpayers still more unwilling to pay. Some of the soldiers' petitions below express the belief that there was a deliberate conspiracy by the army's enemies in Parliament to make them unpopular by withholding their pay, while others suggest that the problem was a reluctance to squeeze the defeated royalists sufficiently, the fault of poor administration, or (as above) the multiplication of officials in the financial departments of government.

Like several others that followed, this petition suggests an alternative, decentralised and hopefully cheaper method of paying the army, by direct appropriation of taxation from specific counties. This idea was in tune with the Levellers' decentralising ideals and it was popular with army petitioners. It went against the grain of all England's public finance institutions, however, and could result in soldiers being ordered to collect their own regiment's pay, which was equally if not more undesirable (see 38 below).

Related sources

Commons Journal, vol. 6, 18 October 1648.
Ashton, *Counter-Revolution*, pp. 57-70.

Gentles, *New Model Army* (index free quarter).
ODNB: Toby Barnard, 'Fleetwood, Charles, appointed Lord Fleetwood under the protectorate (c.1618–1692)'.
Wanklyn, *Reconstructing the New Model*.

7: FOUR NORTHERN COUNTIES

24 October 1648

Context

This petition was evidently the outcome of a meeting, reported in several newsbooks, between the 'Northern Gentlemen' and Oliver Cromwell on 24 October 1648, at the market town of Barnard Castle in Teesdale. Cromwell was returning from Edinburgh through the north of England, and had not yet been diverted to the siege of Pontefract (see 16 below). Given the political importance of the participants, it is hard to believe that there was no discussion at Barnard Castle of the Newport negotiations, or the trial and punishment of royalist leaders on the national scene. It may have been difficult to reach agreement on these issues at the meeting, not least because Sir Henry Vane Junior, a friend of Cromwell's whose family was influential in the locality, was currently one of the six Independent MPs on Parliament's team in the Isle of Wight.

A Commission of Oyer and Terminer (Law French for 'to hear and determine'), demanded by the petitioners, was part of the work of the judges of assize on their annual regional circuits, when they acted along with members of the local gentry. In many counties, assizes were not held regularly during the civil wars, and some or all of the Northern Circuit judges' meetings at Durham, Newcastle, Carlisle and Appleby may have been cancelled during the Scottish invasion.

Text

The Moderate Intelligencer, No. 190, 2-9 November 1648. BL/EEBO: E.470[24]

To the Honourable House of Commons, The humble Petition of the Gentlemen of the foure Northern Counties at their meeting at Bernard [*sic*] Castle.

Humbly sheweth
That your petitioners had formerly some hope that lenity towards those who had been in armes and otherwise active against the Parliament, would so far have prevailed with them, that your petitioners might have peaceably enjoy'd their own habitations, but we have lately found by wofull experience, that the permitting such persons, especially those of Interest in the Country to live amongst us hath brought most unsufferable misery upon these Counties: In so much as we may justly feare the perishing of many Families this Winter for want of bread; Gentlemen of quality and their Families having no other drink but water, and as an exceeding addition to our former sorrows, suffered this Summer by imprisoning our persons, dis peopling our Towns, compelling all able to beare arms, betwixt the ages of 60 and 16, to assist against the Parliament, and by destroying our corne and goods, and killing our Neigbours and Countrimen, and driving away our cattle: And also by bringing into the

Kingdom a forreigne Nation; and by treacherously surprizing and most basely delivering into the Scots hands the two considerable Towns of Barwick and Carlile, and by further aiding and assisting of them, towards the subduing and enslaving of our Kingdom, that many of the actors, contrivers, and assisters in that horrible and traiterous designe, not only against our Countries, but the Parliament and Kingdom, are after all their Summers abominable treason and out-rages, now returned with much confidence and boldness to their own houses, intending to hatch (as wee have cause to believe) new plots this Winter amongst us.

The premises considered, your Petitioners pray that Justice may be speedily executed upon such implacable enemies and declared traitors to the Parliament, Kingdom and their Countries, and to that end a Commission of Oyre [sic] and Terminer, with learned and faithfull judges may be forthwith sent down into these Northern parts, or such other legall Courses resolved on as to your wisdoms shall seeme best for their speedy trials in these Northen Counties, where they have committed the offences, and that a Sollicitor may be forthwith sent down into these parts, that such as are fled out of the Kingdom, or gone beyond Sea, may be proceeded against according to Law, we know no other way under God to prevent a new war, for many delinquents late in Arms, are not onely returned to their own houses, but meet, and have already their private consultations pretending Articles for their peaceable living at home, and are thereupon so insolent, that they ride armed to publike places, and do not stick to say that they yet expect a turn for all this, and we finde by experience, that unlesse the house doe severely proceed against such notorious Delinquents, many of the people in these parts will adhere to them, and justifie their actions, and be ready to rise up in Arms with them upon all occasions. We presse more earnestly the granting of this, knowing that the peace and quiet of the North, if not of the whole Kingdome, depends upon it.

And we shall ever pray

Background

Rumours had reached London that a 'great petition' from the north was being promoted by either John Lilburne, who visited his family property near Bishop Auckland about this time, or Oliver Cromwell, or both. The above petition was the only one to reach Parliament, though letters from some regiments stationed in the north were being addressed to Fairfax and his officers in late September (see 10 below). The issue of justice is presented here as a regional one, and no opinions concerning the treaty, the king, or any kind of revolution are stated. This was evidently the kind of petition that Parliament now preferred to receive, having put aside those from Newcastle and Yorkshire (4 and 5 above).

A majority of MPs elected in 1640 for the sixteen constituencies in Northumberland, Westmorland and Cumberland (the bishop's palatinate territory of Durham had none) became royalists, and of those sitting after the 'recruiter' or by-elections in 1645-8 only six would remain or return after Pride's Purge. The parliamentarian minority of the gentry in these four counties, with Yorkshire, formed an important political group known as the Northern Gentlemen. These had been the backbone of Parliament's support in the region since the start of the war, and were now giving voice to a bitter reaction against the occupation of their counties by Scottish armies three times since 1639. Their region was crucial in the second civil war, and the breakdown of order as a result of that conflict laid the region open to the depredations of 'moss troopers', the traditional Borders banditry. A letter published by the same newspaper the previous week informs us that the gentlemen at the Barnard Castle meeting had asked for 'some active men of each County, who know the Borders', to assist the army in dealing with these. A second letter, dated 31 October, complains about what the writer regarded as the invidious consequences of the lenient terms of surrender granted to the royalists at Appleby Castle in Westmorland, allowing them to return to their homes, with their horses, 'so that with much boldness they ride armed up and down where they please, having full liberty to act their own designs'. The writer's concern that the defeated royalists 'do not stick to say that they yet expect a turn for all this', and apprehension that they would be able to raise support locally if they did get such another turn, reminds us that the fear of a renewal of civil war was part of the background to the politics of late 1648.

Meanwhile, Colonel Ashton had quartered his forces in Westmorland until the money allocated to them from the profits of royalists' sequestered lands was paid to them (see 6 above and 38 below). The condition of the county, the writer claims, was now worse than under the earlier Scottish occupations. The letter is followed by the text of another petition addressed by the gentlemen of the four northern counties to Parliament from Barnard Castle on 25 October, recommending precise numbers for the forces that should be kept in the region and maintained by the whole of England, 'because they are the frontire Garrisons between the two Kingdoms, and have ever been maintained by the publike'. It is clear, however, from the Commons' response minuted on 6 November that the petition they received (also dated at Barnard Castle on 25 October) was the one reproduced above rather than this alternative version. The journal records their approval of a Commission of Oyer and Terminer as requested — before passing on to the still important business of which seven individual royalists were to be exempt from pardon in any Act of Oblivion.

Related sources

Commons Journal: vol. 6, 6 November 1648.
The Moderate Intelligencer, No. 89, 24 October – 2 November 1648.
     BL/EEBO: E.470[1].

David Scott, 'The 'Northern Gentlemen', the Parliamentary Independents, and Anglo-Scottish relations in the Long Parliament', *The Historical Journal*, vol. 42 (1999), pp. 347-75.

William Wardell Bean, *The Parliamentary Representation of the Six Northern Counties of England* (Hull, 1890).

8: WILTSHIRE

2 November 1648

Context

Unlike the Berkshire petition brought to the Commons at about the same time (9 below) this one was received and read to the House. The Speaker's reply, affirming the House's commitment to a treaty with the king, reflected the fact that the Newport negotiations had now begun to produce results. The king's answers had been received on 24 October, and both Houses of Parliament agreed to accept those concerning Ireland, payment of the public debts, the abolition of the Court of Wards and Liveries, and the addition of £100,000 p.a. to the royal revenue in compensation for this last. A committee had been appointed to draw up bills on these things for future royal consent, despite two major obstacles remaining. One of these was Parliament's demand for the exclusion of seven royalist leaders from pardon, though the two Houses had not yet agreed who the seven should be. The other was religion. The king had refused to accept the permanent abolition of bishops and sale of their lands, and rejected the Confession of Faith agreed by Parliament's Westminster Assembly of ministers — still a touchstone of Calvinist belief throughout the English-speaking world. A parliamentary committee had been appointed, however, to rewrite the Covenant of 1643 in a form that the king might be prepared to swear to. The original timetable of forty days had been extended by not counting Sundays and fast days, and a last-minute deal may have seemed possible, though it would come nowhere near the constitutional programme in the 11 September petition (1 above), explicitly supported here.

Text

To the Right Honourable the Commons of England in Parliament assembled, The humble Petition of the Well-affected Inhabitants of the County of Wilts.*

Sheweth, That the Maine end of the Peoples entrusting you, is chiefly to remove Oppressions, that they may live in peace, freedom, and safety. That it is their undoubted priviledge to be Judges of their grievances, and of the time and manner to present them to this Honourable House. That it is the duty of this Honourable House to hear and answer all, and especially grant those Petitions intending freedome; or at least give reasons to instruct the people, wherein any part of their desire is or will be hurtfull to the Petitioners or Common-wealth in generall.

That contrary hereunto, the Freedome of this Nation hath been of late much violated; Petitions have been burned by the hands of the Common Hangman; Petitioners imprisoned onely for petitioning; Petitions unanswered; yea, a Petition of Thousands in and about London presented to this

---

* This text, fuller than the other referenced below, survives in Goldsmiths' Library of Economic Literature (catalogue No. 993), and can be viewed online in *The Making of the Modern World* (Gale website). No printer or publisher is named.

Honourable House. Sept. the 11. 1648. wholly sleighted; though of that nature, with such Foundations of Government therein held forth to be established, and such oppressions to be removed, as we verily believe, till the former be confirmed, and the latter banished this Nation, it will be impossible for this Honourable House to settle this Common-wealth in solid peace and true freedome.

We beseech you consider: can people feed themselves with empty names of Peace, Freedome and Liberty, when the Supream Power is still by you undetermined, that was the first cause of all our warres, distempers and miseries: when Tithes, Excise, the chargeable proceedings of the Law, &c. remaine in the same, or a worse manner, then it was in the dayes of Ignorance, Popery, and Superstition, enforcing maintenance from all sorts of Industrious people, to their extreame prejudice and continuall vexation.

The premises considered, your Petitioners humbly pray this Honourable House, immediately to take the Petition of the 11. of September 1648. into your serious consideration, and vouchsafe answerable actings to every desire therein; then will the Tongues of men be silent that say, Many of you feare to doe justice, and bend your endeavours to preserve corrupt interests; So shall this Honourable House give more life to the present endeavours of your Petitioners, the Army, and all other the Free-people of the Land, to declare their Union, to Centre therein; that so this long distracted Nation may be at length restored to build their peace upon Foundations of equall Government; as not knowing for what other use the bloud and treasure of this Nation hath beene thus freely expended, but at least to procure the desires mentioned in that petition. In pursuance whereof your Petitioners are resolved to adventure their lives to preserve your authority against al opposition whatsoever.

And your Petitioners shall ever pray, &c.

The Honourable House of Commons being informed that divers Gent. (entrusted by the Well-affected Inhabitants of the County of Wilts) were at the door of this House to present their humble petition; and being called in, John Long Esquire, spake to it as followeth:

Mr Speaker, I am entrusted by the Well-affected of our County to present this their humble Petition to this Honourable House, wherein neither my selfe, nor these other Gentlemen entrusted with me, know anything insisted on, but the prosecution of justice, and the removing of burdens. To this we humbly desire the answer of this Honourable House, to return to those that employed us; which we hope will be such, as will send us home with such honourable expressions of you, as may become those that are honourers of God and faithfull Patriots to this Common-wealth.

The Gentlemen being called in againe, the Speaker returned this Answer: Gentlemen, your Petition hath beene read, and this House hath commanded me to let you know, That they are engaged upon a Treaty with the King, and that they are resolved therein, to take care of the LAWES, your LIBERTIES and RELIGION.

That the people of this Nation may at length enjoy the happinesse of equall Government: That all oppressions may be removed, and by doing Justice, establish a lasting Peace to future Generations: We the people of the County of Wilts, whose names are hereunto subscribed, doe nominate and entrust our lawfull Commissioners, viz. Walter South, William Eyre, John Long, Thomas Eyre, Edward Stokes, John Reade, William Ludlow, Nicholas Greene Esquires; James Heely, Richard Crowch, Edward Frippe, William Adlam, William Mountjoy, George Dyer, Thomas Wansey, John Stevens of the Devises; J. James, Bennet Swaine, Christopher Merriweather, Henry White, Thomas Neate, Adam Gouleney, Gentlemen; To present our humble Remonstrance, and Petition, to the Right Honourable the Commons of England in Parliament assembled; and they are hereby desired and authorised, to use their utmost endeavours, by all good waies and meanes, as shall seeme meete unto them, or any seven or more of them, to obtaine those foundations of Government to be established, and those oppressions removed, that are held forth in the large Petition presented to the Honourable House of Commons, upon the 11th of September, 1648. And what our Commissioners, or any seven or more of them, shall doe in pursuance thereof, we shall esteeme it as our acts and deeds, as if we were personally present, and did the same. In testimony whereof we have hereunto set our hands this 26 th day of October, 1648.

Another edition

Perfect Weekly Account, 1 - 8 November 1648, BL/EEBO: E.470[15]

Background

Wiltshire was a predominantly parliamentarian county, though many areas of it changed hands repeatedly under successive military occupations between 1643 and 1646. The county also saw a rising in 1645 of rural 'clubmen' opposed to both sides. In February 1648 the inhabitants of Westbury petitioned Fairfax against being forced to quarter troops of his army, despite having paid the taxes required of them; but they nevertheless declared that they would 'cheerfully undergo [these charges] for the furtherance of the publique good in relacion to the parliament and armie' if they knew for certain how much would be required.

In David Underdown's important discussion of social and geographical fault lines in south-west England, his distinction between open-field, grain producing areas, predominantly conservative in religion and Royalist in allegiance ('the chalk'), and woodland or upland areas dominated by pastoral farming and dairy production ('the cheese') inclined to be puritan and Parliamentarian, cuts right across this county from east to west. The woollen cloth industry was also widespread in the 'cheese' areas, especially the classic cottage broadcloth industry then dominated by rich merchant clothiers. According to the celebrated local antiquary John Aubrey, north Wiltshire was a puritan area where 'The Bible, and ease, for it is now all upon dairy-grassing and clothing, set their wits a-running and reforming.' But Salisbury, the county capital where the long-standing conflict between the corporation and the cathedral establishment had sharpened the support for reform, also had a history of pre-war puritanism.

Although the *Concurrent Testimony* of eighty-two Wiltshire ministers in June 1648, calling for the suppression of heresy and errors, shows the strength of Presbyterianism in the county, there were also significant pockets of religious radicalism. Two touring Baptist preachers, Thomas Lambe and Jeremiah Ives, were joined by some of Colonel Ireton's soldiers when they interrupted a church service in September 1646 at Devizes. Two months earlier two local men there had been charged with breaking a window in a house there where people were 'at conventicle'. When John Rede (or Reade), one of the 'commissioners' named in this petition, brought together a Baptist congregation on his farm at Porton in 1653, it gathered in members from Salisbury and many local villages who may have previously had their own separate meetings. Many historians have noted a connection between Baptists and Levellers, though the relationship was not without tensions; and the possibility of the most radical petitions coming from this historic conjunction of faith and politics will arise throughout this collection.

This petition's support for the Large Petition of 11 September, its highlighting of the constitutional principles the petitioners believe necessary for a lasting settlement, and pinpointing of tithes among other economic grievances, certainly place it at the Leveller end of the spectrum. In addition, much evidence for John Rede's participation in radical army politics at the times of greatest Leveller activity has recently been traced. His appointment as governor of Poole (see 62 below) on the last day of the Putney Debates suggests he was very probably the 'Lieutenant-Colonel Reade' who participated in the historic discussion of the constitution there. John Rees describes Rede as belonging to an outer circle of activists influenced by the Levellers, though not at the heart of their organisation. Despite these radical connections Rede, along with the majority of the other commissioners named by these petitioners, can be found participating in local government from at least this time. There was in Wiltshire no great gulf between people attracted to Leveller ideas and the 'honest' or more moderate party who according to David Underdown rejected social revolution and replaced the traditional elite in the government of English counties under the Commonwealth and Protectorate.

The men whose names the petitioners listed may not all have been the chief promoters of the petition, but they were undoubtedly regarded as reliable by those who were. This was no temporary alliance, either. Among the commissioners named in the petition, Nicholas Greene and Edward Stokes had served on the militia committee for Wiltshire during the first civil war; and Stokes, together with Richard Crouch, William Eyre, John Long, and William Ludlow were appointed by the House of Commons to the reformed committee on 2 December 1648, four days *before* the Independent party took over Parliament at Pride's Purge. John Rede himself had served briefly on the the county committee in 1644, along with Edward Stokes, before joining Sir William Waller's regional army. Rede also appears as a Justice of the Peace from 1649 to 1654, along with William and Thomas Eyre, Nicholas Greene, John Long, Edward Stokes, and Walter South. Bennet Swaine too seems to have been a JP in 1653, but is not recorded as attending any quarter sessions in the order book recently published by the Wiltshire Record Society.

William Eyre or Ayres, not to be confused with the Leveller soldier of the same name, would be elected an MP for Chippenham seven days before Pride's Purge and did not take his seat until 15 January 1649. He was the first new member to be excused from taking the oaths of allegiance and supremacy, but was not named to the commission for the king's trial and played no part in the regicide. Thomas Eyre (not William) was the 'Col. Ayers of Wiltshire', governor of Hurst Castle where the army leaders had the king confined after the Newport negotiations, described by a correspondent of the *Moderate* as 'our dear friend, and true Patriot ... whose fidelity can never be poysoned.' Along with Nicholas Greene, Thomas Eyre would be nominated to the 'Barebones Parliament' in 1653. James Hely would be elected an MP for Salisbury in 1656, and expelled from Salisbury corporation in the 1662 purge of Cromwellians from that body.

George Dyer of Heytesbury hundred, Henry White of Melksham and John Stevens of Devizes appear in the JPs' order book of 1642-54 as local constables. The post was a civic duty rather than paid employment, and became increasingly unpopular among those called upon to serve, as the responsibility of collecting new taxes such as Ship Money was imposed on them under Charles I. In 1639 Christopher Merriweather, high constable of Melksham hundred, was committed to London's Fleet prison after Walter Long, a leading opponent of Ship Money, successfully contested his own 'undue and unequal' assessment. Long was awarded costs of £93 16s against Merriweather and the Privy Council refused to release him, despite the sheriff Sir Edward Baynton, coming to his defence. Since 1647, however, Walter Long had been one of the eleven Presbyterian MPs whose expulsion was demanded by the army, and would soon be among the first to be excluded at Pride's Purge (see 32 below). It would not be surprising if Merriweather felt a degree of personal animosity towards his old antagonist, but he was also part of a network based on shared political commitments that lasted throughout the Commonwealth and Protectorate. Indeed, when the Long Parliament was restored in the crisis of 1659-60, Crouch, Rede, the two Eyres, Hely, Ludlow and Swain appear again in its ordinances for the militia and its financing in Wiltshire. Like Rede, Swayne lived to a great age: he was 83 when he died in 1697, according to a memorial in St Thomas's, Salisbury. Both saw out a later and very different revolution1689; did they ever share reminiscences of a more radical revolution they had once hoped for?

Related sources

Commons Journal, vol.6, 27 October - 2 November 1648.

The Concurrent Testimony of the Ministers in the County of Wiltes ... as also, Against the Errors, Heresies, and Blasphemies of these times, and the Toleration of them. (London, 1648) BL/EEBO: E.449[27].

Firth and Rait: *Acts and Ordinances*.

Clarke Papers, vol. 2, p. 61n (Col. Eyre).

VCH: *Wiltshire*, vol. 5: 'Parliamentary history 1629-1660', 'County Government 1530-1660'.

VCH: *Wiltshire*, vol. 8 (for Westbury).

VCH: *Wiltshire*, vol. 10 (for Devizes).

Ivor Slocombe (ed.), *Wiltshire Quarter Sessions Order Book 1642-1654* (Chippenham, Wiltshire Record Society, 2014).

B. Howard Cunnington (ed.), *Records of the County of Wiltshire, being extracts from the Quarter Sessions Great Rolls of the Seventeenth Century* (Devizes, Simpson, 1932).

Peter Sherlock (ed.), *Monumental Inscriptions of Wiltshire: an edition, in facsimile, of Monumental Inscriptions in the County of Wilton, Sir Thomas Phillipps, 1822* (Trowbridge, Wiltshire Record Society, 2000).

Tony Macfarlane, *The Civil War in Wiltshire* (Salisbury, Rowan Books, 1997).

George Daniel Ramsay, *The Wiltshire Woollen Industry in the Sixteenth and Seventeenth Centuries* (2nd edition, London, Cass, 1965).

David Underdown, 'The chalk and the cheese: contrasts among the English Clubmen', *Past and Present*, vol. 85 (1979), pp. 25-48.

David Underdown, '"Honest" radicals in the Counties, 1642-1649', in Donald Pennington and Keith Thomas (eds.), *Puritans and Revolutionaries, Essays in Seventeenth-Century History Presented to Christopher Hill* (Oxford: Clarendon, 1978).

John Rees, 'Lieutenant Colonel John Rede: a West Country Leveller and Baptist Pioneer', *The Seventeenth Century*, 30/3 (2015).

Stephen Wright, *The Early English Baptists, 1603-1649* (Woodbridge, Boydell, 2006).

Colin Mason, 'The General Baptists and the Levellers', *Baptist Quarterly*, 44/8 (2012).

9: BERKSHIRE

22 November 1648

Context

The promoters of this petition explain that they had first attempted to present it to the House of Commons in October, which seems likely in view of the fact that its avowed model is the Leicestershire petition of 2 October (3 above). The laying aside of petitions on 10 October (see 4 and 5 above) may have been one reason for the House's refusal to hear this one until Wednesday 22 November, when a decision was made to read it on 'Friday morning next'. Its high language, calling for the execution of justice on leading offenders in order to purge Parliament and the nation from blood guilt — though not naming the king — may have been another reason for ignoring it. No actual reading is recorded by the *Commons Journal*; if the 'Friday next' referred to was 6 December (rather than 24 November), this business was forestalled by Pride's Purge. The petition from Berkshire presented to Fairfax and his Council of Officers on 30 November (47 below) was printed along with this text, in a pamphlet naming no publisher or printer.

Text

A True Copie of the Berkshire Petition: Which after a Moneths attendance, the House would not permit to be brought in.

Fiat justitia, et ruat Mundus. [Let justice be done, and let the world perish.] Arise, o GOD, judge thou the Earth.

Totum majus & melius Quolibet sui Parte. Reale majus & melius suo Representativo.
[The whole is greater than any of its Parts. Truly greater and better than its Representative.]

London, Printed Decemb. 2, 1648. No printer or publisher named. BL/EEBO: E.475[2]

To the Honourable Commons of England in Parliament Assembled. The Humble Petition of divers of the Committee, Gentry, Ministry, and other well affected of the County of Berks.

Sheweth, That the Petition lately presented to You by our Countreymen of Leicester shire, in behalfe of themselves, and the whole Nation, did fully expresse our Sense of the present condition of Affaires, and our Desires thereupon.

That the answer You were pleased to give therunto, cometh short (in our understanding) of full Satisfaction to their and our humble Desires represented therein: The speedy and impartiall execution of Justice, the main Scope of that Petition, not at all remembred in Your answer: The Occasion of this our Addresse unto You.

That for those high Concernments (Religion, Lawes, Liberty, and Protection,) whereof in Your Answer You expresse so much of Care, We thankfully acknowledge, But humbly conceive there can be no Exercise of Religion, no Use of Lawes, no Assurance of Libertie, or Protection without such Desir'd Execution of Justice, upon all great Offenders, Notorious Invaders of them.

That (to say nothing of the horrid Murders, acted upon some, and attempted upon more of Your Selves and Friends) even since your Overture of Treaty with the King, (contrary to Your former Votes of Non-addresse, for which You gave such weighty Reasons) His Adherents English, Scottish, and Irish, by divers Insurrections, Invasions, and Combinations in His behalf, have given You such Cause to take up more resolv'd thoughts, and vigorous Courses for timely inflicting Condigne Punishment at least on the Heads of them, as that without it, neither You, nor We, can long be safe.

May it therefore please You so far to preferre the Lives and Interests of Your Selves and Friends, before those of Your and Their Enemies, as speedily proceed to Triall, Sentence, and Execution of all such Eminent Offenders, as God by wonders of Providence hath put into Your power, and require from them (that God may not require from You and the Nation) an Accompt of all that Innocent Blood, which hath been spilt, as Water upon the Ground in both the former and later Wars: That by Removall of such Obstructions, way may be made to Your Settlement, Our, and the Nations Enjoyment of the Common Peace, Rights, and Freedomes, so often sought, and long waited for, Wherein Your Petitioners and Thousands more are ready with their Lives and Estates to stand by You.

And ever Pray.

Background

According to Christopher Durston, popular sentiment in Berkshire inclined towards Parliament from the beginning of the civil wars: in January 1643 its Justices of the Peace claimed it was impossible to raise money for the king because 'the common voice of the multitude' regarded Parliament as 'the people's prop and upholder of their privileges'. The county's constituencies sent a number of radical members to the House of Commons, including Henry Marten, a committed republican who was elected unanimously by the freeholders of the shire in 1640. Marten's views were so unusual among the landowning class to which he belonged, that the Royalist press at the time could not resist attributing all popular mobilisation in the county to his influence, claiming that thousands of the common people had become his followers, and that he was 'resolved to level all in Berkshire'. It should be borne in mind that such statements from a Royalist perspective were not designed to flatter but to vilify him. Sarah Barber's biography characterises him as a 'revolutionary rogue' who as a member of the gentry was prepared to raise his radical tenants in arms in order to protect his own property rights. Other historians have been less judgemental of Marten, who was a notable friend of the Levellers. John Rees describes him as 'a constant champion of plebeian mobilisation' who 'operated with a constituency and allies different to any other Leveller, but he was of their movement'.

The volunteer cavalry regiment which Marten raised in the county in June 1648 worried both the civil and military authorities, and unlike similar forces raised by individual commanders in the emergency circumstances of the second civil war (see 26, 34, 38, 40 and 42 below) it was not given official recognition until the following year. Marten's commissioning of William Eyres, a known Leveller and former adherent of the mutiny at Ware in 1647, as one of his captains, together with incidents of the forcible requisitioning of horses from the stables of the local gentry, aroused a display of political paranoia in the royalist press, but the wilder accusations of plunder and even massacre as they progressed through the Midlands were no more than headline-grabbing inventions. Whatever the truth about his regiment, Marten was certainly close to some of the Leveller leaders and the author of tracts sympathetic to their views, but it is unlikely that he made any direct contribution to this petition, as he and his soldiers were out of the county for several weeks before it was first brought to parliament, and were reported to have reached York by early October.

Although radical religious and political groups sprang up during and after the war in Abingdon and Reading, both within Marten's sphere of influence, the tradition of revolt from below was both more widespread and more deeply rooted in these towns and others in Berkshire, as Durston has shown for particular communities such as Newbury, whose involvement in movements of political and religious dissent dated back to the 1450s, and the 'rebel town' of Windsor, whose inhabitants stood by their popular MP, the radical ex-courtier Cornelius Holland.

Related sources

Commons Journal, vol. 6, 22 November 1648.
Mercurius Elencticus, No. 45, 29 September – 4 October 1648. BL/EEBO: E.465[33].
Chris Durston, 'Henry Marten and the High Shoon of Berkshire: The Levellers in Berkshire in 1648', *Berkshire Archaeological Journal*, vol. 70 (1979-80), pp. 87-95.
C. G. Durston, '"Wild as Colts Untamed": Radicalism in Newbury during the early modern period', in Barry Stapleton (ed.), *Conflict and Community in Southern England* (Stroud, Sutton, 1992), pp. 36-52.
Manfred Brod, *The Case of Reading, Urban Government in Troubled Times 1640-1690* (Peterborough, Upfront, 2006).
Manfred Brod, *Abingdon in Context, Small-Town Politics in Early Modern England* (Peterborough, Fastprint, 2010).

Raymond South, *Royal Castle, Rebel Town, Puritan Windsor in Civil War & Commonwealth* (Buckingham, Barracuda, 1981).

Sarah Barber, *A Revolutionary Rogue, Henry Marten and the English Republic* (Stroud, Sutton, 2000).

PART TWO

GENESIS OF THE ARMY'S
REMONSTRANCE

SEPTEMBER - NOVEMBER 1648

10: THREE LETTERS TO FAIRFAX
22-30 September 1648

Context

As the flow of petitions to Parliament dried up following the Commons debate of 10 October 1648 (see 4 and 5 above), a new wave was forming in the parliamentarian army. Because the texts in the next four sections were addressed not to Parliament but to the army leadership, there is no official record of their reception. A handful of manuscript copies survive in the archives of William Clarke, the army secretary, and some were published in batches by the army administration; but for the majority we have to rely on the weekly newsbooks, one-off pamphlets and broadsides circulating in greater numbers than ever.

Many of these were printed and published anonymously, or under initials and pseudonyms. A number of publications claimed to represent the views of the army as a whole, though none could legitimately make that claim before the Remonstrance agreed on 18 November by the General Council of army officers meeting at St Albans (18 below). One example, *The Declaration of the Armie Concerning the Kings Majesty, and the Treaty*, is an amalgam of of the first two letters below, which the title page claims was presented to Fairfax by Paul Hobson 'and commanded to be printed and published'. There is no other evidence of such a command, and the publisher is a 'C.W.' who cannot be identified. The most obviously suspicious of this kind is *The Demands, Resolutions and Intentions of the Army*, claiming to have been 'sent from a great commander in the army, and desired to be printed and published in the name of the rest' on 26 September, with a long list of demands drawn mainly from the Levellers' Large Petition of 11 September. One of these demands, for the abolition of tithes with no mention of compensation to proprietors, goes further than the Large Petition itself. Despite many historians' speculation that its author was Henry Ireton, his unwavering belief in private property makes this very unlikely. Whoever sent it to the printer was certainly not authorised to issue it in the name of the whole army; while the incorrect rank of 'Major-General Cromwell' on the title page arouses suspicion from the start. Publishers of such claims may have been cashing in on the heightened political awareness of the reading public, responding to some patron's prompt, or spreading fake news as we would recognise it today. All were aiming to profit from the expanding news medium of one-off 'separates' containing an amalgam of news from everywhere and nowhere.

The three letters below do not take the form of petitions. The '&c' in the first leaves it unclear how many people have signed it, and in the second we do not know who 'we' are. The third was addressed by Constable's soldiers to their colonel by eighteen of his officers, but it presumably reached Fairfax thereafter, since a manuscript copy survives among the papers of William Clarke, the army secretary. All three are included here because a few sentences, particularly concerning the king's blood guilt, have frequently been quoted out of context as examples of petitioners' attitudes to the king; though the second, from the Newcastle and Tynemouth garrisons, has a great deal more to say about the authors' expectations of Parliament.

Texts

[i] *Letters from Lieutenant General Crumwel's Quarters... with Letters to his Excellency the Lord General Fairfax concerning the great Petition comming from the North, to the Parliament of England.* London, Printed for R. Smithurst, neer Pye: corner 1648. BL/EEBO: E.466[7]

A Copie of a Letter to his Excellency the Lord Fairfax, from the Garison of Newcastle and Tinmouth.

May it please your Excellency, We make bold being prest in spirit, to represent to you, as the ground of our fears, so the matter of our desires. It hath pleased God after much plottings and endeavours of the old and new Malignants, to Crown the Army under your conduct with great successe; and although God by that calls for justice, little or none is done, to the great grief as to the Kingdom in generall, so unto us in particular; and lesse is like to be done, unlesse your Excellency presently appear to do something, and the Army with you, to be a leading cause to us; we wait for it. Instead of Justice, behold a Treaty with them for Peace, that God speaks no Peace to; and instead of owning just Petitions, they are laid aside, and not countenanced; some imployed in the Treaty not long since [in April 1647] voted the Army Rebels; what that prognosticates in the future, when they have power, we leave to your Excellency to judge. We can hardly forbear but Petition the Parliament; (remembring our Engagement at New-market Heath) but we are very unwilling to do any thing without your Excellencies pleasure, being desirous in all good things to be led by you: and being confident (as formerly, so still) you will stand by the Kingdom and the Army in their just Rights. So hoping you will so far honour us, as to make a favourable construction of our expressions, and give an answer to encourage us to joyn with the well-affected, in their Petitions, for their just Rights and Priviledges. We subscribe ourselves in the behalf of the Officers and Souldiers of this Garison and Tinmouth, Your Excellencies humble Servants, Lieut. Col. Paul Hobson, Major Cobbett, Cap. Clark, Cap. Hutton &c.

Newcastle 22. Septemb. 1648

To his Excellency Thomas Lord Fairfax, Generall of all the Forces raised by the Parliament, for the Common-wealth of England.

May it please Your Excellency, Seeing it hath pleased God to exalt you into a place of Eminency and Trust in the Common-wealth of England, for the Redemption thereof from Captivity and Bondage, and to that End God also having blessed You and us with prosperous Success and Conquests, (beyond the ey of human sense) both in the late and present Wars, over Yours and the Peoples most inveterate Enemies; and seeing that we and all the well-affected of the Land ventured our lives, and all that was deer unto us, not sparing chearfully and faithfully to passe through all dangers and difficulties with you attending that Engagement; we are imboldened now at last (having looked round about us, and finding neither Your Excellency, the Army, nor the People yet answered as to those ends) to make our humble Address unto Your Excellency in this Juncture of time, wherein we apprehend, that the blood that hath bin spilt, The Conquests that God hath crowned us withal, the treasure and wealth of the People expended, is all upon the point of being rendred in vain and of none effect: For, to the sorrow of our hearts, we find that even those particulars of Common Right and Freedom, for which we took up Arms and still continue them, are not regarded, though by way of humble Petition lately presented to the House of Commons by the well-affected in and about London; and insteed of answering their just Desires of Freedom and Safety to the People, we find a Treaty with our conquered Enemy (who hath not so much as himself to Treat for, and on whom we must, and that of right, lay the guilt of all the bloud that hath bin spilt in these wars) is now chosen, and vigorously pursued; and Compositions at easie rates made with the new Delinquents for their late Rebellions and Treasons against the Common-wealth; though we justly expected that their Lands should be made over to us; and the whole Souldiery for their Arrears: and no Justice likely to be done to perfideous Hambleton [the Duke of Hamilton], or to his Adherents, who invaded our Land, and made war upon us; nor yet upon those Lords and Commons, Aldermen, and Common Councel men of London, whom that Invador profest to invite him in: Nor yet upon the Earl of Holland whom the House of Lords lately and most unjustly voted out of his imprisonment in Warwick Castle; nor yet upon the Lord Goring, Lord Capel Lord Louthbury, Laughorne, Powel, Poyer, &c. Neither any thing done to those insolent Common Councel men of London, that durst joyn with the Prince, while in Armes against the Parliament and people, in his Desires; and petition the Parliament for a Cessation of Armes, even with Hambleton himself, after the House of Commons had voted him and his Army Enemies, and those Englishmen that invited them into England, Rebells and Traytors, and notwithstanding the same, the House of Lords abetted and joyned with him and his Army, by publishing his poysonous Declaration by a special Order of their own House, to seduce the People into his Rebellion against our Common-wealth: yet all these wickednesses must be salved up with a Personal Treaty, putting our Capital and Bloudy Enemy into an equal Ballance with all the People and their Representatives, which is more then ever he had from his Coronation, as appeareth by his Oath, which the Parliament hath often publikely declared to the Common-wealth; so that of necessity our Indempnity, our Lives and Freedoms are left at his mercy, and what mercy when our Enemy is received, and the Adverse Party advanced can be expected, we leave your Excellency to judge. Wherefore, May it please your Excellency, we having seriously weighed the foresaid Petition, Intituled, *The humble Petition of Thousands Well-Affected Persons inhabiting the City of London, Westminster, the Burrough of Southwark, Hamblets, and places Adjacent, Presented to the Parliament Sept. 11. 1648.* Together with a second Petition endeavoured to be presented Sept. 13. Intituled, The humble Petition of the presenters of the late large Petition, &c. As also a Letter from our deer friends of the Garrisons of Newcastle and Tinmouth, and finding the common safety of us all wrapt up in those desires; we cannot in duty to God, to our own Native Countrey, and in honour to your Excellencies safety, and al that have adhered unto you, but resent [feel] the said Desires as our own: and humbly implore, That your Excellency will be pleased so to appear before us in the cause of the People, even in the midst of these our dangers and fears, that we and all the People, with the Generations after us, by your Excellencies happy conduct, may have just cause to bless God on your behalf: And that the same may come to pass, shall ever be the faithful prayers and endeavours of

Sir, Your Excellencies most humble servants, wholly Devoted to live and dy with you therein.

[ii] *The Moderate* No. 14, 10-17 October 1648. BL/EEBO: E.468 [2]

This letter coming to our hands, being from the officers of Sir William Constable's regiment, take at large.

Sir, The Officers and Souldiers of your Regiment lying far from the rest of the Army, and having seldome or never any seasonable knowledge of the sence and proceedings of the rest of their fellow souldiers in things relating to Common good, crave leave to offer to your consideration as followeth, *viz.*

 That they together with so many of known faithfullnesse in the Army, have by severall engagements made before God expressed their resolutions & grounds; And the same principles remaining with them, they desire not to lead but to follow; Yet as reasonable men, acting according to Judgement and conscience, doubt not but their highly honoured & heartily beloved Commanders will receive and consider what shall be offered, with freedom and plainnesse, as the sence of any part of those under their Command, and that it will be no otherwise look't upon by any unprejudiced Judgements; They therefore desire your approbation and furtherance (if you think fit, and shall have opportunity) to represent to the Lord Generall, and his honourable Councell of war, these their present apprehensions.

1. That especially in the last declaration for adhering to the Parliament in their non-addresses, the Army cannot count themselves free and disengaged by any unconstant actings of others, the dangerous consequences being as fatally eminent now as ever, and the opportunity,

if lost, not like to be recovered.

2. That they are ashamed to beg pardon of any for their many, and those most honest services done by them for the kingdome, the which if acted by them, might render them guilty of a crime not much unlike to that of *David* in the businesse of *Absalom*, viz. 2 Sam. 19.5.6.7.

3. That they shall never prove good Cavaliers.

4. That they are very much sadded [*sic*] to think how successlesse all their honest endeavours for the subjects ease and liberty have hitherto proved.

Sir, the consideration of the premises we commend to your Honours wisdome, humbly subscribing our selves, Sir, your Humble and most devoted servants.

[In the manuscript, the following names are added, in one hand: Marke Grimes, Wroth Rogers, Laurence Nunny, Matthew Cadwell, Samuell Rose, Arthur Bromley, Edmund Atkinson, Edward Tomson, James Clark, William Jhonstone, James Loving, George Harrison, John Dun, ? Meyer, Robert Baldwin, Richard Oliver, John James, Rise Jhones.]

Manuscript

Letter to Sir William Constable, Worcester College Oxford, Clarke Ms. No. 114, fo. 83v.

Other editions

A copie of two letters, sent from divers officers of the army in the north; to his excellency Thomas Lord Fairfax; concerning the late large petition, presented to the Parliament upon the eleventh of Sept. 1648... BL/EEBO: 669.f.13[27]

The Moderate, No. 13, 3-10 October 1648. BL/EEBO: E.467[1]

The Declaration of the Armie Concerning the Kings Majesty, and the Treaty.... 9 October 1648. Printed for C.W. and are to be sole [*sic*] near the Royall Exchange in Cornhill. BL/EEBO: E.466[10]

A Perfect Diurnal, No. 225, 15-22 November 1647. BL/EEBO: E.520[7]

Background

The royalist newsbook *Mercurius Pragmaticus* claimed that the first two 'divellish' letters above 'had their frame from Ireton, and countenance from his Father[-in-law] Cromwell, and that the prosecution of it among the Souldiery is left to Sir Arthur Hesilrige, Harry Marten, Paul Hobson, and Major Cobbett'. Hobson and Cobbett were experienced activists who would not need their compositions to be 'framed' by a superior officer. Hobson was a Baptist lay preacher and deputy at this time to Sir Arthur Hesilrige as governor of Newcastle, while Major John Cobbett had taken part in the army agitation of 1647 and narrowly escaped cashiering at that time. Commissary-General Henry Ireton was currently at Windsor, having unsuccessfully offered his resignation to Fairfax, and Cromwell had crossed into Scotland on 21 September, so it is unlikely that either of them was directly involved. Henry Marten and his Berkshire troop are known to have been in Leicestershire during the first week of September, and were reported to have reached York by early October (see 9 above). Despite rumours that Marten was leading a force of desperate men fighting under his banner 'For the People's Freedom against all tyrants whatsoever', and determined to 'levell all sorts of people', no petition or declaration from his own regiment has survived.

The forces at the siege of Berwick were drawn from Harrison's and Overton's regiments and the Northumberland Horse, all of which will reappear with their own petitions below. After its surrender the town was garrisoned by the Northumberland Horse and 'some odd companies' of Overton's under Lieutenant-Colonel Thomas Reade, with Lieutenant-Colonel Fenwick as deputy to the governor, Sir Arthur Hesilrige; while the rest of Overton's regiment moved on towards Carlisle, John Lilburne himself visited Berwick on 30 September and left for London the next day with the news of Berwick's surrender.

Constable's regiment was not the one he had commanded during the first civil war, but was raised in Cambridge and the Isle of Ely by Edward Montagu. It had fought at Marston Moor and been quartered at Newport Pagnell in 1644 (see 53 below). Incorporated into the New Model Army, it served at Naseby, Bridgwater and Bristol, and passed to Colonel John Lambert when Montagu resigned in October 1645. By the spring of 1648, under Constable's command, it was split up in garrisons on the southern marches of Wales: six companies were stationed at Gloucester, one at Chepstow and several at Hereford; and some also fought at Bristol and Wallingford during the second civil war. Given the prominence of cavalry regiments in histories of the New Model Army's politicisation, and the frequently expressed belief that regimental petitions were composed by their colonels and imposed on their men, we can see here a group of infantry officers acting and organising independently of their commanding officer, though clearly in sympathy with him.

Constable was a Yorkshire gentleman of reduced fortune who had actively opposed the forced loan and other royal policies in the 1620s. While in the Netherlands (1637-41) he and his wife Dorothy – Thomas Fairfax's great-aunt – attended the English separatist church at Arnhem led by Philip Nye and Thomas Goodwin. The Constables returned to England in 1641 and William obtained a seat in Parliament for Knaresborough, emerging as a loyal supporter of the Independents in the divisions that split the Commons from 1646 onwards. The regiment of foot he raised in 1642 fought at Edgehill; and from July 1643 he commanded the East Yorkshire forces under Ferdinando, Lord Fairfax. He resigned his command under the Self-Denying Ordinance of 1645, but returned to take over this New Model regiment in late 1647, when Lambert resumed his former command in the

Northern Association. From November 1648, Constable was to become a key person on the Council of Officers, especially in the committees which ultimately determined the fate of the king.

The first five of his officers named in the manuscript had been involved in the army's resistance to Parliament in 1647, while under Lambert's command. The radical beliefs of William Erbery, their chaplain then — tending towards the rule of the saints rather than democracy — may have been an important influence. Major Thomas Kelsey left them in December 1645 to join Ingoldsby's regiment (see 12 below). Lieutenant-Colonel Mark Grime and Major Wroth Rogers, with Cadwell and three other captains, signed the New Model officers' *Petition and Vindication* of 27 April 1647; and Cadwell, along with a Captain Blethin, had represented the regiment's officers on the army council in 1647. The regiment attended the rendezvous at Ruislip Heath following the Putney Debates, and it was reported there were 'no other expressions, but of continued concurrence with and submission to the Generall' when they got there.

Wroth Rogers, from Llanfaches near Newport in Monmouthshire, will appear again at Hereford (60 below). He was probably named after William Wroth, minister of the parish from before 1620 until 1638. Both opposed the ceremonialism of King Charles and Archbishop Laud, and Rogers joined Wroth's Independent church following 'the New England pattern' in 1638-9. The church members dispersed early in the civil war, as Monmouthshire fell under royalist domination, and Rogers next appears in Montagu's regiment in 1644 alongside Francis Blethyn, probably also from the Llanfaches area. Both became captains when their regiment joined the New Model. In 1645 Rogers was appointed governor of Barnstaple, and by May 1648 was governor of Hereford Castle, where he remained in post until the Restoration (see 60 below). Grimes was cashiered in 1649, after complaints about his conduct from the corporation of Gloucester; but Rogers and Cadwell were still serving when six companies were disbanded in May that year.

Related sources

Malcolm Wanklyn, *Reconstructing the New Model*.
Firth and Davies, *Regimental History*, pp. 175-83, 389-90, 399-40.
ODNB: David Scott, 'Constable, Sir William, baronet (*bap*. 1590, *d*. 1655)'.
Stephen K. Roberts, 'Rogers, Wroth (*d. c.* 1604) of All-tir-fach, Llanfaches, Mon. and Hereford', (unpublished), courtesy of The History of Parliament.

11: IRETON'S REGIMENT

16 October 1648

Context

Contemporary Bulstrode Whitelocke described this petition as 'the beginning of the design against the king's person, but not discerned till afterwards'. To begin with, the text seems clear on the question of Charles's responsibility for all the bloodshed of the civil wars for which god requires vengeance; yet the fourth demand, which appears in every edition of the text, is that it should be considered treason for anyone to speak on the king's behalf 'till he shall be acquitted of the guilt of shedding innocent blood'. Whitelocke called the petition's approach 'subtle', and modern historians have seen in it signs of ambiguity or hesitation. If we discard the royalist news writers' belief that it was written by Ireton alone, the inconsistency may be explained as the outcome of disagreement and compromise among the officers, and probable authors, whose names are stated in the text.

Text

The True Copy of a Petition Promoted in the Army, and already presented to His Excellency the Lord General, by the Officers and Soldiers of the Regiment under the Command of Commissary General Ireton. London, Printed in the year 1648. BL/EEBO: E.468[18]

To his Excellency the Lord Fairfax our ever honored General; The humble Petition of the Officers and Soldiers of the Regiment of Commissary General Ireton;

Sheweth, That although we are as earnestly desirous of a safe and well-grounded Peace, and that a final end were put to all the miseries and troubles of the Commonwealth, as any sort of men whatsoever: Yet considering,

I. That there is no Justice done against, or tryal of the Contrivers or Abettors of the Rebellion in Wales, Kent; that of Holland, Buckingham, and their Accomplices: or of the Confederates with the Apostate Scots: and indeed little Justice by the Parliament done upon any Offendors of that kind, By which we have too much cause to fear, that there may be a party in the Parliament abetting and corresponding with (if not guilty of) the same Designes.

II. That notwithstanding the King hath betrayed the trust reposed in him, and raised War against this Nation to enslave it, violating his Oaths and trampling under foot our Laws, (then which no Engagement now taken can be more binding:) notwithstanding he is guilty of all the blood-shed in these intestine Wars, as may appear not only by the Declaration of the Parliament of England, and that of Scotland, but even by his own confession in his late agreeing to the Parliaments first Proposition [at Newport]: being also a person who was so far concluded incapable to govern, that the Parliament voted no Address should be made to him. There is yet a prevalent party of his Creatures, who in Parliament, and elsewhere, act his Design, and endeavour to re-inthrone him, and are (as we conceive) the Authors of our present Distractions.

III. That through the evil Designs and Practises of the foresaid Party, the intolerable burthen of Free Quarter is continued upon the people, notwithstanding the unreasonable taxes daily extorted from them, in the name of pay for the Army: By which mean we are not only rendred odious to others, but a burthen to our selves, not being able to cloth our selves, shoe our horses, or free our Arms.

We therefore cannot think any thing can be safely done in order to a peace, until some speedy and effectual course be taken, which we humbly desire your Excellency will be pleased, to your utmost power, to endevor,

1. That there may be a strict scrutiny, for the full discovery of such persons as were contrivers or encouragers of the Rebellions aforesaid, and that Justice speedily be executed on them according to the late orders of Parliament.
2. That impartial and speedy Justice may be done upon all criminal persons, and especially such as have or shall endeavor to obstruct the course thereof, or have betrayed their Trust, or bin Authors of shedding that innocent blood, which calls to Heaven for Vengeance, that so we may be at peace with God.
3. That the same fault may have the same punishment, in the person of King or Lord, as in the person of the poorest Commoner.
4. That all such may be proceeded against as Traytors, who act or speak in the Kings behalf, till he shall be acquitted of the guilt of shedding innocent blood.
5. That the Army may speedily have their pay, or a present course taken against those who unjustly with-hold it; and that they may have the Arrears due since January 15. before they be ordered to pay Quarters, and effectual provision made for the payment of former Arrears.
6. That the intolerable oppression of free Quarter be immediately taken off, and that for the time to come, whilst there is necessity for an Army, there may be Assignations given to each Regiment, Troop and Company, which may be constant, during the Establishments of the Army, that the money may not pass from hand to hand till it is half imbezelled, but be paid immediately from the Countries to the Souldiery, that so all free Quarter for ever avoyded, it may return from the Souldier to the Countryman again.

And now fearing, lest the inveterate malice of our Adversaries should asperse us with a design to destroy Magistracy and propriety [property]; we cannot but declare, that we shall constantly endevor to defend them both with our lives and fortunes, and in expectation of your Excellencies favour in the Premises, we shall ever pray &c.

The great necessities and pressing Grievances of the Soldiery have inforced us to make these our addresses (by way of Petition) to the Lord General, for the redress of them; and knowing that our present undertaking will ere long be presented to publike view, the Officers in the Regiment, under the command of Commissary General Ireton, by whose appointment this is already presented to his Excellency the Lord General, have (to prevent any prejudice, which might otherwise accrue to our present proceedings, by any false or mistaken Copy, surreptitiously gotten and published in their name) desired me to print the same, with the name of an Officer of each Troop subscribed, in the behalf, and at the request of the Officers and soldiers of the said Regiment, that the reader may be the better satisfied. H.C.   [Henry Clare]

Anthony Morgan, Sampson Tongood, James Gennings, Jervice Jefferie, William Rauce, Henry Clare, junior.

Other editions

The Articles and Charge of the Officers and Souldiers in the Armie, concerning the Kings Majesty, and all persons whatsoever, who shall endeavour to re-inthrone Him, or to act or speak in His Majesties behalf, till he shall be acquitted of the guilt of shedding innocent bloud...Commanded to be Printed and Published by the Authority and Consent of the Officers and Souldiers in the Army. October 20. 1648. (No named printer or publisher.) BL/EEBO: E.468[23]

The Moderate, no. 15, 17-24 October 1648. BL/EEBO: E.468[24]

The Kingdoms Weekly Intelligencer, No. 282, 17-24 October 1648. BL/EEBO: E.468[33].

Background

All six of the officers named in the petition appear in records of this regiment. Captain Anthony Morgan was an ex-royalist who was commissioned in the New Model Army in 1647, remaining loyal to the army leadership throughout the events of 1647-9 and later serving the Commonwealth in Ireland. In May 1649 Lieutenants Sampson Twogood, James Jennings and Jarvis Jefferie were named, along with Cornet William Raunce, in a list of those who took part in suppressing the mutineers who refused to serve in Ireland. Henry Clare appears to have been a regimental surgeon.

Cromwell's physician Dr George Bate claimed that the army leaders deliberately agreed to 'suffer the common sowldiers, in their bands and regiments, and officers of lesser note to have their private meetings and to frame petitions', adding that many people found it hard to believe these regiments' colonels were not the actual authors. Yet in the spring of 1647 many officers and common soldiers had been active in discussing and drawing up their grievances, and took an active part in the New Model Army's political intervention at that time. The late Austin Woolrych, in his detailed study of these earlier events, concluded that the soldiers showed they had minds of their own, and even in the few cases where they produced identical grievance lists it was by their own consent. Though elected agitators were allowed no formal role after November 1647, many officers and men of the regiments now producing petitions had previous experience.

According to a letter from Captain Morgan published in the Leveller-friendly *Moderate*, Ireton's regiment had recently been brought together at Farnham in Surrey, but refused to disperse into neighbouring counties as ordered, fearing that they were about to be disbanded altogether; instead, they sent this petition to Fairfax from Farnham and marched into Sussex together. Not all of Ireton's six cavalry troops had been with him throughout the siege of Colchester, some being deployed to deal with royalist insurgencies in the southern counties. Exchequer records confirm that between 14 and 19 October 1648, soldiers from five troops — including Ireton's own, under Major Gibbons — were quartered on householders in Farnham and several villages between there and Guildford (see also 48 below). A soldiers' meeting could certainly have taken place in that area. It is not clear where Ireton himself was: in the last few days of September he had gone to Windsor under orders from Parliament's Derby House committee to interrogate prisoners in the castle. According to several contemporaries, he spent his time there drafting the remonstrance which was to be agreed by the army council in November (18 below); but in the first week of October he was reportedly seen attending the House of Commons, where he had sat for Appleby since 1645.

Related sources

The National Archives, Commonwealth Exchequer Papers, SP28/57, vol. 1, fos. 47-81.
Worcester College Oxford, Clarke Papers, MS 16, fos. 103-8, 113.
Mercurius Pragmaticus, No. 30, 17-24 October 1648. BL/EEBO: E.468[37].
New Propositions from the Armie... Printed for R.W. and are to be sold at the Royall Exchange in Cornhill, 1648. BL/EEBO: E.468[34].
Mercurius Militaris, No. 2, 10-17 October. BL/EEBO: E.468[35].
CSPD, 1648-1649, p. 290.
[George Bate], *A Short Narrative of the Late Troubles in England*, translated from Latin & edited by Edward Almack, 1649 (facsimile edition London, Robinson, 1902), p. 100.
Bulstrode Whitelock [*sic*], *Memorials of the English Affairs from the Beginning of the Reign of Charles the First to the Happy Restoration of King Charles the Second* (Oxford, Oxford University Press, 1853), vol. 2, p. 424.
Ian Gentles, *New Model Army*, pp. 266-70.

Woolrych, *Soldiers and Statesmen*, pp. 55-90, 338-40.
Firth and Davies, *Regimental History*, vol. 1, pp. 115-25.
Wanklyn, *Reconstructing the New Model*.

12: INGOLDSBY'S REGIMENT

30 October 1648

Context

There were a number of reports at the time of this petition that new agitators had been elected by some of the army's regiments, and were demanding the recall of the previous year's General Council, including the soldiers' representatives. Although this petition is not specific about the soldiers' representatives, the regiment would go on to demand that they be brought back to the council in September 1649. Fairfax's response to the petition below was to call to St Albans in early November a Council of Officers, whose attendance lists show that no representatives of the rank and file were there.

Text

A Perfect Diurnall, 30 October - 6 November 1648. BL/EEBO: E.526[25]

Dateline Monday 30 October.

To his Excellency the Lord Fairfax, our Noble Generall. The humble Petition of the Officers of Col. Inglesbyes Regiment, in the behalfe of themselves and private Souldiers, now lying in the Garison of Oxford.

Sheweth, That your Excellencies endeavours, and ours, for common Freedoms, have been so hazzardous to us so chargeable to the people, and so wonderfully owned by God himselfe, that once before, and now againe, God hath given us a totall victory over the enemies of our libertie, and given those unto our hands that would have inslaved us; so that nothing remains to be done, to make and keep us, and all honest people of the Nation free men, and to make the hazzards of our lives, and losse of so much bloud, to be effectuall to us, but an immediate care that justice be done upon the principall invaders of our liberties, namely the King and his party, whom the Parliament have formerly declared non addresses to, The Army likewise declared, to live and die with them in the prosecution thereof.

That likewise sufficient Caution, and streight bonds be given to future Kings, for the preventing the inslaving the people hereafter. And that grounds of encouragement be given to the people of succeeding Generations for defending themselves against the like attempt: Then might we with cheerefulnesse return to our severall callings, hoping to live in peace, blessing God for his goodnesse.

But we are almost past hopes of obtaining these things, and it cannot but lie heavy upon our spirits, to apprehend that all our harvest should end in chaffe: And what was won in a field may be given away in a Chamber. For the Treaty now in hand is the matter of our present doubts, the issue of it can neither be just nor safe; and seeing that upon the well or ill closing of our late and yet continued distractions depends the outward weale or woe of us and our posterity, and that it is a thing ought to be looked after, as to the making successful all our former Victories which God hath blessed us with. We therefore humbly pray your Excellency, That you would be pleased to reestablish a generall Councell of the Army under your command, to consider of some effectuall remedies hereunto, either by representing the same to the house of Commons, as the Petitioners of London, and divers other places have done, or by such other way as your Excellency with your Councell shall think fit in a businesse of so high concernment to three Nations, having expended such vast quantities of blood and Treasures in hopes of better things.

And your Petitioners shall pray, &c.

Background

Although some newsbooks also reported agitation in Ewers's, Rich's and Rainborowe's regiments in Hampshire at this point, this regiment's is the only petition to survive from among them. Ingoldsby's foot had originally been raised and commanded by the parliamentarian leader John Hampden under the Earl of Essex in 1642. Richard Ingoldsby took command in 1644, and it was incorporated into the New Model Army in 1645. The radical millenarian William Erbery had spent time as its chaplain, and it was among the regiments that resisted disbandment and elected agitators in 1647. Ingoldsby himself, a cousin of Oliver Cromwell's, is not known to have played any part in the political actions of the army at that time; but his Lieutenant-Colonel Thomas Kelsey, a yeoman's son and member of the London Drapers' Company (described by a contemporary as a 'godly button-maker') played an active part as deputy governor of Oxford from 1646, purging the university there of royalists. During the second civil war, half the regiment remained at Oxford, while the other half joined Fairfax to put down royalist risings in Kent and Surrey and pursued the rebels to Colchester. In May 1649 Ingoldsby's officers wrote to Fairfax recalling the demands of the army's *Remonstrance* and the *Agreement of the People*, and in September that year its five companies in Oxford mutinied after Leveller literature was seized from the quarters of John Radman, who had been one of the common soldiers' agitators in 1647.

Kelsey was shortly to sit on the committee appointed at St Albans to prepare the army's *Remonstrance* for presentation to Parliament and for publication (below, 18), and would represent the soldiers in discussions with the London Levellers about a new *Agreement of the People*. In the army council meetings of December 1648 and January 1649 at Whitehall, he defended the council's intervention in the political situation against the disapproval of the prophetess Elizabeth Poole, despite declaring his readiness to recognise divine intervention if he believed it to be genuine. He played no part in the king's trial or execution, but supported the Commonwealth and Protectorate regimes. As one of the Major-Generals appointed by Cromwell in 1655 to oversee local government he is said to have displayed both puritan zeal and political radicalism.

Colonel Ingoldsby was nominated to the High Court of Justice that tried the king, but attended only to sign the death warrant. His famous claim after the Restoration that Cromwell had forced his hand is not supported by the clarity of his signature on the document. He too served both Commonwealth and Protectorate, and was made a lord of the new upper house of Parliament in 1657. He was one of the few regicides pardoned after the Restoration, and the only one to be honoured as a Knight of the Bath by King Charles II.

Related sources

The Kingdoms Weekly Intelligencer, No. 184, 31 October - 7 November 1648. BL/EEBO: E.470[10].
The Moderate, No. 17, 31 October - 7 November 1648. BL/EEBO: E.470[12].
The Moderate, 11-18 September 1648. BL/EEBO: E.574[4].
Mercurius Militaris, No. 3, 24-31 October 1648. BL/EEBO: E.469 [10*].
Firth & Davies, *Regimental History*, vol. 2, pp. 372-40.
Woolrych, *Soldiers and Statesmen*, pp. 302-40, 347-8.
Firth (ed.), *Clarke Papers*, vol. 2, pp, 54, 61, 167, 262.
ODNB: Timothy Venning, 'Ingoldsby, Sir Richard, appointed Lord Ingoldsby under the protectorate (*bap.* 1617, d. 1685)'.
ODNB: J. T. Peacey, 'Kelsey, Thomas (d. in or after 1676)'.

13: FLEETWOOD'S REGIMENT

October 1648

Context

Meanwhile, Charles Fleetwood's regiment presented a short petition concerning free quarter to Fairfax, along with their petition to Parliament (6 above) annexed.

Text

The Copies of Two Petitions From the Officers and Souldiers of Col. Charles Fleetwood's Regiment, concerning their severall Grievances, One of them presented to his Excellency the Lord Gen. Fairfax. The other to the Right Honourable the Commons of England in Parliament assembled. Signed by the Chief Officers present with the said Regiment ...

William Coleman Major.	Robert Stanard Lieutenant.
Richard Sankie Captain.	William Bucke Cornet.
Steven White Captain:	William Williams Cornet

Printed by John Clowes, 1648. BL/EEBO: E.468[32]

To his Excellency the Lord Fairfax,
The humble Petition of the Officers and Souldiers of Colonell Fleetwoods Regiment

Sheweth, That your Petitioners taking into their serious thoughts, the intolerable burthen which the Kingdom lyeth under by reason of free Quarter, the many sad complaints which our eares are dayly witnesses off, and the odium which hereby reflects on your Excellency and the Army, somthing we are duly paid, because the Countrey payes all thats demanded of them, and that we are neglective of our duties in not discharging our quarters, as likewise considering the great inconveniences that may ensue, both the Kingdom and the Souldiery being impatient under this insupportable expression [*sic*]. We could no longer delay to use our endeavours for redresse.

Your petitioners therefore humbly pray that your Excellency will be pleased to cast your eye on this annexed petition [6 above], and after perusall thereof, to represent it for us to the Parliament in such manner as your Excellency shall judge meet.

Background and related sources

See 6 above.

14: 'SEVERAL REGIMENTS'

7 November 1648

Context

In response to pressure from Ireton and other leading figures in the army, as well as the letters and petitions above, Fairfax summoned a Council of Officers to meet at St Albans. Its debates began on 7 November 1648, and were reported in a number of newsbooks and pamphlets at the time, but none of these were published under any official imprint before the *Remonstrance* (18 below) appeared on 20 November. A few notes on attendance and committee membership survive, but no minutes like those we have for Putney and Whitehall debates. The petition or petitions described in this text may have been brought in, along with 15 below, on 11 November 1648, the second day of discussion touching 'the present affaires of the Kingdome'.

Text

Packets of Letters from Scotland and the North of England, No. 34 (7 Nov. 1648). BL/EEBO: E.470[17]

A Letter from the Lord Generall's Head-Quarters at St. Albans.

SIR, This day a Generall councell is to meet here; what the event of it will be, it is impossible for any yet to know: But here are Gentlemen with instructions from severall Regiments to presse two things at the said Councell.

1. That the execution of Justice may bee done upon those who raised the former and later warres against the Parliament of England, And that there may not be any exemption of persons from Justice, to neither King nor Subject.
2. That the Treaty may not conclude a Peace with the King and his party, without care taken to preserve the Liberties and Freeedomes of the people of this Nation.
3. That limits may be set to binde Kings for the future, that they shall not have power to enslave the people, by Tyranny and oppression, and triumph upon them as over conquered slaves.
4. That provisions be made for the free people of England that both we and future generations may defend our selves against insulting Kings.
5. That there may be some course taken for pay for the Souldiery, that have served and beene faithfull to the Parliament. And sufficient security thereunto, for them to guard them in what they have done.
6. That these and such other things as shall be agreed on by the General Councel, may be sent to the House of Commons by the Lord Generall, and his Excellency to desire a speedy answer therein.

Another edition

A Declaration of the Armie, Presented to the Kings Majesty in the Isle of Wight; Declaring, their full Resolution touching His Majesties Reign and Government, and wearing the Crown of England; and their Proposals upon what Terms and Conditions they will re-inthrone Him....... Printed for C.W. neer the Royal Exchange. 1648. BL/EEBO: E.470[23]

Background

It is clear from the surviving attendance lists that only officers were invited to this General Council. The forces currently serving under Cromwell and Lambert in the north of England do not seem to have been represented for the first few days. Though there were persistent rumours that Cromwell himself was on his way from Yorkshire, he had only recently arrived to take over the siege of Pontefract Castle and set up his headquarters at Knottingley, from where he wrote to Parliament on 5 November and to his cousin Robert Hammond the following day.

According to a report generally accepted by historians as reliable, although its publisher cannot be identified, the council's proceedings commenced on 7 November with the reading of 'papers formerly presented to the Lord-Generall in the name of some particular regiments of the army' but nothing was concluded that day. The next two days were spent in discussion of the army's urgent practical concerns of free quarter, wages, and indemnity for their wartime actions; and it was only on 10 November that debate on the political situation began. Some of the colonels are said to have started by expressing a desire for peace, and there was some discussion of 'the former Proposalls' (perhaps the *Heads of the Proposals* rejected by the king in 1647) and 'bringing Delinquents to triall'. Some historians have suggested that the bringing in of petitions from various regiments demanding stronger action, from 11 November, was stage-managed by Ireton and others to turn the debate in the more radical direction they desired, but there is no reason to doubt that they had come in from actual regiments.

Of the two sources which provided the public with the text above, the weekly newsbook *Packets of Letters* is considered reliable and widely used by historians. Its report is clear and informative: these proposals were brought to St Albans by the officers under instructions from those they represented. The other publication, however, is a characteristic mishmash of news published by the unidentified 'C.W.', some of it unconfirmed by any other source. The 'gentlemen' who carried these instructions have become 'Agents' in this pamphlet; and it also includes a letter allegedly sent directly to the King by 'divers Officers and Souldiers in the West of England', promising to work for his 're-investing' on two conditions: that justice be done against 'the capitall Offenders of this Nation' and that no treaty be concluded 'without care to preserve the Liberties and Freedomes of the people of this Nation'.

The very notion of re-investing the king was unlikely to be acceptable to Charles, as he had not been, and in his own view could never be, divested of his crown.

Related sources

The Representations and Consultations of the Generall Councell of the Armie at St Albans... Printed for R.A., 1648. BL/EEBO: E.472[3].
Firth (ed.), *Clarke Papers*, vol. 2, Appendix D.
Gardiner, *Great Civil War*, vol. 4.

15: FLEETWOOD'S, WHALLEY'S AND BARKSTEAD'S REGIMENTS

11 November 1648

Context

Following the first three days of the St Albans meeting, which were spent discussing free quarter and soldiers' pay, Fairfax addressed these concerns in a letter to Parliament's committee for the army at Derby House, dated 9 November. It is possible that Ireton presented his draft of the lengthy document which was to become the army's *Remonstrance* the following day. On 11 November the petition below was read in the name of three regiments: Fleetwood's, Whalley's, Barkstead's.

The demands of this petition were circulated, without any preamble, in a number of newsbooks and pamphlets that attributed them to unnamed regiments, the soldiers in general or, in one case, to Rich's regiment alone. The text below was published by George Whittington, one of the army's regular publishers, and can be regarded as the official version. Some newsbooks had reported that a petition was being drawn up at a meeting or rendezvous of Rich's, Rainborowe's and Ewers's regiments in Hampshire on 28 October and would shortly be made public; but whether or not this was presented at St Albans, no further evidence survives.

The petitioners' hope that when peace is secured on the terms they wish for, 'we may with safety be released, from this troublesome and hazardous imployment' is a reminder to us that despite the presence of many professional soldiers in all the civil war armies, men like these did not see themselves as permanently employed in war, nor the New Model as a potential standing army. For the killing of Colonel Thomas Rainborowe at his lodgings in Doncaster, which had occurred on 30 October, see 16 below.

Text

A Petition From Severall Regiments of the Army, viz, Colonell Fleetwoods, Colonell Whalies, Colonell Barksteads, &c Presented to his Excellency, Thomas Lord Fairfax, at St. Albons, on Saturday 11. of this present November. 1648.

WHEREIN They set forth their Desires for a speedy, safe, and just settlement, that thereby the Kingdom may be freed from the heavy burthens that now they lye under, especially that of Free-Quarter... Printed for George Whittington. BL/EEBO: E.470[32]

To his Excellency, Thomas Lord Fairfax, Generall of all the Forses raised by the Parliament, in the Kingdom of England, and Dominion of Wales.

The humble Petition of the Officers and Souldiers in Col. Fleetwoods, Col. Whalies, and Col. Barksteads Regiments, under your Excellencies Command.

Sheweth, That through the blessing of God upon the Army, under your Excellencies Conduct, the enemies of this Nations Peace and Freedom, have twice been subdued.

That as we ingaged in Judgment and Conscience against them, to preserve this Nation from slavery, so we hope the Parliament (by whom we were invited to ingage) would have executed Justice, upon the publike and grand Enemies thereof, and immediately have setled a just Government, under which every mans freedom, right, and property might have been preserved.

That your Petitioners had some hope of that happy fruit of their labours, hazard, & expense of bloud, when the Parliament voted no more addresses to the King, and hereupon your Excellency and your Petitioners did testifie their approbation of those Votes, and did engage to adhere, and stand by them, in the settlement of the Nation without, and against the King, or any other that should partake with him, & your Excellency, and your Petitioners received the thanks of both Houses for the same.

That notwithstanding a bloudy Warre hath been since raysed by the Prince his Commission, a forraign Nation [the Scots] invited to (which did) invade us (and as there is ground to believe) by the Kings consent, thereby to inslave us, to his exorbitant will and lust.

Yet when through the great mercy and favour of God, All their Forces were supprest, instead of having our expectations answered (as to a just settlement) we find.

That the wicked and bloudy Designes of the Enemies of this Kingdom still continue, As of that of Ireland by Ormond, & that [at] home, threatning the lives of every wel-affected person. And this we humbly conceive they are the more imboldened unto, because of the prevalency of some in greatest authority, that will not let Justice be executed upon the grand fomentors, contrivers, & actors, in the first and late Warre. So that the innocent bloud of many of our dear friends (that hath bin spilt) the Rapines robberies, burning & spoiling many wel-affected Towns and Persons, of all livelyhood is forgotten, just government subverted, and such Petitions tending to a setling of a just and equall Government, (as that of the 11. of Septemb. last, from the City of London and Westminster) slighted the intolerable burthen of free Quarter still continued, no redres of publike grivances, by reason of which the implacable malice of our twice conquered Enemies, seemes to steal credit in the hearts of many (whose weaknes hinders them from discerning their evil ends) so that their bloudy intentions against the wel-affected in this Nation, doth begin to manifest it self, both against the Parl.men [*sic*], and the Army, as is apparent by that most desperate and inhumain murthering of Col. Rainsborough.

That as we conceive, your Excellency and the Army, next under God, are the only Barre, that lyeth in their way, hindering the accomplishing of their ends: so their main design is, how to destroy you and it. And that they endeavour by continuing us on free Quarter, yet providing Ordinances, against it, and instructions to enter into no mans house (except Inns, Ale-houses & Taverns) against their wills, which was by us joyfully excepted [*sic*], that thereby the Country might be eased of that devouring Creature free quarter, yet when the Army was thus quartered for the ease of the Country, we were content to make hard shift to maintain our selves out of our pay though it was small, as 2s per diem for horse, and 8d for foot, but that through the subtilty of our Enemies, hath been kept from us, we not having received any pay in 5. months together. So that we must either starve and lye in the streetes, or else still oppresse the Countrey by free Quarter, which renders us odious to the people. And it cannot be otherwise, seeing the Assesments of 60000 l. per mensem, if it were all assessed and gathered (besides money for providing Armes for the Horse and Foot, Recruit Horses, Ammunition for the Army and Garrisons, Coles, Stockings, Shooes for Foot Souldiers, and other incident Charges) will not amount to the Personall Pay of the Army by 12000 l. per mensem.

Now we being pressed in our Judgments, by our Enemies hellish & bloudy designes, & their insolent & barbarous Carriage, and also our hearts burthened with the unsetled condition of this poor Kingdom, are bold to present to your Excellencies consideration these things following.

1. That speedy and impartiall Justice may be executed upon all the fomentors, contrivors, and actors in the first and late Warre.
2. That inquisition be made for the bloud of Col. Rainsborough.
3. That the supream power may be declared and determined, that the want thereof may not be the ground of future, (as it hath been of these former) Warres.
4. That a period be set for this present Parl. to end as soone as may be with safety, and provisions made for future Parliaments to meet certain without writ or sumons.
5. That rules may be set down between the people and their Representatives.
6. That Lawes may be made in things civill to bind all men, so that no man in case of offence, may be freed from that Law whereunto another is subject.
7. That all those common grievances and desires in our Declarations of June 14. and June 23 1647, and expressed in the London Petition, be speedily granted and redressed.
8. That prsent [sic] provision be made for the Constant pay of the Army.
9. That the arrears due from the 15 of January: may be paid off, before we be Commanded to pay Quarters; and that there may be noe other abatement from Officers or Souldiers for free Quarter, then according to the rates set downe in the Ordinance of Parliament, of the 24. day December last.
10. That the Country may be paid for our free Quarter, according to the Deduction out of our pay our of their Assesments.
11. That in as much as the Assessments fall short to pay the Army. That therefore there may be Additionall supplyes monethly out of the Estates of the old and new Delinquents, that there be noe more Tax or Charge to

the Commonwealth.
12. That forth with an Accompte be called for from all persons that have been betrusted with any thing for the State, that the Kingdom may be satisfied therein.
13. That the Deanes, and Chapters Lands may be given to pay the Souldiers Arreares, seeing the Parl. have given away the Delinquents Estates that should have done it.

These things being the proper Issue of our serious thoughts, we implore your Excellency through the many blessings, deliverances, Victories and successes, the Lord hath crowned you withall, The dangers you have been preserved from, the miseries of this bleeding Nation, the bloud of the innocent, the Outcry of the Widdow, and Fatherlesse, the sad Omen of future troubles, to consider the necessity of attaining these things, that we may be no longer the scorn & contempt of the Nation, nor the object of our enemies malice, by the want of just peace and settlement; but with an undaunted courage, to desire the Parl. that these things may be forthwith established, that we may with safety be released, from this troublesome and hazardous imployment, which by reason of the grievous oppression thereof, we professe we are weary of which things we challenge as ours and the Kingdoms due, twice bought with our blood: In the doing of which your Excellency shall not fail of their assistance, who are ready to wade through a Sea of troubles to have them established, although they perish in the work.

And your Petitioners shall pray, &c.

Other editions

The representations and consultations of the Generall councell of the armie at S. Albans. With severall propositions to the L. Generall, from the officers of divers regiments of the army, about the present settlement of the kingdome... London : Printed for R.A., 1648. BL/EEBO: E.472[3]
Perfect Weekly Account, 8-15 November. BL/EEBO: E.472[10]

Background

Whalley's regiment had been formed in 1645 from part of Oliver Cromwell's original volunteer cavalry. Presbyterian minister Richard Baxter later wrote that he had found many 'hot-headed sectaries' in this and other regiments, who 'took the King for a Tyrant and an Enemy, and intended absolutely to master him, or to ruine him', when he preached after the battle of Naseby. Like Fleetwood's, it was one of the first regiments to elect agitators and present their grievances to Fairfax in 1647. 'I find that both my officers and souldiers are not transported or carryed away by passion. Reason sways them,' Whalley reported at that time. The regiment continued to be at the forefront of radical politics in the army, including the controversial appointment of 'new agents' in October 1647, up to the closing of the

General Council after the Putney Debates. During the second civil war, it fought at Maidstone and pursued the Earl of Norwich's force to Colchester. Though the petition below was clearly in line with the army leaders' agenda for the council at St Albans, there is no reason to believe that Whalley's officers and men were any more passive instruments than they had been the previous year. Whalley himself in the following months would attend almost all the meetings of the High Court of Justice and sign the king's death warrant.

Barkstead's was a foot regiment, commanded by Richard Fortescue from 1645 to 1646. In 1647 its men did not at first resist being sent to Ireland, but turned back before leaving England to join the protest movement in the New Model Army. From January 1648 they had been based in London until they were sent to Maidstone and Colchester in the summer campaigns, and after Colchester's fall went on to Great Yarmouth. Lieutenant-Colonel Ralph Cobbett of this regiment was sent to the Isle of Wight to remove the king to the mainland on 30 November, and five companies were at the rendezvous for the army's march on London on 1 December. Barkstead himself, a London goldsmith, would attend all but one session of the High Court of Justice and sign the king's death warrant. Undisturbed by mutiny in 1649, the regiment guarded Parliament and the City of London during the 1650s, and became notorious for suppressing illegal recreational activities. There seems to be no further evidence of political activity within this regiment, but it was clearly regarded as reliable by the army leadership.

Though it is not clear where Whalley's regiment was stationed at this time, Fleetwood's and Barkstead's were both in East Anglia, and communication between them in preparation for the St Albans council was quite feasible.

Related sources

Gentles, *New Model Army*, Chapter 9.
Underdown, *Pride's Purge*, Chapter 5.
Woolrych, *Soldiers and Statesmen*, Chapter 12.

16: RAINBOROWE'S REGIMENT

c. 16 November 1648

Context

Though this petition appeared in print a few days after the army's *Remonstrance*, the absence of any reference to the latter suggests that it was written and subscribed in the week between the death of Colonel Rainborowe at Doncaster on 30 October and the commencement of the meeting at St Albans on 7 November. Thomas Rainborowe had died at the hands of a party of cavaliers from Pontefract Castle who arrived at his lodgings in Doncaster early on 30 October, claiming to be parliamentarian gentlemen bringing a message from Oliver Cromwell. His killing, which still gives rise to intense debate, was a deeply felt loss to the Levellers, whose best friend among the officers he was. One of the largest demonstrations of the period was his funeral procession from Tottenham High Cross to his home parish of Wapping on 14 November. It was also the reason why Oliver Cromwell took over the siege of Pontefract Castle. It was reported on 7 November that the lieutenant-general was on his way to Nottingham to the trial of three parliamentarian colonels who had turned royalist in the second civil war, and would have gone on to the Council of Officers at St Albans had not Rainborowe's death 'altered the course of things'.

Text

The Moderate (19), 14-21 November 1648, pp. 161-2. BL/EEBO: E.473[1]

Dateline 20 November 1648

A Remonstrance of the Regiment of the late Col. Rainsborough to his Excellency, for revenge of their Colonels death.

May it please your Excellencie. Though the sad sense of the unhappy losse of our highly esteemed Colonell, may cause us to beare low in our reputation, and sink us into a slowness to such high actings, as the vigor of his noble spirit might have enabled us unto; yet as Christians and souldiers, indeavouring after just principles of Justice and Freedome; we humbly crave leave, to take advantage from this much lamented occasion, to offer to your Excellency these our disturbed thoughts.

That we feare we are deluded into the hopes of a safe peace, by the expectation of an unsafe Treaty.

That if the utmost purchase of the losse of so much pretious, and now declared righteous bloud, be onely a Liberty to Treat with our capitall Enemy, whether with his dissembled consent, we shall enjoy these liberties, that the sword of the Lord, and the sword of his people hath wrung from his bloudy hands; we are consigned to the most fruitlesse imployment, to be always fighting for that we can never obtaine. Armies can subdue powers, but not change minds; Much treasure might have been spared, and we long ere this been slaves, if we dared to have trusted sacred protestations; That wee are much perplexed with the intricate condition the late resolution of Parliament have put us into, at the same time engaged to fight with an enraged Enemy; and perswaded to believe that all our differences shall be wrapped up in the sweet complyance of a Treaty: And when it was declared to us, that because the King had so often attempted to enslave the Nation, by raising of Armies contrary to many Protestations, he was no more to be trusted, nor no more addresses to be made unto him; and when they kenned the truth of that their Declaration by the confederate risings of all his active parties, in the Kingdome of England, and Scotland; we do much wonder from thence, there should arise any reason to invite them to a new addresse, or fright them to any other application; then [than] to that Army, that under the protection of the Almighty, had rescued them from such dangers, and had unanimously declared, to live and die with them in their former resolutions. Upon all which we ground these our humble desires, That impartiall Justice might be done upon the eminent undertakers of this second warre, especially upon such, who formerly acting as friends to the Nations freedome, have (by betraying its confidence) had greater opportunity to enslave it, That so the cruell mercies shewed to our implacable enemies, might now indanger the lives of our dearest friends. That wee might be aswell satisfied in the reasons, why new applications were made to his Majesty, as wee formerly were in their non addresses; that so, if possible, wee might live and die with them in those resolutions. And if it be found necessary a Treaty should compound the divisions, why such an one, wherein some of both parties are knowne enemies to the Kingdomes Army? That it might be knowne to us, why the Country duly paying their Taxes, The Taxes might not as duly pay the Army, the burden of free Quarter being looked upon by most as a voluntary oppression, not as a necessary grief of the soldier. That by this meanes, concurring with the presented desires of many well affected persons in the City of London, and other Counties, with some of our fellow souldiers in Armes, we might under your Excellencies conduct, be made serviceable to the Nations welfare, and be honoured in being the Kingdomes, and Your Lordships humble Servants, &c.

Background

Thomas Rainborowe's surname will be more familiar to many readers as Rainsborough, the form most frequently used in army documents and printed newsbooks at the time; but it is now usual to use his own spelling, as here. His father and grandfather were merchants and sailors, and Thomas spent the first year of the civil war in the parliamentarian navy, before becoming an army colonel in 1643. His use of amphibious tactics to reduce the royalist stronghold at Crowland in the Lincolnshire fenlands was highly regarded, and after his regiment joined the New Model Army he conducted several other successful sieges, as well as fighting in the battles of Naseby and Langport and storming Bristol. His radicalism emerged in public at the Putney Debates, where he was one of the most eloquent speakers in support of the right of propertyless men to vote. He put himself in the front line politically again by trying to present Fairfax with a copy of *An Agreement of the People* during the mutiny of 15 November 1647 at Ware. Shortly before the Putney Debates he had been appointed Vice-Admiral of the navy, overcoming fierce opposition from Cromwell. The unfortunate outcome will be discussed below in relation to the naval mutiny of May 1648, but here we are concerned with his return to the army and appointment to command the siege at Pontefract, a task for which he was clearly well qualified.

The operation against Pontefract Castle was first commanded by a local gentleman, Sir Henry Cholmeley, and many contemporary sources testify to its ineffectiveness. Raids by the castle's royalist defenders had seized cattle and prisoners, and when Cromwell arrived after Rainborowe's death he estimated that it was sufficiently provisioned to hold out for another year. Cholmley and his cavalry colonels delayed Rainborowe's arrival, protesting that they could not serve under 'a bare colonel of foot in the Army, and a younger Colonel than any of us'. While Rainborowe waited in Doncaster for these 'questions of honour' to be resolved by Parliament, refusing to share command with Cholmley as a temporary compromise, a small party of royalists from Pontefract Castle gained access to his lodgings on the pretext of bringing a message from Cromwell. As he drew a blank sheet of paper from the packet they handed to him, they took him prisoner. Once downstairs Rainborowe tried to escape, and as he was grappling with one of them his lieutenant picked up a dropped pistol and was immediately run through with a sword. Rainborowe died, not in his bed as some reports said, but slaughtered on the street as he bravely fought back.

To Captain Thomas Paulden, one of the royalists involved, his resistance made it 'only his own fault that he was killed and not brought Prisoner to the Castle', where they intended to ransom him in exchange for the life of royalist general Sir Marmaduke Langdale. It is hard to believe that they expected such a 'Person of great Courage and Conduct' as they knew Rainborowe to be, to come quietly. A parliamentary enquiry found no conspiracy or negligence on their own side, but the lack of effective response from Rainborowe's guard has never been satisfactorily explained, and as his biographer Whitney Jones says, a cloud of suspicion inevitably continues to hang over the whole scenario to this day.

Rainborowe's current regiment, quartered around the countryside to avoid too heavy a burden on Doncaster, was not the one he had commanded in 1647. It was the former Tower Guard, originally part of Fairfax's foot but later placed under Colonel Robert Tichborne. Tichborne was another participant at Putney who spoke strongly in favour of representative government, and a future regicide. The regiment left the Tower to fight in the second civil war, losing two replacement colonels under royalist fire at Colchester before being allotted to Rainborowe in July 1648. It is tempting to adapt Oscar Wilde's famous line and suggest that losing a third looks like carelessness, but no fault was ever conclusively found of them. According to Firth and Davies's classic study of the New Model Army regiments, some of its officers can be identified as Independents thrown out of the London militia by the Presbyterians in 1647, not necessarily close to the Levellers but surely sharing some of Rainborowe's principles.

Related sources

A full and exact relation of the horrid murder committed upon the body of col. Rainsborough... Printed for R.A. (London, 1648). BL/EEBO: E.470[4]
Packets of Letters from Scotland and the North of England, No. 34, 7 November 1648. BL/EEBO: E.470[17].
The Moderate, No. 17, 31 October- 7 November 1648. BL/EEBO: E.472[15].
Mercurius Militaris, No. 4, 31 October – 7 November 1648. BL/EEBO: E.470[14]
Thomas Paulden, *Pontefract Castle. An Account how it was Taken, And how General Rainsborough was Surprised in his Quarters at Doncaster, Anno 1648* (London, 1702).
Edward Peacock, 'Notes on the Life of Thomas Rainborowe, Officer in the Army and Navy in the Service of the Parliament of England', *Archaeologia or Miscellaneous Tracts relating to Antiquity* (Society of Antiquaries of London), vol. 46 (1880), pp. 9-64.
Whitney R. D. Jones, *Thomas Rainborowe c. 1610-1648, Civil War Seaman, Siegemaster and Radical* (Woodbridge, Boydell, 2005).
Adrian Tinniswood, *The Rainborowes* (London, Jonathan Cape, 2013).

17: OVERTON'S REGIMENT

14-21 November 1648

Context

This is another petition apparently sent before the Council of Officers met at St Albans, but published towards the end of its sessions. A manuscript version survives in the papers of William Clarke, differing from the printed text only in spelling and punctuation, and includes a list of eighteen of the regiment's officers. Its four demands are very similar to those of others at this stage, but it seems to break new ground with its religious intensity and biblical quotations. The first demand focuses on 'the late war', i.e. the second civil war; while the second, urging that neither king nor lords be treated any differently from others, uses Old Testament examples to insist there can be no peace without justice.

Much has been written about the influence of the bible in bringing about the death of Charles I. While the first reference here is a straightforward one to the notorious Jezebel, King Ahab's wife, who promoted the worship of other gods in Israel, frequently compared to Queen Henrietta Maria, the second, from the Book of Micah (3:12), is as interesting for what it omits as what it contains. It cites examples of mercenary judges and priests that seem to go off at a tangent from the business in hand. Whoever drafted this skipped the preceding verses (Micah 3:9-10) directly attacking the *princes* of Israel who 'build up Zion with blood, and Jerusalem with iniquity'. Is the issue of royal blood-guilt deliberately being side-stepped; or is it a hint that those who knew their bible could place in context?

Text

The Moderate, No. 19, 14-21 November 1648, p.162. BL/EEBO: E.473[1]

The humble Petition of the Officers of Colonel Overtons Regiment, now in the Garrison of Barwick.

May it please your Excellency, When we consider how gloriously the right hand of our God hath exalted itself in power, to the dashing in pieces the Common Enemy of this Kingdom, and the overthrow of all those that have risen up against us; we cannot but confesse there is none so glorious in holinesse, fearful in praises, doing wonders, as our God, and therefore desire to wait upon him in the way of his judgements, and confesse, that according to the greatnesse of his own heart hath he done these things, but lest we may manifest ingratitude for what we have received, in not laying hold on those precious opportunities (which in a way of Justice he hath given in unto us) for the freeing of our poor Nation from oppression, and violence, the execution of Justice on those that have gone on in iniquity and blood & obtaining a blessed peace, the just end of our ingagements, we cannot but (being conscientiously thereunto moved) offer unto your Excel. these few considerations, which we humbly request, your Excel. to present (on our behalf) to the Honorable Houses of Parliament, who, we hope will clear themselves from the iealousies of men, in being a terror to evil works, and a praise to those that do well. 1. We desire that a diligent inquisition may be had for the innocent blood shed in this late War, and that all contrivors, actors, or abettors of it may be brought to exemplary Justice. 2. That in the distribution of Justice, neither King, Lords, nor any such persons be exempted from being proceeded against, according to their demerits, knowing that the many whoredoms, and witchcrafts of Iesabell hindred the peace of Israel [II Kings 9:22], and Princes judging for reward, and the Priest teaching for hire, caused Sion to be plowed upon as a field, and Ierusalem to become an heap [Micah 3:12] 3. That the severall Petitions of the wel-affected of the Kingdom, viz London, Leicester, tending to the execution of Justice, without partiality, securing the rights of the subjects, and setling the peace of the Kingdom, may be seriously taken into consideration, and not so slighted as they have been. 4. That while we are necessitated to be active in the present service, for the security of the Kingdom, we desire that the Parliament would be pleased to finde out some way for our subsistance, that we may not be burthensom by free-quarter as we have been. Lastly, in the prosecution of these our just desires, we shall not account anything dear to adventure, under your Excellencies command, for the honour of Parliament, peace and liberty of the Kingdom.

Manuscript

Worcester College Oxford, MS 16, fos. 8-9. Adds:
Ensigns: William Jackson, Richard Borne, Samuel Martin, John Wheeler, John Barnes, Joseph Nichols, Thomas Russell.
Captains: Robert Reade, Robert Anderson, Ed[ward] Orpin, William Gough, William Knollys, Matthew Fenn.
Lieutenants: Richard Clifton, John Thorpe, Thomas Hunt, Henry Collingwood, Anthony Belcham.

Background

Robert Overton's foot regiment had served under Colonels Lloyd and Herbert during the first civil war, and formed part of the force commanded by Rainborowe at the siege of Berkeley Castle. Overton took command in spring 1647, when Herbert and some of his officers had left for Ireland. Captains William Knowles and Edward Orpin were chosen agitators on behalf of the regiment's officers in October 1647; but the regiment followed Fairfax's orders to appear at the Kingston rendezvous on 18 November without further disturbance. Meanwhile, Overton had been appointed as Fairfax's deputy governor in Hull at Oliver Cromwell's request, and remained there when eight companies were sent to Wales in the second civil war. During September 1648, 'some loose companies' of the regiment joined the siege of Berwick while others went over to Carlisle, and these were reunited to garrison Berwick after its surrender (see 10 above). Most of the officers named in the manuscript are found later serving under George Fenwick, who was in 1648 colonel of the Northumberland Horse (26 below). Their colonel meanwhile remained in Hull, but retained nominal command of this regiment until May 1649, when Fenwick took it over together with the governorship of Berwick. Overton did not attend any sessions of the Council of Officers at St Albans or Whitehall, and although he was named as one of the commissioners to try the king he did not attend the trial or play any other part in the regicide. For his personal political views and style, see 44 below.

Related sources

Clarke Papers, vol. 1, p. 437 (agitators in October 1647)
Firth & Davies, *Regimental History*, vol. 2, pp. 384-7.
ODNB: Barbara Taft, 'Overton, Robert (1608/9–1678/9)'.
Barbara Taft, '"They that pursew perfaction on earth ..." The Political Progress of Robert Overton,' in Ian Gentles, John Morrill and Blair Worden (eds.), *Soldiers, Writers and Statesmen of the English Revolution* (Cambridge University Press, 1998), pp. 286-303.

18: THE REMONSTRANCE OF THE ARMY
16 November 1648

Context

The *Remonstrance* was the principal outcome of the Council of Officers' meetings at St Albans, addressed to the House of Commons but also offered in print 'to the consideration of the whole kingdom'. Many contemporaries attributed it to Henry Ireton, and it cannot be doubted that he was responsible for most of its content, particularly the long preamble. After its unanimous acceptance by the council on 16 November, a committee of six leading officers was appointed to 'fitt it for to bee tendred to the Parliament'; and the final version was signed off by the council's secretary John Rushworth on 18 November. This was read to the House of Commons two days later by their own clerk Henry Elsynge. The reading was reported to have taken four hours, and *Mercurius Pragmaticus* mockingly commented that Elsynge 'was glad when he came home to consult with an Apothecary for the mending of his Lung-pipes'.

The same writer lambasted the document as so long-winded that its essential content could have been printed on three sheets of paper rather than ten. Seventy closely-printed octavo pages containing over 17,000 words, with many highly complex sentences that would challenge any orator, were rushed off the presses by two of the army's regular publishers, and George Thomason was able to purchase it on 22 November. Never reprinted in full since the eighteenth century, it is now accessible in digital form thanks to Early English Books Online. Because almost all the petitions that followed the *Remonstrance* were reactions and responses to it, the text is essential to their story; but in order not to interrupt that story too drastically only the last eleven pages are presented here. These include a numbered list of points leading into the proposals for action and constitutional settlement that have most frequently been reproduced, giving a taste of the preamble and demonstrating the confusing numbering and repetitions which suggest that this part of the document at least is a composite creation, rather than Ireton's alone.

A few salient points from the preamble may be summarised, however. 'The public interest of the kingdom' is repeatedly counterposed to the king's interest, and representative government to his 'court maxims' of absolute royal power. Charles I's persistence in seeking absolute power by making war on his own subjects confirms his guilt for all the bloodshed requiring expiation, from which he cannot now be spared. No restoration would be safe without his undergoing trial and judgement; though if 'there were good evidence of a proportionable remorse in him … his person might be capable of pitty, mercy and pardon'. Many examples are marshalled to prove that Charles cannot be trusted to abide by any agreed settlement. He is known to have written to his son and supporters that he is making concessions under duress, and is waiting to resume his pursuit of absolute power once he is back on the throne.

Does the *Remonstrance* explicitly demand King Charles's head? Readers must make their own judgement, but historians are not agreed on this question. It calls for the king's trial and assumes his guilt, and directly demands capital punishment for his chief followers; but it goes on to discuss what should happen *after* 'Capitall punishments upon the principall Author and some prime instruments'. The ambiguity may arise from hasty amendments made by the 16 November committee, perhaps reflecting some participants' fear of committing treason, the offence that since 1351 had included imagining or 'compassing' the monarch's death. It could also be read as a conditional statement: if Charles himself did not suffer the death sentence, more of his friends would need to pay that price. It is surely also important that the final list of demands (so often reprinted at the time and since, without this paragraph) is introduced by a recognition that the final judgement must await a trial: 'Therefore, the power of justice and mercy being reserved, we proceed to the actual dispensing thereof…'

Religion features in Ireton's preamble as one of the 'more particular or special interests' dividing Charles I from his Parliament, which has tried 'to protect and encourage religious men and godlinesse', while the king was promoting 'an out-side religion and Church government'. God's judgement against the king, as revealed in Parliament's victories, is discussed at length; but overall there is little religious language, and few if any biblical quotations. The Solemn League and Covenant's pledge to preserve the king's person is explained away as a 'covenant between man and man', rather than between man and god. The appeasement of god's wrath for the blood shed is treated as a matter for civil trial and judgement, which would not require the sacrifice of the king's life if he agreed to submit to it; while the 'Man of Blood' rhetoric is notably absent.

Text

A Remonstrance of his excellency Thomas, Lord Fairfax, Lord Generall of the Parliaments Forces. And of the Generall Councell of Officers Held at St Albans the 16. Of November, 1648. Presented to the Commons assembled in Parliament, the 20. Instant, and tendred to the Consideration of the whole Kingdome. Printed for John Partridge and George Whittington, 1648. BL/EEBO: E.473[11]. pp. 60-70.

Having thus endeavoured to Remonstrate the danger and evil of the way you are in, and cleared the way unto what we have to propose, we shall with the same plainnesse and faithfulnesse give you our apprehensions of the remedies; for which purpose upon all the reasons and considerations aforegoing, we proceed to offer, as followeth.

First, we conceive and hope, that from what hath before been said, you may find abundant cause to forbeare any further proceeding in this evil and most dangerous Treaty, and to returne to your former grounds in the Votes of Non-addresses, and thereupon proceed to the settling and securing of the kingdome without and against the King, upon such foundations as hereafter are tendred; but if notwithstanding all the evils and dangers remonstrated to lie even in the Treaty it selfe, you will yet proceed in such an evill way, we shall at least desire that you make sure to avoid that maine venome and mischiefe attending it, viz. The Kings restitution with impunity, &c. and that imperfect bargaining for partiall justice against inferiour offenders; And for the avoidance of these, we propound,

1. That you would reject those demands of the King, sent to you on his and his Parties behalfe, and (especially in relation to that concerning his restitution or returne to London with freedome, &c) that it may be expressly declared and provided by you that, notwithstanding any thing concluded or to be concluded in this Treaty, the Person of the King may and shall be proceeded against in a way of justice, for the blood spilt, and the other evils and mischiefs done by him, or by his Commission, Command or Procurement, and in order thereto shall be kept in safe custody as formerly.
2. That for other delinquents you would lay aside that particular bargaining Proposition, which as we understand, the King hath refused in the termes you offered, and whereby all your justice and mercy too would be rendred, (both for the matter, qualificiations and circumstances thereof) to be dependant upon particular contract with, and grant from the King, and not upon the judiciall power of the Kingdome in Parliament; and that in stead thereof it may be declared and provided by you, that all Delinquents shall subject and submit to the aforesaid judiciall power, to be thereby proceeded against, according to justice, or with mercy, as cause shall appear, and that none shall be exempt or protected therefrom, nor pardonable by any other power, then that of the Kingdome in Parliament, by which they shall be judged; this we propound, to the end that publick justice, and the interest of the Kingdome therein may be vindicated, salved, and satisfied, and yet (when that is so provided for, (and in some fittest examples of justice upon chief offenders,) shall be effectuated) we wish as much mercy and moderation to the generality, upon their submission, as formerly we have both desired and used, or as can consist with the publick interest and safety, and with competent satisfaction to those that have engaged and suffered for it.

If (in relation to the former of these Provisions, viz. concerning the Person of the King,) it be thought an unreasonable or unbeseeming demand in a Personall Treaty, that one Partie (after Concessions to the other in all matters of right, and other things in question,) should agree, besides, to be punished himselfe for having made the past contest about them, we confesse it might be thought so in a Treaty, betwixt Parties standing both free, and in an equall balance of power or possibilities to obtaine the cause; but so farre as a Treaty can rationally or properly be with a Party wholly subdued, captivated and imprisoned, or in the power of the other to such a Treaty, such demands, (if otherwise just) are very sutable and proportionable, and to any Treaty.

It seems surely, no lesse suitable to demand the principall to justice then the accessories, (that were but his necessary and proper Agents in the Contest,) especially where he is as much, (if not more), within the other Parties power as they, and where it is not so much a demanding him to justice, as a Proviso, that (being already in the power of their justice) they will not exempt him from it.

Thus therefore the power of justice and mercy being saved or reserved, we proceed in order to the actuall dispensation thereof, in relation to the late wars, and thereby to peace with God, and quiet amongst men, to propound as followeth:

1. That the capitall and grand Author of our troubles, the Person of the King, by whose Commissions, Commands or Procurement, and in whose behalfe, and for whose interest only, (of will and power,) all our warres and troubles have been, (with all the miseries attending them,) may be speedily brought to justice for the treason, blood, and mischiefe, he is therein guilty of.
2. That a timely and peremptory day may be set for the Prince of Wales and the Duke of Yorke to come in and render themselves, by which time (if they do not) that then they may be immediately declared incapable of any Government, or trust in this kingdome, or the Dominions thereunto belonging, or of any kind of Right within the same, and thence to stand exiled for ever, as enemies and Traytors, to dye without mercy, if ever after found and taken therein; (or if by the time limited, they or either of them do render themselves, that then the Prince for his Capitall Delinquency (being in appearance next to his Fathers) may either be proceeded against in justice, or remitted, according as upon his appearance he shall give full satisfaction or not; concerning his being drawn into the rebellious engagements, he has appeared to head; and the Duke, as he shall give satisfaction or not concerning his carriage in and since his going out of the kingdome (being without leave) and in opposition or contempt of the Parliament, and to the prejudice of the publique Peace, may accordingly be considered as to future trust, or not; But (however) that the Estate and Revenue of the Crown may be Sequestred, and all the matter of costly pompe or state suspended for a good number of yeeres, while the desolations and spoyles of the poore people made, by and in behalf of that family, and for that vaine interest (the state and greatnesse thereof) may be in good measure repaired or recovered; And that the Revenue (saving necessary allowances for the Childrens mainteynance, and to old servants and creditors of the Crowne, not Delinquents) and also the 10000.l per annum, voted to the Crown in Liew of the Court of Wards, may for those yeeres be disposed towards publique charges, debts and dammages for the easing and

lessening of the peoples Contributions towards the same; so as the Estates neither of the friends to publique interest, not alone of the inferiour Enemies thereto may bear wholly the burthen of that losse and charge, which by and for that Family, the Kingdome or the good people thereof have bin or (for future security) shall be put unto.

3. That for further satisfaction to publique justice, Capitall punishment may be speedily executed upon a competent number of his chiefe instruments also, both in the former and latter Warre, and (for that purpose) some such, of both sorts, may be pitch upon to be made examples of justice in that kind, as are really in your hands or reach, so as their exception from pardon, may not be made a mockery of Justice in the face of God and men.

4. That exemplary Justice being done in Capitall punishment upon the principall Author and some prime instruments of our late Warres, and thereby the blood thereof expiated, and others deterred from future attempts of the like in either capacity; The rest of the Delinquents (English) in relation to the warres, may upon their submission and rendring themselves to Justice, have mercy extended to them for their lives, and that only Fines may be set upon them (with reasonable moderation, but with respect to publique damages) and their persons further censured and declared to be incapable of any Office or place of power or publique trust in the kingdome, or of having any voice in Elections thereto (at least) for a competent number of yeers; that also a short and peremptory day may be set, by which time all such Delinquents may have finall warning to come in and render themselves to Justice, and to tender their submissions to such Fines and censures as aforesaid, and, that such of them as shall so do by the day assigned, and shall (withall) pay in or secure their Fines, according to reasonable time given, may have their Sequestrations taken off, and be restored to their Estates; and that to all such (as also to all those that have already submitted to Fines or Compositions, and paid in, or secured the same) a generall pardon may be granted, made and published by Parliament, extending to absolve them from any further censure, damage, trouble, or question, (either in the behalfe of the publique, or at the suit of any private person,) for any thing said or done in prosecution of, or in relation to the late Warre or troubles, and to restore them to all priviledges, benefits, and immunities equally with all other people (excepting only, the capacity to places of power or publique trust, or to voyces in Election thereunto as aforesaid) that so they may not (as heretofore,) after Fines or Compositions to the State for their Delinquencie, remaine subject to any mans action for any particular act of their Delinquencie to their endlesse trouble or undoing, or the driving of them to desperate ways of publike disturbance for their own preservation; but that such of them as will for future live in peace and subjection to the Lawes and Government of the Nation, may enjoy the benefit thereof, and have quiet and protection under the same, & their

posterities (yea, or themselves in time) partake fully and equally with others of the common Interest contended for, and obtained. But as for such delinquents, who (having mercy tendred to them for life, as aforesaid) shall not by the day to be set, come in, and render themselves, submit, and pay, or secure their Fines as aforesaid, That it be declared, their Estates shall from that day be absolutely Confiscated, and sold, or disposed of wholly to the publike use, and their persons to stand perpetually exiled (as Enemies and Traytors) and to die without Mercy, if ever after found and taken within the Kingdom, or the Dominions thereto belonging, and upon their default of appearance, &c. as before, or at the said day, That they be from thenceforth proceeded against accordingly.

5. That the satisfaction of Arrears to the Souldiery, with other publike Debts, and the competent reparation of publike Damages (especially and primarily of such as voluntarily engaged for, and have constantly adhered to the common Cause, and suffered for the same) may be put into some orderly and equall, or proportionable way; wherein (as to Debts and Damages) care may be taken for some precedency of satisfaction to such, whose Loans, or losses appear to have been great, and livelyhoods small, so as they can worst bear the want, or delay: And towards these things (not impairing any other security already given for Arrears to the Souldiery, in an equall way, or for just Debts of other kindes) we propound, that the Fines, or Compositions of Delinquents may be disposed of, and imployed to those uses only, as also the Confiscations and proceed of their Estates who shall be excluded from pardon, or not come in by the day to be assigned, as in the last precedent Article.

Now (after publique Justice, and therewith the present quieting of the Kingdom thus far provided for) we proceed in order, to the generall satisfaction, and setling of the Kingdom, as followeth:

1. That you would set some reasonable and certain period to your own power, by which time that great and supream trust reposed in you, shall be returned into the hands of the People, from, and for whom you received it; that so you may give them satisfaction and assurance, that what you have contended for, against the King (for which they have been put to so much trouble, cost, and losse of blood) hath been only for their Liberties, and common Interest, and not for your own personal Interest, or power.

2. That (with a period to this Parliament, to be assigned as short as may be, with safety to the Kingdom, and publike Interest thereof) there may be a sound settlement of the peace, and future Government of the Kingdom, upon grounds of common Right, Freedom, and safety, to the effects here following:
    1. That from the end of this, there may be a certain succession of future Parliaments (Annuall, or Biennall) with secure provision,

1. [sic] For the certainty of their meeting, sitting, and ending.
2. [sic] For the equall distribution of Elections thereunto, to render the House of Commons, as near as may be, an equall Representative of the whole People electing.
3. For the certainty of the Peoples meeting (according to such Distributions) to elect, and for their full freedom in elections, provided, That none who have engaged, or shall engage in War, against the right of Parliament, and interest of the Kingdom therein, or have adhered to the enemies thereof, may be capable of electing, or being elected (at least during a competent number of years) nor any other, who shall oppose, or not joyn in agreement to this settlement.
4. For future clearing, and ascertaining the power of the said Representatives; in order to which, That it be declared, That (as to the whole interest of the People of England) such Representatives have, and shall have the supream power and trust, as to the making of Laws, Constitutions, and Offices, for the ordering, preservation, and Government of the whole; and as to the altering, and repealing, or abolishing of the same, the making of War, or Peace; and as to the highest and finall Judgement, in all civill, things, without further appeal to any created standing power, and that all the people of this Nation, and all Officers of Justice, and Ministers of State (as such) shall, in all such things be accountable and subject thereunto, and bound, and concluded thereby, provided, That,
    1. They may not censure, or question any man after the end of this Parliament, for any thing said or done in reference to the late Wars, or publique differences, saving in execution of such determinations of this Parliament, as shall be left in force at the ending thereof, in relation to such as have served the King against the Parliament.
    2. They may not render up, or give, or take away any the foundations of common Right, Liberty or Safety contained in this settlement and Agreement. But that the power of these two things (last mentioned) shall be always understood to be reserved from, and not entrusted to the said Representatives.
5. [sic] For liberty of entring dissents in the said Representatives, That, in case of corruption, or abuse in these matters of highest trust, the People may be in capacity to know who are free thereof, and who guilty, to the end only that they may avoid the further trusting of such, but without further penalty to any for their free judgements there.
2. [sic] That no King be hereafter admitted, but upon the election of, and as upon trust from the People, by such their Representatives, nor without first disclaiming and disavowing all pretence to a negative voyce [veto], against the determinations of the said Representatives, or Commons in Parliament; and

that to be done in some certain form, more clear then heretofore in the Coronation Oath.

These matters of generall settlement (viz. That concerning a period to this Parliament, and the other particulars thence following hitherto) we propound, to be declared and provided by this Parliament, or by the authority of the Commons therein, and to be further established by a generall Contract, or Agreement of the People, with there subscriptions thereunto, and that (withall) it may be provided, That none may be capable of any benefit by the Agreement, who shall not consent and subscribe thereunto; nor any King be admitted to the Crown, or other person to any Office, or place of publike trust, without expresse accord, and subscription to the same.

We have thus plainly, and faithfully propounded our apprehensions, how the evill and danger of the present Treaty may in good measure be avoyded, and our further conceptions of a way, wherein, hopefully through the blessing of God (if most men be not given up, some to unjust domination, or particular Interest, the rest to servitude) the Kingdome may be quieted, future disturbances prevented, the common Rights and Liberties provided for, and the Peace and Government of the Kingdome setled, to a just publick Interest; and this wee have set forth in such heads and particulars, which (if you but set aside, for the time, lesse important matters) may most of them be brought to effect, and the rest assured, and put into a good way of effect, within a few Moneths, so as you might then ease the Kingdome from the burthen of the greatest part of that force, which otherwise (in case of Accommodation with the King) you will be necessitated, for a much longer time (probably for many yeares) to keep on, upon the publick charge, unlesse, upon the Accommodation you would give up all to the Kings power againe, and expose those that have engaged against him, as sacrifices to his and the Cavaliers Revenge: And (for our parts) let but that way of Justice be effectually prosecuted, and the settlement of the publick Interest (upon such foundations as are afore propounded) be assured to us and the Kingdome, and put into a course of effect (which as we said before, might well be in a few moneths) and we shall not only imbrace with chearfulnesse, but shall with eagernesse desire discharge from our present service, and shall be most ready to disband all, or part, as shall be thought fit, the Arrears of the soldiery being satisfied. We shall therefore earnestly desire, that these things may be minded, and prosecuted effectually, and that nothing may interrupt them, save what shall be for immediate and necessary safety; And that (to avoid interruptions from such things as are not necessary, or lesse proper for Parliamentary considerations or Debates) you would leave all private matters, and things of ordinary Justice and Right, to the Lawes and present proper Officers, and Administrations thereof, until better can be provided, and commit all ordinary matters of State to the mannage of a fit Councell of State (sufficiently impowred for that purpose, and assisted with the addition of some Merchants, in relation to the ballancing, security, and advance of Trade) so as you may be the more free for the present, to intend those foresaid Considerations of publique Justice, and the settlement of the Kingdom upon just and safe foundations of publike interest, and that when you have effectuated them, or put them into a way of effect, you may (for the after time of this Parliaments continuance) more entirely apply your Councels to such other things, as are the most proper work of Parliaments, and by, and for which Parliaments have had their esteem in this Nation, and the Kingdom most benefit by them (viz. the Reformation of evils, or inconveniencies in the present Laws and Administrations thereof, the redresse of abuses, and supplying of defects therein, and the making of better constitutions for the well Government, and prosperity of the Nation, as also the due proportioning of rates, and providing of moneys in the most equall, and least grievous wayes for all necessary uses of the publike, and the like,) and in Order to such things, that you would in due time and place (viz. after publike justice, and the generall settlement) consider such speciall overtures of that kind, as have been tendred to you in the Petitions of the well-wishers to publike good, and particularly in that large Petition from many about London, Dated the 11 of September last, and also what shall be tendred of like kinde from others, that so what is really for the remedy of common greivances, or the advancement of common good may not be slighted, or neglected, but that evils in that kinde being removed, and good things ordained, and provided by you, for the ease, benefit, and prosperity of the people (in all things possible,) you may (when you come to lay down your trust) leave a good savour behinde you, both to the name of Parliaments, and also of men professing Godlinesse (so much as this House hath done) and therein (chiefly) to the Honour of Almighty God, who hath (in his rich Grace and mercy) done such wonders for you and us: And for furtherance to all these ends, (since the heart of man is deceitful, and corrupt above all things, and most apt to answerable Counsels and actings, where it can hope to walk in the dark, undiscerned, or undistinguished, though but to the eye of man) we must again desire, That even from henceforth the aforesaid liberty of entering dissents (as it is in the Scotch Parliament where lately there hath appeared a most usefull Effect of it so also) may be admitted amongst you, or (at least) that in these transactions, of such high moment to the publique, and all honest Interests, and in times, so apt to deceit, defection, and Apostasie; that liberty may be taken by all honest faithfull Members, that desire to appear (as their hearts to God, so) their wayes to good men; yet still we wish not (whoever should be that meanes be detected for corrupt Counsells) that for his judgement there, any advantage should be taken out doors, but only that men may avoid the further trusting of such persons, and that the innocent may not be unjustly prejudiced or suspected.

Thus, as the exigence of the case, and nature of the businesse requires (being of such vast importance to all Publike, Religious and honest interest, not in this Kingdom only, but in neighbour nations) we have dealt with all plainnesse and cleernesse, as God hath enabled us; and now to conclude, we hope, that in an age of so much light, meer will or resolution will not be held forth, or pursued against it; but that, what reason, or righteousnesse there is in the things we have said, will be considered and followed: nor let it finde prejudice with you from any disdain towards those from whom it comes, (being in the condition of an Army, looked upon as servants under you) since servants may speak to their masters, and ought to be heard and regarded, even when they speak for their own right only, and rather when they speak for the good and safety of them they serve, but much more when they speak of that wherein they have some joynt interest with them; and yet more when (those their immediate masters being themselves also servants, and Trustees for the benefit of others) the speak for the interest of those, for whom both are imployed.

By the appointment of his Excellency, the Lord Generall, and his Generall Councell of Officers.

St Albans Novemb. 18. 1648. Signed, John Rushworth.

Manuscript

Worcester College Oxford, Clarke Ms 16, fos 10-13v: rough draft, with amendments, of the first seven pages as printed.

Other editions

Photographic reproduction of the original at eebo.chadwyck.com.
The Parliamentary or Constitutional History of England, vol. 18 (London, 1763), pp. 161-238. Free to access at archive.org.

Background

It is not clear what happened at St Albans between 10 and 15 November. The fullest account published at the time states that on 10 November, 'further time was spent in debate on the present affaires of the Kingdome', with several colonels speaking to the effect that they wished to see peace and unity between the king and the people. There was also some discussion 'concerning the former Proposalls, and bringing Delinquents to triall' and a desire was expressed that 'those who indeavour to render his Excellencies Army odious' should also be brought to justice. The petition from Fleetwood's, Whalley's and Barkstead's regiments read on 11 November (15 above) may have swung subsequent debate in the direction in which the army leaders wished it to go.

In the next few days several publications claimed that the council had resolved not to interfere with the treaty, and had even promised the re-enthronement of the king, while others rushed supposed 'declarations of the army' into print before the *Remonstrance* appeared. It seems that a section of the army leadership, perhaps those reported to have met at the Bull's Head tavern in St Albans on 14 or 15 November, were opposed to the regiments' petitions, and hoped that by spreading their own version of the news they could alter the council's direction. *Mercurius Pragmaticus* claimed that the debate was being prolonged until Oliver Cromwell should arrive; even reporting that the Lieutenant-General's arrival had 'turned the tide' on 15 November, when he is known to have been writing from Knottingley to the House of Commons about the supplies he needed and the infantry units expected to join him the following day. Considering the facts of Rainborowe's death and the insistence of local military leaders on Cromwell taking charge (see 16 above), these were anything but trivial matters keeping him there. The factor that turned the tide (if that were needed) could have been the news from Westminster that both houses of Parliament had voted to restore the king to full dignity and honour once the treaty was concluded, ruling out a trial; news that would certainly have reached St Albans by the evening of 15 November.

According to John Lilburne, writing in June 1649, the London Levellers had found negative references to themselves in the draft *Remonstrance*, and ensured that these were removed.

Surviving army records note that on 16 November after the council agreed *nemine contradicente* (no one voting in the negative) to adopt 'the paper now read', a committee was appointed to read it over and prepare it for submission to parliament. Its members included some of most radical of the army's officers: Colonels Sir William Constable, Edward Whalley, Isaac Ewer, Adrian Scroop (all soon to sign the king's death warrant) and Major Thomas Kelsey, as well as Ireton himself. The final version singles out for special mention the Large Petition of 11 September, though at Whitehall a few weeks later Ireton was to justify his opposition to the Levellers' insistence on religious freedom by claiming, 'When we had desired the whole we did not insist upon every particle of it.'

The radical newsbook *Mercurius Militaris* claimed that Colonel Rich and Captain Cecil (of Ireton's regiment) dissented, but Fairfax told Parliament that the decision had been unanimous. The Commons agreed after some debate (a heated one according to *Mercurius Pragmaticus*) to postpone further consideration of it for a week, then postponed it again. On 30 November, when news arrived that the Army leaders were planning to seize the king on the Isle of Wight, a motion 'That the House now proceed upon the Remonstrance of the Army' was soundly defeated.

The army's attempt to achieve a change of policy through the 'proper channels' had definitively failed, and the leadership were already making preparations for direct action. Many historians have believed that they also made one final approach to the king, as some publications claimed at the time. In his classic history, Gardiner unfortunately treated as fact the Dutch ambassador's belief that the army council had addressed to the king a list of proposals (extracted from *The Heads of the Proposals* that Charles had turned down over a year earlier) and assumed that Ireton had agreed to the move. This is in such stark contradiction to Ireton's lengthy argument against dealing with the king in the preamble of the *Remonstrance*, with its expressions of regret for the army leaders' own previous attempts at doing so, that it is frankly incredible.

Related sources

Clarke Papers, vol. 2, p. 54; Appendices B (extracts from Lilburne, 1649 as below) and D (attendance lists).

The Representations and Consultations of the Generall Councel of the Armie at St Albans... London: printed for R.A. 1648. BL/EEBO: E.472[3].

The Moderate Intelligencer, No. 192, 16-23 November 1648. BL/EEBO: E.473[15].

Mercurius Pragmaticus, No. 34, 14-20 November. BL/EEBO: E.473[7].

Mercurius Pragmaticus, No. 35, 21-28 November. BL/EEBO: E.473[39].

Packets of Letters, From Several Parts of England, No. 36, 21 November 1648. BL/EEBO: E.473[12].

The Perfect Weekly Account, 15-22 November 1648. BL/EEBO: E.473[13].

Propositions sent in a Letter from Lieutenant-General and his Officers... Printed for Robert Ibbotson. BL/EEBO: E.472[24].

John Lilburne, *The Legal Fundamental Liberties of the People of England, Revived, Asserted, and Vindicated* (1649), p. 35.

David Farr, *Henry Ireton and the English Revolution* (Woodbridge, Boydell, 2006)

Underdown, *Pride's Purge*, pp. 117-19.

Gardiner, *Great Rebellion*, vol. 4, pp. 238-42.

PART THREE

ARMY PETITIONS

FROM THE REMONSTRANCE TO PRIDE'S PURGE

NOVEMBER - DECEMBER 1648

19: HARRISON'S REGIMENT

7-20 November 1648

Context

Events in the northern army at this time are uncertain. Two anonymous pamphlets describe a meeting in that region, but on different days and with different content. According to one, at a meeting near York on 10 November 'the Agents of the respective Regiments in the Northern Brigade' agreed a resolution supporting the demands of the army in the south, 'for the speedy executing of Justice upon all persons whatsoever, even from the highest to the lowest'. According to the other, an army meeting on 11 November agreed after 'much debate in an argumentary way' to stand with the southern army, 'for preservation of the Rights and Liberties of the Free-born people of England, and the establishing of the Laws of the Land'. This version adds that Cromwell agreed that a letter be written to the king, urging him to accept the Presbyterian terms at Newport and take the Covenant oath. It would be unwise to dismiss the report of a meeting as entirely untrue, but whether regimental 'agents' as well as officers were involved seems doubtful. The Lieutenant-General is unlikely to have travelled far from Knottingley (27 miles from York) in the snow and ice then prevailing according to a report from the siege of Scarborough. Since surviving letters were signed by him on 10 and 11 November at Knottingley, any meeting he held is more likely to have been there

Whatever the nature or venue, it seems unlikely that Cromwell proposed to approach the king directly. On 6 November he wrote to his cousin Robert Hammond, governor of the Isle of Wight, that negotiating with the king would be 'meddling with an accursed thing'. Peace 'is only good when we receave it at our father's hand', he wrote, but 'its dangerous to snatch at it, more dangerous to go against the will of God to attayne it'. Sir Henry Vane might be making a mistake in working with the Presbyterians, he wrote, but 'I can be passive and let it go, knowing that innocency and integrity loses nothing by a patient waiting upon the Lord'. It is hard to believe that he agreed to contacting the king recommending the Presbyterian terms to him only a few days later (unless he was just prevaricating); and his next letter to Hammond, on 25 November, suggests no change of heart.

Text

Severall Petitions presented to his Excellency the Lord Fairfax. By The Lieut. Generals, Col. Harrisons, Coll. Prides, Coll. Deanes Regiment. Together With Lieut. Gen. Cromwels Letter To His Excellency Concerning the Same

Printed In The Year. MDCXLVIII. BL/EEBO: E.474[5]

The Humble Petition of the Officers and Souldiers of Colonel Harrison [*sic*] Regiment.

May it please your Excellency, In Conscience to the Kingdom and your Excellency, our publique Engagement for its Redemption and private Obligation of addressing to your self for the regular accomplishment of that end; We presume (in confidence of your Excellencies favorable construction of this attempt) to prostrate our present dissatisfactions to your serious thoughts. Our exactest and most impartial Observations dictate to us a Resurrection (if 'twere ever buried) of the old design to continue Englands Slavery; which though we acknowledg to be covered, yet we conclude with two [sic] thin a vail for being concealed from an ordinary piercing eye. We are not unacquainted with the proceedings of many Commoners in a Petitionary way to the Parliament, or of several Regiments to your Excellency in the like course; though not yet sensible [aware] what satisfactory answer hath been received of either. Nor can we be ignorant that the carriage of the Houses in their Treating Overtures with the King, and obstructing Demurs of impartial Justice-execution upon most notorious Delinquents, speaks audibly a negligent Remissness to our Liberty, if not a covert Resolution to comply with what may add to our Yoke. Hence, acted from better principles, (not forgetting our publike Protests and Engagements) we take the boldness humbly to beseech a Contribution of your Excellencies interest to our ensuing requests.

1. That some speedy and effectual course may be taken for the tryal and just punishment of all English, Welch and Scotch convicted enemies, and that neither birth, or place, may exempt any from the hand of Justice; without which, as the wrath of God will not be appeased, so neither can we expect a happy issue of all our labors.
2. That the Parliaments former Declaration of No farther Addresses to the King may not be unworthily deserted, but He speedily either acquitted or convicted of the Charge therein contained.
3. That all Fomentors and Abettors of the late Rebellion, whether in Parliament, City, or Kingdom, may be discovered, and condignly [appropriately] punished.
4. That the Concurrence to a safe and lasting peace may be dispatched according to the many Petitions to that purpose, especially the late large Petition.

And because even Nature it self prompts us to a Self-provision, no way repugnant to the aforesaid ends, we further implore your Excellencies favor.

1. That provision be made for our constant pay whilest we must be continued as an Army, and the Counties payable to the respective Regiments therein assigned to quarter.
2. That Arrears, since Jun. 15. be payd us before we pay our Quarters; and the accompts of all former Arrears so perfected, that a certain and speedy way be offered for obtainment of the same.
3. That with the deductions for free-quarter in the late service (if any must

be) it be considered, where we have been, and the hardship of our Service.
4. That the Horse-quarters be not confined solely to the Market-towns, it having been experienced how many inconveniences did thence accrew, as to our selves, so unto travellers, and the inhabitants.

These our Requests (being so necessarily tendent to the Kingdoms welfare, that (to our best understanding) there is not another way visible for its recovery) if by improvement of your Excellencies wonted vigilancy they be promoted, (for which our fervent prayers are continued) as we are confident shall have your name a praise on earth unto posterity; so you may be assured your very appearance for that end will more closely engage the honest hearts in England for you, and give a fresh occasion to your Petitioners to profess themselves against all opposers in prosecution of them, even unto death.

Your Excellencies most faithful Servants, &c

Background

This petition was evidently written before the content of the *Remonstrance* reached the regiments in the north of England, though according to Cromwell's covering letter he did not forward it to Fairfax until 20 November, after Captain George Joyce had brought news from St Albans to Knottingley. George Thomason did not purchase his copy on the London streets until 30 November. The covering letter from Harrison's soldiers indicates that they had sent it to Cromwell from Wakefield nearly three weeks earlier, however. Though no printer or publisher is named, the whole pamphlet's authenticity is strongly supported by the survival of the original letter addressed to Cromwell by his men (see 20 below). Cromwell's own letter expresses his wholehearted support for the petitioners, praising their 'very great sence ... of the sufferings and the ruine of this poor Kingdom, and in them all a very great zeal to have impartial Justice done upon Offenders'.

In their letter, Harrison's officers celebrate 'so many wonderfull, and glorious appearances of the Lord with us, in our unwearied paines, and labour, for the reducing this poor Kingdome out of its miserable thraldome' and complain that 'those wicked Incendiaries, should through the corruptness of our Judges, not onely hitherto (but as we have great cause to fear, without redress some other way,) will still escape the hand of Justice, whose lives we beleeve the Lord requires to appease his Wrath.' This language is stronger and more religious than in their actual petition, suggesting that the authors may have moderated their approach to gain support. They do not, however, aim at the king's person any more than the petition text itself.

Colonel Thomas Sheffield's horse regiment had become Thomas Harrison's in June 1647. At that time its men had refused to leave for Ireland, demanding their 'just rights and liberties', as well as arrears of pay owed to them, before they would go. When the regiments were dispersed after the Putney Debates, Harrison's went to the rendezvous at Ware against orders, but quickly submitted to Fairfax on arrival. During the second civil war, they were part of the campaign in north-west England that culminated at Preston in August, and accompanied Cromwell to Edinburgh in late September. Some may then have stayed with Lambert in Scotland until November, though others are said to have been quartered in the English midlands; some were evidently at Wakefield by 7 November, and the main body of the regiment was at Pontefract by the beginning of December, when it set out with Cromwell for London.

Harrison himself presumably supported his men's petition, though its moderation with regard to the king suggests that his was not the decisive voice. Harrison had fought from the start of the civil war in the armies of Essex and Manchester, where he already had a reputation as one of a 'cluster of preaching officers'. After joining the New Model Army he took part in many major battles, including Langport (July 1645), where Richard Baxter saw him 'break forth into the praises of God ... as if he had been in a rapture' when the battle turned in favour of Parliament's forces. As a leading officer in Sheffield's regiment he was active in the army revolt of 1647, although he was not present at the Putney Debates. By November 1647 he declared it 'lay upon his spirit ... that the king was a man of bloud ... and that they were to prosecute him'; and in January 1648, as a member of the House of Commons, he wholeheartedly supported the Vote of No Addresses. He attended the General Council at St Albans in November 1648, and took part in the discussions with the Leveller leaders that produced the new version of *An Agreement of the People* for the army council at Whitehall in December. He was a committed participant in the regicide, attending almost every session of the High Court of Justice, and would serve the Commonwealth regime, After opposing Cromwell's Protectorate (1653-8), he was particularly brutally executed at the Restoration.

Related sources

The Declaration of Lieutenant-General Cromwell, Concerning the King's Majesty, and the Citizens of London, and his Protestation for peace, and re-inthroning of the King: Together with his Propositions to the Army, and their resolution thereupon ... Printed in the Year of joy, 1648. BL/EEBO: E.472[20].

A Declaration of the Army, Concerning the King's Majesty, the Prince of Wales, and the Citizens of London ... Agreed upon by the Officers and Souldiers, under the Command of the Lord Gen. Fairfax, to be read and published throughout the respective Counties within the Kingdom of England, and Dominion of Wales ... Printed for R. Williamson. BL/EEBO: E.472[6].

The Moderate Intelligencer, No. 192, 16-23 November 1648. BL/EEBO: E.473[15].

Clarke Papers, vol. 1, p. 417, vol. 2, pp. 274-5.
Firth and Davies, *Regimental History*, vol. 1, pp. 175-89.
ODNB: Ian J. Gentles, 'Harrison, Thomas (*bap.* 1616, d. 1660)'.
BL: Egerton Ms 2620, fo. 3 (Cromwell's letter before leaving Pontefract).

20: CROMWELL'S REGIMENT

before 20 November 1648

Context

The similarities between this petition and the last above make it a good example of a text written by one group of people being adapted by another. This is neither simple plagiarism nor an artificial exercise in 'changing the words' to conceal its common origin. In the light of the accompanying letter from Harrison's men, it is most likely that their version came first. The concluding recommendations with regard to the supply of money and horses also make more sense as an addition by Cromwell's troopers than as a cut by Harrison's. The preamble now gives a greater role to divine agency in 'stirring up' previous petitioners; while 'pretended friends' have been added to the obstructers of justice, and the 11 September Large Petition is mentioned more specifically in relation to the demand for justice. Among the numbered demands, the necessity of appeasing god's wrath has disappeared from the first, the second reinforces the reference to the Vote of No Addresses by recalling the army's published support for it, and the possibility of acquitting or convicting the king has been reworded. These do not seem to be random alterations, but rather the kind of redrafting job which seventeenth-century guildsmen, town councillors, grand jurymen, or anyone who has ever agreed a document in committee would recognise.

Text

Severall Petitions presented to his Excellency the Lord Fairfax... [as last]. BL/EEBO: E.474[5].

The Humble Petition of the Officers and Souldiers in the Regiment of Lieutenant General Cromwel.

Humbly sheweth, That in disharge of our duty to the Kingdom our publique ingagements for its redemption and private obligations of addressing to your self for the regular accomplishment of a speedy settlement, we presume, and in confidence of your Excellencies favorable construction of this attempt to prostrate our present thoughts and desires to your serious considerations, our exactest and most impartial observations, dictate to us the designed ruin of us, and the faithful in the Kingdoms, which though covered with fair and specious overtures, yet with sadness and sorrow we are affected with beholding thereof; but rejoyce in this, that the Lord hath stirred up many well affected, especially the large Petitioners, to appear for Justice in a Petitionary way to the Parliament, and of several Regiments unto your Excellency: We cannot be ignorant of the hindring and obstructing of impartial Justice, by the powerful influence of pretended friends, which speak audibly, a negligent remisness to our liberty, and a covert Resolution to comply with what may add to our yoke; therefore we are prest in spirit humbly to beseech a Contribution of your Excellencies Power and Interest for obtaining these our ensuing Requests.

1. That some speedy and effectual course may be taken for the discovery, tryal, and due punishment of all English, Welch and Scottish Enemies, especially those that are principally guilty of all the bloods and treasures that hath bin spent in the Kingdoms, and particularly all those that have abetted, contrived and countenanced the late Rebellions, that impartial Justice may be done upon them, according to the many Petitions to that purpose, especially that large Petition of Sept. 11. 1648. without which we cannot expect a happy issue of all our hazards and labors.
2. That the former Declarations and Concurrences of the Army therewith of no further addresses to the King, may not be unworthily deserted, without he being acquitted or convicted of the charges therein contained.
3. That the Kingdom may be forthwith postured and settled in the way of a safe and lasting Peace, for the preservation of honest men, and discountenancing of our Enemies.

And because nature it self prompts us to an honest self-provision, no way repugnant to the foresaid ends, we further beg your Excellencies favor;

1. To that end free quarter may be presently take off, and provision be made for our constant pay, whilst we be continued, and that Counties may be assigned to every respective Regiment to that purpose.
2. That our Arrears, since the 15. of January last past, be paid up before we pay our quarters; and the accounts of all former Arrears be so perfected, and put into a present way, that they may be obtained.
3. That in the deductions for free quarter (if any must be) in this last Summers service it be considered where we have bin, and the hardships we met withal therein.
4. That the Horse quarters be not confined solely to market Towns; it having bin experienced how many inconveniences did thence accrew, as to ourselves, so unto travellers, and the inhabitants.
5. That in our future pay effectual care be taken to supply us with currant, and not clipt, money; the Country, and our selves, suffering abundance of damage, (and as we suppose) our Enemies designing thereby to divide us.
6. That effectual course may be taken to supply the Regiments of Horse, with recruit [replacement] horses, many having lost their own horses in prosecution of the late Service, and are altogether disabled to mount themselves out of their pay, which comes so slowly: it will not furnish them with other necessaries, and many having exhausted all they had, or could get from friends, to mount themselves.

These our Requests being so necessarily tendent to the Kingdoms and our own welfare, that if by improvement of your Excellencies wonted vigilancy they be promoted, (for which our fervent prayers are continued,) as we are confident shall leave your name a praise upon earth to posterity; and you will more closely engage honest men, and give a fresh occasion to your

Petitioners to profess themselves. Your Excellencies most faithful Servants.

Background

The regiment commanded by Oliver Cromwell at this time was not his original 'Ironsides' recruited in London at the start of the civil war, whose command he had resigned in accordance with the Self-Denying Ordinance in 1645. After being exempted from the Ordinance to serve under Fairfax as Lieutenant-General in command of the cavalry, he took over the horse regiment previously commanded in Manchester's army by the Dutchman Bartholomew Vermuyden (nephew of the military and drainage engineer Cornelius Vermuyden). Raised in Norfolk, this regiment had fought at Marston Moor and Newbury before joining the New Model. The Presbyterian Thomas Edwards heard reports from Northamptonshire of radical religious and political opinions among its members in 1646. In the spring of 1647, its agitators included Capt. Joseph Wallington and Lt Edward Scotton for the officers, and Samuel Whiting for the common soldiers, all three of whom signed the letter to Cromwell that accompanied this petition. After fighting in Wales and at Preston in 1648, the regiment went with Cromwell to Scotland at the end of September 1648, returning to England via Newcastle and York. Their march south was diverted to Pontefract by the news of Rainborowe's killing, and the Yorkshire county committee's insistence on Cromwell taking over the siege.

The officers' letter survives among the Clarke Papers, with seventeen signatures. 'We are bold (in discharge of our duties, and upon very serious considerations)', they say, 'to beseech your favourable assistance and approbation in presenting the inclosed, ours and our Soldiers just, most necessary and (as we hope) modest desires.' Using language distinctly more religious than that in the petition text itself, they believe that 'the well-affected and godly of the Land' look to Fairfax and Cromwell as 'principally under God their Deliverers and Saviors from Tyranny and Slavery ... as God shall direct, who (as we are perswaded) will yet further appear for his peoples salvatione.' In that event, they hope that they will not 'act any thing rashly, irregularly, or unbeseeming us, as Christians or Soldiers ... so as it shall be obvious we seek neither our own interest nor particular parties, but the well-being of the whole Kingdom.' The officers who signed — Henry Huntington, Henry Hall, Samuel Whiting, William Stafford, William Cobb, John Byfeild, John Fox, John Hardman, James Goodwin, Francis Browne, Edward Scotten, John Blackmore, Joseph Wallington, Edward Southwood, Edward Warren, Thomas Savage, and Theophilus Barnard — can all be found in Malcolm Wanklyn's list of New Model captains and junior officers known to have served in this regiment.

Many historians have been suspicious of Cromwell for remaining in the north while the army leaders prepared to intervene in political developments at Westminster. Published letters from soldier correspondents at Pontefract explain that they were waiting for the arrival of Major-General John Lambert, who had stayed in Scotland to support a radical Presbyterian takeover but was now marching southwards with three regiments of horse. Cromwell also had to deal with Colonel Ashton's Lancashire force, whose men feared they had been scheduled for disbandment (see 38 below). Lambert arrived on 24 November, but Fairfax was still writing to request Cromwell's presence at headquarters on 28 November, when steps had already been taken to secure control of the king's person and the Council of Officers had resolved to occupy London. 'By the Remonstrance which was lately tendered to the House of Commons', Fairfax wrote, 'I believe your apprehensions are full of the weightines of our present affaires', hoping that with Cromwell's arrival 'a mercifull furtherance wil bee given to the very great business now in agitation.' Cromwell replied with regard to the *Remonstrance*, he 'could see in it nothinge but what is honest, and becominge Christians, and honest men'. On Tuesday 5 December he was marching south at last, with his own regiment, Fairfax's, Okey's, Harrison's, and some other unspecified troops. They arrived in London on the evening of Wednesday 6 December, after the purge of parliament had begun.

Related sources

Worcester College Oxford: Letter to Oliver Cromwell from his officers, Clarke Ms 267/1, fo. 18.
British Library: Oliver Cromwell to Thomas Lord Fairfax, November 1648, Egerton Ms 2620.
Clarke Papers, ed. Firth, vol. 2, pp. 62-3.
Packets of Letters, No. 36, 21 November 1648. BL/EEBO: E.473[12].
Perfect Weekly Account, 15-22 November 1648. BL/EEBO: E.473[13].
The Moderate Intelligencer, No. 192, 16-23 November 1648. BL/EEBO: E.473[15].
The Moderate, No. 20, 21-28 November 1648. BL/EEBO: E.473[31].
The Moderate Intelligencer, No. 193, 23-30 November 1648. BL/EEBO: E.474[3].
Packets of Letters, from Severall Parts of England, No. 37. BL/EEBO: E.474[9].
Firth & Davies, *Regimental History*, vol. 1, pp. 200-04.
Wanklyn, *Reconstructing the New Model*, p. 142.
Wilbur Cortez Abbott (ed.), *The Writings and Speeches of Oliver Cromwell* (Cambridge, University Press, 1937), vol. 1, pp. 670-700.
Gardiner, *Great Civil War*, vol. 4, pp. 233-53.
Underdown, *Pride's Purge*, pp. 119-23.

21: PRIDE'S AND DEANE'S REGIMENTS
before 20 November 1648

Context

This petition specifically demands action against the king, who is held to have admitted his blood guilt by accepting the first clause presented to him at Newport, exonerating Parliament. This widely held interpretation was possibly never accepted by Charles himself. On being taken from the Isle of Wight a week after this petition was directed to Fairfax, he apparently smuggled out a declaration in which he questioned it: 'Hath not all the blood that hath been spilled these seven years been called upon My Head, Who am the greatest Sufferer, though the least Guilty?' This was the only version of Charles's reaction to the *Remonstrance* and the end of the treaty (among many in circulation at the time) reproduced in the officially sponsored volume of the 'martyr' king's works in 1662. It would, of course, have wrecked the whole treaty if published before Parliament's discussion of his final answers on 4-5 December, but it seems to have hit the streets for the first time a few days after the king's death.

Though the text of this petition was forwarded by Cromwell as coming from both Pride's regiment and Deane's, another and more radical one in the name of Pride's regiment was published in London soon after they took part in the purge of parliament on 6 December (22 below). The date of this other petition is uncertain, and part of its content may have been added after the army's *Remonstrance* was read in parliament, but it is possible that it was already circulating when the regiment also subscribed to Deane's men's petition.

Text

Severall Petitions presented to his Excellency the Lord Fairfax... [as last]. BL/EEBO: E.474[5].

To the Right Honorable His Excellency the Lord Fairfax, Commander in Chief of all Forces raised or to raised [*sic*] by the Parliament.

The Humble Petition of the Officers and Souldiers of Col. Prides, and Col. Deans Regiments.

Sheweth, That your Petitioners looking back, and taking a serious view of those many mercies and great deliverances which God hath bestowed upon this poor Nation, in making your Excellency, with those under your command, Instruments of its deliverance, by being twice victorious over those numerous bodies, that were convened in several places of this Kingdom to the utter ruin and destruction thereof, had not God by his mighty power prevented it: And now after all this our unwearied pains, and great hazard of our lives, we hoped to have reaped some Freedom to our selves and the Kingdom, but instead thereof (if not timely prevented) we fear the same miseries, if not worse, are like to return upon us again, by setting up the same usurping power, against which we have contested so long, and, as we conceive, hath bin the chief cause of all our misery, and hath cost this Kingdom so dear to subdue: And the people of this Kingdom being also very sensible of their neer approaching danger and misery thereby, as appears by those many Petitions presented from London, and several Counties: We also being ear witnesses of the peoples dayly and sad Complaints of the heavy Taxations that lye upon them, more especially, because they see the Kingdoms Treasure perverted to wrong uses, and the Souldier unsatisfied, for whom it is pretended to be raised; whereby a heavier burthen then these Taxes lye upon them, by reason of Free quarter, which proves so great a discouragement to the Conscientious Souldiers, who have cheerfully undergone all other hardships.

Therefore our Humble Desires to your Excellency are, (That as God hath hitherto crowned you with faithfulness, and made you an Eminent Saviour to this poor intended ruined Nation) that you would yet continue (which we question not) to stand by us, and the just Desires of this Kingdom, both in presenting them to, and procuring them from the honorable House [sic] of Parliament, as followeth, viz:

1. That the Parliament be desired to take a view of their late Declarations and Charge against the King, as also to consider his own Act in taking the guilt of bloodshed upon himself, and accordingly to proceed against him as an Enemy to the Kingdom.
2. That strict inquiry be made after the chief Fomentors, Actors and abettors of this late [second] War, especially those who were the chief Incouragers and Invitors in of the Scots Army, and that exemplary Justice may be accordingly executed to the terror of evil doers, and the rejoycing of all honest men.
3. That all those, through whose hands the publike treasure of the Kingdom hath run, may speedily be called to give up their Accompts, that thereby the Kingdom may be satisfied, how those vast sums of money that have bin raised therein are disposed of, and that so soon as the necessities of the Kingdom will permit, that [they] may be eased of all unnecessary charge and burdens.
4. That that which is so insufferable for us to take, and so intollerable for the people to bear, namely free quarter may be forthwith taken off, by sending some speedy supplies to the Army; and by appointing several Assignations to every Regiment of the standing Army; without which neither we, nor the people can have any assurance to be freed from that great burden.
5. That all unnecessary officers of the Kingdom may be taken off, by which means great sums of money have needlessly been wasted, and that none of the moneys, which shall hereafter be raised and collected, may be imbeseled or suffisticated; but as it comes to the Souldiers, so it may pass

to the Country again.

6. That no person whatsoever that hath bin active, either directly or indirectly, in this late War, shall be admitted to any place of trust, either Military or Civil in this Kingdom, who by that means may have opportunity to involve the Kingdom in new troubles, and all such persons who are so imployed may be discharged from such imployment.

These our desires we humbly offer, as being of absolute necessity to the present and future well-being of this Kingdom; and seeing God hath hitherto made you faithful in the trust reposed in you; and there being such an opportunity once more to appear for the publike Interest, you may be confident of the Providence of God, who delights in the way of Justice, Truth and Equity; and for our parts we are resolved, by Gods assistance, to stand by you, and all those that joyn with us, in our just desires.

Background

Pride's regiment of foot had originated as Barclay's in the Earl of Essex's army, joining the New Model in 1645 under Colonel Edward Harley. As Harley was recovering from a recent wound, his Lieutenant-Colonel Thomas Pride commanded the regiment at Naseby, where it played a crucial role. Its men refused service in Ireland in 1647, and when the Presbyterian Harley left it, Pride became their colonel. During the second civil war they fought with Cromwell in Wales and at Preston, and at Winwick Pass on 19 August. They were reported to have taken Tweedmouth on 24 September, and probably accompanied Cromwell to Scotland later that month, as he was said to have taken 'all the foot' from Berwick with him. Cromwell left Edinburgh on 7 October, and Pride's forces were reported to be quartered around Richmond (North Yorkshire) on 19 October. They evidently marched southwards ahead of Cromwell, as they were listed among those to appear at the rendezvous on 1 December near London, where Pride and his men were to leave their mark on history during the purge of parliament.

Thomas Pride was a Somerset yeoman's son, who served his apprenticeship in London's Haberdashers' Company. He went on to prosper as a brewer in Southwark, where he belonged to a separatist congregation that rejected the established church. During the Commonwealth and Protectorate Pride would call for the suppression of drunkenness, swearing and 'uncleanness' (a word whose connotations at the time were sexual rather than hygienic) and take vigorous action against cock-fighting, bear-baiting, bull-baiting and prize fencing matches. He won praise for his role at Naseby and at the storming of Bristol and of Dartmouth; and played a leading role in his regiment during the New Model's revolt in 1647. Though he was accused of threatening his men with expulsion from the army if they refused to support him, it is clear that he had commanded the loyalty of the regiment long before Harley left. His own loyalty to the army leadership was solid throughout the political crisis of late 1648, and as a member of the

High Court of Justice he would attend every session and sign the king's death warrant.

Thomas Rainborowe's former regiment was assigned to Richard Deane in September 1647 when Rainborowe was appointed Vice-Admiral of the navy — much to the latter's annoyance, as he had hoped to keep his army command (see 16 above). In April 1647, when he was in London seeking approval for an attack on Jersey, the regiment had mutinied and marched from Hampshire to Abingdon near Oxford, where they joined with Ingoldsby's regiment to try to secure their arrears of pay, and reportedly seized the artillery there as a bargaining tool. Rainborowe restored order and the regiment gave no further trouble, but submitted to Fairfax's command, and took part in the army's occupation of London in August that year. Under Deane in 1648, they fought with Cromwell from Wales to Preston, but it is not known where they were from then until 18 November, when two London newsbooks' correspondents mentioned their presence at Pontefract. They may have been with Cromwell during his brief visit to Scotland and subsequent march from Carlisle and Newcastle to Pontefract, but like Pride's they rejoined the southern army in time for the 1 December rendezvous.

Richard Deane was a merchant from a Gloucestershire family who traded from London and Portsmouth, and a relative of Sir Richard Deane, Lord Mayor of London in 1628-9. At the start of the civil war, he helped to secure the Kent ports for parliament, and had joined Essex's army by 1644. As comptroller of ordnance for the New Model Army, he commanded the artillery at Naseby, Langport, Sherborne and Bristol. He played a small part in the Putney Debates, siding with Cromwell and Ireton against the radicals, and Cromwell was said to have preferred Deane rather than Rainborowe for the post of Vice-Admiral. During the army's occupation of London in December 1648 Deane was sent to commandeer the treasuries at Goldsmiths' and Weavers' halls to pay the army, in order to prevent free quarter being imposed on the city. He would play an active part in the trial of the king and sign his death warrant, and die in a sea battle against the Dutch in 1653.

These four regiments whose petitions were forwarded by Cromwell had evidently formed strong and effective bonds. They had fought together on many occasions in both civil wars, and had good reason to feel that the launching of the second by royalists and Scots had been a pointless infliction of unnecessary suffering, given that god (as they believed) had given them victory in the first. They had also shared the experience of politicisation in 1647, and were accustomed to organising and acting to achieve a consensus. In this latest political crisis, they may be regarded as the hard core of the New Model Army's northern campaign, marching southwards to join their general at headquarters for a historic intervention.

Related sources

Firth & Davies, *Regimental History*, vol. 1, pp. 359-66 & vol.2, pp. 417-23.

Good News from Scotland ... As it was sent in a letter from Lieut. General Crumwells quarters near Berwick, to a Friend in London. BL/EEBO: E.465[34].

The Moderate Intelligencer, No. 188, 17-26 October 1648. BL/EEBO: E.469[1].

Packets of Letters from Several Parts of England, 21 November 1648. BL/EEBO: E.373[12].

His Majesties Declaration Concerning the Treaty: and His Dislike of The Armies Proceedings. Delivered by his majesty to one of his servants at his departure from the Isle of Wight: and commanded to be published for the satisfaction of his subjects, anno 1648. No printer or publisher named. BL/EEBO: E.541[1].

John Gauden (ed.), *Basilika: The works of King Charles the Martyr* (1662), p. 672.

ODNB: Ian J. Gentles, 'Pride, Thomas, appointed Lord Pride under the Protectorate (d. 1658)'.

ODNB: J. K. Laughton, 'Deane, Richard (*bap*. 1610, d. 1653)', revised by Michael Baumber.

22: PRIDE'S REGIMENT

November/December 1648

Context

This petition was published by the Independent *Moderate Intelligencer* on 14 December, but its insistence that 'we abhor Anarchy, Confusion, and the Levelling of mens Estates, so often charged upon us' also suggests a link to the Levellers. It appears under the dateline 8 December, but its reference to parliament's 14-day extension of the deadline for the treaty negotiations, granted on 3 November, suggests an earlier date of composition. The possible objection that 'we put violence upon Authority' seems to anticipate the regiment's notorious participation in just such an act on 6 December, but it advocates a different strategy, calling on members opposed to the treaty to withdraw from Parliament. This was the approach of the army's official declaration on 30 November in response to Parliament's rejection of the *Remonstrance*.

The text of the petition was copied by some of those anonymous or pseudonymous publishers who regularly issued miscellaneous and dubious news pamphlets. In one of these, it appeared with a typically inflated headline, claiming that this was a *New Remonstrance* addressed by 'the Souldiery' to Fairfax 'in the name of themselves, and all the Commons of England'.

Text

The Moderate Intelligencer, No. 195, 7-14 December 1648.BL/EEBO: E.476[24]

To the Right Honorable Thomas Lord Fairfax our faithfull generall. The humble Petition of all the Officers, and Souldiers of the Regiment commanded by Collonel Thomas Pride.

Whereas it hath pleased the Lord of Hosts (who was called upon to decide the controversie of this Nation, to write his name upon your Sword in very legible characters, as appears upon record twice, viz. in the yeare 45, where we had 114 Victories, and now this last Summer above 30, even to our astonishment, who were used by you in that service, that those proud Billows in Wales, England and Scotland have been bounded and calmed, in lesse then six moneths; and when through many tiresome marches and conflictings with many deaths (to say no more, least we be counted boasters) we thought when the North and South winde had thus blown upon the Garden, that the spices would have flown out [Song of Solomon 4.16]; Behold, we have our sorrows repeated, and our fears increased, making our wounds even to bleed afresh. For,

1. We finde many good and just Petitions from City, Countrey, and Army, not onely un-answered, laid by, and slighted, but also things contrary to their honest desires practized, which appeares. First, By treating with a

conquered enemy, contrary to the Vote of non-adresses, against which this Army is engaged by life and death, yea, and to make the Treaty the fruits of our victory over the Scots, resolving to beg mercie of him, the very houre that Army of his was begging mercie of us. Secondly, Not onely Treating, but falling down from their resolved propositions, especially in that of Delinquents from 37 not to be spared to 7, and those neither considerable, nor attainable, mocking the people in their Covenant, which is to bring these to condigne punishment, and as if that were not enough; to abate so much in compositions [fines] of the rest (as if such a complyance were intended, as we should change conditions with the Enemy, and fight and conquer ourselves into slavery. Thirdly, To adde more load to the grieved petitioners, their best friends, and gratifie the worst of enemies, 14 dayes more is granted tendring a complyance upon any terms; yea, though by agreement he hath taken upon him the bloud of the three Kingdoms: and to leave us hopelesse of any good by him, he abets his Son in that Pyracie, and Ormond in that renewed conspiracie against that little Protestant bloud un-exhausted in Ireland. Nor can we but be thoughtfull why some notice might not have been given to your Excellencie and Army, concerning a Treaty, since our Trustees have so often acknowledged God to have sent them preservation by this hand, but we onely point at that.

2. We take leave to tell your Excellencie what you heare of daily to your intollerable griefe, the Army must be made again the burthensome stone to the people (which is no new designe) by their non-payment, and even then (if ever) it had sweat bloud for their safety, by whom thus unworthily neglected, we must professe not an ingenious Souldier of the meanest ranke, but doth blush to receive his unpayed for entertainment, and the rather 1. Because unexpectedly returns to it. 2. Because the Countrey payes their Taxes. 3. Because bad men are enriched by it. 4. Because shame and contempt will be the Souldiers Portion. 5. Because it still sows seed of new broyles, where people are thus abused.

Sir, we have much to complain of, but of nothing more then that the main ends of these Wars, crowned with mercie even to miracle, are not reaped, the Fox stealing that from us by subtilty, which the Lion could not teare by cruelty.

Wherefore, in our own names, and the names of the betrayed, abused people of England, we humbly beseech your Excellencies assistance of us, and concurrence with us in these ensuing requests and groans of our souls, which may not long be denyed us, least [lest] we faint or struggle, as we can, for the life of good men, and a good Cause.

I. That justice may sodainly and equally be dispensed according to the desires of our honoured friends in London, Leicestershire, and others, manifested by their severall Petitions, and the parliaments Declaration concerning the Kings evills asserted; or bewayled, and repented of.

II. That your Army be instantly reckoned withall, and paid, and so dealt with for future (if they must be used) that every Regiment may know their own County, and there receive their pay immediately, without any other Treasurers or wayes of trouble, that so the people themselves may see what they have for their money. In this we are impatient, or so passionately affected, that we gaspe for helpe: This Regiment hath had but one moneths pay since May, having marched 1300 miles this Summer.

III. That the people may know in print, with all speed, which way all publike moneys are disposed of in all counties and places, and that of all kindes, which may be done, if every Collector and Receiver of money be forthwith enjoyned to print their receipts and disbursements, for if the Souldiers be not paid, the people aske whats become of the Revenew, Compositions, Sequestrations, Excise, Lands, &c.

IV. That we may have a just and righteous Government setled in this Nation, advancing Godlinesse, we abhorring Anarchy, Confusion and Levelling mens Estates, so often charged upon us: for which end we desire these two things, in pursuance of which (by help from heaven) we resolve to venture our All.

First, That the Grand and capitall enemies may, without delay, be brought to justice, which is the main root of our misery, we finding all other wayes attempted altogether invalid to carry on this work of common safety.

Secondly, for the dispatch of justice upon all Delinquents, for the rectifying all crooked things among us, and for the good of us, and the generations to come, we humbly conceive our last and surest way will be for your Excellencie and this Army, to make a speedy offer to the Commons House in your name and the Armies, and in the behalfe of all England, that such of them as have been faithfull to the Kingdoms interest, declare with you and the Nation; and that the contrary minded, False, Royall, and Neutrall party may know, that our enemies must not be our Rulers, wee professing that good men, rather then good Lawes, must save us, though we disjoyne them not. And to this last worke we humbly incite, your Excellency, the Army, and all true English hearts; without which we shall not forbeare any meanes, the Lord shall direct us to, whereby we may free our selves, from the guilt of enslaving the Kingdom, to one, or more; And if any shall object, we put violence upon Authority we hereby proclaim to the world, that neither your Excellency, nor our selves, have received Commissions from the Parliament as now constituted, the swaying part thereof, (as lately in Scotland:) brought over to the Kings designes. But from that good party in it, who struggled through many hazards, to modell this army for the Kingdoms safety; nor are we to attend forms, and customes in this extremity; we can as willingly sit down as march, suffer, as act, would but the Godly party in the Kingdom call us thereunto, and thinke themselves preserved by it.

But the people call to us for these things, and wee to your Excellencie, your known worth, inviting us hereunto; in prosecution of which, as an unparallel'd instrument, we shall live or die with your Excellencie, having solemnly promised in answer to the wonders God hath wrought amongst us, to attempt and attend these two last expedient through all hazard.

We cannot so under-value our God, and the rich experience we have had in the behalfe of this Nation, as to see them lie (like Issachar) under these sinfull burdens [Genesis 49. 14-15], our colds, heats, nakednesse, want, hunger, hardship, difficulties, dangers, cares, feares, out of which our blessed and ever to be praised God, hath brought us, suggesting these things unto us, for that flocke of slaughter in this Kingdome.

Sir, we can die, but not endure to see our dear Mother England die before us.

Other editions

A New Remonstrance from the Souldiery to His Excellency the Lord General Fairfax ... with their Proclamation to the Kingdome, concerning putting of violence upon authority.... Published by Robert Williamson. BL/EEBO: E.476[27]

A Declaration to the City and Kingdome from Major General Massey, Sir William Waller, Colonell Birch and the rest of the Impeached Members of Parliament... Published by 'C.W' near the Royal Exchange. BL/EEBO: E.476[33]

New Propositions to the King, from His Excellency the Lord General Fairfax..... Published by W. Fielding. BL/EEBO: E.477[2]

Background

The commitment to bring delinquents to 'condign punishment' is once again a reference to the Solemn League and Covenant of 1643, and it is not the only reference to Scotland here. The recent expulsion from the parliament in Edinburgh, of the majority who had supported the Engagement with the king and invasion of England, had been assisted by the presence of Cromwell with three New Model regiments. Pride's may have been one of these regiments, as the claim of 1300 miles' marching that summer hints. The significance of these events as a possible precedent for an English parliamentary purge was mentioned by Cromwell in his letter of 6 November 1648 to Hammond, and argued by the editor of *The Moderate* on 21 November.

An English precedent for the strategy of secession rather than expulsions from Parliament was the flight of Independent members of both houses to the New Model Army's headquarters after the Commons was invaded by a pro-Presbyterian London crowd in July 1647. According to the Independent MP Edmund Ludlow's memoirs, the army leaders were now urging their supporters in the Commons to secede again, but the MPs close to the army argued that it would be 'more proper to relieve them from those who rendred themselves useless to the publick service, thereby preserving the name and place of the Parliament, than for the members thereof to quit their stations wherein they were appointed to serve'. The decision that the army would purge parliament instead was taken at a very late stage in the course of events, most probably on the evening before 'Pride's Purge'.

The petitioners' demand that the funding of each regiment should be allocated to a specific county, as an alternative to 'other Treasurers or ways of trouble', is in line with the decentralisation favoured by the Levellers, always suspicious of centralised bureaucracy. With regard to Pride's men's complaint of having received only one month's pay since May, Ian Gentles's brief biography of the colonel mentions that during December 1648 and January 1649, warrants totalling £7691 were issued for them. The pay of the regiment's commissioned officers (colonel, lieutenant-colonel, major, and ten companies with a captain, a lieutenant and an ensign each) for the seven months from July to January would have amounted to £2128, leaving the average paid to the remainder of the regiment's 800 men — including non-commissioned officers and a few regimental staff such as quartermaster and surgeon — at very marginally more than the 8d daily wage of an ordinary foot soldier in the New Model Army at that time (8.09 pence per day). If the men of Pride's regiment were, as they claimed, due seven months' pay by the end of January 1649, that seems to be approximately what they received. Gentles comments that hardly any other regiment was so generously treated at the time; but while Pride himself was to grow very rich under the Commonwealth, his rank and file foot soldiers were awarded no bonus for their historic role on 6 December.

Related sources

The Declaration of His Excellency the Lord General Fairfax an his General Councel of Officers, Showing the Grounds of The Armies Advance towards the City of London ... Published by John Field for John Partridge. BL/EEBO: E.474[13].

C. H. Firth (ed.), *The Memoirs of Edmund Ludlow*, vol. 1 (Oxford, Clarendon Press, 1894).

C. H. Firth, *Cromwell's Army* (1962 pb edn, London, Methuen, 1962).

Gentles, *New Model Army*, pp. 279-83.

Firth & Davies, *Regimental History*, vol. 1, pp. 359-66.

ODNB: Ian J. Gentles, 'Pride, Thomas, appointed Lord Pride under the Protectorate (d. 1658)'.

23: NORTH-EAST GARRISONS

24 November 1648

Context

By 24 November the headquarters of the New Model Army had moved from St Albans to Windsor, and this petition arrived the day before the Council of Officers reconvened there to plan for action on the conclusion of the treaty, which now seemed imminent. Given the distance involved, it must have been written and subscribed earlier, though probably not much earlier, as it echoes many points found in the *Remonstrance*.

This text is best known for evoking the biblical example of Agag, king of the Amalekites, to argue that punishing others while King Charles, guilty of the blood shed in the civil wars, is spared cannot be 'an acceptable Sacrifice to the Justice of God'. Only two other petitions (28 and 65 below) came closer to demanding the king's death. The Old Testament tells how, after King Saul had carried out the divine order to kill every man, woman and child of the Amalekites, he intended to spare King Agag and sacrifice instead the best sheep and cattle plundered from his kingdom (Samuel 1: 15). The prophet Samuel denounced this decision, saying that god values obedience more than sacrifice, and hacked Agag to pieces himself.

Text

Two Petitions Presented To his Excellency the Lord Fairfax. ..The first presented at Windsor, Friday Novemb. 24. Printed for John Partridge. BL/EEBO: E.473[23]

To His Excellency the Lord Fairfax; The humble and unanimous Petition and Representation of the Officers and Soldiers of the Garrisons of Newcastle, Tinmouth, Hartlepool, Holy-Isle, together with several Officers of Barwick then present,

Sheweth, That whereas the whole Kingdom hath groaned under the miseries of seven years unnatural bloody war, occasioned by the Kings deserting his Parliament, levying and marching in the head of an Army against them; which (though principally imputed to the seducement of wicked Councellors,) yet it was adjudged by the Parliament, in their Votes of the 20. of May, 1642. to be a breach of the Trust reposed in him by his people, contrary to his Oath, and tending to the dissolution of this Government. But when we consider what latter times have produced, as that Declaration of the House of Commons, February 11. 1647. and the dayly experience we have of him, we cannot but conceive, That although evil Councellors were very instrumental, yet that himself was and is the principal Author, Contriver, Abettor, Manager of all the Bloodshed, Massacres, Devastations, and whatsoever Ruines have befaln, not only this Kingdom, but also that of Ireland: And we are the rather induced to be of this opinion, in regard that no means possible have been left unessayed for the gaining him in: witness the several Treaties formerly had with him; the many Petitions, Propositions, so often tendred to him; and above all the late Treaty of fourty days, which being after a total seclusion, for so many moneths, from all evil Councellors whatsoever, and after those solemn Votes of the Parliament cutting him off from all future hopes of having anything to do with the Authority of this Kingdom; whereupon followed a Charge of many high Crimes; and being, by a special over-ruling hand of providence, disposed not to begin till God himself had spoke so loud from heaven unto him, by destroying all his carnal confidences in a most miraculous manner, as that of Kent, the Scots Army, and the rest; so that had not his heart been wholy shut up and obdurate, and himself resolvedly set upon the Destruction of the Kingdom, he could not but readily have yeelded to all such things as might have tended to the common good: But we find, that he is still as averse as ever; and though some specious pretences are held forth to delude ignorant souls, yet really advantage is thereby made for the laying of a new design to bring about his former wicked intentions, as appears by the Princes continuing still in Rebellion, and the late transactions of Ormond in Ireland, not disavowed by the King; and withall considering, That all endeavours, for the bringing of other Instruments and Incendiaries to condign punishment, while the grand Delinquent is untouched are to little purpose, as being not an acceptable Sacrifice to the Justice of God; to offer him ought else, while Agag is spared; nor answerable, either to the true sence and equity of all former Declarations and Engagements to that purpose (especially that of the Army, upon the Parliaments Vote of Non-addresses to the King,) or to the proper end and intention of them, which was not the Ruine, but the Preservation of the Kingdom.

We therefore Your humble Petitioners, in consideration of the Premisses, and encouraged thereunto by the long experience we have had of Your faithfulness and readiness to serve Your Country, do beseech Your Excellency, that You will now be pleased to shew Your Self, and to use such means as may be effectual; That no further Application be made unto the King, but that, according to former Presidents [precedents] in this Kingdom upon far less Crimes, he may be speedily called to answer to such Charges, as are, or shall be brought in against him; and so, Justice being done upon him, way will be made, with less difficulty and more success, for the prosecution of other Offendors, the prevention of future Insurrections, and firm setling the Kingdom in Peace and Safety.

And we shall ever pray, etc.

Signed by us the Officers of the said Garrisons with the joynt consent of the Soldiers, &c.

Presented to his Excellency the Lord Fairfax, Lord General, at Windsor, Friday Novemb. 24, 1648.

Background

The use of religious language and biblical examples is a striking feature which this petition shares with others emanating from the north-east of England. The post-war parliamentarian regime in Newcastle under its military governor Sir Arthur Hesilrige was closely associated with the Baptist sect, which had recently been introduced there but was already putting down strong roots. (See 4 and 10 above.)

The garrisons of Newcastle and other Northumberland strongholds at this time were largely drawn from two foot regiments of the New Model Army, Skippon's and Hesilrige's, though some local militias were also present, and part of Overton's regiment garrisoned Berwick. Skippon's, which appears to have had no share in the army's political upheavals of 1647, had occupied Newcastle since the departure of the Scottish army in January that year. In December they were joined there by Robert Lilburne's foot regiment, originally raised in Kent. Its men had refused an order at the end of the Putney Debates to join their colonel, who was already in Newcastle as governor. They then drove out all but one of their officers before marching against orders to the rendezvous at Ware on 15 November, where they appeared with copies of *The Agreement of the People* in their hats. Their revolt was crushed, and some of the mutineers were court-martialled and sentenced to death on the spot, though in the end only Robert Arnold was shot. The few still in custody at the end of November wrote to Fairfax denying a rumour that one of them had said it would be lawful 'to murther the king'. This would have been tantamount to assassination or tyrannicide, associated in English Protestant minds with the Jesuits, and shocking also to anyone who believed the king should be tried and executed by public legal process.

The regiment marched on to Newcastle, where Sir Arthur Hesilrige took over their command, and Robert Lilburne returned to the regiment of horse he had raised in his own county of Durham in 1644. The Baptist lay preacher Paul Hobson remained as major of the foot regiment and deputy governor of the city under Hesilrige. Here Hobson and his fellow Baptists may have turned political militancy among this turbulent body of men towards radical religious enthusiasm. The officer accused of spreading the tyrannicide rumour, Lieutenant-colonel Henry Lilburne — a brother of Colonel Robert Lilburne and the Leveller John Lilburne — was placed in command of Tynemouth Castle, which in hostile hands could stop the whole coal trade between Tyneside and London. On the evening of 8-9 August, Henry Lilburne sent most of his men out of the castle and declared for the king. Hesilrige was immediately alerted, and the lieutenant-colonel was killed when Tynemouth Castle was retaken by storm. This experience of betrayal may have intensified the resentment felt throughout the parliamentarian armies at having been called upon — by the rashness of English royalists and the Scottish leaders' change of allegiance — to fight a second civil war which only confirmed the result of the first.

Related sources

The Moderate, No. 20, 21-28 November 1648. BL/EEBO: E.473[31].
A Terrible and Bloudy Fight at Tjnmouth Castle... BL/EEBO: E.459[4].
Clarke Papers, vol. 1 (Letter cited, p. 419).
Howell, *Newcastle-upon Tyne and the Puritan Revolution* (see 4 above).

24: HEWSON'S REGIMENT

25 November 1648

Context

On the same day as this petition was presented to Fairfax at Windsor, 25 November, the Council of Officers made the crucial decision to order Robert Hammond, governor of the Isle of Wight, to secure the person of the king again in Carisbrooke Castle, 'until upon some resolution of our Remonstrance or otherwise further order shall be given by His Excellency'. The reading of this petition as part of the day's proceedings was timely, therefore, though it may have been drawn up earlier as it does not refer to the *Remonstrance*.

To prompt the flow of supportive petitions, a copy of the *Remonstrance* was sent the same day to every regiment, with a letter urging them to 'in a Publicke way expresse to the Generall your regiments Approbation thereof and concurrence therein'. The meeting also appointed a committee 'to consider of such thinges as may be of concernement for the present affaires, & to make transaction thereof', and requested every regiment to send one officer to join the council at Windsor so that all might be involved in the decisions that followed.

The text below was officially published by John Partridge, one of several publishers regularly employed by the army. It also appeared in a miscellaneous news compilation, with the claim that it had been 'Subscribed by the free born people of England, who are resolved to live and dye with their renowned Generall and Army. And commanded to be forthwith printed and published.' Printed at the bottom of the back page, where buyers often turned to find out more about the contents, this was typical of the puffing-up applied to texts picked up from the regular newsbooks by fly-by-night publishers of miscellaneous news in one-off pamphlets.

Text

Two Petitions Presented To his Excellency the Lord Fairfax. ... The first presented at Windsor, Friday Novemb. 24 ... Printed for John Partridge. BL/EEBO: E.473[23]

To the Right Honorable Thomas Lord Fairfax, our noble and faithful General:

The Petition of the Officers and Soldiers of the Regiment commanded by Colonel Hewson

Humbly Sheweth, That whereas your Excellency's approved, worth and fidelity have opened the doors and ears to admit and hear any thing, having tendency to the healing of this bruised and diseased Kingdom; we being many ways provoked to make a present address to the Representatives, know no better nor safer hand to convey it by then your own, which is so dear unto us: Therefore being so sadly sencible of the complaints from all parts, but especially those which seem to crack the axletree of all our hopes; viz. 1. A renewed design upon this Army, by forcing us to free quarter, to make us the contempt and hissing of the people, though we crave your witness that we have not boggled very often, to make brick without straw, and born burden to the cracking of many faithful shoulders, and thereby fill your hearts and ours with unspeakable grief, even almost reluctancies, to despair, had not your firm influence prevented our divisions, and thereby the Kingdoms ruine, which would have gratified the Devil and our enemies, his instruments. 2. As English men we cannot but be sensible of the inconveniences of this late Treaty, whereby it is attempted to null all Contracts, Protestations, Votes, yea to our particular undertaking to bring Delinquents of all sorts to condign punishments, offering thereby more then a conquered, yet implacable enemy, could expect. 3. The exhausting the peoples treasure by many ways, Offices and Officers, and no publique account given thereof, rooted upon cursed self-seeking in some, maintaining the jealousies of many. 4. The Kingdom left naked without any setled Government, so often cry'd for; a Parliament rather being a medicine for mal-administrations, & an Instrument to make Laws with, then a proper Government, as all confess. 5. An inequality of punishments, censures, and compositions, as if we had no net to catch the greater flies. 6. Oppression by Foraign un-English'd Laws and Lawyers grown to swarms, when the best order'd Common-weals have the fewest of that brood, and who have been found by their increase a Pathagnomical Symptome of a crazy State, and Caclecktick Common-wealth. 7. The slighting and contemptous dealing with Petitioners and Petitions, whereby redress hath been sought to the peoples Grievances; a practice as dangerous as unusual, in places where the preservation of the whole is the eye and aym of the Trustees.

We do therefore heartily and fully concur with our brethren in the Army, in their several just Petitions presented to your Excellency, calling for Justice, and just things, and the same we do with those in the City and Country, being the rather prest hereunto, because our late employment hath made some of us eye and ear witnesses of the last transactions with the grand Enemy, and great abettor of Ormond in Ireland, his son in Holland, and any other party that hath but a sword to draw for his destructive designs, we know, and therefore speak.

Wherefore we most humbly pray, that your Excellency would forthwith communicate these our sighs and restless breathings of our spirits to the Parliament. Viz.

1. We cannot, we dare not make such a forfeiture of our unparelled [*sic*] mercies, nor betray our dear bought Freedom, as to leave our selves and the Nation to the Freedom of one mans will, most unhappy in the whole course of his reign, and now dashing this Kingdom into pieces again by his easily discerned subtilties.

2. We desire all the faithful Patriots of the Commons House, may declare and protest against all men, under the same roof with them, that have so plainly betrayed the common safety by pardoning 30. of the 37. that were appointed to death, and these 7. of no note, and but one within reach; for sending most of the rest as their Agents into France, and other parts, which they call banishment.

3. We most earnestly beg, we may be governed and freed from fear of confusion and Anarchy by such a settlement as cannot be expected from 400. men so strangely chosen, and diversely affected: We wish to that purpose, that the Government of Venice, Holland, Switzerland, and other parts, may be examined, that we may not idolize any one Creature, nor ever be any more att his charge, since of 25. Princes of this Nation many have been impeach'd and depos'd by the sword of the people in the hands of their Trustees.

4. We expect that we be not voted against if we do not deliver up prisoners in our power upon those easie terms voted: We are not ignorant how it is design'd, that this Army must be provoked to do evil things, and by those men who are vexed, we have done so many good.

Dearest Sir, In the gaining of these, and other righteous things for the poor tattered Nation, we shall follow your Excellency through Rocks and Mountains of difficulty, or lose all in that work; for we having bin so often dying, that we would choose once to dye indeed, that our dear Native Country may live.

Presented to his Excellency at Windsor, Saturday, November 25. 1648.

Another edition

A Message sent from both Houses of Parliament ... Likewise a New Declaration of the Army ... Published by Nehemiah Wilson. BL/EEBO: E.473[41]

Background

Hewson's regiment's petition is unique in calling for a constitutional revolution modelled on the oligarchic republics of Venice, Holland and Switzerland. Its rejection of the House of Commons as a body of too many men, 'strangely chosen, and diversely affected', is a plea for enlightened oligarchy very far from Leveller thinking; though its condemnation of the use of the Anglo-Norman language in English courts and of parasitic lawyers was found in all radical circles at the time. Another notable feature, remarkable for any political writing in this period, is that it contains no explicit reference to god — though the army's enemies are assumed to be instruments of the devil — despite the strong religious beliefs of the regiment's colonel and lieutenant.

The regiment, formerly John Pickering's, had been under John Hewson's command since November 1646. During the New Model Army's resistance to disbandment in April 1647, their list of grievances was signed by Lieutenant-colonel John Jubbes and Major Daniel Axtell with the common soldiers' representatives. Jubbes proposed at Putney that though the king could be declared guilty of all the blood shed in the civil wars, yet to avoid future conflict he might be received as king again, especially if the people of Scotland and Ireland wished it — an unusual reservation for an English radical. He left the army in April 1648, however, disagreeing with its support for the Vote of No Addresses. Axtell, a member of William Kiffin's Baptist congregation in London, was denounced for lay preaching in 1646. The regiment was accused by *Mercurius Pragmaticus* of having, in September 1648, harassed the population around Hadley and South Mimms and maltreated a group of Scots prisoners taken at Preston committed to their guard.

In January 1649 it was assigned to guard Westminster Hall during the king's trial. At Axtell's own trial in 1660 it was alleged that he had beaten his men with a cane to get them to cry 'Justice', or 'Justice and Execution'. For heavily clothed musketeers, this would have been a humiliating rather than a brutal assault. Axtell argued that the witnesses may have misunderstood: he could have been beating them because they did shout these slogans. His main defence was that none of his actions amounted to treason under any law. 'I was no Counsellor, no Contriver, I was no Parliament-man,' he said, 'none of the Judges, none that Sentenced, Signed, none that had any hand in the Execution, only that which is charged is that I was an Officer in the Army.' His plea is still discussed in modern debates about the defence of acting under orders.

Axtell commanded the regiment's men at the king's trial because Colonel John Hewson was one of the judges. Hewson was a Londoner, a shoemaker or cobbler by trade, denounced by royalist writers for his low social origins, and like Axtell, he was reported to be preaching illegally in 1646; but he belonged to an Independent rather than a Baptist congregation. He was prominent in the army's confrontation with parliament in 1647, and took part in the Putney Debates. Although his interventions there were brief, his later actions show that he opposed the Levellers, and his regiment remained loyal to Fairfax in the aftermath of Putney. At the Council of Officers on 25 November Hewson was (with Ireton, Harrison, Whalley and Constable) appointed to a committee to draw up a further army declaration. In debate on religious freedom at Whitehall on 14 December, he argued for the Calvinist doctrine of the rights of the godly magistrate, against the Leveller belief that the civil state should have no power over religion. As a member of the High Court of Justice in January 1649, he attended regularly and signed the king's death warrant. In May 1649 he would play a leading part in putting down the Leveller-associated mutiny at Burford, some weeks after Axtell arrested Richard Overton in a co-ordinated raid on the Leveller leaders.

We cannot guess who drafted this petition, with its secular republican slant and that curious wording in the preamble's sixth clause. 'Pathognomical symptoms' are those specific to particular diseases, and the expression was also used figuratively by the Independent minister Thomas Goodwin. 'Cacklectick' or catalectic, describes a line of poetry shorter than in the normal pattern, therefore something deformed. The vocabulary suggests an author whose love of learning was greater than his mastery of the jargon, though sufficient to impress his co-signatories.

Related sources

The Moderate, No. 20, 21-28 November 1648. BL/EEBO: E.473[31].
His Majesties Letter to the Parliament ... As also The Armies New Propositions concerning the King ... Published by Richard Robinson. BL/EEBO: E.474[12].
Mercurius Pragmaticus, No. 31, 24-31 October 1648. BL/EEBO: E.469[10].
Clarke Papers, vol. 2, pp. 61, 65.
An Exact and Most Impartial Accompt of the Indictment, Arraignment, Trial and Judgment (according to Law) of nine and twenty Regicides ... Published by Andrew Crook, 1660. BL/EEBO: E.1047[3].
ODNB: Alan Thomson, 'Axtell, Daniel, (*bap.* 1622, d. 1660)'.
ODNB: Christopher Durston, 'Hewson, John, appointed Lord Hewson under the Protectorate (*fl.* 1643-1660)'.

25: HORTON'S REGIMENT AND SOUTH WALES GARRISONS

26 November 1648

Context

A surviving manuscript newsletter from Windsor, dated Sunday 26 November, reports that after the officers had spent the day from nine to five in a prayer meeting, 'seeking God by prayer to direct them in the great business now in hand, that they may be instruments that justice may be done upon those who have caused soe much bloud to be shed', three petitions arrived, from the forces in South Wales and the north of England. This was evidently a crucial meeting: two newsbooks tell us that the officers were unanimous in their resolution to act as quickly as possible 'to bring delinquents to punishment, and settle the Kingdom in peace, with what necessary Laws are wanting for the benefit and ease of the subject'. According to a third, they resolved 'that there might be a sodain [immediate] settlement made in this Kingdom, and wholesome Laws, and a modell of government agreed upon'.

This occasion is not to be confused with two previous prayer meetings at Windsor, which had likewise reaffirmed the army officers' unity in critical circumstances. One of these was the great reconciliation in December 1647 following the debates and mutinies of October and November that year; and the other, the three-day session in April and early May 1648 at which the officers had resolved to have no more dealings with the king and (as later reported) resolved to bring the king to justice as 'that man of blood'. Now, as the army prepared to take the king into custody and remove him from the Isle of Wight, unity was more essential than ever.

Text

The Moderate, No. 20, 21-28 November 1648. BL/EEBO: E473(31)

To his Excellency, the Lord Fairfax, The Petition of your Officers and Soldiers of Col. Hortons Regiment, and of the severall garrisons in South-Wales.

Most Humbly shewing, That your Petitioners, by their distance from the seat of affairs must needs come late to the knowledge of the same; yet they cannot but be sensible all along of the perpetuall designs of the Malignant parties, for the overthrow of Religion, Laws and Liberties of this Nation, which by reason of their great advantages both in City and Kingdom, might easily ere this prevailed, had not the great God himself fought against them, for the deliverance of his people; yet in this only is it acknowledged, they have gotten a great hand (by force) upon the house of Commons, to bring about this Treaty with the King, so derogative to the honour of the Parliament before all Christendom, and how dangerous to the Kingdom, we yet know not, but greatly suspect the tending thereof to abet the designs of the Authors of the same, and that the rather, because of the fear that it is an obstruction in the way of justice, the zealous execution whereof hath saved a Nation, the neglect whereof hath all along in this war, emboldned the common enemy, and all those who (abusing their trust) have unworthily served themselves of the publique, and so not only to impede justice, but also to impower those, whose weaknesse is the strength of the Commonwealth, and whose strength hath been, is, and for the future likely to be the utter ruin thereof; And although your Petitioners sincerely professe before God and the world, that they desire nothing more than a sound and well-grounded peace; yet to imagine the grounds to procure the same, to be with the hazarding of what they have all this while fought for, or by delivering up themselves into the hands of their enemies, whom God hath now delivered into theirs, were in their account an extremity of folly: But in order to obtain that due and direct peace, your Petitioners (though among the remotest and last, yet with reall affections to the publike good) humbly beseech your Excellency would become theirs, and the Kingdoms Mediator to the Parliament, that an impartiall execution of justice upon the grand Incendiaries of this late and former troubles may be speedily inflicted; may the cry of the blood that hath been shed, be so laid to your Honourable heart, that the heads of the Authors thereof go not down into their graves with peace (this is the way of the only wise, and merciful God, and the true way to establish a Nation) and as for this Treaty (which is no childe of prayer, but the product and pernicious scope of their raising it) and the Parliaments voting it, your petitioners being then by the Parliament commanded to fight against the procurers thereof, that there may not be a full ratification and conclusion therein, before a sufficient provision of future safety and liberty be had and given for their satisfaction, who have adventured life and fortunes in this cause, But that your Excellency, First, would rather move the Parliament to hearken to, and accept the petitions of those well-affected in the City of London, and places adjacent, with other Cities and Counties in the Kingdom who have and still would continue to live and die with them, as all under your Excellencies command do so most ardently desire to adhere, then to those specious Declarations of Col Powel, Poyer, Kent, Duke Hamilton, and such others. Secondly, that there may be a way opened, and countenanced, to the impeaching and prosecuting all such person, of what quality, or in what place soever, that have been contrivers and promoters of this late Rebellion, and Justice executed against them. Thirdly, that you would be Honorably pleased to let the Parl. and Kingdom clearly know the causes of the still continuing intollerable burthen of Free quarter upon the people.

Background

South Wales was one of the flashpoints of the second civil war. The revolt there was instigated not by 'ancient Malignants of a deep stain', as Major-

General Rowland Laugharne had described local insurgents in 1647, but by defectors from Parliament's own forces. Dissatisfaction over resources — lack of funds for the maintenance of Pembroke Castle, and the disbanding of local forces without arrears of pay — led to Laugharne and two other key officers declaring for the king in April and' May 1648. His fellow turncoats were Colonel Rice (or Rhys) Powell, a rather obscure figure; and Colonel John Poyer, the merchant mayor and military governor of Pembroke described by one historian as 'a cross between a warlord and a robber baron'. Horton's cavalry, sent down to deal with the revolt in May, were joined by four troops of local forces who had refused to follow the renegades, and together they routed Laugharne and his allies at St Fagans on 8 May. Oliver Cromwell, who had left Windsor with his troops on May Day, then took command and remained in the region until Pembroke Castle fell to him in early July.

Horton's regiment was originally formed in 1643, as parliament's only regiment of cuirassiers. Recruited in Leicestershire by Sir Arthur Hesilrige for Sir William Waller's army, they were nicknamed the Lobsters for their rigid plate-metal armour, now regarded as old-fashioned in England. Re-equipped as harquebusiers from late 1644, they served under Colonel John Butler in the New Model Army from 1645. Butler left the New Model Army in the spring of 1647 along with other officers dissenting from the refusal to disband; but the representatives of the rank and file, along with those of seven other regiments, signed a letter asserting that his former soldiers remained loyal to the army leadership.

Nothing is known of the politics of the regiment at the time of this petition, but six months later, following a number of mutinies resisting orders to join Cromwell's expedition against the Irish, eighty men of the Horton's marched into Monmouthshire under the leadership of a corporal, reportedly expecting to join with a party of Levellers there. When they found no Levellers they returned to their colonel and asked to be accepted back, confessing in terms politically correct for the time that they had been 'misled by Jesuits, and Devils they knew not how'; but when asked who their leader was, 'they cryed one and all'. Despite the brevity of the reference to the London petition of 11 September in the petition above, Leveller influence may already have been present.

Thomas Horton had been one of the most active officers in the army's petitioning of parliament in April and May 1647. He was a minor landowner in Leicestershire who followed his patron Hesilrige into the army, and was wounded at Naseby. By the time he became colonel he was firmly identified with the Independent party, and in due course became one of the most committed of the regicides, attending every day of the king's trial and signing the death warrant.

Related sources

The Moderate Intelligencer, No. 193, 23-30 November 1648. BL/EEBO: E.474[3].
Perfect Occurrences, No. 100, 24 November - 1 December 1648. BL/EEBO: E.526[35].
A Perfect Diurnall, No. 279, 27 November- 4 December 1648. BL/EEBO: E.526[36].
Clarke Papers, vol. 1, pp. 78-9; vol. 2, pp. 58-9.
Worcester College Oxford Ms 114, fos. 124-5.
ODNB: Barry Denton, 'Horton, Thomas (b. 1603, d. 1649)'.
Perfect Occurrences, No. 128, 8-15 June 1649. BL/EEBO: E.530[38]
Robert Ashton, *Counter-Revolution, The Second Civil War and its Origins, 1646-1648* (New Haven CT & London, 1994).
Gentles, *New Model Army*, Chapter 8.
Brian Manning, *1649, The Crisis of the English Revolution* (London, 1992).

26: NORTHUMBERLAND HORSE REGIMENT
26 November - 4 December 1648

Context

Though a copy of this petition was not purchased by Thomason until a week after the 26 November prayer meeting at Windsor, it is most probably the one reported as arriving that evening from 'the regiments of horse in the north'. Substantial extracts appeared in other newsbooks and pamphlets, but the text below is the fullest, and the only one which claims to come from a specific regiment, with a list of those signing on behalf of the rest. Its constitutional programme reflects the Levellers' *Agreement of the People*, though it is not borrowed directly from any single version. The 'Norman Yoke' theory of English history with which it begins arose from seventeenth-century legal and antiquarian thinking and was not unique to the Levellers. The preamble here, in its thoroughgoing opposition to what would later be labelled 'feudalism', is one of the most detailed and passionate expositions ever written. While this petition shares with many others its outright opposition to the Newport Treaty and its demand that the king be brought to trial to account for the bloodshed he has caused, it goes on to envisage an alternative revolution going far beyond any other since 11 September.

The text also appears in a one-off pamphlet issued by an otherwise unknown publisher who claimed it came from the whole northern army under Cromwell. Tempting though it may be to suppose that this was the 'great petition coming from the North' rumoured since September, the regional reference to border tenures and the names appended to it, as well as the dubious nature of the alternative source, favour the authenticity of its claim to come specifically from this regiment.

Text

To His Excellency Thomas Lord Fairfax: General of all the Forces raised by the Parliament, for the Common Wealth of England. The Humble Representation of the Desires of the Officers and Souldiers in the Regiment of Horse, for the County of Northumberland. No publisher or printer named. BL/EEBO: E.475[13]

Sheweth, That the people of this Nation, both by Nature, and as they are Englishmen, are a Free-born Generation, but by conquest and captivity, under William the sixt Duke of Normandies Bastard, they were made slaves, the property of their Lands removed from the Brittish Natives, to the Norman Invaders; the lands which were vouchsafed to their occupation, translated from their own Free-Simples, into strange Tennours, by Knight, Homage, Villain, and other services (to the conqueror and his Norman Earls, Lords, and Knights, which of his Commanders, he made in every County) their free customs abrogated, their Laws subverted, and shut up from the English understandings, into the French Tongue, and all Writs,

Processes, and Proceedings in Law, entred and issued forth in Latin, and the poor Commons (that were used to have all their suits ended in their several Hundreds once or twice a moneth) were forced then to trudge up to London from all parts of the Land, to the new made Norman courts; and none suffered in any Office, either in Church or Common-wealth but those Forraign Invaders. And to infatuate and bewitch the people with an adoration and sacred Reverence of this Bastards Person and his Succession, his Clergy (the better to settle his crown) then preacht him up to be Gods Vicegerent, the Lords Anointed, ascribing a certain Deity to his person, that in process of time, the people (through ignorance) fell down and worshipped the Bastard and his Successors, making the place of his usual presence as holy ground, to be reverenced even in his absence; also preaching up the power the Bastard had thus got over the land, to be the power of God, and he that did resist to resist to his own damnation.

And then, utterly to prevent the English of all recovery and relief by their Parliaments in future, he created Lords by his Patent and Prerogative, to sit by succession in Parliament, as Representers of his conquest and tyrannie over us, and not by election of the people, as Representers and Patrons of the Common-wealth.

And to add unto this, to make his usurpation firm and inviolable, he subdued the Law-giving power of the free people of England in their Parliament, to the Negative voice of Himself and Posterity, and nothing to be had or held, neither Law, Land, or Liberty, but by Grace, by Royal Grant, or the like; as if our selves were naturally their born slaves, and nothing of our own Right. And under the yoke of this Norman captivity and villanage in every of the Premisses, with the most miserable effects and fruits thereof, we have bin held by that succession, even to this Day.

And this King to uphold the constitution and settlement of those principles, and forms of Tyrannie, and in them his Dominion over us, brought a cruel and bloody war upon the Nation; against whom, with your Excellency, under the Authority of Parliament, we have freely engaged: to the end we might rescue the Legislative powers of our English Parliaments, our free customs, and Native Rights, from the bondage of that captivity, and so free our selves and all the people, from the common oppressions of the Land, by a settlement of a just and equal Government of Right and Freedom. And now it hath pleased God to bless our Engagement with an happy conquest over the capital enemy of the people, and to subdue him and his party under the power of the Parliament; we have expected that the Parliament (being fully enabled) should set this Common-wealth at freedom, remove our Oppressions, and bring the capital Offenders and Destroyers of the People to Justice, without respect of Persons. But insted of this discharge of their Trust, we find that they increase and multiply our oppressions, countenance our enemies, reject and slight the just Directions and Petitions of the People for common Right and Freedom; Discourage, and somtime Imprison, and otherwise persecute the Promoters and

Presenters, and burn their Petitions by the hand of the common Hangman: (an Act so abhorred, as never to be forgotten!) and betake themselves to a complyance and Treaty with our conquered enemy, courting his pleasure, and allowing him a Negative Voyce in the passing of all Acts of Parliament; whereby our Indempnity, our Laws, and Liberties, are all subjected to his concession; his Will advanced above all Law, above the Parliament and People; and himself put out of the reach of Iustice, and made accompltable to none.

Unto which yoke of Norman captivity (after all the bloud that hath bin spilt against it) we are loth to be subjected again, as we see both we and all the People must needs be, except the Army interpose betwixt the people and their destroyers, and make good their Engagement at New-Market-Heath, with all their Remonstrances, Declarations, and Promises to the people.

May it therefore please your Excellency, to take these premisses into your timous and serious thoughts, and before it be too late, to improve that opportunity of strength and power which God hath now put into your hands, for the relief and release of this oppressed long captivated Nation; that both we and all the people may thereby be made safe and free: and in Order thereunto, we humbly crave leave to propose these our subsequent desires, in the behalf of our selves and the Common-wealth.

1. That all Monopolies relating either to Sea or Land yet remaining, be forthwith abolished.
2. That the exaction of Tythes, and all manner of Impropriations, be removed; and that the publike Ministry be otherwise provided for.
3. That Excise upon all In-land commodities be taken off, and that no Taxes or Cesments be levied upon the People, but by the old way of Subsidies.
4. That a sufficient competency out of the Bishops, Deans, and Chapters Lands, Kings Revenues, and Delinquents Estates, be ordered and set apart for the discharge of the whole Arrears of the Souldiery, and constant payment of the Army, whereby the people may be wholy eased of all free quarter and taxes for the Army, and the Souldiery also satisfied.
5. That all Parliament-members, Committees, Excise-men, Sequestrators, &c. be called to an impartial account for the monies of the State.
6. That all inclosed Commons, and other ancient donations and rights belonging to the poor (in the several Counties and Parishes of the Land) be restored to their ancient and proper use, for the good of the comunalty.
7. That the ancient Tenures of Lands in the county of Northumberland, Cumberland, &c. which have bin destroyed by several Earls and Lords of late times, to the undoing of the comunalty in those parts, and utterly disenabling them from all good Nurture in Learning or Trades, and forcing them from Generation to Generation, to be hinds, half hinds, quarter hinds, shepherds, and herdsmen, be now enquired into; and if no better, that the ancient right of the old rents (for the good of those counties and

common-wealth) be restored again.
8. That all destitute Widdows and poor Orphans, which have lost their husbands and parents, and all Souldiers that have lost their limbs in the service of the Parliament against the King, be comfortably provided for, by way of constant stipend, and education of the children to Trades.
9. That publike work-houses be erected for prevention of beggars, vagabonds, and idle persons.
10. That till the time of more easie provision of payment for the Souldiery, that no monies for the Army be paid to the Parliament, their Committees, or Deputies; but to such Treasurers of the Army as your Excellency shall appoint, and to be collected by the Souldiery.
11. That a trade of Fishing upon the English coasts be setled by the State, for the good of the common-wealth.
12. That the capital delinquents and incendiaries of the people be brought to speedy justice; and in the first place, that the King (insteed of a Treaty) be brought to a fair tryal, to make answer for all the innocent bloud that hath been spilt in the land, and for other things whereof he stands charged by the Parliaments own Declaration; which showeth the reasons of making no farther Address unto him.
13. That the charge of the Army against the eleven impeached members be made good; and all the members that sate in the Iuncto when the Parliament fled to the Army for refuge, be expelled the House.
14. That encouragement and protection be given to such as shall prosecute any lawful charge or impeachment of treason or other crime against any member in Parliament; and that the members in Parliament, without respect of persons, be disrobed of their protection, and left open and lyable to the Law.
15. That Inquisition be made after the bloud of colonel Rainsborough.
16. That all Iudges, and other ministers of the State, be severely interdicted from receiving any inditement or charge against any person, for any thing done in relation to the first or second war against the King; and that all such so imprisoned, be discharged; with reparations out of their prosecuters estates; and in case of in-ability, the said prosecuters to be answerably imprisoned.
17. That a period be set to this Parliament.
18. That an equal proportion throughout the several counties for the Representatives in Parliament be assigned.
19. That a constant succession of Parliaments be setled, to be called and chosen of course by the people, at a fixed day every year or two years, as shall be judged most safe and needful, and the same to end of course.
20. That our Parliaments for the future be secured and cleered from the Negative Voice of any single person or persons whatsoever.
21. That no man henceforth presume to sit in this, or any other Parliament, by patent or prerogative, or that is not elected by the free choise of the people.

22. That all Statutes, Laws, and Acts of Parliament, be made and run only in the Name of the Commons of England assembled in Parliament.
23. That no persons whatsoever that are Law-makers, be Law-executioners, but that a cleer distinction be preserved and kept inviolable betwixt these two principles and pillars of the Common-wealth for ever, that they be not confounded together in the same persons, for fear of ruine to the freedom of the people.
24. That all Officers of the Common wealth be made to enjoy their places but at a certain limited time: at the expiration whereof themselves to give an accompt of their Stewardship, and continue no longer in their places, except by a new election.
25. That no Parliament Magistrate, or other person whatsoever have power to make any compulsive Law, or execute any Mulct or punishment touching matters of Conscience and Religion: but that all civil people subject to the Laws of the common wealth, though of several opinions and practices, (not being destructive to the State) be protected, and saved from all violence and injury in good Name, person and estate.
26. That all Warrants and Commitments by vertue of any pretended Priviledge or Prerogative, or during pleasure, not shewing the particular fact or crime, be with the greatest severity interdicted and declared void, for ever; with provision for future securitie from such Arbitrary violence upon the people. That all such as are so imprisoned be with Reparations released; and that Liet. Col. Iohn Lilburn and many others that have long suffered in that nature by the House of Lords, may have ample and full Reparations out of their Lordships Estates.
27. That the cruelties and extortions of Goalers [*sic*] be severely provided against; and that for future no Fees be exacted from prisoners; but that fitting accommodation both for lodging and dyet for them, and a sufficient competency of livelyhood for Goalers at the publick cost be provided.
28. That no man be kept in prison above a month; but in that space to be brought to a tryal by a lawful Jury of his equals; or else to be discharged of course.
29. That no man be impressed to serve in the Wars.
30. That our Laws be few and plain, free from all ambiguous meanings, and all in the English Tongue; and to be digested and printed in a Vollume; and one to be provided to be kept in every Church throughout the land; and to be read over at several seasons in open Congregation.
31. That all persons stand alike liable to the Laws of the Land, in all cases, both criminal and civil: and that all protections by any pretended priviledge or prerogative whatsoever, be declared Void.
32. That no more trudging up to Westminster from all parts of the Land, for the tryal of suits of Law be had, but that (as of old) all suits both criminal and civil, be ended in the several Hundreds.

33. That no person whatsoever, that hath born arms for, or asssisted the King, in his Rebellion against the Parliament and people; or that otherwise is found an enemy to this foundation of Iustice and Freedom, be neither chosen, nor have Voice in the choice of any Parliament Members, or other Officers, or Ministers of State, whatsoever.
34. That a solemne Contract upon these and the like Principles of Common Right and Freedom be drawn betwixt the People and their Representors, to be unalterable for ever.
35. That the respective Regiments of the Army (in order to their solemne Engagement made at New market Heath) do with all possible expedition chuse two (or more) Deputies or Trustees (persons of known approved fidelitie, for the freedom of the Common wealth) and each County also to do the like, joyntly to sit, consult and act in the behalf of themselves, the people, and Army; and that the removal of our oppressions, and obtainment of our Freedom, according to the premises above said, be the only work of their Agitation.
36. That the said Deputies or Trustees be limitted in their Session, to the space of two months; at the expiration whereof their Session to terminate; except continued by a new Election: and twelve daies before the said Term be expired, a new choice successively and of course, to be made till the accomplishment of the Work; and that the former Deputies be made accountable to the succeeding.
37. That this Councel be a free Councel, no member thereof to be awed or discountenanced in his Vote, by threats and frowns from any superior Officer: and that no person whatsoever therein have a Negative Voice.
38. That till the accomplishment of this Work, in behalf of the Army and People, that no disbanding of any part of the souldiery be: except of persons ill affected and dissentors from this Expedition.

For these things we declare, and with our Swords in our hands, as we are Souldiers we challenge them as the price and purchase of our Blood; to live and dy for them against all opposers whatsoever: and as we are English men we claim them as our own Inheritance and Birth-right: And humbly beg of your Excellency That you will be pleased to give us and the Souldiery encouragement therein, and so to appear before us for the happy accomplishment of these things: that both we and all the people, and the Generations that are yet unborn may have just cause to bless god for your righteous conduct.

Signed in behalf of the Regiment.

Joshua Wetwang, Edw. Hawnby, Edward Leake, John Moores, John Grice, Francis Bartholomew, Edmund Badger, William Farrow, John Pain, Tho. Baxter, John Baynes, John Griffin, Richard Leake, John Harison.

Another edition

His Majesties Declaration upon his Departure from the Isle of Wight ... Whereunto is annexed, A New Remonstrance from the Northern Army (under the immediate conduct and Command of L.G. Cromwell) ... Published by Giles Cotton. BL/EEBO: E.475[4].

Background

The regiment, commanded by the returned American colonist George Fenwick, was one of many recruited in England at the onset of the second civil war. We first hear of it in July 1648, when it was at Berwick with two 'loose troops' under Major John Sanderson. When the royalists left Berwick to join others in Northumberland, these two forces went with Colonel Robert Lilburne in pursuit of them. The combined body of 600 cavalry and one regiment of dragoons surprised the enemy quarters near Coquetdale on 1 July and took a large number of prisoners, with no casualties on either side. On receiving Hesilrige's report, the House of Commons voted to recognise all the new forces recently raised in Cumberland, Westmorland and Northumberland. The editors of Major Sanderson's surviving itinerary calculate that the Northumberland horse at this time was a relatively small body, probably no more than 130, due to its very recent formation. They later took part in the relief of Holy Island and the siege of Berwick, and remained there in the garrison with part of Overton's regiment. Unlike their neighbours, the Durham horse, who were recruited about the same time and had to be disciplined for plunder almost as soon as they had crossed the Scottish border in October, this Northumberland regiment is not known to have been accused of bad conduct.

Though most of the signatories have not yet been found, Joshua Wetwang features prominently in the history of Embleton parish in Northumberland. His family had been small landowners there since the early fourteenth century, and gradually extended their holdings while another branch flourished in Newcastle. Joshua inherited his elder brother's estate and house at Dunstan Hall (later known as Proctor's Stead) some time before 1657. He prospered under the Commonwealth, and erected a large family pew in Embleton parish church which he is said rarely to have occupied himself. His fortunes declined after the Restoration, however, and his heir sold the estate before 1700. Though much of the content of this petition distinctly echoes the style and works of John Lilburne, who had recently visited his property near Bishop Auckland, there is no reason why Wetwang, or any of the others who may have been schoolfellows of the future Leveller leader in Newcastle, should not have written it.

Related sources

The Resolution of the Army, concerning the King, Lords and Commons, and their Solemn Contract and Engagement to be tendered to the People of England ... Ordered to be printed and published, to be read in all Churches and Chapels throughout the Kingddome... Published by Nehemiah Wilson. BL/EEBO: E.476[16].

His Majesties Declaration and Remonstrance ... Likewise, the further Proposals of the Army, concerning the King and Kingdom... Published by W. Fielding. BL/EEBO: E.476[23].

A Letter from Sir Arthur Hesilrige, 5 July 1648. BL/EEBO: E.451[25].

A Perfect Diurnal, No. 267, 4-11 September, 1648. BL/EEBO: E.526[4].

The Moderate, No. 13, 3-10 October 1648. BL/EEBO: E.467[1].

The Moderate Intelligencer, No. 186, 5-12 October 1648. BL/EEBO: E.467[16].

P. R. Hill and J. M. Watkinson, *Major Sanderson's War, Diary of a Parliamentary Officer in the English Civil War* (Stroud, Spellmount Publishers, History Press, 2008).

H. L. Honeyman, 'Dunstan Hall or Proctors Stead', *Archaeologia Aeliana*, 4th Ser., vol. 17 (1940).

Christopher Hill, 'The Norman Yoke' in his *Puritanism and Revolution* (London, 1958).

A. L. Morton, *Freedom in Arms, A Selection of Leveller Writings* (London, 1975).

Philip Baker and Elliot Vernon (eds.), *The Agreements of the People* (Basingstoke, 2012).

27: SIR HARDRESS WALLER'S BRIGADE AND OTHERS
29 November - 5 December 1648

Context

Like several other petitions coming from garrisons and occupying forces, this one claims the support of sympathisers in the surrounding area. Despite the hardships imposed on local inhabitants in order to maintain regional military forces and garrisons after the end of the first civil war, close relations often developed with 'well affected' inhabitants, particularly among religious minorities. Captain Clarke was to say at the Whitehall debates that the army had been 'a shelter to honest people that had otherwise bin hammer'd to dust'. In some places, a local puritan tradition or history of resistance to royalist invasion may have cemented such relationships.

According to one report, the petition was presented to Fairfax on or about 1 December 1648 by Waller himself, on his way to the House of Commons from the west. In the political crisis of these few days, when the House was debating whether to accept the king's final answers from the Newport negotiations, members were gathering from all over England.

The text below was published in the Leveller-friendly *Moderate*, with a preamble explicitly sympathetic to the London petition of 11 September, including a strong commitment to religious freedom. In another version, the most radical passage of the preamble (marked * to * below) does not appear, and the regional issue of the tin miners is also omitted. A third gives only the numbered demands, omitting clauses 7 (freedom of conscience) and 8 (free quarter) below. Whether *The Moderate*'s version was cut by others, or contains interpolated passages, we cannot know. None of these was an official publication. Different manuscripts — or transcripts of an oral presentation — may have been circulating.

Text

The Moderate, No. 21, 28 November - 5 December 1648. BL/EEBO: E.475[8]

To the Right Honourable his Excellence the Lord Fairfax, Generall of the Parliaments forces for the Kingdome. The humble Petition and Addresses of the well Affected in Devon, and Cornewall. Together with the Officers and Souldiers of the Brigade, under the Command of Sir Hardresse Waller, Knight; now residing in the Western parts.

We your Excellencies Servants, not stirred up by any affection, to meddle with matters besides the business of our respective Imployments, nor any way favouring distempers amongst our selves, or others, neither coveting the vaine glory of being numbred amongst Petitioners, against the evils of the times, nor highly provoked by emulation, from what others our fellow Countreymen and souldiers have done; but singly and faithfully, we come to your Excellency in this Petition, abundantly pressed thereto, from the

Conscience and sense we have of the neere approach of Ruine to all honest Parties of the Kingdome, and your selfe and the Army amongst the rest, whereof the present transactions with the King, the late transactions of the Scots, and of a prevalent party in the houses, are palpable and unhappie evidences to the world, all moulding such a closure of the present differences, as we apprehend, must certainly strengthen all the old corruptions in the former government, and so leave the Kingdome in a more desperate bondage then yet it ever felt; *And farre be it from your Excellencie, and your faithfull servants, to be silent at such a time as this, when all the honest parties of the Kingdome have such deep feares, and heavie thoughts of their, and your approaching Ruine; farre be it from your noblenesse to thinke it, besides your businesse to pitie and plead the Kingdomes cause; We professe the complaints of good men every where pierce our hearts, and our own observations of the just reasons of dissatisfaction, constraine us to this great boldnesse with your Excellencie, to petition you, if it were possible, with teares of bloud, seasonably to interpose your selfe in some just and honourable way, that according to the desires of other Petitioners to the Houses, and to your Excellency (an excellent Modell whereof we have before us, in the London Petition, of the 11. of September last) all disputable matters about the late troubles may be made cleare, Iurisdictions legall and just, duly limited, and ascertained against Tyrannicall and arbitrary Power, Liberty and Property vindicated, and that Antichristian bloudy tenet of destroying mens lives and estates, for not beleeving as the Church beleeves, utterly abandoned;* Among all which generalls, we further present your Excellency with a few particulars following, viz. 1. By what evidences and proofes, or upon what Reasons and grounds the King stands aquitted of the charge of the Houses against him, in their late Declaration to the Kingdome. 2. What persons, especially what members of either House have playd the Traytors, by inviting the Scots to invade this Kingdome, or gave them countenance, or incouragement in that perfidious attempt. 3. That the promoters of the first and second warre be brought to Iustice. 4. That the Arrears and debts of the Kingdome be secured and satisfied, and that the publique faith be not made a publique fraud to the Kingdome. 5. That the Court of Wards be abolished without exacting satisfaction for the same. 6. That the unconscionable oppression of the Tynners by preemption be removed. 7. That the Consciences of men be not cruelly and unconscionably shipwracked. 8. That the cunning device upon the Army for hatefull free quarter, and the Contrivers therof be discovered, and the Army vindicated from the slander thence raised upon it. 9. That inquisition be made after the blood of Colonell Rainsborough. 10. That the Orders for reducing any of the souldiers may be suspended, untill the Commonwealth be setled, and the enemies thereof brought to Iustice. That these, and the like things being satisfied and secured to the Kingdome, Your Excellency and your Army may returne from this present imployment in honour, and good Conscience, as faithfully discharging the Armies ingagements to the Kingdome, and not bear the shame and reproach of men, that only acted for hire, and so that base scandall, so much in the mouthes of your and our treacherous enemies, will not be justified in the hearts of our friends; for the effectuall obtaining of these good things, we shall readily adhere to your Excellency to our utmost ability.

Other editions

A Declaration Collected out of the Journals of Both Houses of Parliament... No. 1, 29 November - 6 December 1648. BL/EEBO: E.475[17]. Omits * to * above and gives numbered headings 1-7 and 9 only.

Perfect Weekly Account, 29 November - 6 December 1648: BL/EEBO: E.475[20]. Omits clauses 6 and 9 above, with consequent renumbering.

Background

Though military control over the whole south-west of England had repeatedly changed hands during the first civil war, Devon and Cornwall were notably different in their underlying alignments, despite the belief elsewhere that they were both solidly royalist (see 54 below). As Mark Stoyle's study of Devon has shown, this was a predominantly parliamentarian county with a history of opposition to royal policies, though some parts of it were basically royalist. While the county gentry veered towards Presbyterian politics after 1645, Independent sympathies had a foothold in certain towns with a pre-war history of puritanism and resistance to the forced loan, ship money, and the Laudian church. Plymouth was a puritan stronghold, while the mayor of Barnstaple, in an area Stoyle says was 'awash with radical clerics' by 1600, was reputed to be leading a local separatist congregation.

Cornwall's lasting reputation as a solidly royalist county seems to be true mainly of its far west, despite the royalists' wider appeal to ethnic identity and resentment of English control. In the second civil war, a royalist rising in the Lizard peninsula in May 1648 failed to spread far, and was soundly defeated at the 'Gear Rout' near Helston. The tin miners of the Stannaries, whose traditional privileges of self-regulation were dependent on the crown, had raised their own regiment for the king in 1642, though those around Plymouth had been more inclined to support parliament. According to a London newsbook, by November 1648 the tinners were now addressing their grievances to Sir Hardress Waller, 'desiring him to improve [make use of] his interest with his Excellency' on their behalf, 'believing themselves a part of the free-born people of England'. This suggests that radicals were at least trying to gain a foothold among the Cornish mining community, and may explain the reference to tinners in the petition above.

In June 1648 Sir Hardress Waller was commissioned by Fairfax to recruit volunteers to combat the royalist revival, instead of relying on the gentry-dominated command structure of the county militias. The Commons ruled in favour of the militia, and the Presbyterian Clement Walker denounced Waller's volunteers as 'the ingaged faction of Independents, Schismatiks, and corrupt persons'. By early August, however, Devon's county committee, made up predominantly of merchants and lesser gentry, were protesting to the Derby House committee against a proposed withdrawal of Waller's forces, fearing that an attack by royalist ships could severely damage trade and encourage further royalist revolt in the west.

The cost of supporting Waller's forces as well as the existing garrisons was a constant grievance, especially in the coastal towns. In May 1648, the mayor of Exeter refused Waller's men admission to private houses and they had to sleep in a church and in sheds. Despite royalist reports that the town was rising for the king, this was a material conflict and it was resolved peacefully. In Plymouth, Waller threatened to billet extra soldiers on inhabitants who had not paid the tax for their maintenance. Despite the hardship and grievances, Waller and the county committees held most of the region peacefully during the second civil war.

Sir Hardress was a cousin of the Presbyterian general Sir William Waller, born in Kent and named (like many English gentlemen) after his mother's family. As an English landowner in Ireland, he fought against the Irish rebels in 1641-2. He joined Sir William's army in England in 1644, and developed radical religious views after his regiment joined the New Model Army. He was one of the delegation who presented the army's declaration of resistance to Parliament in June 1647, and sat on the committee appointed to confer with the agitators about their draft *Agreement of the People* before the Putney Debates. Though supporting the *Agreement* in principle, he was loyal to the army leaders, especially Cromwell. A few days after presenting this petition to Fairfax he stood alongside Pride at the purge of Parliament. He took his place on the High Court of Justice, and signed the king's death warrant, though protesting at his own trial for regicide that he had signed unwillingly.

Related sources

Packets of Letters, No. 35, 14 November 1648. BL/EEBO: E.472[9].
Clement Walker, *The History of Independency, as first published in his Relations and Observations* (London, 1648), p. 161.
Mark Stoyle, *Loyalty and Locality, Popular Allegiance in Devon during the English Civil War* (University of Exeter Press, 1994).
Stephen K. Roberts, *Recovery and restoration in an English County, Devon Local Administration 1646-1670* (University of Exeter Press, 1985).
Mary Coate, *Cornwall in the Great Civil War and Interregnum* (Oxford, 1933)
Mark Stoyle, *West Britons, Cornish Identities and the Early Modern British State* (University of Exeter Press, 2002).
ODNB: Patrick Little, 'Waller, Sir Hardress (*c.* 1604-1666)'.

28: REGIMENTS OF SCROOP AND SANDERS
before 7 December 1648

Context

Events moved quickly on 30 November 1648. While a group of army officers removed the king from the Isle of Wight to Hurst Castle on the mainland, a declaration from the Council of Officers at Windsor announced the army's intention to occupy London. Fairfax wrote to the Lord Mayor explaining that they did not come to plunder the city, but would need a payment of £40,000 of the city's tax arrears to avoid quartering the soldiers in private houses. On the same day the House of Commons, in response to Fairfax's request for an answer to the *Remonstrance*, voted by a large majority to reject it.

The army's declaration that day prioritised 'the speedy obtaining of a more orderly and equal Judicature of men, in a just Representative', and expressed the hope that parliament itself would act 'in the procuring of Justice with the people's ease and quiet, and in the settling of the Kingdom upon a due, safe and hopeful succession of Parliaments ... until a just and full Constitution' could be introduced. Its strategy was still the one reflected in Pride's regiment's petition (22 above): if parliament rejected the *Remonstrance*, all 'upright' members should withdraw, and the army would recognise them as having full authority until a new parliament could be elected. Meanwhile, Fairfax's forces occupied Westminster and the London suburbs peacefully, sleeping at first 'upon the bare boards in Whitehall, St James's and other great houses'.

The events leading immediately to the army's purging of Parliament on 6 December will be discussed below. It is notable that the justifications rushed into print in the next few days included the publication of four recent petitions in one official pamphlet. The first of these, from Scroop's and Sanders's regiments, strikes a very different note from the army's declaration of 30 November, being concerned almost exclusively with justice against the king and his supporters as satisfaction for the blood shed in the two civil wars. It is one of only two known petitions (with 65 below) to invoke the biblical justification, 'Whoso sheddeth mans blood, by man shall his blood be shed' (Genesis 9:6).

Text

The Declarations and Humble Representations of the Officers and Souldiers in Col. Scroops Col. Sanders Col. Wautons Regiment[s], Presented to his Excellency the Lord General Fairfax. As also the Remonstrance of the Souldiers belonging to the Garrisons of Arundel and Rye, and the Officers and Souldiers of Chichester. Printed for John Partridge. BL/EEBO: E.475[24]

To his Excellency the Lord Fairfax, our ever Honored and Renowned Genereall;

The humble Remonstrance of the Officers and Souldiers in Colonel Scroop's and Colonel Sanders's Regiments of Horse.

May it please your Excellency, The consideration of the manifold and wonderful mercies of God manifested unto and upon us, and all the well-affected in the Kingdom, in treading down our Enemies under our feet, because his mercy endureth for ever. The serious thoughts of the hidious cry of innocent blood crying for vengeance to Heaven, together with the Meditation upon that peremptory command of the Creator, Whoso sheddeth mans blood, by man shall his blood be shed.

The necessity of the due and timely execution of Justice, in reference to the appeasing of our present distractions, the setling of a lasting peace and tranquillity in this Nation, the terror of the present and future generations, that they may fear to do any more the like; the dangerous consequence of former lenity, and too much pity, and our observation of a present design by a prevailing party in Parliament, to frustrate all our undertaking and expectations by a (now furiously driven on, and) most unjust Treaty, with our twice conquered Enemy, to the reviving of the hopes of the Common Enemy: Had prest our spirits earnestly to entreat your Excellency, with your General Councel of War, that without delay (according to the wisdom and valor given you by God) you would endeavour that Justice might take place upon all, from the highest to the lowest, from the King to the meanest Subject, that they (who (to satisfie their lusts, to support and continue slavery and Tyranny in this Nation,) by their swords have made many mothers childless, and children fatherless, may (as to a sufficient number of the principal actors) have their children Orphans, and their mothers childless, in that happy day when Judgment without partiallity shall flow down as a stream.

That sufficient and timely provision be made for the taking off from the Country of that unsupportable burden of famine-threatning-free-quarter (the detestation of both soldier and countryman), with divers other things already before your Excellency from other Regiments. But whilst these things were in agitation amongst us, there came to our view the heads of the Remonstrance of the Army, abundantly satisfying our expectations, and preventing [anticipating] our requests, by granting our Petitions before they cam to your Excellencies hands, which we do with all joyfulness receive, and thankfulness imbrace, acknowledging our hands to be much strengthned, and our hearts so encouraged, that we do desire this may be for ever a witness against us, if we do not readily (at your Excellencies command) put our lives in our hands again, resolving by Gods assistance, to break through all difficulties for the accomplishment thereof, and to require the blood of our brethren, and dear fellow Souldiers, at the hands of him (or them) who shall dare to stop the currant of Justice.

Background

It is hard to determine what brought these two regiments together at this time. Neither appears in the list of forces ordered to rendezvous on 1 December for entry into London, though they may have been the two additional cavalry regiments expected but not named in it. This was not these two regiments' only joint production: *A moderate and cleer Relation of the private souldierie of Colonell Scroops and Col. Sanders Regiments* seems to have been written before the purge, though printed later. Its authors, describing themselves as plain-speaking 'old Souldiers', complain bitterly about their living conditions and the great gap in pay between officers and men. They also protest at the condemnation of soldiers and ex-soldiers by local magistrates for acts carried out under orders during the war, or merely for speaking 'seditious words', offering many examples but naming no individuals or locations. They use 'Norman Yoke' arguments claiming that since the king rules only by right of conquest he can justifiably be removed by the same means.

The two regiments had very different backgrounds and histories, however. Scroop's regiment, originally in the Earl of Essex's horse, joined the New Model under Colonel Richard Graves, and fought mainly in the west during the first civil war. Scroop became colonel when they joined the army revolt in mid-1647. In the second civil war, Scroop remained in the south-west with some companies, while others went to Wales, Kent, Colchester and Yarmouth. Adrian Scroop (or Scrope) had raised his own troop of horse in Oxfordshire in October 1642, and served as Graves's major in the New Model. Though his presence at St Albans is recorded only on 7 November, he was appointed to the committee named on 16 November to review Ireton's draft of the *Remonstrance* and prepare it for publication. He would in due course sit on the High Court of Justice and sign the king's death warrant. A possible personal connection with Sanders was his major, Nathaniel Barton, a godly minister as well as soldier, who had joined Graves's New Model regiment after serving with Sanders in Derbyshire.

In his native Derbyshire Thomas Sanders (or Saunders) had from the start of the civil war been in conflict with local magnate Sir John Gell, nominally his commander. After serving under several other commanders and failing to get his own regiment in the New Model Army, he was Colonel Francis Thornhaugh's major by September 1647, and succeeded him as colonel after his death in combat following the battle of Preston. Sanders had the reputation of a religious and political radical, though his only biographer doubts whether this was accurate. At Whitehall in December 1648, he spoke from a moderate position in the army's debate on religious freedom.

The regiment Sanders now commanded was raised in Nottinghamshire early in the civil war, with Henry Ireton as major until he moved to

Cromwell's regiment in 1643. It was never part of the New Model Army, but remained in the midlands under Lord Grey of Groby's command, fighting at the three sieges of Newark and other engagements in that hotly contested area. According to Lucy Hutchinson, whose husband was governor of Nottingham Castle, Thornhaugh's regiment had never been inclined to follow orders unquestioningly. Fairfax reported in July 1647 that they had marched into Buckinghamshire in support of the New Model, 'having delayed Obedience to the Command of many of their Officers, who for some Reason best known to themselves have refused to join with them in their just desires'. In December 1647 they joined with other soldiers protesting against free quarter.

In mid-April 1648 an informant wrote to the Earl of Lanark that 'Colonel Thorney's horse' had marched unwillingly from Lincoln to Leicester, demanded to be disbanded with two months' pay, got drunk and demanded that their colonel drink the king's health. There is no evidence of Thornhaugh's regiment being there at that time, and by 18 May they were marching with Cromwell from Chepstow towards Pembroke, leaving just one company behind in Coventry. They later followed Cromwell to Preston, proving as reliable as any other regiment throughout that time. In the summer of 1643 Thornhaugh's own troop had, however, retreated to Lincoln after the parliamentary failure to relieve the siege of Gainsborough, and returned to Nottingham via Leicester. Lucy Hutchinson tells us that many of the Nottingham soldiers left to join other forces at that time, and a few months later the colonel had lost so many of his troop that he went to London to recruit a new one. The informant's story was apparently five years out of date.

Related sources

The Declaration of His Excellency the Lord General Fairfax, and his General Council of officers, shewing the grounds of the Armies advance towards the City of London ... Printed by John Field for John Partridge. BL/EEBO: E.474[13].

London newsletter, 12 December 1648: National Library of Scotland, Advocates' Mss 33.7.15, fo. 1v.

A moderate and cleer Relation of the private souldierie of Colonell Scroops and Col. Sanders Regiments. Printed for James and Joseph Moxon, for William Larnar. BL/EEBO: E.476[25].

Hamilton Papers, p. 185.

The Moderate Intelligencer, No. 165, 11-18 May 1648. BL/EEBO: E.443[22].

John Rushworth, *Historical Collections of Private Passages of State*, vols 6 & 7 (London, 1721-2).

Lucy Hutchinson, *Memoirs of the Life of Colonel Hutchinson* (ed. N. H. Keeble, London, 1995).

Firth and Davies, *Regimental History*, vol. 1, pp. 277-83.

ODNB: David Scott, 'Sanders, Thomas (*bap.* 1610, d. 1695)'.

29: WALTON'S REGIMENT

before 7 December 1648

Context

This is the second of the four petitions published by the army during Pride's Purge. Walton's men begin like Scroop's, with expressions of confidence that god has been behind the army's victories, and the call for the king to be brought to justice on account of his blood guilt. But while Scroop's and Sanders's men focus on a single issue, calling for the capital punishment of those guilty of bloodshed and throwing in free quarter almost as a routine demand, Walton's add a wide range of reforms, from major constitutional change and the abolition of tithes, to fees charged by England's legal bureaucracy. In the case of this petition and several others like it, the interesting question is not whether it was calling for regicide but whether the fulfilment of its other demands would have amounted to a revolution.

Text

The Declarations and Humble Representations of the Officers and Souldiers in Col. Scroops / Col. Sanders / Col. Wautons Regiment ... [as last]. BL/EEBO: E.475[24]

To his Excellency Thomas Lord Fairfax General of all the Forces raised by the Parliament in the Kingdom of England and Dominion of Wales; The humble Petiton of the Officers in the Regiment of Col. Valentine Wauton, in the behalf of themselves, and Souldiers under their command.

Sheweth, That Your Petitioners observing the good hand of God to this Nation, in the many successes and deliverances to this Army under your Excellencies Conduct, doth justifie that Cause so unanimously undertaking to Gods glory and the Peoples preservation, notwithstanding the secret plots and open force of the common Enemies of our Native Country to destroy the liberties and birth right of the People, purchased by the loss of their Estates and Blood, which Cries to Heaven for Justice against that Capital Destroyer, and his party; the wilful Shedders of the blood of some hundred thousands of the Free-born People of England and Ireland: but our dayly fears are encreased of a third more bloody War, by the sparing of those malicious enemies, which God delivered into your hand, not yet brought to publique Justice, but rather ways found out for their deliverance and escape, by easie Fines, to put them in better condition then those who have suffered the loss of all for their Countries Freedom: Not forgetting that grand Design of Petitions framed by several Counties for a Personal Treaty with Honor, Freedom, and Safety at London, fomented by the Malignant party, to cause Insurrections throughout the Kingdom, that your Army, under your Excellencies Command, might be divided into small parties to suppress the Enemy, thereby to destroy the Army, to accomplish their wicked purposes, by force or fraud, into a Personal Treaty, which God hath hitherto blasted and disappointed; and understanding the pious Resolution of the Army under your Excellencies command, to bring Delinquents to punishment, and settle the Peace of the Kingdom (the desire of an oppressed people, with their just Rights and Freedoms of the Free-born of this Nation.

Humbly pray that your Excellency would not be discouraged because of the opposition and difficulties you meet withal, not doubting but God, who is wisdom and strength, will carry you through this great work, by his own Arm of power, making yours and the Kingdoms Enemies to become as chaff before the wind, we your Officers shal adhere to, and stand by you with the hazard of our lives and fortunes in setling the Peace and Welfare of the Kingdom, as followeth;

1. That the King, that Capital Destroyer of, and Shedder of the Blood of some hundred thousands of his good people in England and Ireland, may be brought to publique Justice.
2. That some of the principal Actors, now in your hand, may have publique Justice done upon them for the innocent blood they have spilt.
3. That the principal Actors and Abettors in bringing in the Scots Army (if found out) be brought to Justice.
4. That no Negative Voyces may be used in this Kingdom against the Peoples Freedom and just Liberty.
5. That the Rights and Liberties of the Free-born people of England be vindicated and cleared.
6. That a just and more equal way for Election of Burgesses to the Parliament.
7. That Free-quarters be taken off, and the Kingdom eased of their Burthen.
8. That the Revenue of the Common-wealth, by Excise, Deans and Chapters Lands, Forrest Lands, the estates of Delinquents, and the parts of Papists Lands, according to their estates so forfeited in any City or County, be for the constant pay of the Army by Assignation, according to the Establishment for Defence of the Kingdom, and satisfying all publique Debts & Damages thereof.
9. That a Treasurer, with two or three Commissioners, in each County, City or Riding, be appointed for such service, with some of the Army, or such as they shall appoint to be joyned with them, whereby the Revenue of the Kingdom may be more certainly known, and not converted to private uses as heretofore, under an Oath for their faithful discharging of their trust, allowing them for their pains two pence in the pound, and no more.
10. That all Committees, Commissioners and Sequestrators be taken away, and some strict course for bringing them to Account, with all Treasurers and Collectors, since the beginning of this Parliament.
11. That abuses in Court [sic] of Justice be reformed; That the People have Justice at their own doors for petty actions.
12. That an Office be set up in every County for the Filing of all Deeds, Bargains and Contracts within such place where the Land lies; Bargain or

Contract made, be Registred in such City and County, for the ease and benefit of the people.

13. That the Clerk of the Peace, for each City and County, do take an Oath for the due Execution of the same; And that four pence be allowed him for Registering every Deed, Bargain or Contract, with the like sum of four pence for every Search.
14. That free Trade may be encouraged, and some stricter course taken to protect Merchants that they be not robbed and spoiled of their Estates at Sea by English and Irish Pirates.
15. That it may be made death to transport Wool, Yarn, or Fullers-earth beyond Seas.
16. That Tythes belonging to the Clergy be taken away, and a Land-rate thorow the Kingdom in every Parish, equal by value, to Tithes for their maintenance.
17. That some publike place in every City or County for a Treasury, be kept for that end onely; and the Justices of the Peace, for such City or County, to receive and pay them their several proportions, as shall arise out of every Parish, to the Ministers of the said place quarterly.
18. That the Six Clarks Office be taken away for their intolerable exactions of eight pence a sheet, for every Bill and Answer fileing in that Court, and ten shillings for every Commission.
19. That the Clerks belonging to the Chancery, may be sworn Attourneys of that Court, who may be allowed two pence a sheet for every Bill and Answer drawing, and half a crown for every Commission.
20. That all Penal Laws may be reviewed, what shall be thought destructive to the people, may be taken away; and what shall be thought necessary, to be continued, such penalty may be imployed for the publique use of every County or City, where the offence shall be committed.

Background

Colonel Valentine Walton, or Wauton (as he signed himself), was Oliver Cromwell's brother-in-law and a member of the Long Parliament for Huntingdonshire, who sat on a number of important committees both before and after the first civil war. When his son died of his injuries after Marston Moor, Cromwell wrote him a celebrated letter with the typical puritan consolation that the young man was now 'full of glory, never to know sin or sorrow any more'.

Walton raised a troop of horse for Essex's army in 1642, and was captured at Edgehill and held prisoner in Oxford. After his release in 1643, he commanded a regiment of foot in the Earl of Manchester's Eastern Association army, and took part in the recovery of the important port of Lynn (or King's Lynn) from the royalists. He was appointed Manchester's deputy governor there, and in the following year he contributed to Cromwell's effort to remove Manchester from Parliament's military leadership.

As an MP, Walton gave up his military command and position in Lynn under the Self-Denying Ordinance in May 1645. He was still involved in the defence of the area, however, sitting on Parliament's Westminster-based committee for the Eastern Association. By November 1647 he was back in post at Lynn, at a time when the Self-Denying Ordinance appears to have been in abeyance. In June 1648 Walton provided the committee at Derby House with a detailed report on the defences of the Isle of Ely, but the committee's letters to him during the summer months suggest that he was reluctant to move his forces out of Boston and Lynn. This was a much more limited perspective than the plan attributed to him by the Presbyterian Clement Walker, to flood the fenlands from Ely to Lincolnshire and break the access bridges in order to create 'a plentifull and strong Fastness' as a last retreat for the Independents if the second civil war turned against them.

Walton's regiment in December 1648 was the same foot regiment he had commanded under Manchester. Never incorporated into the New Model Army, it had garrisoned Lynn and Boston since 1644. In 1651 it was one of 'the several regiments and Troops, that were reckoned as belonging to the marching Army' serving as garrisons. In towns like Lynn, vulnerable to royalist attack, 'soldiers were not by definition unwelcome', says Henry Reece in his study of garrison forces under the Commonwealth. There does not seem to be any detailed information about the presence or influence of separatist congregations or Levellers in this area, though John Lilburne had lived there in the early years of the war. Yet the petition above strongly suggests some radical influence, as well as a distinctively local concern with the cloth industry in its opposition to the export of wool, which was held to deprive Norfolk weavers of employment.

Little seems to be known of Walton's personal views, though he participated willingly in the High Court of Justice and signed the death warrant. After the king's death he was more active in parliament again, was chosen for the Council of State five times running, and reported most frequently to parliament on military matters. 'A brave soldier and a strict puritan' is how a historian of Norfolk has described him, one whose military role has been less studied than his political activity as Cromwell's ally and a regicide.

Related sources

Commons Journal, vol. 6, 20 September 1647, and vol. 7, 2 October 1651.
Calendar of State Papers, Domestic Series, of the Reign of Charles I, 1648-1649
    (London, 1893). All but one of this volume's references to Walton are
    mistranscribed and indexed as 'Colonel Wanton'. A spot check on the
    originals only confirms that it is almost impossible to tell the difference in
    most cursive handwriting.
The National Archives, SP28/28, fos. 206-11.

Abbott, *Writings and Speeches*, vol. I, pp. 287-8.
Clement Walker, *Relations and Observations* (1648), p. 105 [106].
Royal Commission on Historical Manuscripts, *Thirteenth Report* (London, 1892), vol. I, pp. 464-5.
Anon., *A briefe and true Relation of the Seige and Surrendering of Kings Lyn to the Earle of Manchester* (1643).
A List of the Names of the Members of the House of Commons, Observing which are Officers of the Army, contrary to the Self-Denying Ordinance ... [August 1648] BL/EEBO: 669.f.12[103].
ODNB: C. H. Firth, 'Walton, Valentine (1593/4-1661)', revised by Sean Kelsey.
R. W. Ketton-Cremer, *Norfolk in the Civil War, A Portrait of a Society in Conflict* (London, 1969).
Henry Reece, *The Army in Cromwellian England, 1649-1660* (Oxford, 2013).

30: SUSSEX GARRISONS

before 7 December 1648

Context

This is a more basic response to the Council of Officers' invitation to regiments to show support for the *Remonstrance*. Though warm in its expressions of support and solidarity with the army leadership, it only briefly sums up the aims of the *Remonstrance*. What it notably adds more explicitly than most soldiers' petitions is a rebuttal of the accusation that they wanted to keep power in their hands by perpetuating their existence and becoming a standing army. Once rights and liberties are secured, justice executed and peace restored, they say, they will be ready to disband.

Text

The Declarations and Humble Representations of the Officers and Souldiers in Col. Scroops / Col. Sanders/ Col. Wautons Regiment[s] ... [as 28 above]. BL/EEBO: E.475[24].

The humble Declaration of the Officers and Souldiers belonging to the County of Sussex, in the Garrisons of Arundel and Rye, and the officers and Souldiers of Chichester.

Humbly Sheweth, That we having had sad experience, how far our Adversaries have encouraged themselves unto their last trayterous ingagement against the Parliament by the treachery of some, and the dissenting of others, (even of those that at the first joyned hand in hand with us against the common Enemy.) And being also at present fully sensible how far our silence now in this time of greatest action and highest dispatch may give just cause of hope to our Enemies, and of fear to our friends, that we in this County, (though we are under the same command, and have hitherto faithfully and constantly joyned with you both in the first and last ingagement,) yet that now we are either opposers of, or, at least dissenters from you: We therefore for the timely prevention of any such jealousie or suspition, and that we may be no longer a dissatisfaction either to you or to our selves, as to the particular of a ready compliance with you; we having lately seen your seasonable, and (as we hope) satisfying Remonstrance to the Kingdom, in which, as is conceived by us, you are pleased to remonstrate your sense and resolution, as the present affairs of the Kingdom, and now state of things; we cannot with any contentment to our selves, or faithfulness to you, hold it fit to be any longer silent, but we must, and in this our humble Declaration do testifie our general approbation of, and consent unto the particulars declared in your Remonstrance, assuring your Excellency, and those other Officers ingaged therein, that you shall always find us most ready constantly to joyn with you, and unanimously carry on the same things with the body of the Army; we shall willingly, in case of any opposition, as our duty binds us, be ready to hazard our lives with you in pursuance of the things remonstrated by you, and that this our present declaring may not appear to be out of any self-ends, or self-seeking or in any relation to the continuance of our selves in arms, any longer then the condition and common necessity of the Kingdom requires; we have thought it not amiss to add, That the Peace of the Kingdom being once settled and the Peoples Rights and Liberties fully vindicated, and Justice on all Delinquents duly executed, we shall be ready to disband with the first; and this the major part of us have already testified by our willingness to take up Arms, or lay them down, according as the necessities of the Country required.

Background

Historians have paid much less attention to the garrisons located all over England and Wales during and after the civil wars, than to the New Model Army. A number of places were disgarrisoned in March 1647, and their defences slighted in some cases; but the outbreak of the second civil war had made the maintenance of the remaining ones essential. Arundel and Rye were still manned in 1651, with many others along the vulnerable south and east coasts. Although Chichester's garrison had been removed in 1647, by August 1648 the Derby House committee were urging the Sussex county committee to see to the defence of the city and promising to send them whatever forces they might require. There is no further information in the printed sources as to which or how many soldiers were stationed in Chichester at the time of this petition.

Anthony Fletcher's study of Sussex in the civil wars discusses the tension between 'the broad spectrum of gentry opinion' as reflected in the county petition for a personal treaty in May 1648, and the 'explosive nature of the mixture of Puritan fervour and army radicalism' seen in this one. Rye especially had a history of religious radicalism going back many decades, and in November 1648 the local separatist preacher Samuel Jeake collected subscriptions for his own letter of support to Fairfax, claiming that 'our miseries were breeding many generations agoe ... beyond the Norman Conquest', and pleading for justice and righteousness. Fletcher relates the local radicalism in Rye to millenarian expectations of a godly revolution on earth and the drive to build a model puritan commonwealth there which followed in the 1650s.

The roots of puritanism were especially deep in the Weald of East Sussex, the wooded heartland of England's early modern iron industry. Lollard heretics had been found there in the middle ages, and dissent from the Anglican establishment was well established in rural as well as urban areas there by the reign of Charles I, with a network of puritan families providing lay leadership. Puritan ministers were found throughout the county, but more radical religion was less common in West Sussex. Chichester's merchant oligarchy was parliamentarian, although the community of the cathedral close — with which they had a long history of conflict — was naturally royalist. Among the gentry, Sir Thomas Pelham and Herbert Morley were the leading parliamentarians, inclining to Presbyterian and Independent politics respectively. Although six of the MPs for Sussex constituencies were excluded at Pride's Purge, five of those who remained became regicides.

Related sources

Commons Journal, vols 5 (1-2 March 1647), and 7 (2 October 1651) for garrisons.
Calendar of State Papers, Domestic Series, 1648-1649, pp. 247, 256 for Chichester.
Anthony Fletcher, *A County Community in Peace and War, Sussex 1600-1660* (London, 1975).

31: NOTTINGHAM CASTLE GARRISON
5 December 1648

Context

The army's publication of 6-7 December 1648 also included this petition from Nottingham Castle. Though some phrases such as 'Birthright Freedoms' suggest a familiarity with Leveller language, the text includes no specific reforming proposals. The justice it calls for is 'uncorrupted' and 'impartial', naming no targets. On the whole it seems to be playing things safe with a flowery but vague assurance of support; or else — in terms Oliver Cromwell would agree with — waiting to see what opportunities god's providence would offer.

Text

The Declarations and Humble Representations of the Officers and Souldiers in Col. Scroops Col. Sanders Col. Wautons Regiment[s] ... [as 28 above]. BL/EEBO: E.475[24]

To his Excellency the Lord General. The humble Representations of your Officers and Souldiers, in Nottingham Castle, touching their united Concurrence with the late Remonstrance from Saint Albans; and their earnest desires for the speedy and vigorous prosecution of the ends thereof.

May it please your Excellency, We the Officers and Souldiers belonging to the Garrison of Nottingham Castle (being one of the least members of that body, whereof God hath made your Excellency the head) Although design'd to a distinct imployment from the rest of our fellow Souldiers in the Army; and therefore not so well knowing their proceedings, or (at least) uncapable (by reason of our confinement here) of co-acting with them; yet being (as we hope) acted by the same Spirit, to breath after the same happy end of Impartial Justice and Publike Freedom, as we have (with great joy and reciprocal complacency) read them in several of their late Addresses tendred to your Excellency, to that purpose. And especially, having beheld the comfortable Fruit of these, in the late Remonstrance from Saint Albans, sent by your Excellency, and the General Councel of Officers, to the High Court of Parliament at Westminster: Wherein is effectually discovered, the involving depth of mischief and treachery, prepared to devour all the sons of uprightness, covered over with the pretence of composing a safe and well grounded Peace, though founded upon the rotten Basis of an unsafe and hypocritical Treaty.

In consideration whereof, we cannot but with grief express, that our hearts even tremble with amazement, to behold the ambiguous footsteps of our pretended Reformers; who seeming to set their faces towards the Promised Land, hasten to bring us back into the place of Bondage: As if the reinslaving of us under the Iron Yoke of our now seven fold, more enraged Taskmasters, was the deserved purchase of all the precious Blood and

Treasure spent in the former, and later Engagements, for the obtaining of our most endeared Birthright Freedoms. All which, and many more eminent and destructive evils, ready to destroy us, together with the Remedies, are so largely, and with so much plainness and faithfulness, declared in the forementioned Remonstrance.

That it remains (onely) for us to say Amen to your Righteous Undertakings: Exceedingly rejoycing, that we yet hear the Language of a Remnant, so much un-byassed from the rotten principle of self-ish Interest and Sinister respects, as dare adventure to plead for the pure simplicity of uncorrupted Justice: From which, it is given in to our hearts, to hope that Goodness shall (at last) dis-throne Greatness; and the despised plainness of down-right honesty, out-poyze the flashy extravagancies of any Titles. Being bold onely to add the slender weight of our desires, to move your Excellency, and those worthy Instruments with you, to a speedy prosecution of what is so righteously, and (we hope) seasonably proposed with an humble Caution, That you permit not your selves and the Kingdom, to be any more beguiled into, and acquiescenced in a pretended settlement, fixed upon anything less stable, then the real and firm Foundation of Publike Safety; Beseeching God, to protect you from the cheating intricacies of their ways, who can (Camelion-like) assume any colour to deceive. But in what form so ever they appear, will be sure to approve themselves, yours, and the Kingdoms inveterate Adversaries.

And for our parts, as we are really perswaded of the sincerity and uprightness of your intentions, in what you have Remonstrated (and we trust, by the assistance of God, will speedily draw forth into Action,) so do we with singleness of heart, professe our selves ready to run with you the hazzard of all adventures, upon the same publike Bottom, according to our duty in our several places, as God shall enable us; chearfully resigning ourselves to accept what verdict the most righteous Judg shall give in, to be the issue of your godly undertakings: and we hope it will not appear a vanity in us, (though a small inconsiderable handful, and not so early in our appearance, as others,) thus to declare our united humble Concurrence with your Excellency, and the rest of our Brethren in the Army, with all the true lovers of publike Freedom, in seeking the same desired Ends; which as Christians, as Souldiers, and as Englishmen, we are abundantly obliged to do, as well as to manifest our selves,

Your Excellencies, and the Kingdoms faithful Servants. Nottingham Castle, 5 Decem. 1648.

Background

In the first civil war the town and castle of Nottingham were defended by Colonel John Hutchinson as governor, but in March 1647 his foot regiment was reduced to a force of 100 guarding the castle under his kinsman Captain Thomas Poulton. In the spring of 1648 the brother of Lord Byron, a neighbouring royalist, attempted to persuade Poulton to betray the castle, and Poulton strung him along 'to lay the bait', as he felt the castle was not strong enough to resist a direct attack. The story reached the London press, and was retold many years later by Hutchinson's widow and biographer. Though small in number, this garrison was perhaps keen to remove any lingering suspicion of disloyalty. Since the royalists' defeat in Wales and the north, they were holding a number of important prisoners — including Sir Marmaduke Langdale, whose freedom the Pontefract royalists had allegedly hoped to secure by kidnapping Rainborowe at Doncaster. Though the parliamentary commissioners at Newport insisted that Langdale, a leading fomenter of the second civil war, be excluded from pardon, he later escaped from the castle and fled abroad. The renegade parliamentarians Laugharne, Poyer and Poyntz were still in the castle, awaiting Cromwell's arrival for their court martial, when the Lieutenant-General was diverted to Pontefract following Rainborowe's death. Hutchinson, meanwhile, was in London attending to his duties in the House of Commons, where on 26 December he would present a petition with over 300 signatures from Nottinghamshire (63 below).

Related sources

Commons Journal, vol. 5, (1 March 1647).
Lucy Hutchinson, *Memoirs of the Life of Colonel Hutchinson, Charles I's Puritan Nemesis*, ed. N. H. Keeble (London, 1995). Originally published in 1806.
The Moderate Intelligencer, No. 170, 15-22 June 1648. BL/EEBO: E.449[13].
Alfred C. Wood, *Nottinghamshire in the English Civil War* (Oxford, 1937).

PART FOUR

ARMY PETITIONS

FROM PRIDE'S PURGE TO THE KING'S TRIAL

DECEMBER 1648 - JANUARY 1649

32: GENERAL COUNCIL OF OFFICERS
6 December 1648

Context

This important document is not a petition to the army, but a list of demands put to Parliament by the army. It is included here as an essential part of the army's action on 6 December 1648. According to the *Commons Journal*, formal proceedings that day began with those MPs who had arrived before Pride and his men, or were allowed in by them ('about six score' according to Ludlow), demanding that the members prevented from entering should be allowed in. The soldiers refused, and Lieutenant-Colonel Axtell announced that a message from Fairfax and the Council of Officers would shortly arrive. William Pierrepont reported from the deputation sent to speak to Fairfax the previous evening that he had told them to come back in the morning when his officers were present. The rest were now with Fairfax, waiting for his message to be written down. Eventually Colonel Whalley arrived and presented the document to the House. The printed version below appeared next day with the same title as that recorded in the *Commons Journal* and the imprint of John Partridge, the army's regular publisher.

The speed with which this and the four recent petitions (28-31 above) were printed shows how effectively political leaders could deploy the press in a crisis. Official information may have helped to calm the atmosphere in London; while confrontation with the trained bands guarding Parliament was avoided when Major-General Philip Skippon, their commander at the start of the first civil war and throughout the second, persuaded them to stand down. The Commons sent Skippon into the city, 'to employ his best Endeavours to appease any Tumults that may happen there'. Fairfax's troops, who had occupied Westminster a few days earlier, now took over the city, seized its main treasuries, and arranged quarter for the troops, without the much feared storming and plundering that had been forecast. The atmosphere was volatile, however, and rumours were undoubtedly spreading.

Text

The Humble Proposals and Desires of His Excellency the Lord Fairfax, and of the General Council of Officers, In order to a speedy prosecution of Justice and the Settlement formerly propounded by them. By the Appointment of His Excellency the Lord Fairfax, Lord General, and His General Councel of Officers, Decemb. 6. 1648. Signed, John Rushworth Secr'. Printed by John Field for John Partridge Decemb. 7. 1648. BL/EEBO E.475[25]

To the Honorable, The Commons of England assembled in Parliament: The Humble Proposals and Desires of His Excellency the Lord Fairfax, and of the general Councel of Officers, in order to a speedy prosecution of Justice, and the Settlement formerly propounded by them.

Having, with others, for a long while sadly beheld and tasted, in your proceedings, the miserable fruits of Councels divided and corrupted by Faction and personal Interest, even to the neglect, betraying and casting away of all thats publique and good, to the lengthening out of endless troubles, burthen and damage to the Kingdom, to the continuance and widening of that issue of blood, whereby these Nations have been so much polluted and consumed, and to the perpetual hazard of Bondage and Destruction to them at last: And both we and many others having propounded foundations of Justice and Settlement, which are of evident Advantage and Security to the publique Interest, and clear from any thing that's personal or particular; But finding that through th'aforesaid Corruption and Divisions in your Councels, the same can obtain no place or consideration at all: and foreseeing evidently that the condition of the Kingdom will not bear delay of Settlement one way or other, We conceive our selves and others that are sensible [conscious] hereof, to be necessitated into some extraordinary vigorous and speedy way, whereby those roots of Faction, division and private Interests may be weeded out from amongst you, and so your Councels cleared and united, to the timely and effectual prosecution of Justice, with a sound Settlement and publique good to the Kingdom, and to the speedy introducing of such a succeeding Authority, wherein future Differences may be prevented, and a general Acquiescence obtained.

Therefore seeing no better or other way, We propound and demand as followeth:

1. Whereas *Denzil Hollis* Esq; *Lionel Copley* Esq; Major Gen: *Massey*, and others of your Members, (whose Names you well know) were in the year 1647. impeached by your selves for Treason, or for high Crimes and Misdemeanors, in relation to the Treasonable Engagement in the city of London, The violence then done upon the Parliament, and The levying of a new War, and other evils in maintenance and prosecution thereof; and upon clear proofs against them, were by your censure expelled the House, and disabled from further trust therein, and upon new Writs issued out new Members were chosen and return'd in some of their rooms; and yet by the prevalence of their Faction (When in the last Summers War divers faithful Members were engaged abroad upon necessary and publique service, and others through Malignant Tumults and Disturbances could not safely attend the House) the same persons were afterwards re-admitted to sit in the House and Vote as formerly, without any tryal or satisfaction in the things whereof they were accused: We demand, That all those Members so Impeached, may be forthwith secured, to be brought to Justice or Trial for their said Crimes; and that such others of their Faction, by whose Votes, Councels and Confederacy they were so re-admitted, may be secluded from the House, and not sit as Judges for those their confederates.
2. Whereas by the Confederacy of Maj. G: Brown now Sheriff of London, with the said Impeached Members and others, the Scots were invited and

drawn in to invade this Kingdom the last Summer, insomuch as when upon the actual Invasion the House proceeded to declare them Enemies, and those that adhered to them Traytors; yet the said Confederates and other treacherous Members (to the number of Ninety and odde, as upon the division of the House appeared) did by their Councels and Votes endeavour to hinder the House from declaring against their confederate Invaders; We desire, That the said Maj. Gen: Brown may be also secured and brought to judgement, for that and other his treacherous Confederacies or Correspondencies with the publique and declared Enemies of the Kingdom (which we hereby charge him with, and shall be ready to make proof of) And that the rest of the Ninety and odde persons dissenting in the said Vote, may be excluded the House, and not trusted further in your Councels.

3. Whereas in a continued Series of your proceedings for many moneths together, we have seen the prevalence of the same treacherous, corrupt and divided Councels, through Factions and private Interests, opposing or obstructing Justice in all kindes, diverting your Councels from any thing of publique good, hindring any proceedings to any such Settlement, as would consist with Security to the publique Interest, or put a real end to the Troubles, Burthens or Hazards of the Kingdom, and precipitating into treacherous and destructive Compliances and Conjunctions with the acknowledged Enemies thereof; and this we have seen particularly in the corrupt Councels and Resolves of receding from, and recalling the Votes of No more Addresses to the King, &c. (the justness and necessity whereof you had once so cleared to the world) also in the Votes for entertaining or seeking (after all that) a Personal Treaty with the King your Prisoner, upon such Propositions as himself should tender, as well as your own, offering upon imperfect (and those but wrested) Concessions from him, to Restore him, with impunity, to Honor, Freedom, Safety, and his Revenue, exempting all (even the principall) Authors and Actors in the last Summers War from capital Punishment or Tryal, and bringing off the rest with Fines or Censures most inconsiderable to the publique Damage and Mischief they have done; whereby they and others are encouraged to renew the Kingdoms Troubles; And lastly, in the Votes declaring the Kings past Concessions to be a Ground for the House to proceed upon, for the Settlement of the Peace of the Kingdom, notwithstanding the visible insufficiency and defects of them in things essentially concerning the publique Interest, and Liberties of the Kingdom (as those propounded in our late Remonstrance are) and in other matters both Religious and civil (from which, by express Covenant or publique Faith given, you were obliged not to recede; in which Votes and Councels it is apparent, those that are guilty of the[m] have deserted, betrayed and justly forfeited their Trust for the publique; insomuch that we dare appeal to all well affected or reasonable men, Whether there be any hopes by, or with the conjunction

of such men in your Councels, to have any sound or timely Settlement, to have any end of Troubles, Burthens or Hazards, or any publique good done for the Kingdom: We therefore earnestly desire, That all such faithful Members who are innocent in these things, would immediately (by Protestation and publique Declaration) acquit themselves of any guilt of, or concurrence in the several Votes or Councels here before particularly mentioned, as corrupt or destructive, that the Kingdom may know who they are that have kept their Trust, and distinguish them from the rest that have thus falsified the same; and that all such as cannot or shall not so acquit themselves particularly, may be immediately excluded or suspended the House, and not readmitted, until they shall have given clear satisfaction therein to the Judgement of those who now so acquit themselves, and the grounds of such satisfaction be published to the Kingdom.

4. Thus, such as by faithfulness have retained their Trust, being set in a condition to pursue and perform the same, without such Interruptions, Diversions and Depravations of Councels, as formerly, We shall desire and hope you will speedily and vigorously proceed, To take order for the execution of Justice, To set a short period to your own Power, To provide for a speedy Succession of equal Representatives, according to our late Remonstrance, wherein Differences in the Kingdom may be ended, and we and others may comfortably acquiesce; as (for our parts) we hereby engage and assure you we shall.

By the Appointment of His Excellency the Lord Fairfax, Lord General, and His General Councel of Officers, December 6. 1648.

Signed, JOHN RUSHWORTH Secr'

Background

There are some inaccuracies in this document, hastily written while the Commons' deputation waited. The army, on 15 June 1647, had called for the impeachment of the eleven MPs considered the chief promoters of the House's declaration denouncing the petitioners as rebels and of the plan to disband the New Model Army. Denzil Holles and nine others were prominent in the Presbyterian faction; but the eleventh, Sir John Maynard, was not one of them. Lionel Copley was not one of the eleven, but was barred from the House on a different matter and imprisoned with other London Presbyterians in March 1648. The Commons never impeached any of them, but gave them leave to withdraw. When they returned to their seats after the charges were dropped the following June, it emerged that only Sir John Clotworthy (Maldon) had been replaced, and a by-election had been called to replace Walter Long (Ludgershall) but not yet held.

Sir Richard Browne, a Presbyterian coal and timber merchant, was major-general of the trained bands, currently sheriff of London, and foremost among the London politicians accused of inviting the Scots to invade England earlier in 1648. (See also 61 below.) The Commons debated on 14 July 1648 whether to declare the invaders and their supporters rebels and traitors, and passed the resolution without a division. The figure of 'ninety and odde' corresponds rather to the number (92) voting against the Declaration of No Addresses the previous January. Parliament had never agreed that no royalists should be punished for their part in the civil wars, though the number to be excluded from a general pardon was reduced to seven at the Newport negotiations.

The point of this flawed narrative was to demand that those 'faithful' MPs who had defended the New Model, condemned the Scots, opposed the treaty negotiations, and voted against accepting the king's answers on 5 December, should seize the role of representatives of the people for themselves, set a date for their own dissolution, and hold new elections on a reformed franchise. With regard to trial and punishment, the House is asked here and now only to 'take order for the execution of justice', without mentioning any names. The 'faithful' members are still urged to purge the House themselves, though that possibility had just been pre-empted by the army's intervention. A private meeting of MPs and officers had apparently decided on this course of action the previous evening, when Fairfax was refusing to talk to the Commons' delegation until his officers were present.

Though the MPs remaining after Pride's action voted next day (by 50 to 28) to proceed with the army's proposals, it was several weeks before they considered them at all. In late December, they resolved to admit all who would register their dissent from the vote of 5 December on the king's answers, and set up a court to try the king. They never dissolved themselves, set a date for their own dissolution, or considered fundamental constitutional reforms, but sat on until they were forcibly expelled by Cromwell in April 1653.

Related sources

A declaration of the engagements, remonstrances, representations, proposals, desires and resolutions from His Excellency Sir Tho: Fairfax, and the generall councel of the Army... Printed by Matthew Simmons in Aldersgate-street, 1647. BL/EEBO E.409[25].

Commons Journal, vols 5 (1646-48) and 6 (1648-51).

C. H. Firth (ed.), *The Memoirs of Edmund Ludlow* (Oxford: Clarendon, 1894), vol. I, pp. 208-10.

Bulstrode Whitelock [sic], *Memorials of the English affairs from the beginning of the Reign of King Charles I* (Oxford, Oxford University Press, 1853), vol. 2, pp. 468-73.

Commons Journal, vol. 6, 6-7 December 1648.

33: LAMBERT'S BRIGADE

12 December 1648

Context

The meeting that agreed this petition took place as soon as Lambert had effectively taken over the siege of Pontefract Castle. The reduction of this last royalist stronghold in the north, a potential refuge for royalists and provisioned to withstand a long siege, was much more than a footnote to the second civil war, especially after the death of Rainborowe at the hands of a raiding party from the castle (see 16 above).

Despite the rumours circulating for weeks, this is the first evidence of any general meeting in the north since Cromwell's conference with the northern gentlemen at Barnard Castle on 24 October (see 7 above). Though not explicitly mentioning Pride's Purge, news of which had certainly reached Lambert, the petition condemns the Commons' 5 December vote accepting the king's last answers, and implicitly assumes that the army can and will secure the dissolution of the present Parliament and determine the course of the revolution.

Text

A Declaration of the Officers belonging to the Brigade of Col. John Lambert, Commander in chief in the Northern Parts, now lying Leaguer before Pontefract Castle, At a General Meeting of them, to advise upon (and declare their sence of) the present condition of the Affairs of the Kingdom, To his Excellency the Lord General Fairfax and his General Councel. As also Col. Lambert's letter to the General concerning the same. By the Appointment of the Officers at a General Meeting. Pontefract, Decemb. 12. Signed, Tho. Margetts. London. Printed by John Macock, for John Partridge. BL/EEBO E.477[10]

A Declaration of the Officers of Col. Lamberts Brigade, &c.

May it please your Excellency, Divers of us at a late meeting, did make a short address by Letter unto your Lordship, and your General Councel, of what was thought fit at that present, until a more general meeting and consideration might be had, of those things, we, both before and then, had in our thoughts to present unto you. And being now convened at a full meeting, deeply sensible, and fully satisfied in our judgments, of the present dangerous posture, and sad condition of the Kingdom, in relation to the Treaty, and other publike affairs; We have agreed, on the behalf of our selves, and the rest of the Officers and Souldiers under our commands, to express unto you that sence and those humble desires, which God hath been pleased to put into our hearts thereupon, as followeth.

At the beginning of these late differences, the Parliament having acquainted the Kingdom, with the Kings Intentions to draw the Sword of War against them, for the maintaining of His Own Arbitrary Power, and by their several Declarations, Remonstrances, &c. given clear satisfaction to all the well affected, of the justness of a defensive War; and thereby inciting and incouraging all, as they tendred their Native Rights and Freedoms, to rise in Arms for their defence. We were induced out of judgment and conscience, to appear accordingly, and have ever since imployed, and used our utmost endeavours, to the great hazard of our lives, estates, and all that was dear unto us, in that just and necessary work.

In prosecution whereof, this poor Kingdom, hath long lain under most heavy burthens, and oppressions, vast sums of money have been raised by the Parliament upon Excise, Sequestrations, Compositions of Delinquents, Assessments, Bishops Lands, Kings and Queens Revenues, &c. besides the great debts of the Kingdom unsatisfied, many Towns and Countreys [counties] much depopulated and destroyed, thousands of our dear friends and fellow-laborers, have lost their lives and perished in this great service, their wives and children been undone, and many of us yet alive, lost much of our dearest blood.

All which, would yet not seem so grievous to us, the common enemies, being (by the blessing of God upon the Armies) twice vanquished, brought under, and capital offenders apprehended, if after all this (when no visible power hath appeared, or been left, to oppose or hinder the Parliament, from setling the Kingdom, in Peace and Freedom; redeeming it from injustice, slavery, unnecessary taxes, oppressions, and executing Justice upon Offenders) we could once have seen a right use made of those opportunities, which God hath several times put into their hands for doing thereof.

But, to the great grief of our souls, we see not any probable means by them used, to bring about this necessary work: On the contrary, it is apparent, that private designes are carried on, by pretended, even Parliament, friends, with common enemies, (depriving the Nation of reaping the fruit of all the eight yeers labors and services) to introduce that very Tyranny and Oppression, which we were by them invited to oppose; and establish by Treaty, and Act of Parliament, a stronger foundation for (and clearer way to) advancing the Kings destructive designe and tyrannical will, then formerly he had, thereby to subject the whole Kingdom, to a mass of perpetual oppression and injustice; and betray all the well affected in the Kingdom, (especially those who had been most actively engaged against the same) to sudden destruction without remedy.

For proof whereof (omitting many particulars) we need but take a review of the several former Treaties, especially this last, most dangerous, Personal Treaty; having all been gained, by the apparent treachery of the said pretended friends, and the cunning policy of the common enemies, upon the loss or weakness of their power in the field; and so pursued upon the plausible pretence of Peace-making, truly intending nothing but slavery and destruction.

To bring about this great unparaleld design, these treacherous designers did not only raise several great Armies & Forces in all parts (almost) of the Kingdom (to the great hazard of the ruine thereof,) but also invited and procured a numerous and powerful army out of Scotland, that they might the more plausibly, and upon fairer pretences, carry out their destructive designe; suggesting to the Kingdom, that there was no other way for prevention of War, and setling of Peace, then by this Personal Treaty, when they themselves were the causers of the War, and the Kingdoms unsettlement.

To this purpose they endeavoured (the Lords especially, who refused to joyn with the Commons in declaring the Scotish Army, invading the Kingdom under the conduct of Duke Hamilton, to be Enemies) all they could to procure a Cessation of Arms with that (and the English Malignant) Army, when they were in the bowels of the Kingdom, and we were ready to engage with them, that they might thereby get to themselves the greater advantage to carry on their work; Which had they effected, and the good providence of God not prevented, would, in all probability, have brought to pass that their intended compliance with the King, upon his own terms, and their interest only, which now, after the defeate and absolute breaking of those Forces and Armies, they still labor all they can to bring about, contrary to the earnest desires and frequent Petitions presented to the Parliament from the well-affected in all parts of the Kingdom; and strugling, to the utmost, to put the Kings partee, and all the Malignant disaffected people, into a better condition, after their last Rebellion, then they were at the beginning, and all the well-affected, that have done and suffered so much, into a ready way of ruine.

And notwithstanding your Excellency, and your general Councel, had most clearly represented to the Parliament the dangers and evils of this personal Treaty, your Remonstrance & Desires were neglected and refused, so much as to be taken into consideration; But on the contrary, (as we have been informed) the Kings Answers upon the whole Treaty were voted by the Lords to be satisfactory, and by the House of Commons, to be sufficient for a safe Peace to be grounded upon; Which gives us just cause to beleeve, that this Treaty is a clear design to betray the Kingdoms just Cause (which God hath twice pleaded, and judged for them in the sight of all men) into their enemies power again, leaving the unlimited supremacy where it was, as if we had engaged altogether without Cause, and gained nothing by all our losses, hazards and sufferings, but to be thrown, at last, into the cruel hands of our most implacable enemies. And therefore conclude, that all Members of Parliament, or other publique persons, acting such designs, are betrayers of their trust, and perverters of the very end and essence of the power committed to them; charging upon them the cause of the Kingdoms present unsetledness, distraction, oppression, and of all our, and their, fears and miseries. So that,

We cannot longer be silent Spectators of the Kingdoms impending ruin, nor upholders of those that seek it, least thereby we should be involved in their guilt, and make defection from our first principles, but humbly conceive, that we are still bound in duty and conscience to prosecute and pursue to the utmost of our powers, with our lives and fortunes, those principles of Freedom and Justice, that by the Parliaments Declarations, Remonstrances, &c. we were at first called forth to act upon in opposition [to] the Kings unjust unlimited will, for the recovery and defence of the common Rights and Freedoms of the people, greatly rejoycing to see so generall a sympathy in all your Forces (and the wel-affected) by their several Addresses to you, and cannot but take special notice of Gods great goodness to this poor Nation, in preparing, and providentially disposing a people, in the several corners thereof, to stand up for Truth and Justice, in a time of such woful corruption and apostacy, wherein many men in publike trusts and places (perverting the true end of the power they are entrusted with) study nothing more then the advancing of their own ends and interests.

Neither will the same Ground and Principle, which led us forth at the beginning of the Wars, to oppose Tyranny and Oppression, in the King and his Adherents, now give us leave to sit down quietly, as long as we see the Authority and Power of the Kingdom setting up the same Tyranny and Oppression, (in their own or any other Interest whatsoever,) or the Parliament taking away that due and just Liberty of the Peoples chosing their own Representatives, by making themselves perpetual, and thereby in a short time, the little finger of this latter, heavyer then the loyns of the former Oppression.

All which having seriously considered, and that all ordinary means, by the Petitions and cries of the well-affected, have been tryed in vain, (when nothing was expected by us and them but sudden destruction,) we received and perused a Copy of your late Remonstrance, presented to the Parliament, wherein we find the grand Case of the Kingdom very faithfully and discerningly stated and laid open, together with a wise and full discovery of the chief Maladies, Distempers, with sutable Prescriptions for its cure and recovery. We could not but express one [*sic*] full approbation of, and free concurrence in the said Remonstrance, what cause we have to bless God, who hath raised in you such a Spirit of discerning Wisdom and Justice, which we hope proceed from Principles of Common Right, for the publique Good and Interest of the Kingdom; together with our humble Opinions, that the matters therein contained are most necessary to be prosecuted and obtained, as the most visible and probable means for releeving and setling the Nation.

And though they may seem (as civil things) not so properly to come from the Army, yet seeing deliverance no other way, and providence calling in a necessary and extraordinary Case, to walk in an extraordinary Way: We know that God, by whom you are called, who hath so often, so eminently, so experimentally appeared, both to you and us in our faithful endeavors, and great hazards for the Kingdoms Rights, will assuredly (upon your walking after him in the way of his Providence, and humble waiting on him, in the way of his Judgments, without impatiency and distemper of spirit,) make your way plain before you, carry you through, and honor you with being the happy Instruments of Redemption and Deliverance to a poor dying Kingdom.

Our great desire therefore is, That the said Remonstrance may be speedily and effectually acted upon, with such Wisdom, Caution, Self-Denial, Care and Consideration, as that both the common, and bosom Enemy may be prevented in their present, or future, obstructing, opposing, Designs, may not have time and advantage to raise new divisions, troubles; and these good conceptions, which God hath thus begotten in you, and (through you) Remonstrated to the Kingdom, (in which all the well-affected, free, ingenious spirits, will most readily close, and freely act, with you) may not become an untimely birth (as heretofore,) but prosecuted to the life, so as the whole Kingdom may reap the fruit of all our labors, and its own sufferings.*

Though we shall not take upon us to advise or direct your Councel in the prosecution thereof, yet we take the boldness to offer our sense and thoughts, desiring,

That, as on the one hand, your actings may be full and effectual; so on the other, care may be taken, that they may be, with as much satisfaction as can, to all such tender spirits as do agree with you in the justness and goodness of the thing proposed, but notwithstanding are not so clear in using of that means, that you may be forced to take for that end.

That the same care may be had for the taking away of all present and future objections of wilful and unnecessary force, and that all impartial men may be satisfied, that your actings proceed not from your Wills or Interest, nor shal extend further, then singly and clearly to the redeeming of the just Liberty of this Nation, and the setling of it in peace and quietness.

To all which we shall humbly and briefy offer:

That only such things may be insisted on as may put a reasonable and certain period to this present Parliament, and may, for the future, establish free, successive Parliaments, duly elected according to the Provision in the Remonstrance.

That there may be a sure provision made for the more equal distributions of Elections, through the whole Kingdom.

That no person engaged in this War against the Parliament may either elect or be elected to be members of Parliament.

That some certain provision may be made, that no persons that may be elected Members of Parliament, contrary to the provision in the Remonstrance, may be admitted thereto before they are tried whether duly elected accordingly, and approved by some faithful men, to be carefully chosen, appointed and authorized to judg thereof.

All which being setled, the Army provided for, so as no free Quarter may be taken, and such other common and ordinary things as concern the administration of common Justice, the present quiet of the Kingdom, and all

---

* see below.

other things whatsoever, may be left to the power and disposal of the next free and duly elected Parliament, which we conceive may be the most proper instrument in the hand of God for setling the Kingdom.

These Ends and Principles, so long as you are carried forth to pursue (which we hope you never will forsake) you may be assured of our concurrence and assistance to the utmost of our powers.

By the Appointment of the Officers at a general Meeting.

Signed, THO. MARGETTS. Pontefract, Decem. 12. 1648.

Background

In a letter to William Clarke at headquarters, the brigade's Judge-Advocate Thomas Margetts described how, at this 'general meeting of Officers', Lambert 'did expresse himself very sweetly and fully, opposing with aboundance of convincing reason all that gainesaid, so that he gave great satisfaction to all the well affected, and putt much life and strength to the business.' The surviving minutes of a preliminary meeting on 4 December record that Lambert made a speech about the 'great worke' of the army in promoting the *Remonstrance*, 'but left it freely to their owne hearts and judgments either to concurre or dissent as god should direct them therein'. As several important officers were absent, and some had not yet seen the *Remonstrance*, Margetts was instructed to write to Fairfax expressing the brigade's general support. This letter, explaining that they had been unable to respond while they were on the march from Scotland, but now that they had been settled for four or five days at Pontefract a general meeting of officers had been called, was signed by thirty-three officers on 5 December. The minutes of 12 December name thirty-six officers present and include the text of the printed declaration as far as * above. Colonel Bright and Captain Westby were 'unsatisfied in some things in the Remonstrance', and it was agreed that they and any officers of their regiment not present could have their dissents recorded if they wished. Fairfax would be informed of such dissents, 'with the grounds and reasons thereof and with as much care and tenderness as may be'.

Three regiments of the marching army now remained at Pontefract: Lambert's own, Lilburne's, and Bright's, while the others in the north since Preston were marching south with Cromwell. It is not clear which local regiments were still there. Both Lambert and Lilburne were now commanding northern cavalry regiments, while Bright's was the foot regiment under his command since 1644. The presence of Robert Lilburne's major, John Sanderson, and several other officers of his was noted on 12 December; Lilburne's own was not, but he was appointed to a standing council to meet every Friday to deal with public affairs in communication with headquarters. A person of future interest also present was Lambert's quartermaster James Naylor, the Quaker whose tongue was bored for blasphemy in 1656. Captain Adam Baynes, one of the two officers delegated to take the declaration to army headquarters, acted as Lambert's London agent, buying up soldiers' debentures (the promissory notes they received for the percentage of their wages held back during the war) and purchasing property, to the enrichment of both Lambert and himself.

Related sources

West Yorkshire Archives, Ms C469: Council of War of the Parliamentary Army.
Thomas Margetts to William Clarke, 13 December 1648, *Clarke Papers*, vol. 2, p. 70.
William Harbutt Dawson, *Cromwell's Understudy, the Life and Times of General John Lambert and the rise and fall of the Protectorate* (London, 1938).

34: REGIMENT OF JOHN REYNOLDS
5-12 December 1648

Context

Of the two surviving manuscripts of this petition, one is evidently a first draft and the other a revision with less eccentric spelling and handwriting. Some significant passages and phrases, including the definition of a just war as one fought for liberty or justice, do not appear in either printed version. The text offered here, therefore, is the second manuscript version although it is less coherent. The erratic spelling and embedded or unclosed brackets are a common feature of many manuscript texts at this time.

The petitioners' assertion that they are part of the army 'according to the justice of common engagement' points to their origin as a volunteer force raised during the second civil war. The language of blood is thickly sprinkled without targeting the king; while the call to Fairfax personally to show himself 'real' (sincere) to the nation reminds us that he — not Cromwell or Ireton — was the much respected commander to whom they looked for action.

Text

Worcester College Oxford, Ms 16, fos. 23v-25

An humble address to the Generall his Excellencie from Certaine Troopes who voluntarily gave of themselves to oppose ye King in this former Tyrannous warre & also in the Latte Insurrecons in the nation under the command of Coll. Reynolds

May it please your Excellencie, If wee shall speake of the Equall, Common and Just ingagements in bloud for Libertie or Justice (which is that alone that countenances or Justifies war) wee might speake much, and so inlarge our selves that others might in Judgment conscience and Comand reason continually our Inlargements, the bloud and liberty of the Meanest is equally and alike pretious in the eyes of the Just god and just men. Wee have fought against injustice many yeares & against the unjust bloudie Massacreing warre raised by the Kinge as the Declarations of the Parliament manifest, and that which induced us to it was because the Nations Representatives did then seemingly sett their faces towards Righteousnesse & impartiall Justice, but god gave us victory over him & yet when that was done the people of this Nation had to deale (according to the prime lawes of nature, and the declarations of the Parliament themselves (there being corruption & declension from their principles, and seeking the destruction of the Interest of Justice and those that had engaged in bloud for righteousness sake) which the Parliament for their owne and the people's wellfare & safety for the Parliament (being captivated in their Judgments and partiall in their principles) who should have bin An impregnable Bullworke against all Tyrants for the rights of the people, were such as did indeavor to raise an

Army against iustice & right which was a sad reward for those that rolled their garments in woundes & bloud [Isaiah 9, 4-5] for in somme of all they were voted Traytours if they proceeded, but in their and the nations infallible, and just liberty of petitioninge they slighted & imprisoned manie of the petitions and persons of manie of our deare and approved freinds of the nation. But god gave the Army (of whome we were and (as wee humbly conceave) are members according to the Justice of Comon ingagement the Laws of Nature soe much insisted upon, & the declarations of Parliament & Army, speciall particular & solemn ingagement; & alsoe upon a Conscientious consideration of thinges as to god) an honorable conquest and victorie over them. And our declaring for Justice gave the enemies thereoff the Deadley terrifieing blow in the conscience without a stroake, by declareing for Justice our freinds loved us, and justly expected the fruit of our glorious expressions, & declarations. After that there were great Insurrections hatched by Malignants and Apostates, but they were infatuated in their Councells and dissipated in their bloudy and deepe designes. And then the Scottish Army was invited by domestique hipocritts whose guilty harts had the equall guilt of the bloud of Thousands upon them in Insurrections and invasions as aforesaid, and wee ingaged against those insurrections (as contineuing firme & stedfast to our principles by the power of god) against the Comon Enemy for the right of equall peace and Justice, even then when others were delivered over unto a Reprobate some to Apostatize & to turne upon you & your authority against the prime laws of Nature, the declarations & ingagements of the Parliament & Army, even such persons who pretended much Love honour and zeale to your person & authoritie, & by that did (as much as in them lye) indeavour to blast our Reputation, and the love and honor to Justice & you, & by that meanes procured some of us to bee Injured & damnified in the house of our friends. But wee would willingly and hartily wa[i]ve that if wee did but see a cordiallness impartialitie & unity in the Lawes of settlement, & Justice in futuritye. and wee in order unto that ground Excellency and wittness of god would express as much love to authority order and the Reynes of Government (& to your authority in particular) as any men living, & wee cannot but Admire the most high god and praise him and secondarily give you harty thanks for that you have declared your Resolutions as to imminent Impartiall personall Justice upon the Kinge &c and distribut impartiall freedome to the people. And therefore for the love And Honor wee beare to Justice and Righteousness (that one wittnes of god in the world) and for the reall love wee beare to unity upon that accompt, & for the reall Love wee beare to your Excellencies authority in order theareunto we Desire you would give the highest iustest reasonable impartiall & Righteous assurance and satisfaction that may bee to all people and iust men in the Army & Nation (that have a godly Jealousie and that would Advance the Interest of Impartiall Justice and uprightnesse) that you are reall to all the Nation, and to us in particular, (as aforesaid) (as being members thereof) that soe the Lord alone may Acknowledged [*sic*] in Judgment, and impartiall righteousnesse in the Earth. And then our bloud shall not bee pretious in our sight but wee (if god and nature calls for itt) spill itt as water in the streetes to accomplish those ends for the nation, & ourselves as individuall members thereof against all Tyrants whatsoever and Manifest ourselves (though wee would not Compare or boast) as subject to your Authoritye and conducte as any man living in this our Generation.

Another manuscript text

Worcester College Oxford, *Clarke Papers*, Ms 114, fos. 132-3.

Printed version

The Moderate, No. 22, 5-12 December 1648. BL/EEBO: E.476[5]

Background

John Reynolds had been a captain in Oliver Cromwell's horse regiment at the time of the New Model Army's revolt in 1647. For his part in the agitation of April 1648 demanding the reinstatement of soldiers' representatives on the General Council, he was demoted and narrowly escaped imprisonment. In May 1648 he raised his own volunteer cavalry regiment, which according to Gerald Aylmer 'seems to have attracted a more than random number of soldiers with Leveller sympathies'. He commissioned William Bray — the only officer of Robert Lilburne's mutinous foot regiment they did not drive out in November 1647 — as a captain-lieutenant in this force. The regiment fought under Sir Michael Livesey against the Kentish rising, and the Derby House committee ordered Livesey in July 1648 to put down 'great disorders' among them and suppress a 'dangerous' pamphlet they were circulating.

A later defence of Bray by one of his men, John Naylier, explains that they left Kent in September, expecting the Newport treaty to be concluded very soon, after which they would be either incorporated into Parliament's army or disbanded. Reynolds led his men first into Hertfordshire, then marched them towards Pontefract, but after they had taken Peterborough he diverted them into Warwickshire. On learning that he had engaged them to go to Ireland, several troops resisted, and chose 'agents' to represent them. The Derby House committee was still looking for ships to take Reynolds's men to Ireland on 20 November 1648, and this whole account tallies with what is known from other sources.

Their petition was composed after they had seen the *Remonstrance*, and the agents of three troops took it to Windsor. Fairfax's forces had left for London by the time they got there; but they caught them up at Hounslow Heath, and had a stormy meeting with Reynolds himself. At that time, Naylier later wrote, 'we had no Mercenary Troops amongst us, but we were entangled with Mercenary Apostate Officers of Reynolds his own Creatures.'

Though many of those involved had the reputation of Levellers, it is not an overtly Leveller petition. Nor was it written by anyone with the elite education that Reynolds was to display to the king when he walked with him at Hurst Castle to calm his fear of Colonel Harrison.

When Reynolds tried again to take his men to Ireland in 1649, the regiment was split. Bray was arrested for a pamphlet denouncing the army leadership and the Commonwealth regime, and his troop mutinied. Three troops stayed with Reynolds and took part in the suppression of the Leveller-inspired mutiny at Burford in May 1649, then pursued William Thompson's rebel band to Banbury and killed their leader. These troops went on to Ireland, and Reynolds himself sat in the Dublin parliament and was knighted by Cromwell in 1655.

Related sources

John Naylier, *The New made Colonel, or Ireland's Jugling Pretended Reliever* (1649). BL/EEBO E.552[10].

Brian Manning, *1649, The Crisis of the English Revolution* (London, 1992), pp. 201-9.

ODNB: Gerald Aylmer, 'Reynolds, Sir John, 1625 – 1657'.

35: DOVER CASTLE GARRISON
12-19 December 1648

Context

This is, as the petitioners admit, a 'not so speedy' response to the call from headquarters to show support for the *Remonstrance*, explicitly calling for justice against 'him that sits on the Throne'. Its language is full of religious enthusiasm, but the target of the biblical reference to Achan (Joshua 7: 1, 19-26) is not immediately clear. Achan's sin was secretly keeping some treasure looted from the defeated city of Jericho, which had been cursed by god. It is hard to see the analogy here; Oliver Cromwell was more understandably accused of Achan's sin during his rule as Lord Protector. But in one of his letters to Hammond Cromwell himself had described talking to the king as dealing with 'an accursed thing' (see 20 above), so it may refer to the Newport treaty.

Text

The Moderate, No. 23, 12-19 December 1648, pp 211-12. BL/EEBO E.477[4]

The humble Representation of the Officers of horse and foot in, and about Dover Castle, in the behalf of themselves and souldiers.

Humbly sheweth, That as we cannot but look on it as an especiall Act of providence, and manifestation of divine Love, that notwithstanding the power and policy of the publick Enemies of this Kingdom, your Excellencies undertakings should be Crowned from heaven with so great successe and victory, so we are fully sensible of the inveterate Rage, and continued plottings of our adversaries, together with the detestable Apostacy of many that have formerly joyned with us; whereby, after the effusion of so much precious blood, we are likely to be enthralled under a most cruell Yoke, worse then our late Egyptian Bondage, and therefore we most humbly declare:

That we prize it as a great and choise pledge of future blessings, that God hath stirred up your Excellency to Act on such high and raised principles, as are set forth in the late Remonstrance and Declarations, whereby Iustice may be impartially executed as well on him that sits on the Throne, as on the meanest subiect, and the cursed Achans, and troublers of our Israel, removed from among us, that righteousnesse may run down in such a stream, as the God of Iustice may be satisfied for the Current of the blood of his Saints that hath been shed in this Kingdom, and the faithfull reap the benefit of their former fervent prayers and endeavors. In Order to which, we are, and shall be ready to the hazard and losse of what is most dear and precious to us, to engage in any service to promote the ends proposed and though we have not been so speedy in this Representation, and are Restrained to a particular place, (in which we shall endeavour to Act faithfully according to our trust) yet our hearts are enlarged with the earnest desire of the publike Peace, and have, and do unanimously reioyce in your Excellencies righteous undertakings, in pursuance of the ends Remonstrated. And not doubting but the God of our former deliverances, will carry your Excellency through all difficulties, and those mountains of opposition shall become plaine before you. We humbly beseech your Excellency would proceed in what is justly proposed, that the Kingdom may not be beguiled with the specious pretences of our subtile adversaries, but that Delinquents may be punished, our liberties confirmed, and the Kingdom setled, to the glory of God, and comfort of his people; for the effecting of which, without respect to our private interests, we shall willingly, with our lives in our hands, encounter with the great difficulties, and really engage in what may manifest our selves,

Your Excellencies, and the Kingdoms most faithfull servants.

Background

Dover Castle, the 'key to England' reinforced by Henry VIII, was seized in 1642 by the townspeople and held for Parliament throughout the first civil war. When the Kentish revolt broke out in May 1648, extra beds and biscuit were sent to the garrison, but the castle was surrounded, and the nearby ammunition stores occupied by the royalist Sir Richard Hardres, before these supplies arrived. Hardres was reported to have a force of 2000 men, and fired 500 artillery shots at the castle before being driven off by Rich's regiment. He withdrew, apparently considering Dover 'a place of little concernment', and went on to take Deal, Walmer and Sandown castles instead. The two companies of foot at Dover were reinforced in August by an additional company of foot and one troop of horse. The governor of the castle, Colonel Algernon Sidney, was promoted to Lieutenant in October, though he seems to have played no actual part in its defence. That had been left to Captain Brayfield, who purchased supplies for the garrison himself, and local gentleman Sir Henry Heyman.

Algernon Sidney (or Sydney), younger son of the Earl of Leicester, seems to have had nothing to do with this petition either, though he was later known for republican political thought and executed for plotting against King Charles II. In a letter of 1660 he insisted that he had never supported the trial or execution of Charles I. He claimed that he told the only meeting of the trial commissioners he attended, that no court could try the King, and their High Court of Justice had no power to try anyone.

Related sources

A Perfect Diurnal, No. 254, 5-12 June 1648. BL/EEBO: E.522[39].
Commons Journal, vol. 5, 27 May and 2 August 1648; vol. 6, 24 October 1648.
Calendar of State Papers, Domestic, 1648-1649, 6 and 10 July 1648.

Blair Worden, 'Oliver Cromwell and the Sin of Achan', in Derek Beale and Geoffrey Best (eds.), *History, Society and the Churches* (Cambridge, 1985).

Oliver Cromwell to Robert Hammond, 6 November 1648, *Clarke Papers* vol. 2, p. 50.

ODNB: Jonathan Scott, 'Sidney [Sydney], Algernon (1623-1638)'.

Alan Everitt, *The Community of Kent and the Great Rebellion* 1640-60 (Leicester, 1966), pp. 248-9.

36: GARRISON OF BOSTON (LINCOLNSHIRE)
19 - 26 December 1648

Context

This is another brief statement of support for the *Remonstrance* and whatever 'extraordinary' course of action the army leadership feel is necessary, but quite different in tone from the last above. It begins with the reasonableness of the *Remonstrance*, and its religious language goes no further than the conventional piety of hoping for god's guidance. The petitioners' call for justice against the 'chief incendiaries and instruments' of the civil wars makes it clear that they mean a public trial; but as far as individuals are concerned they go no further than the ambiguous phrase 'impartial justice'. By late December this may of course have become a codeword for targeting the king while avoiding explicit mention of him, but that reading should probably not be forced on the text.

Text

The Moderate, No. 24, 19-26 December 1648. BL/EEBO E.536[2]

To the Right Honourable his Excellencie the Lord Fairfax, Generall of the Parliaments Forces for the Kingdom of England, and Dominion of Wales.

The Humble Petition and Addresses of the Officers and Souldiers in the Garrison of Boston.

May it please your Excellency, The sense we have of the present distemperatures, and dangers of this Kingdom, and the strength of Reason we find in your late Remonstrance presented to the House of Commons, have taken such hold of our judgements, as not only to approve of some just course, though extraordinary, in this Juncture of time, for the healing thereof; but withall, Humbly to tender our cheerfull and ready concurrence therein; And here we crave leave to express what we cannot seriously think of without regret, That since the Kingdom hath now been delivered the second time into the Parliaments hand, the chief Incendiaries, and Instruments of these late wars, have not been brought to publick Trial, and Iustice, for their wicked and Traiterous Designs, and attempts, whereby to deter others from the like for the future.

 We therefore beseech your Excellency, as the good hand of God shall lead you, to think of some Expedient, and to endeavour effectually that impartiall Iustice may have its free course, and the obstructions of it removed, that Government may have its due constitution, the people of England their just Rights, and the Kingdom a speedy, and (through Gods blessing) a happy settlement. For the gaining of which, we shall faithfully serve your Excellency with our lives and fortunes.

Background

Before the civil wars, Boston had resisted Charles I's forced loan and ship money. A strong puritan presence had emerged under John Cotton, minister of St Botolph's church, which does not seem to have been weakened by Cotton's departure, with many of the townspeople, to America. The port remained a parliamentarian stronghold throughout the civil wars, supplying food to Hull and importing munitions for the forces in Lincolnshire. Under Presbyterian governor Colonel Edward King, however, Boston was drawn into the internal strife among parliamentarians. King broke up an Independent congregation and incurred the enmity of John Lilburne. After he was removed from his command in 1644, Boston enjoyed stability under Colonel Edward Syler, a local man. By mid-1645 the garrison is said to have been composed of forces from other counties, and the fortifications were in poor shape.

By 1648 Colonel Walton at King's Lynn had taken over responsibility for Boston, and the Derby House committee advised him to move a company of his men from there to the Isle of Ely on 12 June 1648. The Presbyterian Clement Walker believed that Walton was planning to create a defensible refuge for the Independent party extending from the fenlands around Boston and Crowland to the Isle of Ely in the south. In reality, Walton's command was less far-reaching, but it united the subscribers of the petition numbered 29 above with those of this petition.

Related sources

Calendar of State Papers, Domestic, 1648 – 1649. (Wanton in error for Wauton throughout.)

[Clement Walker], *The History of Independency* (1648), p. 90. BL/EEBO: E.463[19].

A. A. Garner, *Boston and the Great Civil War* (Boston, 1992).

37: GARRISONS OF SHREWSBURY AND LUDLOW
25 December 1648 – 1 January 1649

Context

These petitioners' plea that the business of a constitutional settlement should come first, leaving other reforms to 'the ordinary remedy by Parliament' was timely, for the Council of Officers at Whitehall was still discussing a new *Agreement of the People*, though it was soon to be overshadowed by the trial and execution of the king.

The fear of 'new contrivances' leading to a further civil war, also feared by Hewson's regiment (24 above), was an important factor in the events leading up to the king's trial. Ireland was constantly in the news. The Anglo-Irish Protestant Marquis of Ormond, Charles I's Lord Lieutenant in Ireland, was working to make peace with the moderate Catholics of the rebel confederation there. English royalists hoped this would bring them external military and naval support, hopefully in coalition with the Dutch, who had just rejected Parliament's advances. Although neither Ormond's new alliance nor any foreign aid arrived in time to save Charles I's life, the new regime still had to deal with these external threats.

Text

A Perfect Diurnall, No. 28, 25 December - 1 January 1648-9, BL/EEBO E.527[1].

Dateline Tuesday 26 December

To his Excellency the Lord Fairefax Generall of all the Parliaments Forces in this Kingdom; The humble Petition of Col. Macworth, and the rest of the Officers and Souldiers in the Garrisons of Shrewsbury and Ludlow, in the County of Salop [Shropshire].

Humbly Sheweth, That the hearts of your petitioners have never been freed from feares, since they perceived a resolution in the Houses of Parliament, to admit and carry on a Personall Treaty with the King, which being Petitioned for clamorously, cryed out for and at length professedly fought for by the Parliaments professed enemies, could never be imagined to be intended for good to the Parliaments friends, & for that reason alone (beside the many more of great weight against it) could never certainly have been affected, had not some of those intrusted by the Kingdome, by combination which [with] the Kings party vigorously promoted this designe in a Parliamentary way, as that which at length must consummate and confirm what ever was plotted for the Kings ends and purposes: But that God who comforteth the abject, and Loves to turn the wisdome of carnall men into folly, hath in part freed us from our former feares, and hee having disappointed them in their other designes, which were but in order thereunto, hath disappointed them also in this by putting an end (if at this distance we have the truth) unto that evill Treaty: which notwithstanding, and that our hopes are againe revived by that faithfull and judicious Remonstrance, lately sent by your Excellency and your Councell of Officer to the Parliament; wherein the mischiefes of the late Treaty, and miseries lying yet upon the Kingdome with their probable remedies are declared (whereunto we hereby most gladly witnesse our concurrence) yet such is the Apostacy of some, Treachery of many, and cowardlinesse, or to speak the best coldnesse of the most, That new contrivances will not be wanting suddenly, nay already begun in Ireland, (as appeare by the Marquesse of Ormonds Declaration now published to the world) for the destroying of the well affected party in the three Kingdoms and to all adhere to them; under such Notions and names as themselves please to give to them, and for the utter frustration of all that good, which this Parliament while they Acted upon right principles, and unto right ends so happily had begun.

Wherefore your Petitioners humbly beseech your Excellency as you tender the honor of God, the welfare of this Nation, in Generall, and more especially the lives and liberties of those of the Nation that have engaged out of Conscience and honesty for this Parliament, that you would still continue to represent to the house of Commons the desires of us, and of all their reall friends in the Kingdome, and earnestly to Mediate with them, to consider and regard the severall late Petitions from London, Leicester-shire, the Northern Counties and other places sent them, lest it be imputed to their perpetuall dishonour, that they have deserted their first principles, or intend to hearken to the Counsells and perswasions of their enemies, rather then of those who have hazarded their lives and fortunes in theirs and the Kingdomes just quarrell. Not ceasing to lay before them the great distractions and dangers of the Nation, and how needfull a present settlement is by vertue of that authority they have hitherto claimed and exercised, with any more addresses to the King, who is not like to surcease the execution of those mischiefes hee and his party by his Instigations, have unalterably resolved: and to beseech them, that after a Generall invocasion upon God, appointed throughout the Land for direction and successe, that they would set all other businesses of lesser consequence aside till this great businesse of settlement be effected: And because there is little hope of peace with God or man whiles the Authors of our former and late troubles, and of the bloud shed in the three Kingdomes escape unpunished; that your Excellency would be pleased to endeavour, that justice may be done upon them in some exemplary way suitable to their crimes without respect of persons, according to Gods own way of proceedings; who is no respecter of persons. That so such snakes may be no longer nourished in our bosomes, who doe but watch their opportunities at length to sting us to death: many grievances and burdens of free Quarter, unequall taxes, irregular, corrupt, and extorsive proceedings in Courts of Justice; and other grosse miscarriages in Government of the Common wealth) call for speedy redresse: But might the mentioned particulars be once seriously intended: We should not need to dispaire of some reformation in these. In reference to all which we shall depend upon the ordinary remedy by Parliament, till God declare by evident demonstration of his will in the passages of his providence, that that extraordinary is to be resorted unto which is never denyed, in case of extremity, to any people: And having this set before our eyes from what God seemes to have discovered [revealed] by his miraculous past deliverances, and leading us in safety through all the difficulties our enemies could devise to hinder our departure out of spirituall and civill bondage, that there remaines for us yet a promised Canaan. We doe therefore resolve, God strengthening us, to follow your Excellency and the rest, those conductors raised up and spiritted for so great a work, through a Sea of bloud to attaine the fruition thereof.

Signed by us as the severall Officers of the severall Companies in the said Garrisons, for our selves and the said Companyes, by their appointment and agreement.

Background

Although Shropshire was held by the royalists for most of the first civil war, the local parliamentary regime had been in place since 1645. Colonel Humphrey Mackworth, governor of Shrewsbury, successfully defended the town against a royalist attack in April 1648. Two of the four local captains who raised additional volunteers as ordered by the county committee in June 1648 were Shrewsbury drapers and the other two were local gentlemen. All four of them had been involved in the town's puritan circles since before the civil wars. Mackworth himself was a Shropshire landowner and lawyer who divided his time between the county and the London courts.

He was an alderman of Shrewsbury and the town corporation's learned counsel, and had been involved among the town's puritans who refused to bow their heads at the name of Jesus as ordered by Archbishop Laud. He also acted as a trustee of the Feoffees for Impropriations (1626–33), who bought up tithes sold into private ownership after the Reformation, in order to endow preaching ministers. Throughout the civil wars he was in close correspondence with the Earl of Denbigh, a leading Independent politician. His son Thomas was elected for Ludlow in 1646 and sat on after Pride's Purge. Though Colonel Mackworth played no part in the regicide, his remains were removed from Westminster Abbey at the Restoration and thrown into a common burial pit.

Related sources

Robert Jones, *A Great and Bloody Fight in Shropshire*. BL/EEBO E.457[18].
His Majesties declaration and message, to the Marquis of Ormond... BL/EEBO E.475[28].
J. E. Auden, 'Shropshire and royalist conspiracies ... 1648-60', in *Transactions of the Shropshire Archaeological and Natural History Society*, 3rd Ser., 10 (1910).

Barbara Coulton, 'Humphrey Mackworth: Puritan, Republican, Cromwellian', in *Cromwelliana*, 1999.
ODNB: Toby Barnard, 'Butler, James, first duke of Ormond (1610–1688)'.

38: LANCASHIRE OFFICERS

25 December 1648

Context

While declaring support for the *Remonstrance* and the leadership of the New Model Army, this petition does not specify any further aims. Neither the political nor the religious language it uses goes beyond the conventional parliamentarian references to the common interest, freedom and liberty, and the hand of god in Parliament's victories. Perhaps this was all that Fairfax and the council of officers wanted when they sent out copies of the *Remonstrance*, inviting the regiments to show publicly their 'approbation thereof and concurrence therein'. This one's background story, however, reveals that it was far from a routine response.

Text

Heads of a Diarie, No.4, 20-27 Dec. 1648. BL/EEBO E.536[9]

To His Excellency the Lord Fairfax Lord Generall of all the Forces for the Parliament of England. The Humble Petition of certain Officers in the County of Lancaster, whose Names are hereunto subscribed,

Humbly sheweth, Whereas your petitioners have cordially engaged for the common Interest of freedom and liberty against the King and his party, that labour to set up his power and will, ever since the beginning of these unnaturall Wars, and having been therein (through the goodnesse of God) preserved in our Integrities, against the self-interest and faction of all backsliders and corrupted parties, both in our own County and else where. And having with comfort seen how God hath owned the Army under your Excellencies command, with part of which we have often engaged, (especially in this last war) and whom we account the only visible means and instruments next under God to put a period to our miseries, and to preserve us from the evill of wicked and corrupted Parties, and having now at the last extricated our selves from those commands and obstructions that hitherto letted [hindered] us, Doe most humbly declare our earnest desires and ready complyance to joyn with the Army under your Excellencies command, for the pursuance of all those just ends you have remonstrated and declared, and doe further humbly desire (though unworthy) to be entertained under your Excellencies command, and that we may have Capt. Crumwell, son to the Honourable Lieutenant Generall for our Collonel, and this we commend to your Excellencies consideration, wishing that God in his mercy may prosper our undertakings.

Background

In the summer of 1648, Colonel Ralph Ashton (or Assheton) of Middleton raised a Lancashire force of horse and foot to oppose the Scots' invasion.

The Derby House committee approved, and called on the county committee and deputy-lieutenants to send more recruits into Westmorland for this 'prudent endeavour'. After the battle of Preston the committee praised the forces that had 'served with so much distinction under Colonel Ashton', and promised to raise more money for them — in addition to the £3000 they had already received — if they would follow Cromwell northwards. Ashton was promoted to Major-General, at forty shillings a day in addition to his pay as a colonel of both horse and foot. He went on to expel the royalists from Cockermouth and take the surrender of 1000 Scots and royalists at Appleby. So far — despite criticism of the terms he granted the enemy's junior officers at Appleby (see 7 above) — there were no reports of bad behaviour among his troops.

In the last week of October, as Parliament faced the dilemma of either maintaining the 'supernumeraries' raised during the second civil war at the cost of popular discontent, or weakening their security by disbanding them, both houses voted to disband the Lancashire force and pay the money due to them. Ashton and his fellow county committee men were reluctant to obey. In mid-November came reports that Ashton's forces were 'very insolent… and give out big words against the army', and had attacked an officer of Harrison's who tried to take away arms and horses they had allegedly stolen. Shortly afterwards, the Derby House committee complained that a large number of Lancashire soldiers were quartered in Cumberland 'under pretext of raising the pay assigned to them upon that county', though a single troop should be enough to gather it in. This incidentally reveals the downside of the system of payment by specific county assignments urged by many army petitioners.

Meanwhile, a plan to recruit Ashton's forces into a new regiment of foot for Ireland won Derby House's support. Volunteers were to receive their disbandment money first, and individuals who openly opposed the scheme would get none. Ashton and the county committee were still reluctant to comply. Pride's Purge further aggravated the situation because most of the county's MPs were Presbyterian. A cousin of Colonel Ashton's acted as a teller for the Yeas on the vote to accept the king's answers, and all but two were excluded at the purge. Meanwhile, Parliament continued the reform of county militia committees that had begun before the purge.

In early January 1649, a group of officers at Lancaster Castle reported that a Presbyterian minister, Thomas Smith, was hoping for the Scots to return and suppress 'Independents and Sectaries', and praising the Lancashire militia as 'the honestest army in the Kingdome, for they would stand for the Presbyterian Government'. Evidently Ashton's officers were not solidly behind him, and those who signed the report to Derby House may also have organised this petition, which like most of its kind appeared in print without individual names.

These officers also request incorporation into the New Model Army, rather than disbandment with the money due to them. Perhaps they too feared that the civil wars were not yet over, and wished to serve with the New Model if that should happen. Captain Cromwell, whom they request as their colonel, was the Lieutenant-General's younger surviving son Henry, who had been commissioned to command a new cavalry regiment. In February 1649 the House of Commons was still discussing how the Lancashire forces 'may be speedily disbanded, or disposed for the Business of Ireland'. Captain Bamber's troop of horse was resisting disbandment early in May that year, while Captain Cromwell's regiment did not sail to Ireland until 1650.

Related sources

The Moderate, No. 24, 16-26 December 1648. BL/EEBO E.536[2].
Ibid, No. 37, 20-27 March 1649. BL/EEBO: E.548[21].
CSPD, 1648-1649, pp. 263-5, 298-9, 332, 335, 336.
Commons Journal, vol. 6, 25 September, 24 October, and 14-26 December 1648; 10 February and 9 April 1649.
Clarke Papers, vol. 2, pp. 160-3, 187-90.
The Moderate Intelligencer, No. 192, 16-23 November 1648. BL/EEBO E.473[15].
Ibid, No. 197, 21-28 December 1648. BL/EEBO E.536[18].
Mercurius Pragmaticus, No. 36-7, 5-12 December 1648. BL/EEBO E.476[2].
The Kingdomes Weekly Intelligencer, No. 309, 24 April - 1 May 1649. BL/EEBO E.552[21].
Heads of a Dyarie of Some Passages of Parliament, No. 15. BL/EEBO E.529[33].
Ernest Broxap, *The Great Civil War in Lancashire* (Manchester, 1910 & 1971).

39: FOUR SHIPS IN THE DOWNS
28 December 1648

Context

These two declarations are responses to a letter sent out to the parliamentarian navy with the *Remonstrance* a few days after the similar one sent to the army regiments. It is not clear which ship or ships the total of 350 subscribers were on. Though the full strength of the *Unicorn* was 250 men, there had been only forty aboard in July 1648; but the Earl of Warwick, as Lord Admiral, had probably increased the number before the ship sailed with his fleet to Helvoetsluis on the Dutch coast in August. The declarations of loyalty and religious belief in these documents call for at least as much attention as the better known expressions of loyalty to the king and support for Presbyterianism issued on behalf of the revolted ships seven months earlier.

Text

The Declaration and Engagement of the Commanders, Officers, and Seamen in the Shippes, under the Command of the Right Honourable the Earle of Warwicke in the Downes, declaring their free concurrence in the Remonstrance of the Lord Fairfax, and the Army under his Command. London, Printed for John Playford at his shop in the Inner-Temple. Decem. 28. 1648. BL/EEBO E.536[15]

[i] To the Right Honourable Thomas, Lord Fairfax, Generall over all the Parliaments Forces at the Head-quarters London, these present.

Right Honourable, We have had the honour lately to receive foure Letters, with the Armies Remonstrance, all from your Excellencies Councel, with which our hearts and Affections doe freely concurre as well as any, knowing the things therein expressed are just and good, for wee doe verily beleeve the bloud of these precious ones which hath been spilt since this warre, even like water upon the ground, cryeth aloud for the speedy execution of justice upon all such who shall be found guilty hereof: and as the bloud of the Innocent cryeth loud for justice, so we are confident that many thousands oppressed, groane under their intollerable burthens, having long expected to be eased thereof, which God in mercy give deliverance to all. We are sorry the said Letters came no sooner to our hands before our Fleet was disperst; which if they had, God permitting, we should cheerfully have improved our interest to the utmost to have answered your Excellency, with the Honourable Councels present expectations. But now we are but foure Ships here in the Downes; The *St. George, Unicorne, Mary-rose,* and *Fellowship.*

The reasons of our not declaring at present, is namely the Lord Admirals absence from us, for that we think ourselves in duty obliged to his Lordship, as our Head, to motion the same first to his Honour, hoping to have his concurrence therein, knowing we are bound in Conscience acting under his Lordships power to observe all his just and lawfull Commands. We doe heartily wish and desire there may be a faire correspondency between his Lordship and your Excellencie: That as the Lord hath been pleased to use both your Honours as instruments of much good to these poore distracted shaken Kingdomes; so our prayers shall be, that God Almighty from that fulnesse which is in himselfe, would fill you more and more with himselfe: whereby your Honours hearts, together with all the faithfull, may be united as one man, to live and dye together in the Cause of God and peoples Liberties, against all oppositions whatsoever. Now as God hath been pleased to set this upon our hearts, so we may confidently assure your Excellency the same hath root in the hearts of many other the Commanders of our Fleet, and only in us and them, but in many other the Officers and Sea-men under our Respective Commands.

Thus much we humbly thought our selves obliged to hint forth to your Excellency in answer to these received; and we hope so long (by Gods assistance) as we have our hearts and hands, they shall be lift up for Gods glory, and the Kingdomes good, being confident God will perfect his owne work on his time to his owne glory: for we have had many pledges of his favour and goodnesse in owning your Excellency and that Army, against all opposition of yours and our enemies. We have likewise seen his Power, Love and Goodnesse, to the Fleet under our Generall the Lord Admiral in the late Expedition; even to the Admiration of men, and astonishment of our enemies. Now the God of Heaven, who is wisedome it selfe, fill your Councels with the wisedome that is from above, which is first pure, then peaceable. We shall now humbly beg leave of your Excellency to subscribe our selves as we desire to be, Your Excellencies humble servants to command, Robert Moulton, Richard Haddocke, Thomas Harrison, Fra[ncis] Penne [Penrose].

St. George in the Downes, Decem. 24. 1648.

(ii) The engagement of the Commanders Officers and Seamen of the Ship Unicorne, under the Command of Captain Richard Haddock Vice-Admirall for the Fleet Commanded by Robert Earle of Warwick, Lord High Admiral of England, against the revolted Ships and all adhering to them now in Hostility against the Parliament.

Whereas it hath pleased the Honourable Houses of Parliament in consideration of the late revolt of divers ships of the Navy, and their desperate designes against the Cause of God, which the Parliament (we do assured beleeve) doth maintain, and do afford the Navy divers weighty and worthy motives and incouragements to oppose that parts [*sic*], and from the bloudy and barbarous of the Apostate Ships, so especially from the worth of our Liberties as Subjects, and Religion as Christians; We the Commanders, Officers and Seamen in the Ship Unicorne, do not from any slavish Principles of Respects, feare, or credit, but voluntarily and freely from the bottome of our hearts and consciences subscribe to live and die with the

Honourable Earle of Warwick, now Lord High Admiral of England, in this present engagement, for the preservation of the publique good, and the maintenance of that Covenant which we have formerly taken: In testimony whereof we subscribe our hands.

Subscribed by above 350.

Background

The naval revolt of May 1648, whose 'Apostate Ships' these seamen had successfully seen off, involved fewer than one-third of Parliament's thirty-nine ships at sea that summer, and began in just one strategically placed squadron of six. The political and religious views of the seamen in revolt were published in manifestos under inflated titles such as 'The Declaration of the Navy', while the attitudes of the majority who remained loyal received no such publicity. Since personal comments about Vice-Admiral Thomas Rainborowe found in a single manuscript of unknown authorship have also been the foundation of a myth about his background and character, a brief re-examination of the revolt seems appropriate here.

On 26 May 1648, the crew of Rainborowe's flagship, the *Reformation*, repudiated his command. They refused to let him board on his return from Deal Castle, where he had gone under instructions from the Derby House committee to stop the Kentish rebels from occupying it. Rainborowe believed he could have prevented the seamen's revolt if he had not been ordered ashore, but the sailors seem to have feared that they would be ordered to join him on land, and his absence facilitated political interventions by Presbyterian minister Samuel Kem, and former Vice-Admiral William Batten.

Rainborowe was not the 'landlubber' too many historians have assumed, ignoring Clarendon's grudging admission that he was an appropriate choice for command at sea, 'having been bred in that element, and knowing the duty of it very well'. His father had led the 1637 fleet, financed by Ship Money, against pirate bases in Morocco; and Thomas himself commanded the fleet raised in 1642 to harass the Irish rebels. In 1643 he served under the Earl of Warwick in the maritime defence of Hull, before joining Lord Fairfax's Yorkshire army, and later the New Model (see 16 above). He was appointed Vice-Admiral in October 1647, though Parliament's disapproval of his political stance at Putney and Ware delayed his taking it up; but by February 1648 he was actively preparing the summer fleet. The Navy Committee's delay in giving him a flagship, then choosing the *Reformation* (or *Constant Reformation*), which had been Batten's, was perhaps unfortunate; but Rainborowe's correspondence shows he was settled aboard a month before the revolt, not turned away on his first arrival as alleged by several sources then and since.

Local Kentish rebels (see 40 below) also directly canvassed the *Reformation* as it lay with five other ships in the Downs, that strategically important anchorage between the Kentish coast and the Goodwin Sands. The sailors' first manifesto — claiming falsely that the whole fleet was secured for the king — repeated the demands of the petition that had inaugurated the Kentish revolt: a personal treaty with the king, the disbandment of Fairfax's army, observance of England's 'known laws', and the preservation of the subjects' liberty. Committed royalists took advantage of this moderate stance at sea as on land, and a few days later the whole squadron of six, with two ships from the western fleet, declared for the Prince of Wales. A second manifesto, published in Holland and London early in July, declared nine ships 'rescued for His Majesties service', with a statement of royalist and Presbyterian principles.

The total grew to ten when Batten and the *Constant Warwick* joined them. As vice-admiral, Batten was in command from April 1645, when Warwick resigned as Lord Admiral under the Self-Denying Ordinance and was replaced by a committee. In September 1648 Batten resigned in turn, later claiming what is now called constructive dismissal, due to the assistance he had given the Presbyterian MPs suspended from Parliament. He had also been in secret contact with a Scottish agent, who reported on 23 May that Batten had promised to bring over many ships and was confident of the seamen's support.

We cannot know now who wrote the manuscript note in London Presbyterian George Thomason's collection, blaming the revolt on 'the Insufferable pride, Ignorance and insolency of Colonel Rainsborough' and on 'Severall landsmen made Sea-Commanders'. In the rebel seamen's published manifestos Rainborowe is attacked only for his political views, as a man 'not wel-affected to the King, Parliament and Kingdome', holding 'most destructive Principles both in Religion and Policy, and a knowne enemy to the Peace and Antient Government of this Kingdom'.

Despite serious fears of discontent spreading elsewhere, especially at Portsmouth, the naval revolt was contained after Warwick was reinstated as Lord Admiral on 1 June, and repentant rebels were offered an amnesty (which Batten and his crew were to take up six months later). On 30 August, while waiting with fourteen ships at the mouth of the Thames for the arrival of nine more from Portsmouth, Warwick confronted a slightly larger royalist fleet. The royalists were driven off by a storm, narrowly avoiding being caught between the two parliamentarian contingents. In another storm-lashed confrontation off Helvoetsluis in early November, three revolted ships were recaptured and only one of Warwick's taken by the enemy. Though the fleet's return home without further action was controversial, disaster had been avoided, and the loyal seamen might well thank god for their success so far.

In his subsequent report, Warwick described the poor condition of his ships and shortage of supplies, and requested prompt payment of the sailors' arrears of wages. The seamen's protestations of loyalty to the Lord Admiral and solidarity with Fairfax's army above are likely enough to be sincere, therefore; and their declaration of support for the purged Parliament shows that the navy was far from being solidly Presbyterian in politics. A few days before these declarations, six of Warwick's ships had been in the Downs. The other two may have sailed away by the time the declarations were subscribed. Batten was appointed to the Navy Office after the Restoration, to have his image memorably preserved for future generations as Samuel Pepys's corrupt and incompetent boss.

Related sources

The Declaration of the Navie, with the Oath Taken by all the Officers and Commonmen of the Same ... BL/EEBO 669.f.12[37].
The declaration of the Navie ... BL/EEBO 669.f.12 [36].
'The reasons the Navy give for their resolution'. BL/EEBO E.448[3].
A Declaration of the Officers and Company of Sea-men aboard His Majesties [sic] *Ships* ... Printed at Holland, and re-printed in London, 1648. BL/EEBO 669.f.12[69].
A Declaration of Sir William Batten, late Vice-Admiral ... BL/EEBO E.460[13].
Hamilton Papers, pp. 201-2.
Clarendon, *History of the Rebellion*, vol. 4, p. 404.
J. R. Powell and E. K. Timings (eds.), *Documents Relating to the Civil War 1642-1648* (Navy Records Society, 1963).
J. R. Powell, *The Navy in the English Civil War* (London, 1962).
E. Kennedy, 'The English Naval Revolt of 1648', *English Historical Review*, vol. 77 (1962).
ODNB: C. S. Knighton, 'Batten, Sir William (1600/01–1667)'.

40: LIVESAY'S REGIMENT

28 December 1648

Context

The king was now becoming a more prominent focus of petitions, following his arrival as a prisoner at Windsor. An ordinance for setting up a court to try him was introduced to the House of Commons on the same day as the publication of this and the navy's petitions (39 above). The petitioners' prioritising of judicial proceedings suggests that Livesay and his officers were in close touch with the army leadership, since the alternative view that the dissolution and reform of Parliament should come first had now been rejected by the army's allies in Parliament. Despite their alleged radicalism, Livesay's men seem to be following events rather than challenging them, and telling the Council of Officers what its members wanted to hear.

Text

The Declaration and Engagement of the Commanders, Officers, and Seamen in the Shippes ... Also a Representation of the Forces under the Command of Sir Michael Livesey, Commander in Chiefe in the County of Kent. Printed for John Playford. BL/EEBO E.536[15]

To His Excellency Tho: Lord Fairfax, Lord Generall of all the Forces raised in the Kingdome of England, and Dominion of Wales. The humble Representation of us the Officers of the Forces under the Command of the Honourable Sir Michael Livesey, Commander in Chiefe in the County of Kent, in the behalfe of our selves and the Souldiers under our Command.

Sheweth, That we have as deep, and as large a sense as any sort of men whatsoever of the blessings of God going along with your Excellency in your just and righteous undertakings, wading through so many Seas, and passing over so many Mountaines of difficulties, in regard of the many bloudy designes, and contrivements, and the cruell, implacable and restlesse rage of the open Enemy; as also, the odious Apostacy of seeming friends; yet through the exceeding mercy of God towards you, and the Army under your Command, in bearing up, and incouraging your Hosts, even to admiration, and all honest hearts rejoicing, the Lord hath crowned you and the Army with many great and glorious victories and successes, both in the first and late Wars: And when as the Lord was pleased to determine the quarrell of the enemy against them in their subversion, and vouchsafing you once more an opportunity, and put it into your hearts to thinke of, and to endeavour after such things as might conduce and lead unto an happy settlement of this poore distressed, and almost dying Nation, (occasioned by a bloudy, treacherous and wilfull enemy,) Your Excellency and Councell of Warre were pleased in order hereunto lately to present unto the House of Commons a Remonstrance, and latter Declarations, which we having seriously weighed, and considered of the excellency, justnesse, and reasonablenesse thereof, we do fully correspond, and give our hearts approbation thereunto: And in an especiall manner, in order to your desires therein, We earnestly desire that justice may impartially be executed on all offendors, from the greatest to the least, as well upon the Person of the King, as others; And that the prosecution thereof may be vigorous and without delay, for delaies (by sad and frequent experience) have proved to be of a very dangerous nature, and pernicious consequence and tendency; And thereby have rarely recovered, or gained the like, or same opportunity.

In order to the prosecution of all which, we do jointly and unanimously declare unto your Excellency, that we both are, and shall be ready (as God shall enable us) to engage our selves as your Excellency shall command, and direct us, that these things may be effected. And we professe we shall not judge or account our lives, or dearest injoyments neare unto us, so that our deare and native countrey may live, and be delivered out of those miseries and calamities that have so often, and so long threatened its ruine and destruction; And that Tyranny, Oppression and injustice might be removed and supplanted, and the just, deare bought Liberties and Freedomes of the Commoners of England may returne unto them; That this Nation may once more be happy, and crowned with blessednesse, which shall be the earnest, cordiall and constant breathings and desires of we, who do subscribe our selves the Petitioners, and your Excellencies most humble and faithfull servants.

Background

Sir Michael Livesay, or Livesey, was a Kentish magistrate, an active puritan and a member of the parliamentarian county committee from the outbreak of the civil war. He commanded a local regiment under Sir William Waller, and was among those who challenged Waller's authority in 1644. He refused a commission in the New Model Army, however, and his regiment was given to Henry Ireton. Elected for Queenborough in 1645, he supported the army and the Independents in Parliament and worked closely with other radical MPs. He returned to Kent to quell Canterbury's pro-Christmas riots notoriously harshly in 1647. Throughout the second civil war he led the county's forces against the royalists in Surrey and Sussex as well as Kent.

Despite their military successes, Livesay's men were disorderly. On 18 July Derby House warned the Kent county committee of 'very great disorders' among his men, particularly in Major Reynolds's troop, some of whom were in prison in Rochester. 'By means of these disorders,' they wrote, 'the discontents of the people are heightened and their disaffection increased.' They enclosed a 'printed paper' circulated by Reynolds's men, adding 'We need say nothing to you of the dangerous tendency thereof', requesting the committee to act to prevent 'the danger that may come by employment amongst your forces of men so principled as these seem to be'. Unfortunately, this paper does not survive.

Reynolds's troop was indeed a hive of radical activity (see 34 above), as was Captain William Bray's, still lingering around Croydon despite being ordered into Kent. In late August, however, Major Reynolds gave 'a very favourable account' of Livesay's forces at Derby House. Two months later, the troops stationed at Sevenoaks were said to have offered 'great incivility and affront' to the Earl of Leicester (Algernon Sidney's father) at Penshurst. The affront to a nobleman suggests continuing radicalisation among Livesay's forces at this time, though the nature of the incident is unknown. It may have been the defacement of the Sidney family's ancestral images in Penshurst church, which is said to have happened 'during the civil wars'.

By the time of the declaration above, Reynolds had led the radicals out of the county and obtained a commission for a regiment of his own, who subsequently resisted being sent to Ireland but complained of having been ignominiously labelled Levellers. (See 33 above.) Livesay and his remaining officers may have been relieved at their departure, but their own views were radical enough to support this declaration aligned with the army leadership. Livesay went on to take part in the king's trial, attending every day and signing the death warrant.

Related sources

CSPD, 1648-1649, pp. 198, 291-2.
Commons Journal, 11 October 1648.
ODNB: J. T. Peacey, 'Livesay [Livesey], Sir Michael, first baronet (1614 – 1665?)'.
John Naylier, *The New made Colonel, or Irelands Jugling Pretended Reliever* (1649). BL/EEBO E.552[10].

41: DENBIGH CASTLE GARRISON AND LOCAL SUPPORTERS

before 2 January 1649

Context

The Old Testament story employed by these petitioners could be taken to imply that the king should die. Ahab, king of Israel, was reproved by a prophet for extending mercy to his defeated enemy Benhadab (or Ben-ha'dad) king of Syria, befriending him though he had twice made war on the Israelites, and Ahab had been warned that god demanded the Syrian's death (1 Kings, 20). The story offered parallels with the English civil wars – repeated wars, a god-defying treaty — and like Saul's mercy to Agag (see 23 above) it was a favourite text of radical preachers and pamphleteers. Sparing an enemy was shown to lead to destruction.

Text

The Moderate, No. 25, 26 December-2 January 1648-9. BL/EEBO E.536[30]

To his Excellency, Thomas Lord Fairfax, General of the Forces in England and Wales.

The hearty Resolutions, and humble Petitions of the Governour and Souldiers of the Castle of Denbigh, and divers others, Officers, Souldiers, and well affected in the said County.

That the great thunderings and Earthquakes in this British Island, awakened us in this Corner thereof, to enquire after the causes of those Nationall concussions, and finding an unruly and unreasonable party of imperious, selfe-willed men, Resolved to engage in bloud, to stave from us at once our comfort, as Christians in Gods Kingdome, and freedom, as subjects, in our only native soyle; we quickly and cordially adventured our naturall lives, and freely cast over board our estates at the back of our Pilots, to keep this sinfull Nation, and our unworthy selves, and families, from sinking. But since perceiving clearly, that though the firme, faithfull, and famous trustees of the Kingdome, have with much uprightnesse indefatigably endeavoured our common good and security (which we ever with all thankfulnesse acknowledge, yet were they, by whose meanes we hope will yet more manifestly appeare) overborne, and hindred therein, so that instead of a safe haven, we were brought againe upon perillous Rockes; instead of righteousnesse, Behold the bitter worme of Injustice, and enraging hemlock of oppressions growing up in our furrows: Mercy turned to Cruelty, contempt and despite against the faithfull and tryed people, and pillars of the Land; Truth fainting and fallen in the streets, Justice and equity kept out of the Gates; the sonnes of bloud and violence (who had not the hearts in the field to looke the Generation of the just in the face) very insolent, and too much incouraged once more to attempt the tearing out of the bowels of the peaceable of the Land, and having learned out of the books that the Tyde of righteous Judgement must have its course, and after it, all the upright in heart; and minding how that dangerous mercy, and childish lenity of *Ahab*, who called up his brother *Benhadab* (that twice conquered slave) into his own Chariot, which act, with his depriving but of one honest *Nabaoth* of his life, brought that lukewarm professor to tremble in his own blood and just ruine in the third war [I Kings 21, 22], and have intentively observed at a distance, that (though many tooles were in Gods hand for the edifice begun, were blunted, and so laid aside) yet the edge of heaven, and high countenance of the Almighty, is still upon your Honourable self, and faithfull, dreadfull, and (through God) powerfull Army, once despised, dispersed, and (as it were) disbanded, but since made glorious together and a sunder, in removing mountaines of difficulties, breaking through rocks of oppositions, raising up the vallies, taming the rebellious, relieving the Parliament, quieting the Nations heart-city (once and againe distempered) and scattering the Scottish Allies, to the thankfull admirations of the people of the most high God, far and neer.

We therefore being thereunto encouraged by your Excellency, and the Armies late seasonable, and solid Remonstrance, do in full assurance of understanding, faith, and hope, humbly, and unanimously declare our Resolutions, to joyn heart, hand, life, and all, with your truely honourable self, and constant Army, and the many thousands of Israel; for we see of a truth God is with you, and them, for the reliefe and recovery of our late oppressed, and long tried Worthies in the Parliament, in order to the setlement of common Interests, and impartiall punishment of mad men (who are still thirsty, though already drunk with the blood of multitudes of our deare brethren), Humbly praying, that you would (as under full saile) like noble *Joshua*, and *Caleb*, follow *Jehovah* fully in the paths of Justice, Moderation, Courage and Faithfulness, wherein we doubt not of the high and mighty presence of our King, the god and rock of all Ages, to attend you; and to that great Captaine of your Hosts for his direction and successe in all the work entrusted to you, we shall also, whilst we breathe together in this Cause, ever pray, &c.

Background

Although north Wales was held by royalist forces for most of the first civil war, parliamentarian control was firmly established before the second broke out. By contrast with South Wales (see 25 above) there were no prominent defectors to the royalist cause, and the local insurrections of hard core royalists were successfully suppressed. Colonels Thomas Mytton and George Twisleton (or Twistleton) routed Sir John Owen's small royalist force at Y Dalar Hir near Llandegai in Caernarvonshire in early June 1648, and Owen was imprisoned at Denbigh. Lord Byron's takeover of Beaumaris Castle on Anglesey lasted a little longer but did not spread revolt, or even obtain the wholehearted backing of local royalists. When the Independents in Parliament were looking for effective military leaders, they were able to find and mobilise local men, despite the fact that very few of the traditional gentry leadership were sympathetic.

George Twisleton was a Yorkshireman who had settled in the region since arriving in Wales with Parliament's army in 1646, and was appointed governor of Denbigh Castle in January 1648. In July 1648 he quashed a royalist plot to rescue Owen. Later, his staunch support of the Commonwealth was reinforced by acquisitions of confiscated royalist property, and he represented Anglesey in all three of Oliver Cromwell's Protectorate Parliaments. As a member of Denbigh corporation he led the reform of its charities and proposed a 'manufactory' for the employment of the poor.

Meanwhile in Denbighshire, Wrexham was becoming a centre of radical religious enthusiasm. The English Independents saw it as their mission to plant the gospel in 'the dark corners of the land', especially in Wales. Cromwell himself (despite his Welsh ancestry) considered the population of Wales 'a seduced and ignorant people'. Parliament's practical objective in the late 1640s was to license itinerant preachers; their long-term aim of settling preaching ministers with funds acquired from purchasing lay-owned tithes was formalised in 1650 in the Commission for the Propagation of the Gospel in Wales. Though puritanism in Wales is often regarded as an alien import, its leaders were Welsh-speaking preachers whose radicalism was given free rein following Pride's Purge.

One such leader was Morgan Llwyd, minister to a gathered congregation in Wrexham from 1647, who had spent time in England and had preached to parliamentarian forces. In 1644 he joined Sir Thomas Myddelton's army in north Wales, which included Twisleton's and Mytton's regiments. By 1648 he was moving towards millenarianism, believing that events in the British Isles would lead to the thousand-year rule of god's saints on earth. There is perhaps a hint of this in the petition's reference to 'the many thousands of Israel', the present-day saints in Britain. This petition reminds us that radical minorities could have a significant presence even in regions where the traditional elite, and probably most of the common people, were conservative and royalist at heart. Their petitions conveyed the message that those who made the revolution in London were not without effective supporters in regions far from the capital.

Related sources

J. R. Phillips, *Memoirs of the Civil War in Wales*.
A. H. Dodd, *Studies in Stuart Wales* (2nd edn., Cardiff, 1971).
W. S. K. Thomas, *Stuart Wales* (Llandysul, 1988).
ODNB: Stephen K. Roberts, 'Llwyd, Morgan (1619-1659)'.

Roland G. Thorne, 'Twisleton, George (1618-67)', revised by Patrick J. S. Little (unpublished, courtesy of History of Parliament).

Christopher Hill, 'Puritans and "the dark corners of the land"', in Christopher Hill, *Change and Continuity in Seventeenth-Century England* (London and New Haven CT, 1974).

42: OXFORDSHIRE COUNTY TROOP
before 9 January 1649

Context

Despite the very general terms in which it is expressed, the date of publication of this petition suggests informed support for the army's most recent intervention. The king was brought into strict captivity at Windsor on 23 December, and the purged Parliament moved towards setting up a High Court of Justice in early January. The petitioners urge the execution of justice 'without partiality', but refrain from singling out the king or any other individual; while they see the overall purpose of the army's intervention as the removal of tyranny and oppression. The image used here and in other petitions, of justice and righteousness running down like a stream, is from the Old Testament (Amos, 5:24)

Text

The Moderate, No.26, 2-9 January 1648/9. BL/EEBO E.537[26]

To the Right Honourable, and our most Excellent General, Thomas, Lord Fairfax, Lord Generall of all the Forces in England and Wales.

The humble Petition and Representation of the Officers and Souldiers under the Command of Capt. Henry Smith, in the County of Oxon.

Humbly sheweth, How sensible we are of the manifold and glorious appearances of God in and with your Excellency and the Army under your Command, not only in the first and second transactions thereof, in the many engagements and successes against the visible enemies of ours, and the Kingdoms peace and freedom (which fills our spirits with admiration) but also in those late manifestations of his divine glory, in drawing you up to act in that which is so honourable in the eyes of God and his people, viz. the execution of justice without partiality, which speaks no lesse to us then Gods presence with you, his wisdom in you, his power for you, to fulfill the councell of his own will; from these our apprehensions we are drawn out (as Subjects and fellow-Commoners of England) to declare our approbation of, and full assent unto the late large Remonstrance and Declarations thereupon, from your Excellency and generall Councell, presented to the Honourable House of Commons, together with the Agreement and grounds for future settlement, tendred to the consideration of the Kingdom, being assured in our selves (upon a serious view of all the particulars therein) of the justice, reasonablenesse and excellency thereof, in order to the establishment of the peace of the Kingdom, upon such a sure foundation as shall not easily be shaken.

May it therefore please your Excellency to put forth all the power the Lord hath conferred upon you, and all the wisdom he hath placed in you, for the speedy prosecution of all those things declared by you, and the execution of justice upon all those enemies to yours and the kingdoms peace, without respect of persons, that justice being executed in our land, righteousness may run down all our streets, Tyranny and oppression (of what kinde so ever) being removed, the voyce of joy and gladness may be heard in all our Cities; in the prosecution of all which we (though but a handfull of men) do unanimously declare our readinesse (according to the actings of God in us, and your Excellencies command) to stand or fall with you, not accounting our lives deare unto us, so that life, liberty and freedome may be administred to this long inslaved, and late dying kingdome; and we desiring to approve our selves your Excellencies servants in the work of the Lord towards this Kingdome, shall ever pray, &c.

Background

The Oxfordshire county troop commanded by Captain Henry Smith (or Smyth) was attacked in a royalist newsbook of October 1648 as a 'bastard kind of militia', raised without Parliament's knowledge or approval. The official record tells a different story. After Parliament's disbandment of many provincial forces and garrisons in early 1648, the outbreak of royalist risings and news of the army being raised by the Scots required the urgent recruitment of additional forces. Many Presbyterians saw this as an Independent plot to establish a military balance in their own favour (see 29 above). Though reluctant to face the unpopularity incurred by raising additional taxation, both Houses of Parliament agreed to recognise retrospectively the new forces raised on Fairfax's authority, including those of Northumberland, Lancashire and Kent discussed above (26, 38 and 40). Notoriously, the force raised by Henry Marten at his own expense in Berkshire and Oxfordshire was not accepted by Parliament, which repeatedly ordered its disbandment. Not all additional forces were so autonomous or radicalised, though volunteers may indeed have been driven by anger that Charles I had reignited civil war. Enemies were inclined to lump them all together, and perhaps the proximity of the Oxfordshire troop to Marten's catchment area made the accusation more credible.

Mercurius Pragmaticus's correspondent also alleged that the Oxford garrison had 'dealt unmercifully with the poorer sort' in collecting extra taxes to support it. 'It is conceived by many very intelligent men,' it added, 'that this is done without the privity and consent of the Houses of Parliament, only to feed the insatiable Cormorants of our Committee.' In reality, the Derby House committee wrote approvingly to the Oxfordshire county committee on 11 August about Captain Smith's troop, which was raised by commission from Lord Saye and Sele, Parliament's Lord Lieutenant. During the first civil war Saye had been unable to exercise the office in royalist-occupied Oxfordshire, but his office was now functioning. Derby House also ordered 'that money may be levied for its maintenance under the Ordinance for the payment of garrisons appointed by the Parliament', authorising the county committee to raise further forces if the garrison of Oxford itself was insufficient for the city's defence. The conduct of the soldiers at Oxford may have been harsh, but a militia could have no more legitimate birth than the Lord Lieutenant's commission.

It is not clear where the religious language of the petition was coming from. Opposition to royalism and its religious culture among the townspeople of Oxford should not be discounted, for their experience during the presence of the king's court was not a happy one (see 2 above), and the long-standing cross-currents of local politics broke forth again after the retaking of the town by Parliament in 1646. However, Banbury was an Oxfordshire town with a more visible puritan presence and closer ties to Lord Saye, the most prominent Independent politician in the House of Lords.

Related sources

Mercurius Pragmaticus, No. 27, 26 September – 3 October 1648. BL/EEBO E.465[9].
Calendar of State Papers, Domestic, 1648-1649 (11 August 1648).
Sarah Barber, '"A bastard kind of militia", localism and tactics in the second civil war', in Ian Gentles, John Morrill and Blair Worden (eds.), *Soldiers, Writers and Statesmen in the English Revolution* (Cambridge, 1998).
David Eddershaw with Eleanor Roberts, *The Civil War in Oxfordshire* (Stroud, 1995).

43: PORTSMOUTH, ISLE OF WIGHT AND HURST CASTLE GARRISONS

9 January 1649

Context

Though geographically and militarily situated at the heart of the most crucial recent developments, these petitioners still entertained the possibility that 'the grand disturbers of this Nations peace' might be cleared of the accusations brought against them. Though the process of setting up the king's trial was now well under way, he is not named; nor is the outcome of his trial pre-empted, since guilt and innocence must be established by the principles of law and justice. Reasonableness and justice, not blood guilt or god's vengeance, are the comparatively moderate keynotes of this address. The petitioners share with many others the belief that god has been and still is with the army, and they give the London Levellers' 11 September petition and those of 'divers counties' equal approval with the army's *Remonstrance*.

Text

A Perfect Diurnall, No. 287, 8-15 January 1648/9. BL/EEBO E.527[6]

To his Excellency Thomas Lord Fairfax, Generall of all the Land-forces raised by the Parliament, and continued for the defence of the just rights and freedoms of this Nation, and to his generall Councell.

The humble Petition of the Officers and Souldiers, together with divers of the welaffected Inhabitants in the Isle of Wight, Portsmouth, and Hurst.

Sheweth, That our equall sensiblenesse (with our fellow Souldiers and Countrimen of the overflowing miseries, and insupportable grievances by the War brought, and subject to be continued upon the people by common enemies, and apostates, also our sad apprehensions of the late dismall and delucive treaty, with a dangerous, pollitical, and Conquered Enemy, and our earnest love to Righteousness Peace and Union upon just principalls, doth invite us to declare our sincere affection to, and approbation of the just and reasonable desires mentioned in the large Petition of the 11. of September last; with the Petitions of divers Counties, and that seasonable Remonstrance of your Excellency and Councel in conjunction with the said large petition; and calling to mind the manifold blessed dispensations of God to this Nation, by the continued successes given to the unwearied labours of your Excellency, and the Army under your command, against the enemies of our peace in the first and second war; Together with the present inforced and necessary undertakings, (in behalf of all the faithful and cordeal people of this Nation; which hath freely adventured their lives, and all that was dear to them, in that common cause of publique good) encourageth us to believe; that the same God which hath blessed you in the former, will also crown these your honourable endeavours with happy success in the latter.

Wherefore we humbly desire, that your Excellency and Councell will still manifest your constant and sincere affections (in pursuance of Justice) to a righteous settlement, and (by vigorous and speedy actings) not leave place for your selves to be diverted from those your declared Resolutions, but singly and impartially to proceed, that to [*sic*] the grand disturbers of this Nations peace, may either be cleared of those great and heinous crimes publiquely declared, and laid to their charge, or else condemned according to principles of Law and Justice; And that such only for future, may be implyed in any places of office and trust in the Common-Wealth, as are of known fidelity to the publique interest, that the heavy burthens of the wearied people may, (with all convenient speed) be removed; and that (after great expence of blood and treasure) the Nation may enjoy that long desired issue of a firm and lasting peace; for the speedy accomplishment whereof, we do, and shall, in the strength of God, with all readinesse and chearfulnesse, engage our lives, and all that is dear unto us, with your Excellency; and all others, who shall joyn with you herein being willing to cast our whole mite into that common treasury for the obtaining of so reasonable and just ends aforementioned.

And your Petitioners shall ever pray, &c.

Subscribed by above 1600 persons, and presented to his Excellency by Lieut. Cuppage, Lieut. Ward, Ensign Fox, Marshal Templer, and Mr. Darneford, Mr. Ginner of Portsmouth.

Another edition

A Proclamation Of His Excellency: Tho. L. Fairfax, L. Gen. ... With a Petition of the Officers and Souldiers, together with the wel-affected Inhabitants in the Isle of Wight, Portsmouth, and Hurst, presented to his Excellency. Printed for Thomas Turner. BL/EEBO: E.537[36].

Background

Throughout the civil wars Parliament had been intensely concerned for its defences in this area, especially after the revolt of its ships in the Downs (see 39 above). Rumours of a royalist force gathering locally raised fears that Charles might yet escape the Isle of Wight into welcoming English arms, rather than exile abroad. Portsmouth was a naval base of prime importance, vulnerable to attack because of its situation on an island separated from the mainland by narrow channels. The Isle of Wight was of course a prime target, and on 1 June 1648 the Derby House committee asked the Commons for two or three thousand pounds to improve its security. Three weeks later the committee ordered part of the Portsmouth garrison to reinforce Hammond's troops on the island, and 500 men to be raised to replace them. When the treaty negotiations began at Newport the king was released from strict captivity in Carisbrooke Castle on parole, and Colonel Isaac Ewer took over the Portsmouth garrison.

Under its previous colonel, Robert Hammond, Ewer's regiment had been one of the most active in the New Model Army's 1647 revolt; and when Hammond moved to the Isle of Wight as governor in August that year he took with him one company, under Captain Edmund Rolph. A year after the king's unexpected arrival on the island that November, Hammond was still worrying over his unwanted role as Charles's jailer. In the last days of November 1648, when the Council of Officers at Windsor decided to take the king into custody to prevent him leaving for London before his parole was over, they sent Ewer to secure Hammond's co-operation or, if he refused it, remove him from the island.

The main story has often been told. Hammond prevaricated over his dual allegiance to parliamentary employers and a military commander, Ewer took him into custody, and the two set off for Windsor. While Hammond left Edmund (now Major) Rolph and two other officers in charge, Ewer entrusted the further management of the business to his own major, Robert Saunders. Saunders reported from Portsmouth next day that Captain George Joyce had also been on the island, 'privately to agitate businesse with the Governour and other friends,' hoping 'that if possible itt may nott bee knowne hee was there, to take off the scandal of an agitating businesse.' After the parliamentary negotiators left Newport on 27 November, Lieutenant-Colonel Ralph Cobbett of Barkstead's regiment, attended by some of Ewer's men, removed the king to Hurst Castle with the agreement of Rolph and acquiescence of his fellow deputies. Hurst was a Tudor fortress isolated from the mainland by a natural shingle causeway, and the army council ordered the garrison to obey Ewer's officers in the absence of their own commander, Colonel Ayres. According to Sir Thomas Herbert, one of the three attendants the king was allowed, they were joined there by Colonel John Reynolds, whose regiment was quartered in the area (see 34 above). During the king's three weeks at Hurst Castle, he reportedly enjoyed walking and talking with Reynolds.

Throughout this operation, the tasks committed to Ewer's troops in particular could hardly have been entrusted to men who were less than totally politically reliable. Their declared support for the 11 September petition suggests that Leveller influence, present earlier in both Ewer's and Reynolds's regiments, was significant. This petition also claims the support of the 'well affected' in the area, with a total of over 1600 subscribers. The figure cannot be confirmed but is not inherently incredible.

The three army officers presenting the petition to Fairfax were accompanied by two citizens of Portsmouth, whose inhabitants had joined forces with the pro-parliamentarian gentry of Hampshire to take the town from the royalist governor Goring at the start of the civil war. On 6 January 1648 a petition from the port complained to Fairfax about the cost of maintaining the garrison, but also admitted that with the current decay of trade in the town, their livelihood was dependent on its continuance. They hoped it would remain 'what ever becomes of other', and requested on behalf of the soldiers 'as well as our insolvent selves' that additional pay be sent to the troops to avoid free quarter.

Related sources

Clarke Papers, vol. 2, pp. 54-61.
Calendar of State Papers Domestic, 1648-1649, pp. 90-1, 142-4.
Firth & Davies, *Regimental History*, vol. 1, pp. 346-59.
[T. Birch, ed.], *Letters between Colonel Robert Hammond, Governor of the Isle of Wight, and the Committee of Lords and commons at Derby House, General Fairfax, Lieut. General Cromwell, Commissary General Ireton, &c* (London, 1764).
Sir Thomas Herbert, *Memoirs of the Last Years of the Reign of King Charles I* (London, 1813 edn).
Petition from Portsmouth to Fairfax, BL Additional Ms. 18979. fo. 262.
ODNB: Andrew J. Hopper, 'Ewer, Isaac (d. 1650/51)'.
Jack D. Jones, *The Royal Prisoner, Charles I at Carisbrooke* (Guildford and London, 1965).

44: GARRISON OF HULL

9 January 1649

Context

The covering letter from Colonel Robert Overton to Fairfax published with this text is dated 9 January 1648/9. In it, Overton updates the content by welcoming the army's recent moves 'towards the discharge of that great ingagement which lyes upon us all for the settlement of the Affaires of our Nation'. The petition was not printed until early March, however, along with a later one to Parliament from the officers of Fairfax's regiment. The imprint, like that on 39 and 40 above, is that of John Playford (better known as a music publisher), one of several publishers paid by the army for work around this time.

The learned style, including many Latin quotations, leaves little doubt that it was written by Robert Overton himself. Sir James Turner, his Scottish prisoner at Hull, thought him 'a schollar, bot a little pedantic', as well as 'the most Courteous Independent that ever I met with'. The accompanying letter from his officers, however, assures him of their loyalty and proclaims a common outlook. 'You owe not more to us then to your own virtue,' they write, 'that we make bold to request your acceptance of our compliance with your Remonstrance', and go on to defend their intervention in politics with a memorable image: 'we cannot imitate those unworthy Champions who hoped their fish would swim safe when the Republike sank.'

Text

The Declaration of the Officers of The Garrison of Hull: In order to the Peace and Settlement of the KINGDOME. Presented to his Excellency the Lord Generall, and the Generall Councell ... London, Printed for John Playford, 1 March 1649. BL/EEBO E545[17]

We doubt not but the unsatisfied party of this abused Kingdome will wonder that we still renew our reiterated Declarations, as if we intended to turne State Reformers in their stead who have therewith hitherto been intrusted. It is true, we never expected to be put upon such imployments; nor find we any felicity therein: but having by all means submissively shewed our conformity to the old rule of *Cuncta prius tentanda* [there's a first time for everything] *&c.* yet instead of redresse, finding nothing but delay, we are constrained to search into the ground of this ingratitude, and to expose or display it to the view of the world.

Herein we conceive our selves sufficiently authorized by the practice of the best State, and the precept of the best of Oratours [Cicero], who in his Oration against *Verres*, hath taught us, that in *publice crimine quilibet non debet non esse accusator* [no one is barred from being the accuser in the case of a public crime], and where such practices shall appear inconsistent with the welfare of a Nation, opportunity to check them and provide for a remedy.

Nor can we any waies doubt of a success sutable to the rest of our undertakings, being assured, that our prosperous Armies were never supported by a better Cause; and therefore that you no longer be held in suspence, what it is that we (as well as others) declare against, or do desire, be pleased in the first place seriously to consider your condition before these Warrs; secondly, the reason of our ingaging in them; thirdly, The promises of our Publique Trustees in case our successes enabled them to a performance; and lastly we having rendred them such as they desire to be, how well they have acquitted themselves of their promises and trust.

In severall Declarations, especially that of December, 1640. they have represented to us the state of this Kingdome, groaning under the arbitrary pressures of an unlimited Soveraignty by Ship-moneys, Monopolies, innovations of Prelates in Church-Discipline, interruptions of Parliamentary proceedings by the Regall dissolving Vote, with other illegal Taxes and tyrannies, which we only point at in this place.

For these no cure was held out so catholique as a Parliament, though even Generall Councells have foully erred in matters of Faith, and that of the highest nature, yet we hoped better things from our Nationall Convention, insomuch that never any people so thirsted for a free Parliament as we; never any people so assisted a Parliament in theirs and the publike necessity. Have we not rendred their Councells successful, and (through Gods assistance) inabled them to restore us to all those benefits of safety in person, propriety in goods, and purity in profession, which they so frequently declared to assert?

And though we are not ignorant how remote our condition is from those ends, or how little our pressures are abated, yet can they not deny but that we have discharged our parts in the field; which if gainsaid, Pulpits and printed Gratulations would convince them: Had they in their sedentary devoirs been so successful in the service of the State, by whose authority they act, our pressures had by this time been abated, reformation setled, debts payed, *Ireland* relieved, and the streame of publike disbursements reduced to its proper and ancient channell.

But on the contrary, to our great grief we see, our distractions grow greater, and our wounds wider, by the unrestrained appetites of self-seeking parties both in Church and State, as if the enemy of mankind did despaire to accomplish his designes against Christianity by the Roman Jesuite, without a Protestant Priest and pestilentiall Politician; the little fingers of whose insolence and avarice are grown heavier then the Loynes of Soveraignty or Episcopacy. For, besides what our State-mongers have perverted to private ends, some of the Long Robe, who have preached against Pluralities, have annual salaries amounting almost to 1000. l. *per annum*. If we inquire what their imployments are to answer such in-comes, we shall finde amongst many little besides the preaching of themselves and their owne authority over their fleeced flocks: yet whatsoever some of them decree in the Church, or the Parliament in the State; must (as if infallible) be received with an implicite obedience, no dispute, no Petition, no Remonstrance, unlesse it speak the sence of a prevailing party in the Parliament, and be ushered in by a totall resignation of our selves, can be accepted.

To this tamenesse we have suffered our selves to be brought, and might so perhaps have continued, had not the late actings of our Trustees sufficiently informed us, that warr cannot be too much suspected which is obtruded on termes not to be looked into. And therefore if the attempts of such lawlesse usurpers run so high whilest we have a faithfull Army on foot, what will they do when we are disbanded, and they backt with an indisputable power! If they once dare to declare us enemies for but intending to Petition for due pay and deserved indempnity, how boundlesse would they be (if under private and popular Notions) they could without controul pursue their own interests and appetites!

Is not therefore the present actings of our Officers and Army proper to settle Peace, as to disappoint the pursuances and plots of private spirits? would it not better become us to die with our swords in our hands, then (after we have vindicated the publique Liberty against the power and pride of Princes) to succumb under the servitude of our fellow-subjects, how great soever? for which of our good deeds do we deserve to be destroyed? are they angry because we are about to expedite the peoples Peace and preservation? are we not therefore properly provoked to snatch the wreath from off their brows, which (by the mercies of the Almighty) our late conquering swords have crowned them with? is this the requitall and income of all our difficulties undergone, perills past, lives lost? Is this the fruit of our victory acquired? have we for this so frequently removed their foes and feares, secured their safety, or rendred them capable of the full execution of due, but deferred Justice? Was it not for this cause we covenanted, hazarding our lives ao [*sic*] preserve our Liberties? yet after all must we sit still to see oppressions unsuppresst, Justcie [*sic*] perverted, grievances augmented, and Tyranny Re-inthroned?

In this so sad a condition may we not with *Adrian* the Emperour cry out, *Multitudo Medicorum me perdidit?* [the crowd of doctors has destroyed me] may it not properly be applyed to the late prevailing party in our present Parliament, whose apparent declinations from their honoured undertakings (whether we eye their private Interests, or unparliamentary proceedings) looke with so foule a face upon us, as we may justly question, whether there be not as great a necessity of transferring that Trust from its abusers, as erst to make use of their undertakings? Nay, we may boldly assert their carryings on for pretended preservations, have been so costly to us, and so commodious to themselves, that there is no capacity so weak, but too aptly apprehends it for a truth, that it is better to be stung with one Hornet, then a whole nest; better one Pope, or one Tyrant then a multitude; may never so malignant a Genius possesse a Parliament as to render our endeavours to regaine true liberty uselesse.

Yet how is the State of England altered, and from the pity of its enemies become the envy of her false and feigned friends, for whom our care and conscience gave us courage to ingage; our courage begot their present power, their power our servitude and calamity. A strange kind of requitall some will say, that those heads should cut off the hands, by which they have climbed to that dazelling greatnesse, from whence they but giddily discern either themselves or us, whom they still strive to thrust even with the hazzard of the Nation and their owne ruine, beneath the honour of our Armes into a condition of servitude, beggery and basenesse; witnesse the contemptible price of blood paid to some, whilest other impoverished Petitioners are constrained to stand perpetuall Centinells to want and wrong, whilest some of their own indeered darlings lie stowed in plenty and secure reposes, being in as deep Arrears for service to be done, as other for pay that's due.

Certainly, the free and faithfull Commoners of England did not intrust them thus to act their own ends, or to accumalate and divide such vast proportions of treasure amongst themselves and Sycophants, whilest worthier Members, and more publike spirited persons are famished and defrauded: this is so cleare a truth, that he that runs may read. Have we any thing desirable here more then the care of our consciences, the freedome of our persons, community of friends, and propriety of goods? In all which should we declare how much both our Countrey and we have suffered in a patient expectance of a happy issue, we should adde to our calamities one vexation more then ever our Trustees intended us; for had they believed that any durst have been so bold as to arraigne their actions, we may charitably think they would have been more wary in disobliging those for whom they are and ought to act.

For those last six yeares, what hath been the constant cry of the prime Potentiaries in our great Councell, but the Liberty of the Subject, and the Priviledge of Parliament; the former whereof we now see is almost swallowed up of the latter, witnesse the Goale-books of Newgate, the Tower, the Gatehouse, and other places of Purgatory, where publike spirited persons lie impoverished and imprisoned in a hopelesse and helplesse condition, languishing after a legall tryall: Be assured all ye native noble English, that the same contrivance which provides mannacles for their hands, would in time see that no fetter would be wanting for your feet.

But must the Medium whereby we are conveyed into this pretended blessednesse, and by which so many millions have been screwed forth of seduced purses, be no other than that old and ancient Qualepipe [quail pipe], publike necessity; Oh invincible argument! endlesse necessity, which perhaps our abusers did never resolve to have done withall whilest we had either juice to squeeze, or tamenesse to suffer it: Is any Art either ancient or moderne omitted to exhaust the treasure of these times? witnesse the reported dividend of some hundred thousand pounds amongst some select Members, to recruit not so much perhaps their pretended losses, as their crack'd estates, whilest the publike debts of the Kingdome with our dearly earned Arrears, are throwne in amongst things most fit to be forgotten.

Surely strangers might think the Parliamentary Revenues were at a low ebbe, when they are seen, and seem compelled to shuffle off their friends and the peoples supporters; but were some of the Receipts accounted for, it would happily strike amazement into all that have but sleightly considered it; for setting aside all the rooking Committees both in City and Countrey, whose names and natures might almost call the profession of Christianity it selfe in question, do but consider the vast Contributions of Associated and reduced Counties, Deanes and Chapter Lands, Pole-moneys, Sequestrations, old and new loanes on Publike Faith, Seizures on the whole Revenue of the Crowne and Miter, fifty Subsidies at once, fifth and twentieth part, Adventures, free gifts, Taxes for British moneyes for almost ruinated, and (if some say true) cheated Ireland, besides the vast accumulations of treasure by Compositions and Pardons, there being, as we are informed, at the end of the first Warre above 8000. Compounders, whose Compositions if computed but at 200.l. a man one with another, which in the generall is much undervalued, and their pardons at 36.l. a piece, the totall when levied, which undoubtedly was long since done, according to the exactest Computation, would almost amount to eighteen Millions, to which the Customes and Excize throughout the Kingdome addes many thousands more weekly: And yet some of our Stewards have been pleased to put on such a vizard of poverty, that two hundred thousand pounds could not be paid to our Brethren the Scots, without the sale of Bishops Lands; thus a new device and tax must alwaies do the work in hand, still to secure and increase the sacred heap; a bank doubtlesse were it brought together into one bulke, which some of them have courteously carved to one another, would vie with the treasure of all the Jews in Spain or Italy.

Can we then believe that these our friendly Feoffees after the contraction of so much guilt would ever patiently return to their private fortunes? or give up their accompts to their fellow-Commoners of England, whose Stewards they are, and erst had the modesty to acknowledge, that the power was ours by which they acted? which if true, as undoubtedly it is, then we are certaine that the last appeale and resolution must be to and from us. Notwithstanding this they would become our great Lords, some of them having besides the corrupt acquiring of their Burgesseships, sate so long as to bring in their children to sit at the Sterne of State, meaning no doubt to transmit this new principality from Generation to Generation. But have we in the interim any assurance of either Law or Liberty, save what proceeds from their arbitrary breathings? What did any Nation undergo by a forraigne conquest, which hath not in this last eight yeares been practised upon this?

Tacitus the wisest of the Romane historians sets forth, that the times were so base and bad under *Nero* and *Domitian*, that none durst complain of them, the people being grown so tame with sufferance, that they had almost lost their memories. But it may be objected, there was never any Government which pleased all, or hath not upon tryall and experience had it inconveniences. The severall States of Sparta, Athens and Rome it self, thought they had well provided against the Tyranny of their Princes by their *Ephori, Decemviri, &c.* yet these found such a venery in exercising their severall powers on those that gave them, as in fine a new publique necessity was discovered which way to put those down, who had deserved no better whilest they were up.

We might draw the Parallel nearer to our times, should we examine whether some of our Representators have not transcended in their tyrannies, whatsoever hath been acted by those fore-mentioned names of infamy: or secondly whether the injured Freemen of England may not justly reassume their misimployed power, and call the Authors to account for acting contrary to common trust, safety, and satisfaction: but it will be more beneficiall to pitch upon expedients for Peace and Freedome, or for the future to secure our selves against all arbitrary Powers, whether Regall or Parliamentary.

But by the way, peradventure some may object and say, suppose this ill compacted body of Parliamentary power, be by the present moving of the Army either extinguished or reduced to a better temper, and that the disposall of the Supreme Power suffer under the Sword, what assurance is there that the souldier will not misimploy the power which we have intrusted with those whom you are about to take it from?

This is *Argumentum ad hominem* [an argument directed at persons rather than principles], and seeing that the intentions of men cannot be looked into, our best conjecturall light must arise from precedent actions, and in this particular we dare stand the attest of our most crying adversaries; we neither have nor desire better witnesses touching our deportment, then your selves, we wanted neither presidents [precedents] nor opportunities to have inriched our selves by secret fraud or open violence ever after our Army appeared so considerable at Naseby; what might we not have done when we marched from New-market through London, or what can hinder us now that we are in it from making our selves Masters of that whereby others become both wretched and miserable? but we trust, that power which hath hitherto given us so many testimonies of Mercy, will to the end accompany us in all our deportments, which if compared with the tyrannical fleecings of severall Trustees or their substituted Committees, we doubt not but reason will promp you rather to embrace a protection from those for the present, whose civilties have oredone expectations, then longer to lye under their insultings which have hitherto so foully falsified.

Besides, if we had been so base as to chaffer [haggle] for your Freedome, temptations to take us off have not been wanting, even by some of those who have formerly been so fierce against us; we speak not this to kindle a fire-brand to tye *Sampson's* foxes together by the tailes; but rather to stirre you up to take notice in time what danger you are in to be undone: let Westminster witness it by the many red eyes and wet handkerchiefs of poor Widdowes waiting for the wages of their deceased husbands, beside half-starved Officers attending the Returnes to their Petitions, with charges great as the success is little, whilest kindred and creatures have their suggested services rewarded, and their pretended losses plentifully repay'd; the account whereof is frequently cast up false by kindred, airy Courtiers, and oyly mouths, and formall flatterers; yet in the mean time those of more weighty and substantiall worth have neither Oratours nor Advocates to mention their merits, or to write Narratives of their neglected necessities.

Oh! whether is *Astrea* [goddess of innocence] fled? what is become of Common Justice, that most essentiall part of Magistracy! have our politique Bodies lost all the life-bloud of Love? can these Philistines put forth *Sampson's* eyes, and not expect that a free people inraged by the losse of their dear purchased Liberties should pull down the Pillars of their abused power? When Magistracy degenerates into Tyranny, are we not disobliged from our obedience, and put upon the freedome of naturall endeavours for preservation? Surely the Sword of Justice was not committed to their keeping to cut our throats: He is highly ignorant and blind, who thinks humane obedience binds us to sleight a publique preservation. In this respect a free people never want [lack] a full power. Tyranny is Tyranny in whomsoever, and wheresoever resistable. Nature in the inferiour creatures fortifies her self defensively, and hath her nobler peece of wonder a lesse priviledge?

Their own Declarations have taught us, that all power is intrusive and conditionall on our part; therefore King *James* (though he had as great an itch of Monarchy upon him as other men) proclaimed in open Parliament, that, *Nihil aliud potest Rex quam quod Iure potest* [a king can do nothing else but what he can do by law], And *Bracton de Corona* tells us, *Quando Rex non per Legem regit, non amplius Rex est, sed Tyrannus* [when a king does not rule by law, he is no more a king, but a tyrant]. The best of Princes ever kept their bounds, acting to Gods greatest glory, knowing the Soveraigne power to be the Peoples, from whence they derive their Principalities, next that great Law-giver, who assures us, that the service due from man to man is not coercive, or distinguished from equall nature, save for safety sake. It is but the overflowings of Fancy, or an Optique mistake that lets loose the reines to the sence of a lawlesse Soveraignty, provoking Princes to think themselves greater than their Maker ever meant. Surely Parliaments cease to be Parliaments, when they cease to be just Powers; as Kings cease to be Kings, when by overstretching the reines of Government, they forget to be good and just: therefore Justice defines Magistracy, as lawlessnesse doth tyranny and arbitrary usurpation.

How much then are we concerned to oppose all illegal proceedings? how much more as Souldiers obliged, who have been more desperately ingaged, and (for ought we yet find) so dangerously deluded, in being made the unhappy instruments of advancing private interests with publike spirits. Seeing therefore we have hitherto been perverted, as to promote their private projects, who care not if we die like dogs, so they might live like Princes, who give us cause to despaire of any good ever to proceed from them. And in as much as none can merit the title of true Patriot, who indeavour not to deliver their countrey from all her calamities; we do therefore see how necessary it is we be not longer blinded in our obedience, or shackled by our Fellow-subjects, in subordination to their lawlesse lusts, who in the nature of their imployments are the Kingdoms Servants to mannage its Interest, not their own, further then conjoyned with ours, which they have hitherto too much contemned or trampled upon.

Since therefore to their Papall predominance, they would have added a Popish infallibility, whose Decrees admit no dispute or rejection, but resolved to remain the everlasting Land-Marks of our dread, in reference to their own indemerits and our blind obedience. It will behove us now at last to pray Almighty God to restore us to our wits, for if he make us wise (through his goodness and mercy) we may make our selves happy.

Now that the world may know we strike only at the persons of offendors, not at the Parliament, but the corrupted party in it; we do therefore in the presence of Almighty God (whose presence we expect, according to the sincerity of our souls) publish and declare to the whole Kingdom, That upon serious thoughts and due examination, we have found and do believe a prevailing party in the Parliament to be the propagators of many miseries and calamities which now sit heavy on this Kingdum [sic], and that their long continuance in this usurped Soveraignty is utterly inconsistent with all our safeties; not that we are ignorant of, or unwilling to acknowledge the special power of Parliaments, or that we believe all the Members to have deserved this so severe a censure, for we are confident of the contrary: Yet inasmuch as it is rather frequency of Parliaments then perpetuity, that must make us happy, the latter being too great a temptation to Tyranny; we with the rest of our fellow subjects and soldiers (who by the confession of our Trustees, have within our selves the supream and original power to provide for the Common Safety, when we find, as we now do, our trust abused and betrayed,) do therefore declare;

1. That, together with the King and his Capital Creatures, the evil Members of both Houses have justly forfeited their Power and Priviledg; and to the end therefore that others who shall succeed in the managements of this Trust, may know that they act not only in their own business, but ours; therefore that this Kingdom may at last acquire its banished peace and welfare, we do in the first place, with the rest of the Army, desire the speedy execution of due and distributive Justice to all and every Capital Offendor.
2. That all inferior Delinquents do submit to the present judicial Power.
3. That a speedy period be put to this present Parliament, and a new Election of faithful Members made.
4. That there be a succession of free and future Parliaments, with secure provisions for their meeting, sitting and ending; such neither electing, nor to be elected, as were in Arms or otherways pre-ingaged against us.

5. That so many of the old Members as have not crept in by corruption, (and against whom there shall not appear crimes sufficiently scandalous to make them incapable,) may be incouraged and continued, until the dissolution of this present Parliament.
6. That all elections may be according to due and equal distributions.
7. That by an universal and mutual Agreement, it be enacted and decreed, *in perpetuam rei memoriam* [for an everlasting remembrance] that the power of all future Representatives may be inferior only to that of the people, in order to the preservation of them in their just and proper Rights, and that the observation thereof be added to the oath administred to every Member upon his admission into the Parliament.
8. That henceforth the things of Common Right and Justice be left to the Laws well Regulated, and proper Officers being appointed for ordinary matters, a Council of State may more aptly apply themselves to those extraordinary administrations of Parliamentary Power.
9. That the publique Petitions of the people may be more seasonably considered, and speedily dispatched (as is forementioned in the large Remonstrance) it will be requisite to afford Liberty of entring dissents against such Representatives as appear either unfaithful or unpliant to the Trust of the People.
10. That all future Kings be hereafter elected by the Peoples Representatives upon conditional trust. or without claiming any negative voyce [veto] against, or beyond the power of *Parliaments*.
11. That the succeeding *Parliament* may remember the self-denying Ordinance, and speedily pursue an impartial account of the Kingdoms imbezelled treasure, which being discovered we doubt not but sufficient will be found to discharge the publique debts of the Kingdom, and speedily to make *Ireland* pay the price of that blood which it hath so inhumanly shed.
12. That the matters of general Settlement be proposed by the *Parliament*, and agreed unto with the subscriptions of the People, the like Award may be made, and in the same case required to be performed by all succeeding Kings, and other publique Officers of State or Trust.
13. That no future Convention of *Parliamentary Power* be above Biennial, or do henceforth presume to exempt their person from being liable to discharge their debts, or to satisfy their Creditors by this means. If hereafter we should be so unhappy as not to be acquainted with *Parliamentary Justice*, or if future *Parliaments* should prove like this, yet their domination being circumscribed within a limited time, they will (as it is well observed) be afraid to commit those insolencies, which will be avenged them at their return into a private condition.
14. And foreseeing the dis-joynedness of the times, and the opposition we stand in to *Ireland*, and other domestique and forraign enemies; it will be requisite that a standing Militia be continued in experienced and approved hands.

15. That in order to the removal of jealousies and fears, it is further desired by us, (as more conducing to a speedy and perfect Peace) that an Act of Oblivion may be past for inferior offendors, from the benefit whereof we only exclude those whose Crimes are Capital, of which number we put in the forefront the corrupt Members of this present *Parliament*, with their deputed Creatures and Committees, who either cannot or wil not give account of the publique treasure by them purloined; these in the first place we desire may be driven to Restitution, or to make their persons satisfie, if they shall not discover [reveal] upon their own oaths, or of any other whom they shall be required to bring in for the further discovery of their estates, in order to the intended satisfaction: though our professions do not qualifie us to new-mold a State, yet necessity having cast it upon our care, providence puts us to point at these genral conducements to so necessary a work, which we cast in as our mite with the more full and effectual Remonstrance of the Army.

16. That such of the Assembly as claim their Authority in the Assembly *Jure Divino*, may be speedily abrogated *Jure Humano*, unless they can make it appear they have not illegally intruded upon their place and power; And that we may hereafter (by all their great expence of time and treasure) be as much satisfied as themselves. Amongst some of whom the Church Revenues have been parcel'd forth into such large portions as might enable them to maintain the pride and luxury of Cardinals, whilest their forsaken and fleec'd Flocks are forced to attend the Alms of others, prehaps more precious for parts and piety, and yet but pensioners to their pride and pluralities, though exceeding them as far in grace as they do others in good livings: Such Lackwings are the Cankerworms of our souls, as corrupt Committees are the Horsleeches of our Estates; the one devours our goods, the other our good names: The *Tenents* of the one (in matter of Regall Supremacy) are inconsistent with the Laws of the Land, and the other, in point of traiterous practices, for profits sake, are perfectly principled against them.

17. Now, to the end we may live at unity amongst our selves, the stronger not insulting over, but bearing with the weaker, and both glorifying God by an unblameable conversation; there is another sort of publique persons that deserve to pass under as strict a Reformation as any we have yet had to do with, they are such as receive their name from the Law, which they make a nose of wax; these are the great and close suckers of our State, and such as have contributed so much to the honor of Christianity; that the pens of men of honor and quality have delivered to the world, that the grand Signior of *Constantinople* hath more Justice done his Subjects in one moneths time, then all the Christian Princes in seven years: These are the men for whom (if they may be suffered) our swords have cut out pleading work for generation to come And therefore since their abstruse sence in a barbarous Dialect, which they expound as they list, carries with it the monumental badg of our Normane servitude, and the profit the

Kingdom receives by it, no way countervails the mischief that is [*sic*] doth enact: It is our earnest desire, that all the Constitutions of this Kingdom, both penal and others be abreviated, and clad in the home-spun language of our native Nation, that every man might in some sort be able to understand and plead his own Cause.

18. That some strict course may be taken for preventing that horrid practice of Attorneys in putting men out of the protection of the Law, by outlawing, before notice be given them of the Suite, though never so causless: And that all such undue proceedings may make the Suite null, &c. that the Remedy be not worse then the Disease.

19. That to avoyd corruption of Lawyers and their adherents, and to take off mens mindes from litigious contentions, some Expedient of determination of differences may be provided, by the appointment of men of known integrity; and parties authorized in every Town or Hundred to decide ordinary Controversies, so that no man be admitted to commence a Suite (save in grand Causes) without their concession.

20. As also that both Judges and Pleaders may have their respective Salleries from the Publique, upon penalty of abjuring all bribes or underhand obligations Whereupon that example of *Cambices* may happily be renewed, and put into execution: We need not doubt then but every Tribunal in *England* will have something to hang over it, that shall better instruct its several Judges then all the letters of Princes or Potentates, or all the Dividends betwixt them and their purse-bearing Broakers at the end of the Term.

But in [the] case we are now in, what Justice can we expect from any civil Judicature, where the Members of *Parliament*, who should be Law-makers, descend for gain so far as to be Pleaders in each common Court? and seeing no Judge standeth but by their Vote, what dares any of them do in asserting the old known Laws, when upon every Appeal to the Parliament their *Pleaders* become their *Judges*? And how valiant such Justices have been in acquitting them selves where they feared their sitting besides their Cushions, their behavior in the case of Ship-mony sufficiently declare. The several abuses throughout the Kingdom for want of faithful Magistrates, and for lack of due execution of Justice and Judgment, doth not only distract the Army, but also very much discourage and disaffect our best friends; for hereby differences are undecided, because good and godly County-Commissioners are not chosen, nor according to our legal Customs and Constitutions impowered to impeach persons peccant, or to present the *Parliament* with the occasions of their County; Wherein, if Courts of Judicature were established throughout the several Hundreds, and Lawyers appointed to plead at a set allowance, Causes might be more justly and speedily determined, and all oppositions lessened or prevented.

We might in this sence enlarge our selves in several respects, wherein the condition of this Kingdom is so uncomfortable: But, though we take no pleasure to rake in the kennel of so much confusion, yet would we take the pains to clear and cleanse it, that at the last we may attain the true enjoyment of what we have purchased at so dear a price; that so the Authors of our Calamities may receive their wages according to that Justice which their Actions do make them fear. But we hope, by what hath been already said against others, that we have innocence in our hearts and hands towards the Peace of this Nation, for whose freedom we will both fight and pray. We intend not in any kinde to continue our Countries Misery, but to pursue its Peace and preservation, in prevention of those oppressions fit to be repealed, in regard of those great Engagements which are given by us all, rather to make good the happy issue of the old, then the beginnings of a new and wasteful War.

We have fought for Justice and Freedom, the inheritance left us from our forefathers, and it is now become our purchase and price of our blood, spilt in opposition of tyrannical attempts, wherein supremacy of power cannot legitimate scorn or cruelty. And though greatness may make injuries more great, *Power* too much improved sometimes provokes the *Peasant* to brave the *Prince*. Indeed it is easie for boundless ambition to aspire, but not ever to continue uppermost. Love and Justice are the lasting Conquerors, the truest Supporters of a State, without which the most transcendent Acts of Magistracy stand tottering, and do either by the wounds of separation bleed to death, or very rarely perpetuate a power to posterity. But if, by Gods blessing upon our loyal hearts and endeavors, this Kingdom shall receive its wonted *Peace* and Vigor in the condign punishment and suppression of all our opposers, and the Arch enemies of our common Safety; we shall no sooner see *Peace* and *Truth* established, the Liberty of our Consciences, according to the Word of God, in Doctrine and Discipline secured (for we abhor an universal *Toleration*:) but we shall be willing immediately to acquit the happy Management of our hitherto successful Arms, and betake us to such other employment as the great Creator shall call us to.

All we shall in the *interim* desire, is, That the great and wise God may be ever more glorified, for working the deliverance of his people by such poor despised persons; and that they my [*sic*] receive such fair acceptance and acknowledgment, for all their faithful performances, that no age hereafter (looking over their neglects) receive discouragement to sacrifice their lives in vindication of the publique Liberty.

By the Appointment of the Officers at a General Meeting. Signed. JO: HEMINGWAY.

HULL, *January 1648*.

Background

The difference in language and tone between this petition (also 58 below) and the earlier one from part of Overton's regiment, which remained in

Berwick (17 above) is remarkable. Overton himself had been in Hull since October 1647, when he was appointed deputy governor there at Oliver Cromwell's special request, and he held the post intermittently until 1660. Three companies were stated in 1658 to have served there for twelve years, and some officers were recruited from higher ranks in field regiments. Many of the garrison acquired local wives and families; while Overton himself, a native of Easington at the tip of the Humber estuary, described Hull as his preferred command, where he could enjoy 'the comforts of my relations and my country'.

Overton and the municipal corporation of Hull did not get along well, however. The corporation opposed his appointment, though some of the inhabitants supported him, but Fairfax's intervention helped to pacify the councillors who saw him as a dangerous radical. Supporting one of England's largest garrisons was a heavy burden on Hull's 6000 inhabitants, which in 1648 (a disastrous harvest year) was openly blamed for driving up food prices. From 1650 the garrison was involved in a conflict over the religious establishment in the town, and religious divisions intensified to the point at which Holy Trinity church was partitioned between rival ministers and congregations. Henry Reece concludes, however, that 'it was the corporation that lost all the battles that mattered'. The military had more influential allies in London, and the provision of religious choice for the people of Hull was a side effect. At the Restoration, Hull's historian Hugh Calvert says, the corporation 'had the consolation of blaming all their apparent disloyalty of the preceding years on the garrison.'

Robert Overton was no known relation of the Leveller Richard (who may have been born across the Humber in Lincolnshire) and was never directly associated with the Levellers. His regiment had been active in the army's resistance to Parliament in 1647, but remained loyal to Fairfax at Ware. A contemporary thought that Robert Overton's 'forward zeal to justice and right made the Levellers assume to own him', but he could nevertheless be trusted by the Independents. The suspicion of Leveller sympathies still hung around in 1655, when he denied the charge, but wrote to a friend, 'If a Leveller be one, who bears affection to anarchy, destroying propriety [property] or government, then I am none ... [but] for the settling of a well-grounded government, redress of grievances; civil, ecclesiastical or military, or inflicting condign punishment upon capital offenders, &c. if this be levelling, I was and am a Leveller.' In 1649, when some regiments refused to go to Ireland and William Thompson led a Leveller-inspired rising, the garrison of Hull issued their *Humble Remonstrance and Resolves* to disown the divisive opinions allegedly spread by 'secret and under-hand Actors for Atheism and Anarchy'.

Robert Overton's arguments for the sovereignty of the people are largely an academic version of Richard Overton's *Appeale from the Degenerate Representative Body* (1647). The two shared a view of the state as a human institution, whose nature is to be understood in a historical and philosophical rather than a biblical way, essentially no different from the ancient Greek city-state or Cicero's Roman republic. Neither of them rejected religion, and Robert Overton's biographer emphasises the fact that he was a deeply religious person. Their secular theory of popular sovereignty, however, was basically incompatible with the 'godly rule' exemplified in Thomas Collier's view that 'those who are saved spiritually know best what is good for the nations temporal wellbeing' (see 56 below). Though the Commons' declaration of their own sovereignty based their claim firmly on the principle that 'the people are, under god, the original of all just power', many of their supporters accepted the new regime as the best available embodiment of godly rule.

Related sources

The humble remonstrance and resolves of Col. Overtons regiment in his Excellencies garrison of Hull. Printed for Lodowick Lloyd, and Henry Cripps, 1649. BL/EEBO E.560[23].

Henry Reece, *The Army in Cromwellian England, 1649-1660* (Oxford, University Press, 2013).

Hugh Calvert, *A History of Kingston upon Hull from the Earliest Times to the Present Day* (London, Phillimore, 1987).

ODNB: Barbara Taft, 'Overton, Robert (1608/9–1678/9)'.

Barbara Taft, '"They that pursew perfaction on earth …" The Political Progress of Robert Overton,' in Ian Gentles, John Morrill and Blair Worden (eds.), *Soldiers, Writers and Statesmen of the English Revolution* (Cambridge University Press, 1998), pp. 286-303.

Sir James Turner, *Memoirs of his own Life and Times* (ed. Thomas Thomson, Edinburgh 1829), pp. 78-87.

45: FORCES BESIEGING PONTEFRACT

19 January 1649

Context

By the date of this petition, Robert Lilburne had left for London to take part in the king's trial, leaving his regiment behind at Pontefract along with Lambert's and Bright's. Lilburne attended the first session of the trial proceedings, though not every day that followed, and signed the king's death warrant. The present petition endorses the Commons' declaration of their own sovereignty, along with Pride's Purge and the purged House's readmission of all who would repudiate their vote for proceeding to settle with the king on 5 December.

Text

A Perfect Diurnall, No. 287, 22-29 January 1648/9. BL/EEBO E.527[12]

May it please your Excellency,

By understanding that the Commons in Parliament have lately voted the Supream power of the Kingdom to be in the People, and derivatively in them (their Representatives) for the making, repealing, and confirming all Laws; and by vertue of that power have appointed an High Court of Justice for Triall of the King; as also to bring to justice other the captiv'd enemies of our peace and freedomes, we begin to see some hopes of reaping the happy fruit of our hard labours, and long services, for the setling of this Nation in the enjoyment thereof; and are unable sufficiently to express our joyfull recentment of (the Kingdom being like to receive an inestimable benefit by) your late most necessary (wisely managed) action, in securing and secluding those Members of the House that carried on that Series of wicked, corrupt treacherous counsell, and designe (to betray the King[d]ome to perpetuall slavery, for their own ends) largely mentioned in your Remonstrance, Declaration and (more particularly) in your late humble Answer of the third of January instant, to the Parliaments demand of the reason of your secluding and securing the said Members; which (we hope) hath given them (as (we doubt not) all well affected unprejudiced people thereby will with us receive) full satisfaction thereunto; and that they will plainly perceive the good hand of God, leading you to, and acting you in that high and harmlesse service for the kingdom, as a manifest token of his presence, and that very way he had appointed to breake in pieces those strong destructive counsels, which doubtlesse would have soon involved the Kingdome in more Warre and trouble to its utter ruine.

Neither can we hide our great rejoycing, to see your prudence, care, and constancy in the kingdomes present necessary worke; nor our observation of that presence, power and wisdom of God, carrying you on therein; Which as we doubt not but the Parliament, and all the well affected (at least) will clearly see, and the whole kingdome (though (most) unworthy) enjoy the benefit thereof; so you also (upon your humble, carefull, and tender walking in your high and slippery places) will perceive a continuation of this Divine presence, not onely to the silencing and preventing of all your Enemies (who watch and labour for your falling) but even to the perfecting of the same, so as all the people shall acknowledge it is the worke of God alone.

Signed in the name of the Counsell of Officers at the Leaguer before Pontefract Castle.

Tho. Margets, Pontefract, 19 January 1648[1649].

Background

Of the three colonels currently at Pontefract, Lambert never declared for or against the king's trial, while his kinsman Bright was openly opposed to it; but Robert Lilburne's opportunity to play an active part in the trial is explained in letters from Thomas Margetts, judge advocate and secretary to Lambert's brigade (see 33 above). Although Lilburne's name appears on the list of 135 commissioners for the trial passed by the House of Commons on 6 January 1649, it seems that he had not been included in the original list of 150, which had to be revised when most of the peers and judges named refused to take part. Margetts appears to have seen this original list, writing on 6 January to Captain Adam Baynes, 'We finde in the list of the kings Jury there is no officer of our brigade mentioned for those of the Army, is it not a little disobligement?' The 'disobligement' was evidently rectified in time for Lilburne to be present on 20 January.

Robert shared neither the radical views of his brother John the Leveller, nor the apostasy of his brother Henry, betrayer of Tynemouth Castle to the royalists. Though the colonel had played a prominent part in the army's resistance to disbanding in the spring of 1647, he was far from his New Model regiment in November when they marched mutinously to Ware declaring their support for the *Agreement of the People*, having gone to Newcastle as governor three months earlier. He and his officers publicly dissociated themselves from the events at Ware, condemning the *Agreement of the People* as containing 'such things as are in themselves very disputable, whether just or unjust, and which is more then probable, may be more distructive to the Commonwealth if granted, then the refusall of them will be'. Nevertheless, they expressed support for ending the present Parliament and ensuring that 'the whole Kingdome may be prosperous in the enjoyment of a free Parliament, and every particular person of his owne proper Interest.' In Newcastle, Lilburne seems to have drawn closer to the opinions of his major, Paul Hobson (4, 10 and 23 above) and may have helped him to found the first Baptist congregation in the town. Sir Arthur Heselrige replaced Lilburne as governor at the end of 1647, and Hobson stayed on as his deputy while Lilburne campaigned successfully with his own horse regiment and others in the north during the second civil war (see 26 above) and spent the month of October 1648 in Scotland with Lambert.

Meanwhile at Pontefract, it is likely that Margetts was the moving spirit of this petition. The commitment of the judge advocate and his circle to regicide and revolution, well in advance of the actual events in London, is revealed by the correspondence of Adam Baynes, William Clarke and others. On 19 December an unidentified correspondent wrote to Clarke that the majority of the purged Parliament were now 'of our opinions, for the altering of Monarchicall government', preparing 'to loppe that Cedar or grubbe it out by the rootes; and in process of time to destroy every branche thereof ...' Margetts wrote to Clarke on 30 December worrying that the business of dealing with the king was going slowly: 'Tis true the greatness of it may plead for time, but I am sure tis best striking while the iron is hot ...' He hoped to see the army leaders act so vigorously that 'the men of the world ... may still stand amazed at the workings of god through you.' A week later he wrote to Baynes that the well-affected in the north rejoiced in the army's 'gallant proceedings against Charles Stuart', but urged greater speed, before other European monarchs could 'turne Justice aside least it might prove an ill president [precedent] to them in future'. An *Agreement of the People*, he added, required more time and thought than dealing with the king, because 'the one is as the pulling downe of an old house the other as the building of a new one'. Though the brigade's committee for public affairs had not met since Baynes left Pontefract (see 32 above), and most of the three regiments' officers were not currently present, Margetts promised to get the business dealt with as soon as possible.

This petition was perhaps facilitated by Lambert's absence from Pontefract, engaged in disbanding local forces. These included the regiments of Colonels Cholmeley and Rhodes, whose sense of seniority had explicitly motivated their resistance to Rainborowe's appointment (above, 16). They were now, by an irony of fate, being laid off by a superior commander still in his twenties, who in his brilliant career had commanded both 'mere' foot and cavalry regiments.

Related sources

Correspondence of Adam Baynes, BL Additional Manuscript no. 21417.
Correspondence of William Clarke, National Library of Scotland, Advocates' Manuscripts nos. 33.7.15 and 35.5.11.
A Perfect Diurnall, no. 226, 22-29 November 1647 (Robert Lilburne's declaration, reprinted in Rushworth, *Historical Collections*, vol. 7 (London, 1701), pp. 913-4).
ODNB: Barry Coward, 'Lilburne, Robert (*bap.* 1614, *d.* 1665)'.
R. Howell, Jr, 'The Army and the English Revolution: the Case of Robert Lilburne', *Archaeologia Aeliana*, 5th Ser. Vol. 9 (1981), reprinted in Roger Howell Jr, *Puritans and Radicals in North England* (Lanham, NY, 1984).

Cicely Veronica Wedgwood, *The Trial of Charles I* (London, 1964, pp. 106-17.
Sean Kelsey, 'The Death of Charles I', *The Historical Journal*, vol. 45 (2002).

PART FIVE

LOCAL PETITIONS TO THE ARMY

FROM THE REMONSTRANCE TO PRIDE'S PURGE,

NOVEMBER 1648 - JANUARY 1649

46: RUTLAND

24 November 1648

Context

This was not the first time that radical groups in the provinces had addressed their concerns directly to Fairfax and his army. In the spring and summer of 1647, petitions from the eastern counties had rallied support for the army's stand against disbandment and for constitutional reform. Several of those that appear below mention their own petitions at that time. David Underdown divided petitioners who called themselves 'honest' or 'well affected' into two kinds: one pro-Leveller, the other more moderately aligned with the political Independents. The distance between the two increased in the crisis of late 1648, and Underdown has argued that the 'honest' radicals who held power in the counties under the Commonwealth typically suppressed Leveller activity. Some of the petitions below reflect that growing split, and some do not, but perhaps the most marked difference is between those focussing exclusively on 'justice' and those that also urge the securing of constitutional or individual liberties.

The first of these, from Rutland, has much in common with petitions to Parliament in this period. Its approach to the king's guilt or innocence is sly: to ignore the sensational charges against Charles published in February 1648 would be a dishonour to Parliament, it says. Either he is guilty or Parliament was falsely smearing him. They want Charles to be removed from power, but leave open the question of whether this means the abolition of monarchy or its limitation. This text was published by William Larner, who also published many Leveller tracts and showed a strong commitment to their belief in sovereignty of the people and the rule of law.

Text

To his Excellency The Lord Fairfax, General of the Forces Raised for the Defence of the Kingdom, The Humble Petition or Remonstrance of the Well affected Inhabitants of the County of Rutland. Printed by James and Joseph Moxon for William Larner. BL/EEBO 669.f.13[47]

May it please your Excellency, The Consideration of the Honour which God hath put upon You since these troublous Times began, hath cast our eyes on You as (under God) the means of our further good; and therefore we thought it fit to make our Addresses to your Excellency for counsel and relief in our present condition, which is very grievous, and is like[ly] to be worse, the present evils being but presagements of future woes. Indeed our miseries are at that height already, that if some speedy course be not taken, we are like[ly] inevitably to be ruinated. But God having so appeared for his faithful ones already, giveth us much ground of confidence that he will not forsake us nor his owne cause; which is, the deliverance of his people, the advancement of Justice, and the punishment of malicious offenders. And we are perswaded of You also, that you will not be wanting [lacking] to do us good, or omit to seek the welfare of this poor Nation, nor let go the blessed opportunity which the God of heaven hath put into your hands to do us good. And in order to your furtherance herein, we desire that your Honour would be pleased to open your gracious ear to our (as we judge) weighty motions or Proposals, which are the Declaration of our griefs, lawful desires, and firm resolutions; that which in the first place we do offer as a grievance of our distressed souls, is not so much what we have lost in our Estates already, as our undone estate if our greatest enemies shall be made our Judges and chiefest Governour (or King) in order to which, and to the enslaving of us for ever, we conceive this Treaty with our conquered enemy was intended by some, which Treaty giveth a check to all the Parliaments former Declarations, and heroick Votes concerning the King, which Votes and Declarations we thought had not bin easily altered; the crossing of which adds so much to our sorrows, as we are not able to express, and also by this means a horrid contradiction is made to the Parliaments Declaration and resolution concerning no more Addresses: Indeed it is a giving them the ly, as though all that they had said of him, as touching the betraying of Rochell, the death of his Father, the Irish rebellion, bringing in the German horse [mercenary cavalry], the violence done to the Parliament at the beginning of their sitting, with divers other evils of a high nature which they laid to his charge, had no truth in them, but a mere Florish to defame him and deceive the people.

If all these things were justly charged upon him, (as in honour to the Parliament we beleeve they were,) oh how durst our Parliament think of Treating with such a man! And that which also melteth our very souls, is the much bloud already spilt, and yet we like[ly] to return into our former slavery. This is intollerable, and that which leaveth us without all hope is this, we see the Parliament intend not any more to hear our cries, but do lay aside all our Petitions; and although they burned them not by the hand of the common Hangman, yet they make us hang in torment between hope and fear, and so we are like[ly] to do if this Honourable Army help us not. Do you not lay it to heart how many Noble and yet Humble Petitions they have laid aside, as that from the faithfull Citizens of London, that from the Town and County of York, that from Kingston upon Hull, and that well grounded and reasonable Petition from the Town and County of Leicester, and many others to the same effect. Thus many mens desires, all mens good, is laid aside to feed some wicked mens humors: oh for Gods sake lay these things to heart. And further that which vexeth our hearts and thousand righteous souls of the Commons of England is, that still our Worthies are privately murthered, and all our ruines plotted, as appeareth by a Libel scattered abroad our County, and as you may see threatneth the destruction of those honest Gentlemen that were forced to leave the Parliament House [in July 1647] and fly to the Army which engaged at Newmarket.

And further when we see the freedoms of the People, and the security of all the Parliaments Souldiery depend upon the consent of a King, whom they have conquered, and this security to be for years, and if the Militia be intayled to the Crown, then if the King dy before these years be expired it must be returned to the Crown again, for the Father cannot give away the sons inheritance: whereas if the House of Commons had declared themselves the supream Authority of the Nation (as they ought to have done) our securitie had been firm.

And further it may be justly conceived, that what things are done by constraint are void in Law: and concluded by the Kings party that whatever he signes are done by constraint: What shall hinder him (being once impowered) to urge the Letter of the Law against the Parliament and all that adhered unto them, to their utter ruine. And if the King could raise so great an Army when he was in Carisbrook Castle, what will he be able to do when he comes to London among his now Desparados, may he not easily gain the Militia in one moneth, and overturn all that hath been accomplished with so much difficulty? And now if you and the Well-affected in the Army do forsake us, in respect of the help of man, we are utterly undone: and pardon us if we say, God will forsake you, and let you fall by those hands in which you leave us.

These are some of those sorrows in which we must sink, or resolve to take some more noble course, even to defend our selves by our sword, judging it far better to dy honourably in the field in one hour, than to live slaves in our houses for ever. Now the Lord teach you and us what to do; if we sit still, we are like to be massacred in our beds, or as our beloved *Rainsborough* was, whose death addeth to the life of our sorrows: oh trusty *Rainsborough*! thou art but what we are like[ly] to be; but what shall we do? We beseech your Excellency tell us, or hear us with patience, and we will relate what we intend.

First, we will pray to your God and to our God, and when we have powred out our tears to him, and our complaints to one another, as we have in some measure done already; then we will resolve to stand up with you and the rest of the faithful in the Nation, and declare further what we resolve to have: Only (Right Honourable) we thought good to make our humble Addresses unto you, and beg your aid, your countenance and your prayers, your grave Counsel, and Christian advice in this matter. We thought it good as *Mordecai* did *Hester*, to put you upon endeavouring our deliverance [Esther: 2], and let us in all humility and faithfulness tell you, God will find some way to set us free; but how you will answer your neglect, we cannot tell. In times past we have found you ready to venture life and limb for our good, which gives us much assurance you will stand for us and with us still, for our Just Rights.

We are no complementers nor flatterers, but well willers to the good of our Countrey, for which we assure you we will venture life and limb with you, for the suppressing of Tyrants, taking away of oppressive Laws, and all grievous burdens under which the Common-wealth groaneth. Thus having imparted our Desires and present Condition to your Excellency, we commit you to the Teaching, Guidance and Protection of God, and rest,

Yours, The Inhabitants of the County of Rutland

This Petition was presented to the General on Fryday the 24 of November 1648, by Lieut. Freeman, accompanied with three Gentlemen of the same County.

To which the General returned this answer, Gentlemen I have sent to the House, I hope they will do that which will be for the good of the Kingdom; if not, I will venture my life with you for Justice: and return you Thanks.

Background

A short petition addressed to Fairfax in the name of the inhabitants of Rutland in November 1647 appealed to him to represent their grievances to Parliament, particularly the burden of tithes falling on this small and predominantly agricultural county. Recent legislation had allowed local magistrates to impose triple damages for non-payment of these dues in kind to the Church of England or lay landowners whose ancestors had purchased them. This later petition is more political and wide-ranging, but both reflect the religious radicalism that took root in Rutland from the spring of 1647 onwards, promoted by the Baptist preacher Samuel Oates. Oates was a London craftsman from Norwich, who practised his belief that preachers should be supported by voluntary contributions by passing his hat round the congregation. His success aroused alarm among Rutland's ministers and gentry, one of whom wrote in October 1647, 'Hee is a malevolent Depraver of our Church, and I beleive will bee proved allsoe an Adversary to Magisteriall Government.'

Early in 1648 a number of ministers in Rutland and neighbouring counties complained to Parliament that Oates was 'Preaching and Rebaptizing verie manie and drawing a Concourse of people after him', holding weekly meetings in barns and stables, but sometimes also 'thrusting himself into our Pulpits' in parish churches. As well as preaching 'false doctrine', he had 'dispersed and endeavoured to promote that Sedicious paper, called the Agreement of the People'. Leveller ideas frequently went hand-in-hand with religious radicalism, especially that of the General Baptist sect, whose views on salvation were as challenging to contemporary orthodoxy as their demands for religious freedom and political change.

Colonel Thomas Waite, a Rutlandshire man, claimed after the Restoration that he had opposed local radicals and acted against petitions calling for justice against the king. He stayed away from Parliament from mid-December 1648, and although named to the High Court of Justice attended only once, on 29 January. He claimed that he had been tricked into attending by Cromwell, also that Lord Grey of Groby had assured him that the king would not be executed, and that he was forced into signing the death warrant without reading its contents. Though all the evidence from those on trial for regicide must be open to suspicion, Jason Peacey and Andrew Hopper have recently suggested that some of his evidence may not be totally untrue.

Related sources

Two Petitions to the Generals Excellency ... Printed in London by Robert Ibbitson, in Smithfield. BL/EEBO E.412[18].

Alan Betteridge, 'Early Baptists in Leicestershire and Rutland (1)', *Baptist Quarterly*, vol. 25 (1973-4), pp. 204-11. Also at biblicalstudies.org.uk.

ODNB: Stephen Wright, 'Oates, Samuel (*bap.* 1614, d. 1683)'.

David Underdown, '"Honest" radicals in the Counties, 1642-1649', in Donald Pennington and Keith Thomas (eds.), *Puritans and Revolutionaries, Essays in Seventeenth-Century History Presented to Christopher Hill* (Oxford: Clarendon, 1978).

VCH: *Rutland*, vol. 1 (London, 1908), pp. 189-95.

Andrew Hopper, 'The Reluctant Regicide? Thomas Wayte and the Civil Wars in Rutland', *Midland History*, vol. 39 (1), 2014.

Jason Peacey. 'The lies of the regicides? Charles I's judges at the Restoration', Cromwell Association, at olivercromwell.org/wordpress/?page_id=209.

47: BERKSHIRE

30 November 1648

Context

While the promoters of the Berkshire petition to Parliament (9 above) were still waiting at Westminster in hope of a hearing, they addressed more recent events with this petition to Fairfax and the Council of Officers. According to the title page, it was presented at Windsor headquarters on 30 November: the momentous day when the Council took the decision to move towards London, Lieutenant-Colonel Cobbett arrived on the Isle of Wight to remove the king to Hurst Castle, and the Commons voted to reject the *Remonstrance*.

Most of the content is typical of petitions at this date, but its suggestion that the remedy will come from either a purged Parliament or one freshly elected strongly suggests that it was composed at Windsor, where meetings of London Levellers, Independents, and army radicals had been arguing about these alternatives during the preceding week. Though the petition's authors evidently knew about these meetings, they do not take sides on this question, nor on whether the king's trial or a constitutional settlement should take priority. This is despite their insistence in the petition to Parliament (9 above) that there could be 'no Exercise of Religion, no Use of Lawes, no Assurance of Libertie, or Protection without such Desir'd Execution of Justice, upon all great Offenders'.

Text

A True Copie Of The Berkshire Petition ... Together with a Copie of Many of those Petitioners their Representation to His Excellencie, and the Councell of Warre at Windsore. The last of November, 1648... London, Printed Decemb. 2, 1648. BL/EEBO E.475[2]

A Representation to his Excellencie, and the Councel of War, of the Concurrence of many hundreds of the wel-affected of the county of Berks, with them in their late Remonstrance and Declaration.

How much Cause we have to blesse God for You (as having seen so much of God in You) in Your pass'd Action. How much of Satisfaction we have receiv'd, and to how much of Expectation we are rais'd in Your present Declaration. The Ends proposed in themselves so just, and equall, and for the Nation so advantageous, and honourable The Expedients offer'd in Relation thereunto so proper, and suitable. The Wayes and Rules laid down for Advanceing, and carying on these Expedients towards those Ends (in this Iuncture of Affaires, and Counsels) so Necessary, and (with their respective Restrictions, and Qualifications taken in so) Lawfull; The Time lastly for such your Remonstrance so seasonable; (After so long, and vaine Expectation from them, who had so much Power put into their hands by the People, so many Advantages by God himselfe, wanted nothing but Hearts to doe us Good.) Some Petitions for Justice, and just things Vouchsafed no Answer upon hearing, Others not so much as Reception and Reading, Enemies finding more of Favour then Friends of Right Those become Themselves (in the Generality of them) our greatest Burden and Grievance who should have eas'd us of all our Grievances and Burdens, and after so many Pretences for Freedome and Safety. Nothing in Veiw but Tyranny, Rapine and Bloud.

That (the Premisses consider'd) we cannot but cheerfully expresse our free, and full Concurrence with You in the whole of it (though we cannot yet looke upon it as the whole of that which must make us happy) Our firme Resolutions with the utmost of Estate, and Life to adhere to You in all good ways for the most effectuall Pursuiance, and Promoting of it, and whatsoever else of Publike Interest, and Advantage shall be further added by You, or contributed by others: And our undoubted Confidence of such Successe and Blessing from God upon it, and all that cleave to it, with that syncerity and Uprightness of Heart mentioned in it; as (either by this present Parliament, purg'd, or another and more equall Representative chosen) to have a true Accompt requir'd of all the Bloud spilt, and Treasure spent, The Guilt of bloud so throughly purg'd as no longer (in that regard) to lay under the wrath of God, and the Springs of bloud so throughly stopp'd, as no longer to lay open the wrath of men. The Spunges of the Common-wealth so throughly squeez'd, and crush'd as no longer to be subject to their Exertions [*sic*] and Rapines. The Foundations of our Freedom and Safety so deep-layd, and Superstructions so strong built, as neither to be batter'd by Power, nor undermin'd by Policy. See You every way as Instrumentall towards the Setling of an happy Peace, as You have been in waging a succesfull Warre; caried on throughout with such a Frame of Spirit, that all the World shall see it was in Your Hearts only to serve the Necessity of the Nation, not Your selves of it, only to seeke Your Selves in it, not set your selves above it, not to become a new Oppression to us, but (under God) our Redemtion from all Our Oppressions. For the present, and our Bullwarke, and Preservation against them, or the like for time to come. In which Confidence in, and Concurrence with You, We have Subscribed our Names.

Background

The existence of religious and political radicalism in several Berkshire towns before the civil wars has been noted above (9). The Levellers' ally Henry Marten is known to have been in Windsor in the last week of November, meeting with the London Levellers and Independents who had come to urge the army to stop the Newport treaty being agreed by Parliament. According to John Lilburne, Marten was the only MP nominated who attended the meetings of the joint committee then set up, and stayed in Windsor to work with Lilburne on the latest draft of the *Agreement of the People* after its London Independent members had left. Though Marten's influence surely played a part in this petition, it avoids commitment to the *Agreement*, and does not contain any hint of the overt republicanism for which Marten was notorious. Nor does it make any reference to Parliament's published charges against the king which he had helped to draft in January 1648.

Cornelius Holland, MP for New Windsor and former clerk to the Prince of Wales's household, was also present in Windsor at the time and may have been the petitioners' informant. Consistently aligned with the radical Independents, Holland had introduced the 10 October 1648 petition from Yorkshire (5 above) to the Commons, and moved thanks for the army's *Remonstrance* on 20 November. Lilburne's account of the Windsor meetings describes him as friendly to the London Levellers, offering to bring four MPs to the joint committee — though by the time Lilburne wrote this he had turned against Holland, Cromwell's 'present darling' said to be enriching himself with former royal lands. Some historians see Holland's radical religion and politics as a front for his self-advancement, but his most recent biographer judges him genuine. He attended the king's trial regularly, but did not sign the death warrant.

Windsor, though physically overshadowed by its castle, was not a royalist town. Its inhabitants had a long history of stealing timber and hunting deer in the royal park, and radical Protestant roots a century deep. Local puritan congregations dismissed the ceremonialism of the royal chapel, and the town was quick to send funds to Parliament on the outbreak of civil war. Parliamentary forces took the castle in October 1642 and held it from then on. The garrison, recruited locally, mutinied over arrears of pay in 1644, and Parliament tried but failed to disband it after the first civil war. From 1642 to 1645 its governor was Colonel John Venn, who was soon to take part in the king's trial and sign his death warrant. The likelihood of local initiative for this petition is at least as strong as the possibility that it was composed by Marten, Holland or Venn. Though unlikely to have been as widely subscribed as the October petition to Parliament (9 above), it may have gathered support from congregations in Abingdon and Newbury, for example, on the previous Sunday (26 November).

Related sources

John Lilburne, *The Legal Fundamental Liberties of the People of England* (1649). BL/EEBO E.567[1].

Commons Journal, vol. 5, 3 January 1648.

ODNB: J. T. Peacey, 'Holland, Cornelius (1600-1671?)'.

Chris Durston, 'Henry Marten and the high shoon of Berkshire: The Levellers in Berkshire in 1648', *Berkshire Archaeological Journal*, vol. 70 (1979-80), pp. 87-95.

Raymond South, *Royal Castle, Rebel Town: Puritan Windsor in Civil War & Commonwealth* (Birmingham, Barracuda Press,1981).

Sarah Barber, *A Revolutionary Rogue, Henry Marten and the English Republic* (Stroud, Sutton, 2000).

48: SURREY

14-18 December 1648

Context

The Moderate does not give the date of this petition, saying only that it was 'never before printed'. The mention of Colonel Harrison replying on behalf of the Council of Officers enables it to be dated, however, since Harrison was present at Whitehall on 14 and 15 December 1648, but left for Hurst Castle next day, and does not reappear in the Council's records until after the king's execution. The second demand below also relates to the debate about religious freedom at Whitehall on 14 December. A petition with similar demands, including the abolition of tithes and radical control over the county militia, was presented to Parliament on behalf of the well-affected of Surrey on 1 February 1649 (64 below).

Text

The Moderate, no. 28, 16-23 January 1648/9. BL/EEBO E.539[7]

An excellent Petition was presented to his Excellency from the County of Surrey, and because never Printed, take it here at large, with his Excellencies answer thereunto.

To the Right Honorable his Excellency, Thomas Lord Fairfax, and the General Councel of the Army. The Humble Petition of the known well affected Inhabitants of the County of Surrey,

Sheweth, That the Enemies of this Common-wealth, being (by the blessing of God) upon the endevors of the Army under your Excellencies Command, totally vanquished and subdued, and a fair opportunity thereby offered to settle the Peace of this much oppressed, and impoverished Nation, upon Grounds of Freedom and Safety. Your Petitioners well considering the same, and looking upon this Army, as those whom God hath chosen to be Instruments for so good an end; well weighing the miserable consequences that will unavoidably follow, in case you should neglect, or not make a right use of this season and hopeful opportunity Upon consideration hereof, we are encouraged with urgency of Spirit, to importune you, that all private Interests being laid aside, which hath so memorably and lately been the means of our distractions, you would cordially and industriously set your selves as a means to establish the Government, and remove the grievances of this Nation; and in doing thereof, that you would have a special regard to the Desires in that Petition of the 11 of September; and above all things, avoid the perpetuation of Command, Trust or Office, in the hand of any person or persons, it having proved by the sad experience of all Ages and Countries, and of our own in particular, the means of Corruption and Tyranny in those that are trusted, and of bondage to the people. Considering likewise, that the miseries of the wel-affected people have been very much increased for their affection to you and their Country, in that the power of most Counties hath been placed, and still is in the hands of such as have been most opposite to your proceedings, whereby your friends have been, and are lyable to many affronts and abuses; seeing likewise, that such as have assisted the publike enemy, have justly forfeited, at least for a time, their title to places of Trust and Office: Upon consideration of the premises, it is humbly and earnestly desired.

1. That you would speedily and effectually prosecute the particulars in your Remonstrance, and in the Petition of the 11 of September; and especially, that you would be the means for the chusing a new Representative, in such maner, as is expressed in a Paper, intituled, *The Agreement of the people*; that so the affairs of this Nation, may be managed by a legal and regular Authority.

2. That you would be very circumspect, in reserving from the power and trust of succeeding Representatives, such particulars as are mentioned in the said Agreement. Chiefly, that we may not be compelled to any thing about Matters of Faith, nor restrained from the Profession thereof in the exercise of Religion, nothing being more neer and dear unto us; by intrenching upon which proceeding, Parliaments have very much violated the Liberties of the People; kept the Nation in ignorance; occasioned frequent Divisions, Wars, and the miserable Consequences thereof: And that all other grievances, as are generally complained of, May either by the Agreement be removed, or proposed therein, to be taken away by the succeeding Representative, in such a maner, as that the people may, as neer as may, be ascertained of their removal.

3. That the Commissioners of the Militia, the Deputy Lieutenants, Sheriffs, Justices of the Peace in this County, and all other places, may be chosen by the wel-affected inhabitants thereof, and that all such as have assisted the King in purse or person, or appeared in the late tumultuous engagement for a personal Treaty, or that have otherwise abetted the same, or that may be charged with any probable suspition of evils to their countrey, may upon a penalty be for a time prohibited from being chusers, and made uncapable of being chosen into any the aforesaid places, or trusts, that so such as have expressed a constant good affection to their Countrey, and hazarded them selves in times of its greatest necessities, may no longer be trampled upon by their haughty and imperious Adversaries: That all dangers of Future insurrections in this County, and elsewhere, may be prevented, and the hands of yours, and this counties friends, strengthened. And that just accounts may be taken of this Counties disbursements, and its real friends distinguishment [*sic*], from such as under a Cloak thereof, are its secret, and worst of enemies.

Lastly, We humbly desire that your Excellency would make a due construction of what we here present unto you, as proceeding from the integrity of our hearts, and that you would use the most speedy and effectual means for the accomplishment of our Desires: So shall we think our former miseries well recompensed, and daily blesse God for the happy deliverance, which by your means he hath vouchsafed to us: But if you shall now lose this opportunity, which God hath wonderfully put into your hands, and thereby give up this almost ruined Nation, into the hands of its mercilesse enemies. God may shew you, when too late, your fayling, and finish our deliverance some otherway: Therefore we again most humbly and earnestly intreat, That these our Just Desires may be without delay accomplished, that so this poor distempered, oppressed, exhausted, and afflicted Nation may be relieved, and our selves, with all the faithful, engaged to lay all our endeavors for your assistance.

His Excellencies Speech to the Petitioners, upon the reading of their Petition.

The Petitioners having first presented their Petition to the General, after almost half an hours discourse with them, had this Answer returned by his Excellency.

That he did very much approve of their forwardness therein, and gave the Petitioners hearty thanks for their good affection to the publick; and further said (or to this effect,) Although God hath no need of the Creature, upon whom we were not to look, yet every one in their places ought to seek after the good of the publike, as God shall stir them up. and further said, That he doubted not but those who were in Power would indeavor the same.

Hereupon his Excellency referred it to be considered of by the General Counsel of the Army, and the said Counsel gave order to Colonel Harrison to return this Answer, to wit, That they had well considered of the Petition, and was required to return the Petitioners hearty thanks from the Lord General, and General Counsel, and that most of the particulars therein were now in agitation, and the rest should, as conveniently as may be, taken into consideration.

Background

This petition marks a dramatic turnaround in Surrey's post-civil war politics resulting from Pride's Purge. Since 1642 the county had been steered by a moderate leadership determined to hold it for Parliament despite the inhabitants' differences of opinion. Puritanism was widespread in west Surrey's cloth-making towns, and Windsor Forest had seen protests against the forest laws; while religious and political radicalism flourished in Southwark and neighbouring parishes. Sir Richard Onslow, a Presbyterian, was the dominant figure in the post-war years. According to his opponents his conciliatory policies, aimed at calming the conservative gentry's fear of disorder and revolution, had protected the property of local royalists. The poet George Wither, a friend of Henry Marten, was prominent among Onslow's opponents. After being removed from the JPs' bench after the first civil war Wither, believing that this was because he was not wealthy enough, denounced all rule by the rich and moved closer to the Levellers.

Early in May 1648, Surrey's Grand Inquest at the assizes and Grand Jury at the Quarter Sessions — official representatives of the county's freeholders — resolved to follow Kent and other counties and petition Parliament for a personal treaty with the king. They also demanded the disbandment of all armies and the payment of the soldiers' arrears. The petition was promoted through the county's official structures, and included a call for the king to be 'restored to his due Honour, and just Rights' and 'Established in His Throne according to the Splendour of His Ancestors'. It was carried to Westminster on 16 May by a procession of Surrey inhabitants, and the situation turned violent. In clashes with guards from Barkstead's regiment, there were deaths on both sides. Onslow's conciliatory stance, and some petitioners' repudiation of the royalist content even before it reached Westminster, helped to calm the situation; while a parliamentary deputation under the Earl of Northumberland forestalled any attempt by royalists to raise forces to join the rebellion in neighbouring Kent. The burden of free quarter on the county was also reduced by settling bills for the New Model Army's accommodation there as soon as the fighting in Kent was over.

All attempts to maintain consensus politics ended with Pride's Purge, removing all but four of the county's MPs, and Onslow was briefly imprisoned. His opponents purged Surrey's local government and installed the 'well affected'. This declaration of support for the *Remonstrance* and *Agreement of the People* shows strong radical influence, perhaps stemming from Southwark where the Leveller distiller and lay preacher Samuel Hyland sat on the militia committee. The demand for religious freedom without reservations or qualifications was supported by the Levellers, and by many members of Independent and Baptist congregations like those in Southwark at the time.

Following the king's trial and execution, George Wither returned to the county committee with a dozen new members, including Major Lewis Audeley (who had spoken in the Putney Debates) and Samuel Hyland. Despite an even stronger demand for control by the well-affected of Surrey presented to Parliament a day or two after the king's death (below, no. 64), a number of moderate figures from Onslow's regime remained in place and a complete radical takeover was prevented.

Related sources

To the Right Honourable Both Houses of the Parliament of England, The humble Petition of divers thousands, Knights, Gentlemen, and Free-holders, of the County of Surrey, together with the Burrough of Southwark... No printer or publisher named. BL/EEBO 669.f.12[26].

A Declaration of the Knights, Gentlemen, and Freeholders of Surrey: Concerning their late Petition and the Slaughter and Imprisonment of Several of their Countrey-men ... No printer or publisher named. BL/EEBO E.443[8].

The National Archives, Commonwealth Exchequer Papers, SP28/57, vol. 1,
   fos. 47-81.
John Gurney, 'The County of Surrey and the English Revolution'
   (unpublished D.Phil thesis, University of Sussex, 1991).
Henry Elliot Malden, *A History of Surrey* (London, Elliot Stock, 1900).
VCH: *Surrey*, vol. 1: Henry Elliot Malden, 'Political History'.
ODNB: Michelle O'Callaghan, 'Wither, George (1588-1667), poet'.
ODNB: John Gurney, 'Onslow, Sir Richard (*bap.* 1601, d. 1664), politician'.

49: 'COUNTY OF WARE'

before 15 December 1648

Context

It is a mystery where this petition came from, as Ware in Hertfordshire was not even a borough at the time, though it was an important market town and staging post on the main road from London to the north, and the site of the army's rendezvous in November 1647. 'Ware' is printed very clearly in the only known text, in a not especially radical newsbook, under the dateline of 15 December 1648. The text should probably be regarded as a fake petition, but is included here for the relevance of its content alone, which suggests a radical though not explicitly Leveller point of view. The reduction in the number of persons to be excluded from pardon and mention of the Scottish precedent for a purge of Parliament (see also 22 above) suggest that it was composed before Pride's Purge, though not published until after it.

Text

The Perfect Weekly Account, 13-20 December 1648 . Dateline Friday 15 December. BL/EEBO E.477[13]

To his Excellency Thomas Lord Fairfax, General of all the Forces in England. The humble Petition of many well-affected persons in the County of Ware

Sheweth, That to the great grief of our souls, we have found the humble addresses of the well-affected in many parts of this Nation, to their Representatives in Parliament, concerning the danger of the Treaty, the impartial executing justice upon offendors; the taking a course, that oppressions and oppressors may be removed, and the peoples just liberties established, have been neglected, and rendered fruitlesse, as is evident not only in answers given to Petitioners from the County of *Oxon*, *Leicester*, *Wilts*, &c, the laying aside that from the well affected in London of the 11. of September last, but also by their treating with the King, contrary to their former votes grounded upon those just and continued reasons declared to the Kingdom, and followed with the resolutions of your Excellency, and the Army under your conduct, to stand by them in the settlement of the Nation without him: As also by their extenuating of Justice in the number and quality of excepted persons, they being false, and most inconsiderable, and known to be most of them out of the Kingdome. As if the voting of Justice upon so few, were sufficient satisfaction for the blood of so many thousand Innocents crying for vengeance, by all which, we greatly fear this Nation will be desolated, and Parliaments unavoydably blemished; the thoughts whereof, as they do not a little afflict us, so they inform us to send out groans to God: and also by all those never to be forgotten judgments the Lord hath laid upon you, in giving such wonderful successes, not only under authority when right managed, but also against it, when abused by a major part, as in

England, or by a Major part, when with strength added to it, as in Scotland, earnestly to implore and beseech your Excellency,

That you would be pleased to contribute (as you have worthily begun) your utmost assistance, that Justice may be fully and speedily executed, without respect to great or small, Delinquents brought to condign punishment, and those especially, who promoted the last war and risings in the Kingdom, or had a hand in bringing in the Scots this last Summer, and that this oppressed and abused Nation may be set at liberty from their oppressions, and their future peace and the freedomes setled upon firm foundations, So shall we with all our hearts, lives, and estates, freely assist you.

And shall ever pray.

50: BRISTOL

before 19 December 1648

Context

By the time this petition was sent to Fairfax, Parliament had been purged and the members remaining had revoked the acceptance of the king's answers. However, Charles remained in Hurst Castle and no further decision about him had been made, while the purged Commons showed no inclination to dissolve themselves and call an election. Instead, their numbers were slowly increased by persuading members voluntarily absent since 6 December to return. Meanwhile at Whitehall, the army council was debating a radical new constitution based on the latest version of the *Agreement of the People*. Between regicide and revolution, several options remained open, and no decisions had yet been finalised.

These Bristol petitioners appeal for satisfaction for blood shed, but also for a lasting settlement based on 'judgement and equity'. The concept of equity, as used at the time, was not a vague one like our modern 'fairness', but the medieval idea of natural justice above and beyond the law, still current in seventeenth-century political theory. Their accusation of bloodlust against the king is such a personal attack that it may well be read as a call for his death; but even here it is never made explicit. The most important issue seems not to be killing him, but preventing his restoration to power.

Text

The Moderate, No. 23, 12-19 December 1648, pp. 210-11. BL/EEBO E.477[4]

To His Excellency Thomas Lord Fairfax and The Honorable, The Councel of the Army

The humble Representation of divers honest Inhabitants of the City of Bristol, and the adjacent Villages.

My Lord and Gentlemen, When we beheld the glorious splendor of Justice and Righteousnesse, beaming forth itself in your Remonstrance to the House of Commons, Nov. 18. 1648. we were filled with joy and satisfaction, that the divine presence had again overshadowed you, and appeared hereby to us with smiles of love, and pledges of favor, when with the night of ruine we were almost overwhelmed: For which, as we kiss the footstool of that glorious Majesty, who thus rarely brings forth our deliverance; so we chearfully confess you to be his glorious instruments, whereby he hath stilled the enemy and the avenger.

We must seriously profess, That though your former proceedings against that generation were exceedingly prospered, beyond the Parallel of former ages, and had engraven upon them, the kindness of God to a distressed people; yet they had but served to have made us the more exquisitely miserable, if your former Conquests should have acquiesc'd in the Actions of that House; who were bringing your Conquered Prisoner with Honor and Safety, into the Throne of Power, Majesty and Greatness, without satisfaction for the blood that hath been shed, or sufficient provision made for the security of the liberties of England, and their faithful assertors: And should you now (which God forbid) forbear the effectual prosecution of what you have now Remonstrated and professed, we may from that, sadly write all imaginable misery upon us, and our Posteritie for ever.

We were filled with sorrow, when we saw the abominable Apostacy, and degenerated Actings of the Majority of the House of Commons, who after we had bought their security with our most precious blood and treasure, should by their treating with the King, so cruelly sell us into the blood and revenge of him and his desperate Confederates, so contrary to their first Principles and Declarations, and to justice and equity, esteeming the effusion of the most excellent English blood, to be but a just Homage to his lusts, and Tyranny, and all their unhappiness to be but an equitable Tribute to his will and pleasure: the consideration of which, as it filled us with amazement, so it drew from us thereof a sad Remonstrance, which we made ready to present them; but when we saw what would be its portion, in the laying aside of other Petitions of that nature, through the prevalencie of the Royall Faction, we were put into great perplexities, and thoughts, which way we might avoid our destruction, and then were directed to your Excellencie and Army, as those who were the sword of the Lord, and the only way we could imagine for our preservation; To you then, as the last hopes of our dying spirits, did our thoughts hasten, if so be God had laid up in you salvation; and to that end, unbosomed our troubled souls with an Humble Representation, and with our desires, that you would pity your selves and England, and take notice of our Apprehensions, and Condition, in that the Petition was intended to the House, and act in Orders to them both; and we were ready to have presented it, but such was the goodnesse of God, that in the moment of time he appeared upon you beyond all expectation, with the glorious presence of Justice and Equity, and with excellent Remedies for the healing of the Nation, layd down in your Remonstrance; with which, as we are really one in all things, so as life, upon the giving up of the Ghost, was it to us a seasonable refreshment.

In the prosecution of which, go on Noble General, and worthy Gentlemen, in the strength of the Lord of Hosts according to his power acting in you, and his people your friends in England, and cease not till the Cedars of Tyrannie be laid even with the ground, and the happinesse of this the Nation be established upon the pillars of Judgement and Equity: For the accomplishing of which, we do hereby assure you, that with our lives and estates we shall readily follow you in all your engagements.

We who subscribed a Petition to your Excellency, presented at Kingston in August, 1647, do desire our loving friends, Mr. Robert Stapleton, Mr. James Powel, Major Samuel Clark, and Captain Thomas Norris, or any two of them, to deliver this Representation to your Excellency and Councell in our names, and at our Requests.

Other editions

A Letter from Sixteen Gentlemen of Kent ... As also the remonstrance and petition of divers honest inhabitants of the city of Bristol, and the adjacent villages ... Printed for R. White, Decemb. 19. 1648. BL/EEBO E.477[1].

A Declaration, Collected out of the Journals of Both Houses of Parliament, No. 3, 13-20 December 1648, pp. 21-2. BL/EEBO E.477[74]

Background

The earlier Bristol petition addressed to the army by 'divers Free-men of England, Inhabitants in the city of Bristol, and in the adjacent parts' was published, along with another addressed to the House of Commons, in September 1647 by Giles Calvert. The first called for the punishment of the kingdom's and the army's enemies, the honouring of Parliament's liberties, and no disbandment of the army until these aims were secured. The second reproached Parliament for attempting to disband the army, turning away petitions, and imposing an oath of adherence to the Solemn League and Covenant unacceptable to many 'tender consciences'; and advocated specific reforms echoing many points of the Leveller programme at that time. These, together with the present text, are strong evidence for the existence of Leveller-allied radicalism in Bristol and the neighbouring areas of Gloucestershire and Somerset.

Nevertheless, it is hard to establish who and where the promoters and supporters of these petitions actually were, perhaps because Bristol's history during and after the civil wars was selectively edited by contemporaries themselves. The city's experience had been traumatic: after admitting a parliamentarian garrison in 1642, it was taken by Prince Rupert in 1643, but besieged and reconquered by Parliament in 1645. Acute internal divisions surfaced when two citizens were executed for plotting to deliver Bristol up to royalist massacre in 1643; and again when royalist councillors were purged in 1645. For the preservation of Bristol's trade and industry the mayor, aldermen and common council did their best to maintain a front of co-operation and unity. Some historians describe civil war Bristol as neutral, with no strong feelings about religion or politics, excepting only the Independent congregation that later became the Broadmead Baptist Church. Some of this group moved to London during the royalist occupation and returned in 1645, but their meetings were still small enough to be held in private houses in 1647-8. Their history was written later by members of Broadmead church from the recollections of those alive in the 1670s, such as the remarkable Mrs Dorothy Hazzard. (Another strong female role model was a 'Blackymore Maid' whose wisdom and saintliness were an inspiration to the members.) Their history rarely mentions politics, however. They may have been silent on the subject after the Restoration in the way that some politicians after the Glorious Revolution played down their previous religious commitments. The problem for historians is not separating politics and religion in seventeenth-century Bristol, but identifying the evidence for reuniting them.

A few incidents suggest that politics and religion were as closely intertwined here as in any English city. Minister Matthew Hazzard, later a Broadmead leader, was in trouble in 1640 for refusing to read a prayer condemning the Scottish Covenanters as rebels, praying instead that god would reveal 'the traitorous enemies that disturbed the public peace and molested the hearts of the Church and of faithful people'. The mayor and corporation petitioned Parliament in January 1642 to appoint John Tombes, a friend of London congregational leader Henry Jessey, as preacher at All Saints. In an official sermon of thanksgiving for the city's delivery from the royalist plot in 1643, Tombes explicitly justified nobles and commons uniting against tyrannical rulers. In 1648 the authorities petitioned Parliament again to allow the appointment of preachers to the cathedral, where the old ceremonies had been suspended.

One of the two 'loving friends' named above in the 1648 petition, James Powell, was accused after the Restoration of having been appointed as the city's chamberlain in the 1650s only on Oliver Cromwell's recommendation, and was dismissed in 1662 for refusing to take the oath of adherence to the restored Anglican church. Major Samuel Clark, who settled in Bristol after leaving the army, was admitted as a burgess in 1652 after paying the penalties for trading in the city as a 'foreigner' (a native of England but not of Bristol).

Related sources

Two Petitions of Divers Free-men of England, Inhabitants in the City of Bristoll, and in the adjacent Parts ... Printed for Giles Calvert, 1647. BL/EEBO: E.405[23].

Commons Journal, vol. 2, 4 January 1642; vol. 5, 2 September 1647.

John Tombes, *Iehovah Ireh, or, God's Providence in Delivering the Godly*. Ordered to be printed by the House of Commons, 22 April 1643. BL/EEBO E.100[31].

Edward Terrill, *The Records of a Church of Christ meeting in Broadmead, Bristol, 1640-1687*, ed. Roger Hayden (Bristol Record Society, 1974). Earlier editions can be read online at archive.org.

John Latimer, *The Annals of Bristol in the Seventeenth Century* (Bristol, 1900).

Patrick McGrath, 'Bristol and the Civil War', in R. C. Richardson (ed.), *The English Civil Wars, Local Aspects* (Stroud, Sutton, 1997).

John Lynch, *For King and Parliament, Bristol and the Civil War* (Stroud, Sutton, 1999).

51: KENT

23 December 1648

Context

This petition was presented at army headquarters on 23 December, the day that Charles I arrived in Windsor. When the Council of War at Whitehall had ordered his removal from Hurst Castle on 15 December they had also appointed a committee 'to consider of the best ways and grounds for the speedy bringing of the King to Justice'. The king's slow journey was met in some places by cheering crowds, but when he arrived at Windsor Castle he was to be kept under close guard in the upper castle, barred from contact with other royalist prisoners, and forbidden all private conversation or correspondence. On 23 December also, the Commons set up their own committee 'to consider how to proceed in a way of Justice against the King, and other capital Offenders', and welcomed a parallel petition from Kent (57 below). The following day it was unofficially reported that the army had drawn up a list of charges against the king and resolved that 'if they proceed to trial, it will be in a Parliamentary way, and the Army are to manage the proofs'. This is indeed what was to happen; but the 'charges' prematurely reported were mostly extracts from the *Remonstrance*.

Since this petition focuses on the 'execution' or 'prosecution' of justice, we may wonder whether the words mean different things. Does the first imply capital punishment? These petitioners use both at once, urging the army to 'prosecute the execution of justice upon the person of the King'; and in the next few sentences they seem to function as alternative vocabulary. We cannot yet say that they openly demand the king's death, as the January 1649 petition to Parliament from this county does (65 below).

Text

The Moderate, No. 24, 19-26 December 1648. BL/EEBO E.536[2].

Dateline 23 December 1648.

To his Excellency and generall Councell of Warre, The humble Proposals of divers of the well affected in the County of Kent, the City and County of Canterbury, together with the Cinque Ports.

As we desire to eye, and bless the Almighty in those great and almost miraculous things, which he hath done by you for the publique: So likewise we conceive our selves bound, gratefully to acknowledge our reall obligations, viz. to your selves, for all your vigilant care, and indefatigable endeavours therein, constantly and faithfully, notwithstanding all opposition of open enemies, and Apostate friends; And because we believe that there is in you a readiness to hearken to, and a Candor to judge of whatever may be proposed unto you, in the pursuit of those things that may conduce to the reall welfare, and safety of the well-affected people; We doe therefore take leave hereby, to present these ensuing particulars to your serious consideration. First, that you prosecute the execution of Justice upon the person of the King, and to [*sic*] proceed to the prosecution of your Resolves, in your Remonstrance, touching the Prince, and the Duke of Yorke. Secondly that you pursue the prosecution of Justice upon Duke Hamilton, together with the rest of the Invaders, and inviters of them to that treasonable Act, as well English, as Scots. Thirdly that you pursue Justice upon some few of the chief Actors, in the late Rebellion in Kent, and upon the chiefe Agents in the Revolt of the Navie. Fourthly, that Iustice be executed upon some of the chief Actors, in the invasion made by the Prince, and the forces under his command since the revolt of the Navie. Fifthly, that the City of London be setled in such hands, as may disable it for disservice, and Render it in a Posture serviceable to the Publique; so that you may with safety march from, and returne to it upon all occasions. Sixthly, that a way may be thought upon for a correspondency with the Navie, so as that there may be an unanimous consent in all actings, between the forces by Sea and Land, And lastly, that the Militia of this County may be speedily setled.

Background

Kent had been held by Parliament throughout the first civil war, and saw little fighting during it; but it became a major flashpoint of the second. The financial burdens and harsher aspects of parliamentarian rule were unpopular there, as elsewhere, and the harsh punishment of the Canterbury rioters who protested at the banning of Christmas celebrations in 1647 was a cause of particular bitterness. Protesters in spring 1648 demanded peace with the king; by May the county was in revolt, and was joined by the mutiny of the ships in the Downs (39 above). According to Alan Everitt the Kentish outbreak was 'not the rising of a single clique or class of the community' but 'a revolt of a whole countryside'. The intervention of outside royalists with their own agenda, culminating in the landing of the Duke of York in Kent in July 1648, destroyed this alleged unanimity, however. The rising was put down after some fierce fighting, especially at Maidstone, by Fairfax's and Livesay's forces (see 34 and 39). This petition's sharp focus on the leaders of the 1648 royalist risings, as well as the king himself, surely reflects the bitterness of Parliament's supporters at this recent explosion of war in their county.

Everitt's influential study of Kent defined the 'county community' as consisting of the landed gentry, mainly moderate royalists. He saw parliamentary control as an imposition from outside, necessary because of the county's strategic importance and closeness to London. In the landscape of insularity and social harmony before the wars, he saw little room for 'extremists' on either side; but the civil war brought great changes, admitting to local power 'relative nouveaux riches of legal or mercantile origin' lacking the traditional authority. His view that the landowning gentry were the 'natural rulers' of an agrarian society, and that their relative absence from local government during the Interregnum was the weakness that brought its downfall, has influenced a wide range of historical writing on English county societies.

Alternative views of Kentish society have since been offered, both by Peter Clark's in-depth study of religion, politics and social change from the Reformation to the civil war, and by Jacqueline Eales's research into committed parliamentarians among the Kentish gentry and clergy. Both link parliamentarian politics to the history of religious dissent in Kent, which goes back to pre-Reformation times. At least three urban communities — Ashford, Canterbury and Cranbrook — showed their commitment to Parliament by raising volunteer forces even before the king raised his standard. In 1648, some areas made little or no contribution to the rising against Parliament, especially those parts of the Weald where cloth-making and iron-working had brought significant economic and social change.

The puritanism that produced 2,500 subscriptions from the Weald to London's 'root and branch' petition against bishops in 1641 continued to be significant, and Eales points out that the county had become a stronghold of the Particular Baptists by the late 1640s. Kent's best-known religious radical was John Saltmarsh, rector of Brasted, who wrote in 1646 that Christ's people had not only a duty of obedience to secular authorities but an interest in them, 'of consultation, of debating, counselling, prophesying, voting'.

The purging of royalists and moderates from office in Kent after the defeat of the 1648 rising not only strengthened those who had been loyal to Parliament all along, but brought the most radical among them to the fore. Andrew Broughton, elected Mayor of Maidstone in late 1648, for example, was to serve as clerk at the king's trial. Everitt's assertion that such people did not represent 'Kentish opinion in general' is beside the point. The spectrum of Kentish opinion was broad from the start, and these Independents were moving away from the Leveller end of it. In January 1648, a Presbyterian minister reported that John Lilburne had told a gathering at Wapping about a forthcoming meeting at Dartford to receive reports from the Levellers' agents in Gravesend, Maidstone and other Kentish towns, whereupon the House of Commons ordered the county committee to stop all such meetings. It is unlikely that this put an end to Leveller activity in Kent, though there is no distinct sign that they contributed to any of the three Kentish petitions in this collection (see also 57 and 65 below). The focus of all three is the trial and punishment of Charles and his leading supporters, together with the immediate security of the current regime. Their demand for the militia, the navy and the City of London to be kept in politically reliable hands reflects the fact that the process of reconstructing the county militias under the traditional command of Deputy Lieutenants, begun before the purge, was continuing under the new regime. No known names are associated with this petition, unlike the last of the three (65 below).

Related sources

Alan Everitt, *The Community of Kent and the Great Rebellion* (Leicester, Leicester University Press, 1966).

Jacqueline Eales, 'Kent and the English Civil Wars, 1640-1660', in Frederick Lansberry (ed.), *Government and Politics in Kent 1640-1914* (Woodbridge, Boydell, 2001).

Jacqueline Eales, '"So many sects and schisms": religious diversity in revolutionary Kent, 1640-60', in Christopher Durston and Judith Maltby (eds.), *Religion in Revolutionary England* (Manchester, Manchester University Press, 2006).

Jacqueline Eales, 'Alan Everitt and the Community of Kent revisited', in Jacqueline Eales and Andrew Hopper (eds.), *The County Community in Seventeenth-Century England and Wales* (Hatfield, University of Hertfordshire Press, 2012).

Andrew Hopper, 'The impact of the County Community hypothesis', in Eales & Hopper as above.

William Haller and Godfrey Davies (eds.), *The Leveller Tracts, 1647-53* (Gloucester, Mass. 1964), p. 100.

52: GLAMORGAN

23 December 1648

Context

Despite accusations current after the Restoration, nothing in this petition explicitly advocates regicide. It was presumably composed and subscribed some time before it was presented, and may have been held back by the army leadership for this occasion, when their own resolutions and the Commons' focused on the trial of the king. Here, he is named only in connection with the Newport treaty, and those so far escaping justice are rather 'the most desperate incendiaries'. The word 'incendiaries' was often used by parliamentarians for the king's advisers and supporters — who had inflamed relations between the monarch and his people and set his kingdoms ablaze with war — to sidestep direct accusations against the king himself.

These petitioners declare that god has favoured the New Model Army not only on the battlefield but in their intervention in political affairs. It will be shown below that the organisers and subscribers of this petition had especially strong reasons for expressing gratitude and support to the New Model and its leaders, while keeping more radical political views at a distance.

Text

The Moderate Intelligencer, No. 197, 21-28 December 1648. BL/EEBO E.536[18]

At the desire of some of the Authors this is inserted, which other way should not, because the Reader may loath twice-sod Coleworts [twice-soaked greens], and of this kinde neer 100 have been Printed.

To his Excellencie Thomas Lord Fairfax , and the Honorable the Councell of warre: the cordiall congratulations of the Lovers of Justice and Freedom within the County of Glamorgan, in reference to your Remonstrance, of November 18, 1648.

Noble Worthies, When with much patience wee had a long time waited for the setling of the Nations upon the foundations of freedom, and the execution of justice upon capitall Offenders; whom our God with no lesse miracle then mercy, hath so often delivered into your hands; and instead thereof, through the prevalency of a malignant faction, have found our lives and liberties even betrayed into the hands of our enemies, by that unjust and dangerous Treaty with the King, and the most desperate Incendiaries, (especially those who have kindled and added fuell to the flames of Warre in our thereby ruined Country) excused from justice, expresly contrary to the Votes and Declarations of the House of Commons, to the astonishment of all true hearted people; and in all these perceiving our selves surrounded with destruction we were the more ardently drawn forth in our spirits to attend the Lord our Deliverer, who according to his wonted goodness, broke forth upon you in a Glance of Justice and Equity [in a glorious splendor of Justice and equity*], exprest in your seasonable Remonstrance, in the perusal whereof [which we with such joy perused*] our hearts were ravished with so deare a sight of our redemption drawing nigh. In relation to which, we thought it necessary to let you know, that wee are much satisfied with your proceedings, and that for the accomplishment of those things [accomplishing those things and whatever else concerns the Liberty of the Nation*], we are ready to assist you with our lives and fortunes, being perswaded that you will proceed with the same vigour and undauntedness of resolution for the perfection thereof, that our so numerous enemies take not occasion thereby to render us more effectually miserable; and we doubt not but the Lord of Hosts will be with You.

Signed by yours and the Kingdoms Faithfull Servants, Richard James Vic. Com. [sheriff] with Gentlemen, Freeholders, and others of the said County, to the number of 197.

The Congratulation was presented to the Councel of War upon Saturday night by Mr Basset Jones, Son to the Sheriff of Glamorgan: who, after the reading thereof by the Judge Advocate, was desired to withdraw, and then, [Jones] being called in, Col.Rich then President, exprest their cordial acceptance thereof, enjoyning the said Mr Jones to acquaint those Subscribers, That as they had there promised to spend Life and Fortune in assistance to their proceedings; So the Army would be as careful to assist and protect them in the midst of their enemies, upon all occasions.

Other editions

The Moderate, No. 25, 26 December- 2 January, 1648/9, p. 231. BL/EEBO E.536[30] [Passages marked * above appear only in this version.]

Background

The traditional approach to Wales in the period of the civil wars has explained the dominance of royalism throughout the principality as the inevitable product of a hierarchical and conservative society; while Puritanism appears as an alien import, towns and trade being dismissed as insignificant. Along with the rest of South Wales, Glamorgan was occupied by forces raised under the king's Commissioners of Array at the start of the civil wars. No parliamentarian militias were formed, while the rents and estates of the king's opponents were seized by the Commissioners, and many of their owners fled to England. The refugees also included members of the isolated Independent congregation at Llanfaches near Newport (Monmouthshire).

More recently however, some historians have described Glamorgan as a changing society in the century before 1640. Social mobility was most marked among the gentry, where small squires proud of their ancestry were capable of challenging aristocratic patronage. Cardiff and Swansea prospered through trade with England and Atlantic Europe, while the pre-industrial manufactures of wool and leather were expanding along with coal mining. The Anglican Reformation, with its redistribution of monastic property and compromises in worship and belief, was widely accepted, while the pockets of Catholicism that remained were dependent on aristocratic patrons like the Earls of Worcester at Raglan. Puritan clergy were active in South Wales before 1640; but the best-known examples, William Erbery and Walter Cradock, left the country before 1640 and were radicalised after the civil wars. In the complicated interplay of local allegiances among the gentry, opposition to Charles I's policies did not automatically mean adherence to Parliament when war broke out.

By mid-1645, tensions between local and national royalists grew, in reaction to the depredations of royalist general Charles Gerard. When the king came to Glamorgan after Naseby a 'Peaceable Army' of gentry and yeomen confronted him with a list of demands including the expulsion of all Catholics, the replacement of Cardiff's English garrison by a local force, and the remission of £7000 arrears of royal taxation. The recapture of Bristol by Fairfax was a severe blow to Glamorgan's Bristol Channel ports, and disaffection from the royalist cause was spreading. By the start of 1646 Cardiff and Swansea had succumbed to parliamentarian forces landing on the coast with naval support, without any military engagement on land.

A county committee of soldiers and local gentry was consequently 'dropped into' Glamorgan, in the words of Stephen Roberts. In the political vacuum created by the collapse of royalist power and aristocratic patronage this new regime, founded on godly militarism, took advantage of rapid changes of allegiance among local leaders, and maintained control despite tensions among the different factions on both sides. Brief revivals of the Peaceable Army, protesting against Parliament's banning of the Book of Common Prayer, were quashed in 1646 and 1647. Although some puritan preachers returned to South Wales between 1645 and 1648, it was not until after 1650 that radical religion spread significantly enough, under the Commission for the Propagation of the Gospel in Wales, to lay the permanent foundations of Welsh nonconformity. Meanwhile, Glamorgan's attachment to the New Model Army was reinforced when it defeated the South Wales rising in the second civil war. (See also 25 and 37 above.)

This delicate balance of forces could explain the relative restraint of the petition above, and no contemporary evidence can be found for more radical political or religious views. The dominant policy of leaders such as Colonel Philip Jones, described by Roberts as the 'dictator' of Glamorgan in the late 1640s, and Michael Oldisworth, working to revive the influence of his patron the Earl of Pembroke, was to strengthen ties with the Independents in Parliament. The group now in power remained loyal to the Independents throughout the Commonwealth and Protectorate regimes. The political and religious leanings of Richard Jones of Michaelston-super-Ely (Llanfihangel-ar-Elai), county sheriff for the year 1648, are unknown, though he and his son Basset Jones, named in the petition, later fell into conflict with Colonel Philip Jones over a property dispute. Basset Jones (or Jhones) was a scholar and physician who studied at Oxford, Paris and Leiden, corresponding with alchemists, scientists and social reformers in England and on the Continent. Presenting this petition seems to be his only known political act.

Related sources

Stephen K. Roberts, 'How the West was won: parliamentary politics, religion and the military in South Wales, 1642-9', *Welsh History Review*, vol. 21 (2003).

Philip Jenkins, *The Making of a Ruling Class, the Glamorgan Gentry, 1640-1790* (Cambridge University Press, 1983).

Glanmor Williams (ed.), *Early Modern Glamorgan from the Act of Union to the Industrial Revolution* (Glamorgan County History, vol. 4, Cardiff, 1974).

W. S. K. Thomas, *Stuart Wales* (Llandysul, Gomer Press, 1988).

A. H. Dodd, *Studies in Stuart Wales* (2nd edition, Cardiff, University of Wales Press, 1971).

ODNB: Ariel Hessayon, 'Jhones, Basset (b. 1613/14), physician, chemist, and grammarian'.

53: NEWPORT PAGNELL

26 December 1648

Context

By the time this petition was presented at Whitehall, the purged Parliament had moved towards setting up a court to try the king and other 'delinquents'. The text appears to have been composed some weeks earlier, expressing fears about the outcome of the Newport negotiations officially terminated on 13 December. It may have taken time to gather subscriptions; or perhaps it had arrived earlier but was made public now, when its opening demand for the king to be brought to justice was most useful. The officers in council were still debating the proposed *Agreement of the People*, but had passed on from the argument about freedom of religious belief and worship after agreeing on a narrower toleration than these petitioners demanded. On the day this was presented, the Council voted on the 'sixth reserve' — which would have outlawed prosecution under charges not already existing in law — after amending it to make an exception for 'calling to account and punishing publique officers failing in their trust', to allow for the trial of the king.

Text

A Petition presented by the Inhabitants of Newport-pagnell and the parts adjacent to his Excellency the Lord Generall Fairfax, and the Generall Councell at White-Hall on Tuesday, Decemb. 26. 1648, Desiring the person of the King might be brought to speedy Justice, and other matters of the like Nature. No publisher or printer named. BL/ EEBO 669.f.13[61]

To the Right Honourable His Excellency the Lord Fairfax, Generall of the Parliaments Forces, and to the Officers of the [*sic*] Excellencies Army now met in Generall Councell.

The Humble Petition of the well-affected in Newport-Pagnell, and the Parts adjacent.

Humbly sheweth, We are very sensible [aware] by whose meanes, and to satisfie whose Prerogative Fancy, our Lives and Liberties have bin ruined and almost destroyed, which our Representatives well resenting (at their first Convention) did by severall Declarations sufficiently satisfie the Kingdome: And for prevention of future Arbitrary Practises over our persons and Estates, did dismount the tyrannicall Courts of Star-Chamber, High Commission, and Councell-Table; going yet further, that if the King (in dislike of their just endeavours for the Peoples safety) should make Warre upon the Parliament, it should tend to the dissolution of his Government: in order to which (the King guilty of breach of the Trust aforesaid) That satisfactory Declaration of no more Addresses did abundantly witnesse their just Proceedings, puting us upon expectation of their candid intentions to a

53: Newport Pagnell, 26 December 1648

just settlement of Peace and Freedome: But now (to our greatest griefe be it spoken) we have found resolutions in our Electives, implying a notorious contradiction of their former just and equitable Principles, giving the King that by Vote which by all the strength and policy of His Royall Party he could never yet attaine by the sword. All which mischiefes we doe interpret to obnoxious humours (hoping no errors in the Vitals) But in case these Votes should arrive to their intended accomplishment, we are given to beleeve (notwithstanding all the Bloud and Treasure (since the Wars began) that hath been exhausted) we shall be left in a worse condition then before; and by so much the more the rage of that professed Tyrant and his Creatures incensed against us. And in the midst of these our feares and jealousies [suspicions], there appeared not from our Representatives the least hope of Recovery (notwithstanding Petitionary means hath bin used to rectifie their judgments).

All which, as the subject matter of our saddest thoughts, we humbly present to your Excellency and Officers under your Command: Beseeching you, by all the Deliverances and Victories that God hath duplicated upon this Army, That you be not deluded by the sophistry of a corrupt Party, but to improve your power to the utmost for the establishment of Justice and Freedome: And that your Excellency will be pleased to mediate the Parliament in our behalfe, for these our just desires; And in prosecution hereof, we shall assist your Excellency to the utmost of our Lives and Fortunes.

1. That the Author of the Bloud and Ruines of the Three Kingdomes (as we conceive) the person of the King be brought to speedy Tryall.
2. That a strict Enquiry be made after all Persons (of what quality soever) that had a hand in the first or second War, and Justice done according to their demerit.
3. That the heavy burthen of free Quarter be wholly taken off, and effectuall care taken for constant pay of the Army, and provision thought upon for paiment of their Arreares.
4. That the Capitall and most Antichristian oppression of Tythes be taken away, and that Gleabe-Lands be sold to satisfie Impropriators: Provided their Tenure be not from Bishops, Deanes and Chapters, or Colledges, or their Estates under Sequestration; And Gospell-Ministers to be maintained by a free Contribution, according to Gospell Order.
5. That no Law be made or continued for the punishing of our persons about matters in Religion, seeing every soule shall stand or fall to his owne Master, no need of tormenting before the time.
6. That the Lawes of this Land be translated into English; and that there be a Court of Judicature in each Hundred of every County, where Causes may be equally determined by twelve sworne men Annually chosen by the Freemen of the said Hundred, and not left to depend upon Prerogative Lawyers for Justice, the Obstructors of the Peoples Freedomes.

7. That a speedy course may be taken for the suppressing of Ale-houses, They being the very Receptacle and Nursery of Rogues to plot and contrive all manner of villany, and Cause of the great dearth and famine in this Kingdome; And unlesse it be timely prevented, will occasion the starving of many thousand Families.
8. That the Desires of the large Petition presented Sept. 11 be taken into speedy Consideration; That it may not discourage the well-affected from making future Addresses.
9. Lastly, we protest against Community or abridgement of the least title of any mans Property. This being the period of our desires, That the Lawes being grounded upon Reason and Religion, all Persons may be bound alike to subjection.

And your Petitoners shall pray, &c.

The Answer of the Generall Councell in White-Hall on Tuesday, Decemb. 26. 1648

To the Petition of Newport-Pagnell, and the Parts adjacent.

That they had read the Petition, and did very kindly resent [appreciate] and thankfully accept those Expressions first in the preamble of the Petition, of their affections and faithfulnesse, in relation to the publique Justice and Liberties of the Kingdome, and for their desires in the Prayers of the Petition concerning the prosecution of Justice and Freedome: We doe heartily close with your desires in it, and shall endeavour to prosecute the same, as God shall direct and inable us in all honest wayes. And for the last part of the Prayer of the Petition, for mediating with the Parliament concerning those particulars following, They were acquainted, that the most part of the particulars are such as doe relate to publique Justice, and a generall settlement of the Liberties of the Kingdome. The Councell hath taken many of them already into consideration, and are in consideration of some other things remaining; which so soone as they have passed the Councell, you will see publique, and we hope to your satisfaction; and the other particulars that you desire mediation in, either concerning the Reformation of Lawes in being, or the making of new, Particularly the Councell doe let you know, that such things as those are matters of the publique Justice and of the Kingdome; they shall so farre as they are proper for their Cognizance take them into consideration in their places and time.

Background

Newport Pagnell, today the site of a motorway service station, has been an important stopping place on the road north from London for centuries. During the first civil war, it often lay close to the line between opposing armies, and became one of the most important of Parliament's garrison towns from 1643. Oliver Cromwell, second son of the Lieutenant-General, died of smallpox there in 1644. John Bunyan served in the garrison; and the future Quaker founder George Fox may have visited the town in 1642-3. The Presbyterian Sir Samuel Luke, governor from 1644 to 1646, took Newport Pagnell's religious life firmly in hand, writing that seven 'able divines' were now preaching there, and the garrison were attending prayers every morning. He had dispersed one unauthorised late-night religious gathering, announcing that the inhabitants were free to hear whatever preachers they wanted in private houses, but must notify the authorities. When he demanded that all inhabitants take the Covenant, only one refused: a silk weaver denounced by Luke as 'a villain ... that under pretence of holiness practices all manner of looseness and villainy, neglects Parliament and condemns the Assembly of Divines'. The Westminster Assembly had been set up by Parliament to make recommendations on the reform of the national church and was disliked by religious separatists and sects. Luke worried that religious dissent was spreading to local villages beyond his control, and appealed to friends on the county committee to suppress unauthorised religious gatherings.

A few days before Naseby, while Fairfax waited for Cromwell at Newport Pagnell, Luke arrested two of Fleetwood's captains, Paul Hobson and Richard Beaumont, for unauthorised preaching. They missed the battle, and when barred from the official thanksgiving service next day, they preached at a gathering in the village of Lathbury. Luke sent them to their colonel, Fleetwood — 'beleeving them to be Anabaptists, which cannot consist with Magistracy or Government', but both Fleetwood and Fairfax defended them. Hobson and Beaumont left the army, Hobson going on to spread the Baptist message elsewhere. This petition's religious clauses suggest that the townspeople of Newport Pagnell continued to frequent more radical religious gatherings outside the town, though we lose sight of religious dissent there until 1659. The local vicar, John Gibbs, was ejected then for refusing to administer communion to the whole parish — the sign of a 'gathered' congregation of self-identified saints within a parish church.

There was widespread support in Buckinghamshire and neighbouring counties for the abolition of tithes, intensified by Parliament's August 1647 ordinance punishing non-payment with triple damages. Contemporary pamphlets and petitions, such as *The Husbandman's Plea against Tithes* (1647), gave several reasons for abolition: the heavy burden on the farming population, arguing that it was much more than the biblical one-tenth in practice; the superseding of the Old Testament's ten percent for the support of a priestly tribe by the coming of Christianity; and, most radically, the view that every individual should support their chosen minister by voluntary contributions. The petitioners propose here that only lay impropriators should be compensated, and the necessary funds raised by selling the glebe lands and others belonging to the established church. This points to a radical conclusion, dissolving the Tudor Reformation's bond between church and state for good. The petitioners' support for unqualified freedom of religion is not based on thinking we would recognise as liberal or tolerant today, however. They argue that the punishment of heretics and unbelievers should be left to god alone: they will burn in hell like other sinners; but there is 'no need of tormenting before the time'.

Related sources

Clarke Papers, vol. 2, pp. 149-50.
The Husbandmans Plea against Tithes (London, 1647).
VCH: *Buckinghamshire*, Vol. 4.
Frederick William Bull, *A History of Newport Pagnell* (Kettering, 1900).
The Letter Books of Sir Samuel Luke, (ed. Harry Gordon Tibutt), (Bedford, Great Britain Royal Commission on Historical Manuscripts with Bedfordshire Historical Record Society, 1963).
Original Letters Illustrative of English History (ed. Henry Ellis), 3rd Series vol. 2 (London, 1846).
Alexandra Walsham, *Charitable Hatred: Tolerance and Intolerance in England, 1500-1700* (Manchester University Press, 2009).
Norah Carlin, 'Toleration for Catholics in the Puritan Revolution', in Ole Peter Greel and Bob Scribner (eds.), *Tolerance and Inolerance in the European Reformation* (Cambridge University Press, 1996).
Peter Clark, 'The alehouse and the alternative society', in D. H. Pennington and K. Thomas (eds.), *Puritans and Revolutionaries, Essays presented to Christopher Hill* (Oxford, Clarendon, 1978).

54: HERTFORDSHIRE

9 January 1649

Context

This is another petition that does not refer to the most recent events at the time of its publication: the latest it mentions is the purged Parliament's repudiation of the Newport treaty negotiations (13 December 1648). Since then, the House of Commons had declared itself the supreme power in the constitution, a High Court of Justice had been set up to try the king, and his trial proclaimed in Westminster Hall. But because the charge against him was not finally agreed until 19 January, the day before the trial began, it was still not clear that the more sensational accusations published in the days following the Vote of No Addresses would be included.

The petition's reference to the by-elections that took place from August 1645 onwards to replace members who had died or defected to the royalists, raises a more general issue. According to Underdown's classic analysis of 'the purgers and the purged', over half the members of the Commons just before the purge had been elected since 1645. Overall, the new recruits included a higher proportion than the house as a whole of 'revolutionaries', who supported the purge or accepted its results. Oliver Cromwell's early exemption from the Self-Denying Ordinance that barred army officers from the House is well known; but after the end of the first civil war a clutch of New Model Army colonels — Ireton, Fleetwood, Harrison, Ingoldsby and Skippon — had obtained seats at by-elections. By late 1648 also, a number of sitting MPs, such as Livesay, Marten, Walton and Lord Grey of Groby, had raised or led forces in the second civil war. By contrast, the majority of those imprisoned by Pride had sat since before the first civil war, though among those merely excluded, the percentage of 'recruited' MPs was proportional to their presence in the House.

Text

The Moderate, No. 27, 9-16 January 1648/9, pp. 251-2. BL/EEBO E.538[15]

Dateline 9 January (1649).

To his Excellency Thomas Lord Fairfax, Lord General, and his general Counsel. The Humble Petition of the well-affected in the County of Hartford, &c.

Sheweth, That your Petitioners do with much thankfulness acknowledge the mercy and goodnesse of God to them, and all the well-affected of this Nation, in stirring up your Excellency, and the Army under your Command, to interpose between them, and their intended ruine, who (having constantly adhered to the publike interest) th[r]ough the various mutations of times, and not been wanting in contributing due and cheerfull assistance towards suppressing the common enemy, even much beyond proportion), have long waited with much patience, on those from whom we hoped for relief, yet have had no deliverance: But as in Egypt Pharaoh dyed, and another that knew not Joseph arose in his stead, who afflicted Israel [Exodus 1:8]; even so, in our Parliament, many of our worthy patriots are dead, and such new Members come in their room, as have doubled our afflictions; as in particular, they have gathered in our moneys under pretext to pay your Excellencies souldiers, but have kept the moneys, and made us keep the souldiers; some also chosen by this County, have strongly endeavoured to hinder the success of such means as hath been used to secure the County, writing down to the Parl. Committees, to desist raising money, thereby to discourage the souldiers for want of pay, when indeed we were in great danger to be overrun, an enemy being then (as it were) in our bosoms; besides the great indignities put upon many, who with all uprightness and faithfulnesse have served the publick, by sequestring, and excluding them from those Offices and imployments, wherein they were most usefull, as Committees, Commissioners, &c. And giving countenance and incouragement to such as might rather be esteemed enemies, and dangerous to the State, by making them Iustices of the Peace, Committees, Commissioners, &c. which makes us more then suspect they had no good design upon us; and when we consider what Ordinances have past the Houses for suppressing the Book of Common Prayer, and how long Members of Parliament at our Counties Sessions, have not only reasoned, and pleaded for those Laws which binde the people in Conformity thereunto, but punished divers [some] by imprisonment, for not observing the same: we can in reason expect no ease, but rather torture for tender consciences: but above all, we must needs look upon the late Treaty, wherein they so strongly engaged, as the most prodigious and horrid thing they could have attempted, to the utter, and inevitable ruin of the whole Kingdom, and their own perpetual shame and Infamy, especially, if their Declaration of no more Addresses have any truth in it.

We therefore humbly beseech your Excellency (whom by many sweet experiences we have found to be *Pater Patriae*, a Friend and Father to your Countrey) to look upon our miserable distresses and distractions, with a tender and regardfull eye, to take care for the speedy settlement of our almost ruined Nation. To make good your severall Declarations, Remonstrances, and Proposals lately set forth, (that we may not languish in a tedious expectation of benefit by them) not forgetting your ingaged care, that the Petitions presented to your Excellency and the House, by the wel-wishers to the publick, especially that of 27 Heads, of the 11 of September last, may have their timely consideration. That Iustice may be administred to all, and that those that have been Capitall offenders, may have due punishment, and be presidents [precedents] to future Generations: More particularly, that secure and timely provision may be made against persecution for conscience sake by the usurped power of the Magistrate, as also against the exercise of Arbitrary power, over any mans person, or

Estate, and against the in tollerable oppression of tythes free-quarter, &c.

And in your Excellencies prosecution of these, or the like things, as matters of Iustice and Freedom, (though it should be in wayes extraordinary) your Petitioners will stand by you, and assist you with their Estates and Lives.

Background

By the beginning of 1649, Hertfordshire's activists were accustomed to petitioning. Previous examples had included a petition to the House of Commons, protesting against tithes, in 1647. Militant puritanism had been present there since before the civil war, when local troops recruited to serve in the Bishops' Wars against the Scots (1639-40) mutinied, rioted and destroyed altar rails. Radical preaching and opposition to tithes flourished in and around the Chiltern Hills (including parts of Buckinghamshire, Bedfordshire and Oxfordshire). Travelling Baptist preachers visited Hemel Hempstead and St Albans in the mid-1640s, while Kensworth (now in Bedfordshire) was an established Baptist centre by 1650. Leveller influence may have arrived in the mid-1640s with Richard Overton's writings against tithes; for Hertfordshire people contributed in February 1647 to a petition demanding Overton's and his wife's release from imprisonment, along with that of their fellow Levellers John Lilburne and William Larner.

Hertfordshire radicals offered support to the New Model Army's revolt in 1647, with petitions addressed to Fairfax in June and assistance from local troops on the army's march to London in August. A joint petition to Parliament from the 'well affected' in Oxfordshire, Buckinghamshire and Hertfordshire the following month urged the expulsion of the Presbyterian leadership from the Commons, the execution of justice on all offenders, the abolition of tithes, the freeing of unjustly imprisoned activists, and the removal of 'intollerable burdens of the distressed Commons on their Conscience and Estates'.

This broad alliance between radical Independents and Levellers was disrupted by the events at Ware in November 1647, when several regiments arrived against orders at the rendezvous declaring their support for the *Agreement of the People*. A few days before this event, however, a Hertfordshire petition to Fairfax had described the authors of the Leveller-influenced manifesto, *The Case of the Army Truly Stated*, as men 'much dis-affected to the armies Declarations, and Kingdoms peace'. Local backing for Fairfax and Cromwell's suppression of the disturbance reflected the views of those Independents who had run Hertfordshire's militia committee during the first civil war, and of local men among the officers in Hewson's regiment (Daniel Axtell, see 24 above).

The influence of prominent committee men such as Gabriel Barbour of Hertford and Dr John King of St Albans had been much reduced after the first civil war, when local government institutions like the Justices of the Peace and the county lieutenancy were revived. Hertfordshire's June 1647 petition already complained of the appointment of 'malignants' and disaffected individuals to local offices, 'whereby the most cordial friends of the Parliament are slighted and disregarded; and upon very slender Causes indicted, imprisoned'. An attempt to indict soldiers before the JPs at St Albans for conduct under orders during the war — 'there being but little Favour or Mercy to be had for Parliament Soldiers by the Justices of our County' — led the soldiers to fear they might be disbanded without indemnity. Blaming by-elections for the failure of the House of Commons to address their concerns, the Hertfordshire petitioners at that time had called for the disenfranchisement of Devon, Cornwall and Wales, areas they believed to be 'wholly disaffected to the Proceeds [*sic*] of Parliament'. This was unjust to Devon, at least; but several Hertfordshire politicians had acquired vacant seats in the south-west, some of them 'rotten boroughs' created to boost crown influence in Tudor times.

Leveller support in Hertfordshire did not disappear after Ware. John Lilburne was in Watford in January 1648, on day release from his imprisonment in the Tower of London. The Levellers' 11 September petition is singled out for special mention in the text above, while the loyalty of the county's radical Independents to Fairfax is also reaffirmed by the use of the phrase *pater patriae*, formerly conferred by the Roman senate on eminent citizens. At a time when the county's more conservative politicians were urging the reduction of military forces and relief from taxation in expectation of a peace treaty, these petitioners still saw Fairfax's army as their salvation.

Related sources

The husbandmans plea against tithes. Or, Two petitions presented unto the House of Commons ... Published by some of the Petitioners ... BL/EEBO E.398[2].

To the right honourable ... the Commons House of Parliament (Englands legall Soveraign Power, Assembled,) the humble petition of the inhabitants of Buckinghamshire and Hartfordshire ... [No printer or publisher, 1647] BL/EEBO 669.f.10[115].

Four petitions to His Excellency Sir Thomas Fairfax ... Printed for Laurence Chapman, June 18. 1647. BL/EEBO E.393[7].

The copie of three petitions as they were presented to the Honourable, the House of Commons ... Printed for William Larner, 1647. BL/EEBO E.407[29].

Two Petitions to the Generals Excellency, One from the County of Hertfordshire, concerning the Papers of the five Regiaments ... Printed by Robert Ibbitson, 1 November 1647. BL/EEBO E.412[18].

Alfred Kingston, *Hertfordshire during the Great Civil War and the Long Parliament* (London and Hertford, 1894).

Alan Thomson, *The Impact of the First Civil War on Hertfordshire, 1642-1647* (Hertfordshire Record Society, 2007).

Alan Thomson, *The Ware Mutiny, Order Restored or Revolution Defeated?* (Ware, Rockingham Press with War Museum Trust, 1996).
Underdown, *Pride's Purge*, Appendix A.

55: WORCESTERSHIRE

25 January 1648

Context

Though framed as a 'declaration' rather than a petition, this claims to have been subscribed by a few hundred individuals, including office-holders and grand jurymen as well as citizens and soldiers; and its subscribers hope that their support will be shared by many more when the aims of the *Remonstrance* are achieved. It is, like others in this section, an indication of local support sufficient to secure the English provinces under whatever new regime would follow the king's trial. Its moderation fits Underdown's picture of 'honest' radicals distancing themselves from religious and political extremes, and its avoidance of more specific demands or any direct reference to the king suggests a minimum platform. In secular language (though with the customary nod to god at the end), it extends the idea of patriotism to describe the army leaders as 'patterns' to all other nations.

Text

A Petition of the Justices of Peace, Grand Jury men, and other Gentlemen, at the Quarter Sessions holden at Hereford ... With a Ioyfull Acclamation From the wel-affected in the City and County of Worcester. Presented to the Lord General Fairfax, and Councel of Officers. Thursday Ianuary 25. 1648. Published by Authority. Printed by Giles Calvert. 1649.
[Herefordshire Record Office (courtesy of Stoke Edith Estate)]

Upon Thursday, January 25, there was presented to his Excellency, and his General Counsel of War, an Acclamation from the Wel affected Gentlemen of the Committee, Ministers, Common-Councel, Grand Jury, Souldiers, and divers hundreds of the Inhabitants of the County and City of Worcester, as followeth:

For his Excellency Thomas Lord Fairfax, and the honorable Councel of War. The joyful Acclamations of the well-affected, in the City and County of Worcester.

Blessed Patriots; for you have been blessed: And the real pursuance of your late Remonstrance (so uprightly stated) will record you so much more to all posterity, Founders of our Peace, as well as confounders of our foes.

We cannot but send you our Acclamations to strengthen and quicken your hands in that mighty work; and few, though we be, that yet appear, yet assured we are, that suitable actings to such just Principles (you neither seeking yourselves, nor too much the compliance of others) will soon bring in all the upright in the Land unto you. And not onely so, but will further make you glorious Patterns to all other people, for the good of all Nations.

Proceed therefore (or else undoubtedly you soon ruine, both your friends, and selves) vigorously, and th[o]roughly in the name of the Lord, and you will eternize your own, while we subscribe ours: In life and death:

Yours in all righteous ways, for Publike Interest.

Mr. Moor was desired to return thanks from his Excellency and General Officers, to the foresaid Gentlemen, for their good affections; and that their desires should be promoted.

Another edition

The Moderate, No.30, 30 January – 6 February 1648/9. BL/EEBO E.541[15].

Background

Worcestershire presents one of the paradoxes of the first English Civil War: the county is regularly characterised as royalist, but the two county MPs elected in 1640 developed into the most fiercely radical Independents, and were joined from 1645 by a contingent of mainly like-minded recruits. Though royalist forces occupied Worcestershire throughout the war and local royalists ruled until the New Model Army gained the upper hand in 1645-6, its people were not uniformly royalist in sympathy. We need to re-examine the idea — long a favourite in student essays — that the whole county lay in a royalist area, famously characterised by Christopher Hill as 'the economically backward areas of the north and west', by contrast with parliamentarian 'economically advanced' south and east of England.

Worcestershire is not easily categorised within this scheme. From the Malvern Hills to the fringe of modern Birmingham, it embraced a wide spectrum of economic activities by the 1640s, with nearly one in five of the population occupied in industries such as textiles, coal mining and iron-working. Worcester and other ports on the Severn linked the marches of Wales and the west midlands to Bristol's international trade. The county was a valuable prize for either side, and war was profitable to its entrepreneurs who supplied weapons, gunpowder and clothing. Social tensions were evident before the civil wars: wealthy clothiers profited from the work of poor spinners and weavers, the government tried to suppress tobacco growing in the Vale of Evesham (to protect Virginia), and local inhabitants rioted in defence of their common rights when royal forest land was parcelled out for enclosure. Puritanism had arrived in towns such as Kidderminster, where Richard Baxter as preacher was beginning his struggle to build a godly minority. These and other conflicts of interest combined to produce, according to Worcestershire's historian Malcolm Atkin, 'a suspicious and quarrelsome atmosphere of rising rancour' on the eve of war. Atkin suggests that people tended to ally with whichever side in the national conflict seemed more ready to attend to their grievances, or was simply opposite to the one supported by their antagonists.

In March 1645 a popular rising against the 'outrages and violence' of the royalist soldiers called for king and Parliament to unite against evil advisers and arbitrary government. Before the end of the year a group of gentry openly declared their adherence to Parliament and raised a force in support of the New Model Army. Discontent among the townspeople of Worcester when Colonel Thomas Rainborowe laid siege to it forced the royalist governor to capitulate after a few weeks rather than endure a blockade or storming. The county was then occupied by parliamentarian troops, Rainborowe remaining governor of Worcester until April 1647. A new local regime was formed of parliamentarian supporters, while like-minded individuals who had left the county for the duration of the war began to return. Some, like Richard Salway — whose father Humphrey was one of the county MPs — arrived with Rainborowe's army. Others returned from Coventry, where Richard Baxter and his fellow puritans had taken refuge. The radical preacher John Tombes (see 50 above), now fully committed to adult baptism, returned to his native Bewdley to found a Baptist congregation there.

Pockets of royalist support nevertheless remained, and the regime was constantly on the lookout for opposition. In January 1648, Worcester rioters protested against the excise tax, and further trouble was averted after a group of parliamentarian officers from the forces currently being disbanded met at Broadway to discuss resistance. In March, Captain Edward Wogan of Okey's regiment led his troop out of Worcestershire to join the Scots mobilising for the king in Edinburgh. There was little or no fighting in the county during the second civil war, however, and a planned royalist revolt under Colonel Dud Dudley was nipped in the bud in July.

Meanwhile, Worcestershire's two county MPs supported the Independents in post-war parliamentarian politics. Humphrey Salway was among those who fled to the New Model Army after the House of Commons was invaded by a pro-Presbyterian mob on 26 July 1647; and Serjeant-at-Law John Wylde was the assize judge who delivered a radical resolution from the grand inquest of Somerset to Parliament on 10 October 1648 (see 4 above, 56 below). Both were as anti-Leveller as they were anti-Presbyterian, and both survived Pride's Purge. Wylde, now Chief Baron of the Exchequer, joined the rest of the judges in refusing to have the king tried in any regular court. Although Salway was nominated to the High Court of Justice he never appeared there; but he and Wylde both returned to the Commons after the king's death. MPs joining the Commons from Worcestershire in 1645 included Colonel Thomas Rainborowe and a cousin of John Wylde for Droitwich, where this family had long had influence. After Rainborowe's death John Wylde's brother George arrived in the Commons the day after Pride's Purge and dissented from the acceptance of the king's answers along with his kinsmen. It seems likely that the county's 'joyful acclamation' above was framed by this Independent clique, seeking political reinforcement by obtaining subscriptions among the county's office-holders and others.

Related sources

Malcolm Atkin, *Worcestershire Under Arms, An English County during the Civil Wars* (Barnsley: Pen and Sword, 2004).

W. R. Williams, *The Parliamentary History of the County of Worcester ... 1213-1897* (Hereford: privately printed, 1897).

Richard Greaves and Robert Zaller, *Biographical Dictionary of Seventeenth-century British Radicals*, vol. 3 (Humphrey Salway, John Wilde or Wylde).

ODNB: C. H. Firth, 'Salwey, Richard (*bap.* 1615, d. 1686)', rev. Sean Kelsey.

ODNB: Robert Zaller, 'Wilde, John (1590–1669)'.

David Underdown. '"Honest" radicals in the counties, 1642-1649', in Donald Pennington and Keith Thomas (eds.), *Puritans and Revolutionaries, Essays in seventeenth-century history presented to Christopher Hill* (Oxford: Clarendon, 1978).

PART SIX

PETITIONS TO PARLIAMENT

FROM PRIDE'S PURGE TO THE KING'S EXECUTION

DECEMBER 1648 – FEBRUARY 1649

56: SOMERSET

21 December 1648

Context

The presentation of this Somerset petition in Parliament was followed by a 'Day of Humiliation' with prayers, fasting and sermons, marking a return to the business of the king. The members still sitting in the purged Commons had reinstated the Vote of No Addresses, 'and annulled the vote accepting the king's last answers as sufficient grounds for proceeding to a settlement. They had heard the army's other demands of 6 December (32 above) read twice, but refused to reach any resolution before they had an answer to their requests for the release of the imprisoned members, which only began on 20 December. On the same day, they began to readmit members willing to register their dissent from the vote on the king's answers, which would gradually increase the numbers sitting. But it was not until 23 December that they set up a committee 'to consider how to proceed in a way of Justice against the King, and other Capital Offenders'.

The petition below does not target the king by name, and its other points are moderate. Though urging 'a settled sufficiency' for ministers, it avoids explicitly advocating the abolition of tithes. Its plea to Parliament to 'accept that peace which God ... tenders, and not take one from flesh, or from the hands of your Enemies' resembles a passage in Oliver Cromwell's letter to Robert Hammond a few weeks earlier, but it is unlikely that Cromwell had anything to do with this petition.

Text

To the Honorable, The Commons assembled in Parliament, The humble Petition of divers Gentlemen, Ministers, and well-affected Inhabitants in the County of Somerset. London, Printed for Edward Husband, Printer to the Honorable House of Commons, Jan. 5. 1648 [1649]. BL/EEBO: 669.f.13[66]

That your Petitioners calling to minde the continuate actions of your Enemies for years past (especially those mentioned in your several Declarations) and their late Design for a second War, finde their Ayms destructive, and their Malice adusted [*sic*], and can expect no Peace from them (their specious pretence notwithstanding:) But when your Petitioners reflect their thoughts on that powerful Providence which hath still attended your Preservation (even to the height of Miracle) and frustrated that late Design (laid confidently for your Ruine) by the hands of a few of your dispersed Army, weakned by neglect of Friends, and fighting a potent enraged Enemy (emboldened with assurance of Success) We your Petitioners rest in admiration of Gods mercy towards you; and do hope shortly to enjoy a well-grounded peace (if the Vote of No further Address be not too much forgotten) and a Reformation, according to the Word of God (the result of our wishes and prayers) and to see Justice executed, the ends of the National

Covenant. In pursuance of which we humbly pray,

That you accept that peace which God, your Protector; tenders, and not take one from flesh, or from the hands of your Enemies, lest the Kingdom, yourselves, and we, become their prey.

That a Reformation be speedied and setled, according to Gods Word.

That Justice be done upon great Offendors (a second time brought before you) in satisfaction of the blood shed in your quarrel, confessed by your very Enemies to be innocent, and not to be quieted (we are confident) by an Act of Oblivion, or otherwise, then by an impartial Justice.

That your Armies (approved faithful) be encouraged, duly paid, not laid aside, until your Enemies have laid down their thoughts of Blood and Slaughter.

That the pious Ministery may have a setled sufficiency, and not deprived of their augmentation; the fruits of your Justice, and reward of their sufferings.

Die Jovis [Thursday], 21 Decembr. 1648

The House being informed, That some Gentlemen of the County of Somerset were at the door, they were called in; and there presented a Petition, which was entituled, *The Humble Petition of divers Gentlemen, Ministers, and well-affected Inhabitants of the County of Somerset*, which after the Petitioners were withdrawn, was read: The Petitioners being afterwards called in, Mr Speaker gave them this answer:

Gentlemen, The house hath read your Petition, which consists of three Points, which sheweth your great care of Justice, Safety and Religion; wherein you deserve extraordinary Thanks, and the House hath commanded me to give you Thanks, and I do give you Thanks accordingly. And the House hath commanded me to tell you, That it is their Resolution with all speed to take into their serious consideration the three Points of your Petition, consisting of Justice, Safety and Religion.

Ordered by the Commons assembled in Parliament, That this Petition be forthwith printed and published.

H. Elsynge, Cler. Parl. D. Com.

Background

Despite the reputation of Somerset's leaders for extremism at the time and since, the only Somerset MP nominated to the committee for proceeding against the king, Lislebone Long (Wells), played no part in the trial or execution, but stayed away from Parliament after 25 December. The county's history during and after the civil wars suggests that a group combining religious Presbyterianism with political Independency, rather than a radical Independent one, held power in the county by late 1648.

During the first civil war, Somerset had passed from parliamentarian into royalist hands and back again, with much fighting and bitterness on both sides. Local royalist Sir Francis Dodington's execution of prisoners secured him a permanent place on Parliament's list of delinquents to be excluded from pardon after the wars. West Somerset clubmen in revolt against Goring's royalist army in the spring of 1645 called on both sides to make peace under the king's rule; but later risings in east and north Somerset inclined towards Parliament, and helped Fairfax to retake Bristol. David Underdown largely based his polarisation of clubmen's risings between neutral or royalist insurgents in the 'chalk' lands and those more favourable to Parliament in the upland or wooded 'cheese' areas on this and neighbouring counties.

After the first civil war the parliamentarian County Committee was restored, but the political differences in Parliament were reflected here in a way that was unusual but not unique (see 3, 4 and 5 above). The most prominent committee members, Alexander Popham from a leading gentry family and John Pyne the squire of Curry Mallet near Taunton, were committed to a Presbyterian religious settlement but politically favoured the Independents. Neither played any part in the regicide; nor did Sir Thomas Wroth, despite his January 1648 speech in Parliament praying 'from devils and Kings Good Lord deliver me ... I desire any government other than that of kings'. In the hotly contested by-elections of 1645-46, fourteen of Somerset's MPs who had died or been disqualified as royalists (out of a total sixteen) were replaced, and among the new recruits the anti-Independent Clement Walker won Wells's second seat. Walker's voluminous polemics against the Independents' alleged anarchy were matched by his fellow Presbyterian and Somerset native William Prynne, who took a Cornish constituency in November 1648. Both accused John Pyne of bullying and manipulation, and dismissed the rich clothiers and successful merchants on the committee as unfit to rule because of their inferior social standing.

Pyne was accused by his enemies of packing the Grand Inquest of freeholders at the Taunton assizes in September 1648 to push through a radical petition addressed to Parliament. The survival of an annotated list of freeholders suggests that he may have vetted some names for loyalty to the current regime; but it would be naïve to suppose that the royalists had not done the same when in power. In this case the presiding judge, Serjeant-at-Law John Wylde (see 4 and 55 above), may have been the chief influence on the petition, whose actual text does not survive. A version of the 10 October 1648 debate published in an eighteenth century compilation, based only partly on *Mercurius Pragmaticus*'s contemporary account (see 4 and 5 above) describes it as being expressed 'in a much higher strain than the other two'. The *Commons Journal* records only a 'presentment' from the Grand Inquest, which normally meant a list of formal indictments arising from the cases heard; and the House formally thanked Wylde for his good service. This slender evidence of Somerset 'extremism' has greatly influenced views of the petition above.

This text is far from extreme, compared with others. Clement Walker condemned it as sectarian, originating from 'private interest in Conventicles and corners; as are all the bloudy Petitions for justice against capitall Delinquents', and labelled Somerset's well-affected 'all the Anarchists and Cheaters'. Though the accusation of anarchy was commonly aimed at England's Baptist sects (evoking the Anabaptist takeover of Munster a century earlier), the author of this petition is unlikely to have been the Baptist preacher Thomas Collier, as later alleged. Collier visited Somerset in the early 1640s, and by 1648 Taunton had a Baptist congregation; but the text bears no sign of his individual style or beliefs. Defending the *Remonstrance* at the time of this petition, he called on the army to set up a godly government rather than an elected one, since 'those who are saved spiritually know best what is good for the nations temporal wellbeing.' The petitioners do not draw this political conclusion from god's almost miraculous intervention in the wars. Nor do they explicitly call for the king's death, which Collier did elsewhere, appealing to the biblical passage calling for the shedding of the blood of killers (Genesis 9:6, see 28 above and 65 below).

The petitioners' demand for 'a reformation according to Gods Word' echoes the Solemn League and Covenant of 1643. Collier, however, had denounced the Westminster Assembly set up by it to design a religious settlement for England, finding 'no rule in the Book of God' for it. The petition may have obtained some support Taunton's Baptists, but it is unlikely to have originated with them or with Collier, as it seems to be appealing to religious Presbyterians rather than Independents.

Along with Wroth, John Pyne (MP for Poole in Dorset) was named to the High Court of Justice, but each attended only one session, and neither signed the king's death warrant. Nine Somerset MPs took their seats in the Rump, but only two of them before the king's execution. Clement Walker was imprisoned at Pride's Purge, along with his fellow Presbyterian William Strode, and two more were excluded; while two others simply stopped attending, and the sixteenth, Walter Strickland, served the new regime as a roving diplomat. The majority of the Somerset contingent therefore acted in the role of Underdown's 'honest' radicals, running the county under the Commonwealth and supporting the new regime as a bulwark against a more radical revolution, a prospect they feared as a dangerous threat to social stability and private property.

There is no surviving evidence for Leveller activity in Somerset before April 1649, when troops billeted around Taunton were reported to be spreading radical ideas. Local Levellers were later reported to be 'exceedingly dishartned' by the defeat of the mutineers at Burford and William Thompson's Midlands rising; though they were also said to have refused their support to Thompson. Parliament thanked Wroth and Pyne for raising a volunteer force to deal with the Leveller threat, but they appear to have dispersed peacefully.

Related sources

Commons Journal, vol. vi, 21 December 1648.
Mercurio Volpone, 5-12 October 1648. BL/EEBO: E.467[22].
Mercurius Pragmaticus, No. 29, 10-17 October 1648. BL/EEBO: E.467[38].
Thomas Collier, *A Vindication of the Army-Remonstrance*. BL/EEBO: E.477[6].
'Theorodus Verax' [Clement Walker], *Anarchia Anglicana, or The History of Independency, The Second Part* (1649). BL/EEBO: E.570[4].
Old Parliamentary History, vol. 18 (pp. 31-2).
David Underdown, *Somerset in the Civil War and Interregnum* (Newton Abbot, David and Charles, 1973).
ODNB: David Underdown, 'Pyne, John (*bap.* 1600, d. 1678)'.
ODNB: John Wroughton, 'Wroth [Wrothe], Sir Thomas (1584-1672)'.
ODNB: John Wroughton, 'Long, Lislebone [created Sir Lislebone Long under the Protectorate] (*bap.* 1613, d. 1659)'.
ODNB: Stephen Wright, 'Collier, Thomas (d. 1691)'.

57: KENT

23 December 1648

Context

The Kentish petition above (51) was presented to the army and this one was read in the House of Commons on the same day, after the House had set up a committee to consider ways of bringing the king and other 'capital offenders' to trial. Since the army council had appointed their own committee for the same purpose on 15 December, and had by now removed the king from Hurst to Windsor, the business could no longer be avoided. The Kentish petitioners may have decided to address both Parliament and the army while the outcome remained uncertain.

Despite the difference in the language and content between the two petitions — directing the more religious preamble to Fairfax and his army as god's instruments, while the approach to Parliament praises its actions since Pride's Purge — the content of both is centred on bringing those responsible for the civil wars to justice, while indicating a more general support for the *Remonstrance*. The focus here is more specifically on the king himself.

The version of the Commons' answer given in the text below differs from the official record in the *Commons Journal*, which does not include the words, 'especially in the eastern part', leaving us in little doubt that East Kent (which includes Canterbury) is where this petition originated.

Text

The Kentish Petition: To the Honourable The Commons now sitting in Parliament: The humble Petition of diverse [sic] *well-affected in the County of Kent, the City and County of Canterbury, together with the Cinque Ports, in the behalfe of themselves and others.* Printed for Hanna Allen, at the Crown in Popes head Alley, 1648. BL/EEBO: 669.f.13[64]

Humbly sheweth, That we cannot but with all thankfulness take notice of, & acknowledge those Votes that passed this Honourable House, December, 13, 1648, for the disanulling of certain Votes formerly made, and now appearing to be dishonourable and destructive to the publike good, viz. for the nulling of those former Votes which were made for the recalling of those former votes of Non-addresses to the King; and also for the nulling of those Votes which were for the approbation of the Kings answer to the Propositions as a ground for peace; and for Voting the whole Treaty in the Isle of Wight, as dishonorble [*sic*] and destructive to the publike, &c. As being fully convinced of the justice, honour and necessity of the said Votes: and forasmuch as we are confident that justice is the best foundation of a Nation, and the punishment of offenders a chief branch of justice.

We do therefore humbly beseech this Honorable House according to the Armies Remonstrance (that great and best expedient hitherto proposed for

57: KENT, 23 DECEMBER 1648

the publike settlement) to proceed to a speedy bringing to justice (that grand Author of all our miseries) the Person of Him, who as a King ought to have defended us, but as a Tyrant hath actually levied Arms and waged War against us, together with all other great Delinquents, both in the first and second War, as well those of your own House as any others.

And to continue in a speedy vigorous and undaunted acting, with that ever faithfull Army, in all things that tend to the wel-fare, safety and settlement of the wel-affected people.

And your petitioners resolving with their lives and all that's dear to them, to stand by you, shall ever pray, &c.

The Gentlemen of Kent presented this Petition unto the House on Saturday the 23 of December. 1648, The House called them in, and Master Speaker told them, the House looked upon the honest men in Kent, had ever proved faithfull to the Parliament, especially the Eastern part: And for the things, petitioned, the House was now in consideration of them: and for the Subscribers, who now shew their good affection, the House gives them thanks.

Background

See 51 above for a discussion of the Kentish background and the nature of the county's dominant form of radicalism at this time, and 65 below for further information about petitioners in Kent.

58: GARRISON OF HULL

25 December 1648

Context

It is not clear that this petition was ever read in the House of Commons. The *Commons Journal* entry for 25 December (a working day, as the Christmas holiday was banned) does not mention it, though it may have been obliterated with part of the day's proceedings in 1659. Several newsbooks reported only a debate on whether members who had been excluded at Pride's Purge could be re-admitted, and an order for the committee to consider proceedings against the king and others to meet in the afternoon.

The message of the petition is straightforward, demanding justice against 'capital offenders' and supporting the *Remonstrance*. Some of the language used is little more than padding, with the conventions common to many other petitions. The Yorkshire petition to which the petitioners say they contributed in October (5 above) was far more startling in its language, with explicit belief in divine intervention and the necessity of appeasing god by cleansing the land of blood guilt. Indeed, the strongest contrast is that this one does not mention god at all — an omission which might be thought unusual in any seventeenth-century political document and is shared by just two others in this collection (24 above and 66 below).

Text

A Perfect Diurnall, 25 December - 1 January 1648-9

Dateline Monday 25 December.

BL/EEBO: E.527[1]

For the Right Honourable the Commons of England Assembled in Parliament. The humble Petition of his Excellencies Officers and Souldiers in his Garrison of Kingston upon Hull.

That your Petitioners having with the late addresses of this County ineffectually offered their own desires for civill Justice to be done upon the persons, and Estates of Cappitall offenders in the former and later Wars. But finding that in the un-Masqueing of this most just desires [*sic*], the reprehensions of the House by their denyall or neglect, have hitherto stamped so great a discouragement on our minds and memories, as had almost silenced truth and innocency it self, did not the satisfaction we have received from the Remonstrance of our most Renowned Generall, and his generall Councell of the Army; reinforce our courage and resolution, to cast off that discommendable crime of blushing at a vertuous action, or succumbling under the burthen of so unsuitable a silence in so common a concernment, as hath throughly ingaged us in these readdresses to your honours; wherein we devote our adherence to his Excellency and the Army in their Remonstrance, and the perticulars of it; In which pursuance we

Repetition your Honourable and speedy comportment, not doubting but the effectuateing thereof will Crown your former Councels, and perfect our present peace, nor want we further hope, that the great reason and Justice therein rendred, will so powerfully on your parts perswade, that you will not repent the grant of which we have Petitioned or sewed for. Thus not fearing that our duty therein shall arive at labour in vain, we do assert unto our selves, that our love and service to the publique good, and your just Power and Priviledge shall ever run in an undevided Channell. Which would otherwise by the wounds of seperation bleed to death; that your Honours may prove the repayrers of our breaches, and true proper Parents of Peace.

Your Petitioners will ever pray, &c.

Background

Compared with the full revolutionary programme addressed to Fairfax and the Council of Officers by the same garrison on 9 January 1649 (44 above), the scope of this short petition to the House of Commons is limited. Its encouragement to the Rump to get on with the business of bringing those responsible for the civil wars to justice backed the Commons' decision two days earlier to set up a committee for that purpose.

For additional background and related sources, see 17 and 44 above.

59: NORFOLK

26 December 1648

Context

The *Commons Journal* records the presentation of this petition on 26 December 1648 by 'divers gentlemen of Norfolk', and the answer that was given to them: 'Most of the Particulars of your Petition they have already taken into Consideration, and the other Things they shall so take into Consideration, and proceed so therein, as shall be to the Satisfaction of the Kingdom'. Perhaps significantly, the Commons' very next business was to extend the scope of the committee they had appointed to consider proceedings against the king: it was now also 'to consider of, and present to the House, some general Heads concerning a Settlement'.

Text

A Perfect Diurnall, no. 238, 25 December 1648 – 1 January 1649. BL/EEBO: E.527[1].

The Kingdomes Weekly Intelligencer, 26 December – 2 January 1649. BL/EEBO: E.536[33].

The humble Petition of the well affected Gentry, and other Inhabitants of the county of Norfolke, and County of the City of Norwich.

Humbly sheweth, That after a vast expence of blood and treasure for many years continuance, we have expected a firme establishment of our Native Liberties; but by the just hand of God upon us for our old and new provocations in our unchristian divisions, and abominable self-seeking that is amongst us, even of all conditions; and through the restlesse malice of our secret and open adversaries, wee are under the shadows of hope cast back into as great fears and dangers as ever, having no greater security against our first removed evils then at first, if so much. Now to the end wee may not deliver up our selves to ruine, by neglect of our first principles, sealed with Oathes, Vowes and Covenants, as well as the naturall ties of sense and reason, assuring Common and publique, if not Universall good hereby. We humbly offer these following offers to the honourable House for redresse of present, and prevention of future evils, *viz*.

1. That present enquirie be made who have been the chiefe Instruments of the King in the former or this latter war, and the late inviting and bringing in of the Scots; and that he himselfe, and all such as have been the most notorious Incendiaries and Instruments in shedding blood, may without further delay bee brought to due and impartiall Justice. The remissnesse in which upon serious inquisition wee fear to be one of the chiefest causes of Gods so great displeasure, in the severall judgements now in this Nation.

2. That Courts of Justice both for law and equitie, Judges, Officers, and Fees certain, and Laws in the vulgar Tongue, and all other things concerning the administration of Justice in this Kingdome may without respect of persons be so speedily setled as may agree most with the rule of Christian duty, just reason, and the true birthright and priviledge of Englishmen; And that accordingly impartiall Commissioners be forthwith authorized and employed to try the severall persons that had any hand in the mutinies in Norwich, Kent, and other Counties.
3. That some speedy course be taken whereby the way of discharge of the debts, especially the publique debts of the Kingdome may be ascertained, and to that end that no more Compositions be made with Delinquents till they be all discharged, and the last penny due as arreare, or shall become due to the Army satisfied; and such as shall be thought fit to be sold to be ascertained, and the same accordingly performed, extending as well to the new as to the old Delinquents, and that all further Taxes for the security of the Kingdome, may throughout the whole Kingdome be made as easie and laid as proportionably, and so to be levied as can by your wisdomes be contrived.
4. That such as have been in action in the last war, or formerly against the Common-wealth, may be disabled from all offices and places of trust in Parliament or elsewhere, that under the notion of a Peece wee be not voted or contrived into ruine by them that could not beat us into it, and to that end that a speciall Committee be ordained to order and regulate affaires of State during the intervals of Parliament.
5. That the power of the Militia of the Kingdom may not bee conferred by your Authority on Malignants or Newters, but that the same may be put into such hands onely, whose integrity, fidelity, and affection to the Parliament cannot justly be suspected.
6. That the Army whose faithfulnesse and constancy wee cannot but acknowledge, may be vindicated against all unjust odiums and aspersions cast upon them, especially for their late proceedings in order to impartiall Justice upon the capitall offender, the best means to establish this dying and almost miserable destroyed Nation, and the better preventing the odium of the people against them occasioned by free quarter, that constant pay be provided for them. And your Petitioners shall pray, &c.

Background

It is difficult to identify the 'well-affected gentry' who supported this petition. Most modern studies of Norfolk emphasise the conservatism of that class, who were strongly inclined towards peace in late 1642, and delayed their military preparations until Parliament's Eastern Association established firm control the following year. Norfolk MP Sir John Potts believed that the people 'generally' were for Parliament, but confessed he would not feel safe 'when soever necessity shall enforce us to make use of the multitude'.

Norfolk had seen a serious rural rebellion in 1549 and widespread enclosure riots in 1611, and the destruction of fences on crown land in June 1641 may well have aroused other landowners' fears.

Despite the gentry's reluctance, the people of Norfolk mobilised for Parliament when choice became unavoidable. A volunteer company was raised in Norwich for defence against supposed Catholic threats in 1641, and the county militia was raised in September 1642. While attempts to raise forces for the king were prevented, Captain Robert Swallow raised a troop for Parliament 'at the charge of the young men and maids' in Norwich, and was granted £61 from city funds to equip them for Cromwell's cavalry regiment. Lord Grey of Wark took fifty more Norwich men to serve under Cromwell, 'as an inducement to the Parliament to relieve the said city in time of need'. Yarmouth banned the reading of the king's commission of array, and in 1643 Sir Miles Hobart raised a foot regiment of 'Norfolk redcoats' for the Eastern Association. Captain John Jubbes, arming himself 'in conscience and judgement ... for the recovery of my Countries Rights & Freedom', recruited men for Hobart in his own locality (thought to be Wymondham) and later served in the New Model. There was little military action in the county after King's Lynn was regained from the Royalists in 1643 (see 29 above). Royalist plots were nipped in the bud, while the coasts and inland frontier were held firmly for Parliament.

Religious issues divided the people of Norfolk, with dissenting roots going back more than a century. An intrusive visitation of parishes by Matthew Wren, Bishop of Norwich from 1635 to 1638, exposed differences of opinion and practice. A Norfolk trust was set up in 1631 to purchase privately owned tithes to endow preaching ministers, while sympathetic patrons placed preaching ministers in rural parishes like Hingham, whose pastor Robert Peck led a party of emigrants from Norfolk (including an ancestor of Abraham Lincoln) to Massachusetts Bay. Pressure for further reform of the church met with opposition, and religious discord was most intense in the city of Norwich, where some parish churches confronted puritans with provocative ornamentation and were denounced by the puritan ministers of others. The town council of Great Yarmouth had quarrelled for years with the bishops over the appointment of preachers, while King's Lynn maintained a preaching lectureship but avoided conflict with the ecclesiastical authorities. In 1644 puritan aldermen led an attack on religious images in Norwich cathedral, burning their plunder after 'a kind of Sacrilegious and profane procession', according to Bishop Joseph Hall.

After 1645, the Presbyterian system found many supporters in Norfolk; while the growth of Independent congregations and sects added to religious tensions. Politically, Presbyterians dominated the mid-1640s by-elections, and five of those elected across the county would be excluded at Pride's Purge. But Thomas Atkins — a Norwich-born merchant who served as Lord Mayor of London in 1644-5 — was elected for Norwich in 1646, and acted with political Independents such as Miles Corbett (MP for Yarmouth), despite his own religious preference for Presbyterianism. King's Lynn, where Valentine Walton (MP for Huntingdonshire) returned as governor in 1647, elected Independent Thomas Toll, along with a royalist who was expelled from the House.

Just as civil war was breaking out again in 1648, political and religious conflict in Norwich produced a singular tragedy known as the Great Blow. Resentment against the parliamentarian regime crystallised there (as in Canterbury) in agitation for the restoration of Christmas festivities in 1647, but Puritan citizens opposed to Christmas petitioned the city council for further godly reformation. They accused the mayor, Richard Utting, of laxity and corruption, and in April 1648 had him arrested on a parliamentary warrant. Rioting broke out, a troop of Fleetwood's horse was sent to quell it, and rioters raiding the committee house for weapons and gunpowder triggered an explosion that killed at least forty people. The religious reformers saw the carnage as God's punishment on the rioters. Their party took over the city, voted money to Fleetwood's troops, gave Fairfax a warm reception in August, and sent Cromwell a congratulatory address a few days before the king's execution. Many rioters were tried, and eight hanged in January 1649.

It is not known who organised the petition above, or how they did so. The most likely candidates are the corporation of Norwich, MPs Corbett and Atkins, and Colonel Walton at King's Lynn. The demand for laws and legal proceedings in English suggests some Leveller influence, but it is hard to locate any local source. Compared with the thorough-going radicalism of Walton's regiment's petition (29 above), such input may have been deliberately avoided in order to appeal to a wider base.

Related sources

Clive Holmes, *The Eastern Association in the English Civil War* (Cambridge, Cambridge University Press, 1974).
R. W. Ketton-Cremer, *Norfolk in the Civil War, a Portrait of a Society in Conflict* (London, Faber, 1969).
Francis Blomefield, *An Essay towards a Topographical History of the County of Norfolk* (Fersfield, 1739).
Champlin Burrage, *The Early English Dissenters* (Cambridge, Cambridge University Press, 1912).
Matthew Reynolds, *Godly Reformers and their Opponents in Early Modern England, Religion in Norwich c. 1560-1643* (Woodbridge, Boydell, 2005).
C. B. Jewson, 'Norfolk Baptists up to 1700', *Baptist Quarterly*, vol. 18 (1960).
ODNB: Richard L. Greaves, 'Bridge, William (1600/01–1671)'.
ODNB: Sarah Barber, 'Corbett, Miles (1594/5–1662)'.
ODNB: Keith Roberts, 'Jubbes, John (*fl.* 1643–1649)'.

60: HEREFORDSHIRE

9 January 1649

Context

Though agreed at the JPs' Hereford quarter sessions on 9 January 1649, this petition was not read in the House of Commons until 3 February. It may be that subscriptions were still being canvassed until then, or that it was held back until the king's trial was over. The burden of the war and the current military occupation of Herefordshire are central to the petitioners' concerns. Their call for preachers to be sent to 'those that sit in darkness' was to be repeated by another petition from the same quarter sessions in March 1650, shortly after an Act of Parliament was passed 'for the better Propagation and Preaching of the Gospel in Wales'. This was a long-standing missionary project currently led by the Cornish-born Independent minister and friend of Cromwell Hugh Peter, though historians have seen its outcome as an influx of English influence into Wales.

The manuscript copy bears the autograph signatures of two Justices of the Peace, John James and Thomas Rawlings, and lists fifteen jurors. All the printed versions add four more JPs and thirty-five gentlemen. The manuscript may have been conveyed to Sir Robert Harley before the subscriptions were completed.

Text

A Petition of the Justices of Peace, Grand Jury men, and other Gentlemen, at the Quarter Sessions holden at Hereford for the same County. Presented to The Right Honorable House of Commons Assembled in Parliament ... Published by Authority. Printed by Giles Calvert. 1649. Herefordshire Record Office: E12 BG 46/48. [By permission of Mr. Foley of Stoke Edith Estate.]

To the Right Honorable, the House of Commons in Parliament Assembled.

The Humble Petition of the Justices of Peace, Grand Jury men, and other Gentlemen at the Quarter Sessions holden at Hereford for the same County, the 9. day of January, 1648.

Sheweth, That being sensible of the miseries of this poor almost wasted Kingdom, and of the long continued sufferings of this County in particular, and finding by experience we had been all brought to extream miserie, and total ruine before this day, had not God appeared as wonderful with, and for the General, Lieutenant General, and their faithful Commanders and souldiers of late, as ever he did by miracles for his people of old; and in our apprehensions, there being under you no other visible means or power, by whom God doth appear to save this poor Kingdom from the bloody Irish, that party of perfidious, plundering Scots that last invaded our Kingdom, together with the Malignant, Trecherous English, then this present Army, whose valour God hath made a terror to all our enemies; do therefore humbly propound, That you will hear the General, and General Councel of the Army, in all things tending to the speedie settlement of this Kingdom, that as one man we may joyn together to oppose what force soever shall invade us. That you will take a speedy course that all Treasurers, Committees, and Sequestrators be brought to a speedy and strict account. That the best advantage be made of all Sequestrated estates, and the general receipts of the Kingdom may be improved for the publike, with the best advantage. That you will take a special care for the payment of the Army, and with all possible speed take of the great burthen of Free Quarter. That no man be forced to give Free Quarter, unlesse he deny, or delay payment of his Assessment. That the Salary, or allowance of men in publick Imployments, may not exceed, during the continuance of our great payments. And that no man may be forced to serve the State at his own charge, from the greatest, to a petty Constable, That all such persons as be in any publick imployment, that lengthen our miseries, by turning with all windes and tides for their own advantage, may be put out, and all opportunities taken to putt an end to our troubles, that the generation to come may bless God for some that continued faithful. That you will send forth men of able gifts and parts to preach the Gospel to those that sit in darkness. And lastly, give us leave to present the great sufferings of this County, by paying in all paiments, almost, (if not altogether) double as much as any adjacent County, occasioned formerly by difference, and malice between some of the chief houses, and families of our County, and our great sufferings when the Scots lay so long before *Hereford*; the many thousand pounds that have been collected from us to disband Col. *Birches* Regiment, of which (we never received one peny) and others raised since; and yet never being freed from free quartering, unlesse it were for some few weeks.

All which, we hope, you will take into consideration, in conve[n]ient time, and in all your good endeavors, tending to a speedy settlement of this Kingdom, we will to the utmost of our power, as God shall enable us, assist you and your faithful Army under the Command of the General.

And shall ever pray, &c.

Justices of Peace: Thomas Baskerville, John James, Thomas Rawlings, Francis Pember, Henry Williams, Thomas Seaborne, Esquire, Major [Mayor] of the City of *Hereford*.

Grand Jury: John Vernal, Thomas Andrews, Iohn Lenitoll, Anthony Carwardine, William Clark, Iohn Taylor, Richard Gwatkin, Thomas Church, Iohn Leech junior, Iohn Lufton, Thomas Eynion, Iohn Simmonds, Rowland Bethel, Iohn Colley, William Marsh, Thomas Williams, Francis Sheward, William Brown, Thomas Danet.

Gentlemen: Sir Iohn Bridges, Knight and Baronet, Robert Higgins, Thomas Higgins, Arthur Cockerham, Robert Flacket, Thomas Careles, Oliver Chambers, Francis Walker, Miles Hill, Francis Pember junior, Henry

Williams, Iohn Herring, Verney Higgins, Thomas Hewet, Francis Bifield, Alexander Garston, Iohn Pembridg, William Careles, Iohn Wolfe, Philip Sterky, Ioseph Patshal, Edward Hussey, Iohn Adis, Iohn Cholmley, Thomas Williams, Iohn Walsam, William Williams, Iames Woodhouse, Iohn Harris, Edmund Orub [Grubb], Walter Wallaston, William Hoper, Richard Putney.

The Gentlemen that presented this Petition, were by the Sergeant of the House, called unto the Commons Bar, where Mr Speaker told them, that he was commanded by the House, to give them hearty thanks for their Petition, and for their affectionate expressions therein, who did assure them, that the House would take all possible and speedy care for the setling and ease of the Kingdom, and that the particulars in their Petition, should be taken into their serious consideration in convenient time.

Manuscript

British Library Additional Ms No. 70,006, fo. 56.

Other editions

The *Moderate*, No. 31 (6-13 February 1649). BL/EEBO: E.542[11]
The Armies Modest Intelligencer, No. 3 (1-8 February 1649). BL/EEBO: E.541[28]

Background

The Scottish parliamentarian army referred to in the petition besieged Hereford in August 1645. The English parliament did not pay them adequately, and many local people refused to sell them food when they did have money. Hungry Scottish soldiers took 'apples, pease and green wheat' from the fields — even bread from the housewives' ovens, it was said — intensifying the local community's hostility. Herefordshire's English identity as a marcher county was entrenched over many centuries, and it lay at an intersection of the major ethnic tensions within the Stuart kingdoms. Herefordshire clubmen also protested against Irish troops in the royalist armies, though these seem to have been few.

This clubmen's rising is said to have mustered between 12,000 and 16,000 supporters in March 1645. They came to Hereford and demanded that the king's men should collect taxes by legal means only, that nearby Canon Frome's garrison should be removed, and that Hereford's should be replaced by 'native countrimen'. Parliamentarian Colonel Edward Massey offered help but was told, 'They will not as yet declare themselves for the Parliament.' Colonel John Birch later took Hereford for Parliament after a feinted withdrawal and dramatic night march back to the city through the snow. The plunder that followed was conventionally justified by the royalist commander's refusal to surrender; but as £870 16s 8d was subsequently raised from inhabitants redeeming their property, this was no orgy of destruction. The cathedral's vicars choral were, however, outraged when Birch allocated their quarters to inhabitants made homeless by the siege.

As Hereford's governor, Birch presented a challenge to the county's parliamentarian leaders, the Harleys of Brampton Bryan. The Harleys' circle of puritan gentry and ministers had been isolated during the royalist occupation of the county, when Brampton Bryan itself was besieged and famously defended by Lady Brilliana, wife of Sir Robert Harley. Staunch Presbyterians in religion and politics, their traditional commitment to public service was inseparable from a sense of entitlement and intolerance of newcomers. At the 1646 county election, Sir Robert Harley spent £402 12s 6d on 577 suppers and 2,898 dinners to secure the victory of his son, Colonel Edward Harley, over Birch. Birch too was Presbyterian in religion and politics, but he was born in Lancashire and made his fortune as a wine merchant in Bristol. He provoked the County Committee by posting his communications with them in the market place; and although defeated in the county election he won a seat at Leominster, where the future Baptist John Tombes had been minister in the 1630s and a Baptist church existed in the 1650s.

Birch's troops presented problems when Hereford's garrison was reduced to 160 men in the castle only, early in 1647. Birch himself resigned and agreed to his surplus troops being sent to Ireland; but for six months they remained in Herefordshire, resisting removal and demanding their arrears of pay. In February 1648 Major Robert Harley (Sir Robert's second son, known in the family as Robin) complained in Parliament about the 'mutinous Carriage' of Captain French's troop, who had come to Herefordshire from Lord Grey of Wark's regiment. Mutinies against disbandment without payment of arrears were, as John Morrill has shown, not confined to New Model regiments during the nationwide political conflict over the cost of the army that followed the first civil war. In Herefordshire the pattern was to be repeated after the second.

In the spring of 1648 Hereford Castle's new governor, Lieutenant-Colonel Wroth Rogers of Constable's regiment (see 10 above), had to repair and provision it immediately against Sir Henry Lingen's local royalist rising. Lingen's success was short-lived, but the rising in Wales further alarmed the county regime. As late as September 1648, the assessment commissioners were authorised to raise £100 per week for three months to maintain a troop of horse under Major Robin Harley and four companies of foot, 'for suppressing tumults etc' while other local forces were being disbanded. When Harley's troop's turn for disbandment came on 18 December 1648, it seems that not enough money had been raised in the county to pay them all; and on 2 January 1649 fifty or more of those who remained came armed to Hereford with a 'mutinous petition' demanding their arrears. Thomas Blaney reported that he and his fellow tax commissioners were forced to take £810 6s 2d from the county's monthly assessment (for Fairfax's army) to pay the troopers.

Events in Herefordshire following the arrest of Sir Robert Harley, his elder son Edward, and Colonel Birch at Pride's Purge are very unclear. On 26 December, the parliamentarian *Moderate Intelligencer* published a report that 'the false dealing of many intrusted by Parliament' had been discovered and some sent to Gloucester to be charged. The following week, the royalist *Mercurius Elencticus* reported that Blaney (a neighbour and friend of the Harleys) and Major Harley himself had been arrested in Radnorshire by Horton's regiment and imprisoned in Hereford Castle, while Harley's remaining troopers sought sanctuary in Kingsland church, 'beleeving that Hortons men would dismount them'. Robin Harley wrote to King Charles II in 1671 that he had fled in fear of his life because his secret actions against the king's enemies, ensuring that frequently 'one or other of their maine wheeles became disserviceable', had become known. He was released from prison early in 1649, however, and sat on the Herefordshire militia committee for some months longer. On 16 February 1649, Blaney acknowledged the receipt of £911 'out of the money that came from Bristol being appointed for the disbanding of supernumeraries' from Major Harley.

The above petition was agreed at the Hereford quarter sessions in the middle of this murky affair. The Independent-led alliance that it signals ran the county for the next decade, bringing back some of the Harleian old guard from 1653. According to Gerald Aylmer, thirteen members of Herefordshire committees under the Commonwealth (for taxation, the militia, and sequestrations) had sat before 1648; while nineteen were 'new men' including middling and lesser gentry, urban professionals and traders; and ten were 'outsiders' like Wroth Rogers. Those names on the petition that can be identified also suggest a broad base. John James was from Worcestershire, but married to a Herefordshire woman, while Francis Pember and his son were of old Herefordshire gentry stock. Thomas Baskerville was related to the Pembers by marriage; and Thomas Seaborne, mayor of Hereford (not to be confused with his royalist brother Richard) was an apothecary. Thomas Rawlins, from the middling gentry, served on every known committee in Herefordshire from 1643 to 1660.

At least six of the 35 other gentlemen named were appointed to the county's militia committee a few days before Pride's Purge. Among the others, Sir John Bridges was upper gentry; while the Higgins family were apparently old antagonists of the Harleys. Thomas Careless, former high constable of Broxash, had played a leading role in the clubmen's rising of 1645 that would not 'as yet' side with Parliament. Miles Hill of Weobley, a lawyer, advised Birch's county election campaign, but his own account, published in 1650, tells how he turned against the Scots and their 'pretended appearance of religion and zeale' when dealing with surrounding villagers' claims for damages incurred during the siege of Hereford. The later assertion that he was an Independent preacher is unverifiable, though his 1650 pamphlet is rich in millenarian language. The above petition's agenda suggests that these were 'well affected' and gentry-centred Independents rather than radical extremists. The unique demand that no official should be required to serve at his own expense may reflect the local case of Ambrose Elton Jr, who complained to Parliament about being nominated as sheriff for 1647 because he was heavily in debt and reduced to selling his future inheritance.

Wroth Rogers (see 10 above), was the key figure in this new regime though less the stereotypical 'county boss' than Sir Robert Harley had been. He was joined by Colonel Thomas Harrison (see 19 above) and Stephen Winthrop, the son of Massachusetts Bay's governor and Thomas Rainborowe's brother-in-law, who was praised by Roger Williams as 'a great man for soul liberty'. Their circle's enthusiasm for godly rule appears in the March 1650 petition urging Parliament to continue 'that blessed worke that you have begun, in Propogatinge the Kingdome of Christ by sending furth & Countenancinge godly & fitt men to preach the Gospell'. It also appealed for a strict law against adultery, laws in English, the abolition of tenure-in-chief (by which landowners owed wardship to the crown) and the removal of weirs from Herefordshire rivers.

Related sources

The National Archives: Commonwealth Exchequer Papers SP28/229.
BL, Additional Ms.11053, fos.110-11.
BL, Additional Ms. 70006, fo. 74.
BL, Additional Ms. 70035, fos. 47-50.
Royal Commission on Historical Manuscripts: *Portland Manuscripts* vol 3, fos. 139-63.
CSPD, 1645-7, 1648.
Commons Journal, vols 4-6.
Mercurius Elencticus, no. 58, 26 December 1648 – 2 January 1649. BL/EEBO: E.536[31].
A Continuation of the Proceedings of the Scots Army before Hereford (1645). BL/EEBO: E.296[24].
Miles Hill, *A True and Impartiall Account of the Plunderings, Losses, and Sufferings of the County of Hereford by the Scottish Army* (1650). BL/EEBO: E.607[3].
Nathan Rogers, *Memoirs of Monmouth-Shire* [1708] (Chepstow, Moss Rose, 1983).
Firth and Rait, *Acts and Ordinances*, p. 1246.
Jacqueline Eales, *Puritans and Roundheads, The Harleys of Brampton Bryan and the Outbreak of the English Civil War* (Cambridge, Cambridge University Press, 1990).
G. E. Aylmer, 'Who was Ruling in Herefordshire from 1645 to 1661?', *Transactions of the Woolhope Naturalists' Field Club*, vol. 40 (1972).
VCH: *Herefordshire*, vol. 1, ed. William Page (London, Constable, 1908), pp. 381-98.

John and T. W. Webb, *Memorials of the Civil War between King Charles I and the Parliament of England, as it affected Herefordshire and Adjacent Counties*, vol. 2 (London, Longman, 1879) pp. 150-57, 249-54, 287-301, 417-8.

Paul Gladwish, 'The Herefordshire Clubmen, a Reassessment,' *Midland History*, 10 (1985).

Christopher Hill, 'Puritans and the "Dark Corners of the Land"', in his *Continuity and Change in Seventeenth-century England* (London, Weidenfeld and Nicholson, 1974).

ODNB: Newton Key, 'Birch, John (1615-1691)'.

ODNB: Julia J. Smith, 'Tombes, John (1602-1676), clergyman and ejected minister'.

Stephen K. Roberts, 'Wroth Rogers' (unpublished), by courtesy of History of Parliament.

61: COMMON COUNCIL OF THE CITY OF LONDON
13 January 1649

Context

On 1 January 1649 the purged House of Commons declared it treason, under the fundamental laws of England, for a reigning king 'to levy War against the Parliament and Kingdom of England'. The twelve members still sitting in the House of Lords rejected this ordinance, along with another for setting up a court of justice to try the king, and adjourned themselves for a week. The Commons then declared their own house, as the representative of the people of England, 'the Supreme Power in this Nation', with power to pass laws without the consent of the peers or monarch (4 January 1649).

England's revolution was so far developing piecemeal, overcoming obstacles as they arose rather than following an overtly republican plan, while the Council of Officers were still amending the latest draft of *An Agreement of the People*. The Commons committee for the king's trial and the settlement of the kingdom commissioned a new great seal, an important instrument required to validate official documents, that would represent the supremacy of the House of Commons; while another committee was consulting lawyers on how to replace the use of 'the single person' in judicial proceedings (e.g. 'the king vs Joe Bloggs', and 'the king's peace'). Two weeks before the king's trial began, however, a parliamentary clerk reported to MP Bulstrode Whitelocke that the revision of legal proceedings was being considered 'upon the alteration like[ly] to be'.

Parliament's intervention in the City of London developed similarly. On the recommendation of a Commons committee including London's two radical MPs, Aldermen Isaac Pennington and John Venn, both Houses on 18 December 1648 barred from city elections, for one year, anyone who had assisted the king in the first or second civil war, or the Scottish army in its invasion of England. On the eve of the Common Council elections, 20 December, any citizen who had subscribed to the city's petition of 27 June 1648 for a personal treaty with the king was also barred. When the Lord Mayor and aldermen protested against this interference, the Commons appointed a committee to review the oaths of office taken by the city officials. Its scope was then extended to oaths of office throughout the country, to remove the pledge of loyalty to the king. This could be seen as part of a process of creeping republicanisation; or alternatively, as a pragmatic measure depriving the oath-takers of an opportunity for conscientious objection to the king's trial.

Text

The Humble Petition of the Commons of the City of London in Common Councel Assembled, To the Honorable, The Commons of England, in Parliament Assembled. With a Narrative of the Proceedings of the Court of Common-Councel: And the Vote of the House of Parliament, and their Answer thereupon....Ordered by the Commons assembled in Parliament, That this Petititon and Narrative, and Answer of the House thereunto, and Vote thereupon, be forthwith Printed and Published: H. Scobel, Cler. Parl. D. Com. London, Printed by Peter Cole, 16 January 1648[9]. BL/EEBO: E.538[16]

To the Honorable, The Commons of England assembled in Parliament: The humble Petition of the Commons of the City of London in Common-Councel assembled, Sheweth

That seriously weighing those unspeakable toils, difficulties, dangers, and temptations, in every kinde, wherewith you have been hotly assaulted for many years together, by the powerful influence whereof, many great pretenders to the publique interest have been wrought off from the same; And withal, considering that all these, notwithstanding you have stood like a mighty Rock, firm and constant to your Trust, and are now acting after such a Rate as our dead hopes break forth with triumph from their Graves, We cannot but with enlarged hearts bless the God of Heaven for you, and (if it were possible) in the hearing of the whole world, proclaime our thankfulness to you for the same.

And apprehending, That the Non-Execution of Justice, the Intrusting of the Militia, and Navy in the hands of Neutralists, unfaithful, and dis-affected Persons; the great decay of Trade, the protecting of many mens Persons and Estates from the due course of Law, and the unsettled condition of this Nation, are some of the great and principal Evils under which the hearts of thousands of your friends (yea the whole Land) groan; We humbly pray,

1. That as you have begun to advance the Interest of unpartial Justice, so you would vigorously proceed in the Execution thereof upon all the Grand and Capital Authors, Contrivers of, and Actors, in the late Wars against the Parliament and Kingdom, from the highest to the lowest; that the wrath of God may be appeased, good men satisfied, and evil men deterred from adventuring upon the like practises for the future.
2. That the Militia, Navy, and all Places of power, may be put in the hands of none but such as by a constant and uniform tenour of their words and actions, have approved themselves faithful unto you, and the just rights of the Nation.
3. That with all convenient speed you would think upon some effectual course for the recovery, and increasing of the almost lost Trade and Manufacture of this City and Kingdom.
4. That no Priviledge whatsoever may exempt any from the just satisfaction of their due debts.
5. That having by your Votes of the 4th of this instant January, Declared, that the Commons of England in Parliament Assembled, have the Supreme Power of this Nation; you would (as far as you are able) endeavour the setling thereof upon foundations of Righteousness and Peace; In the maintenance, and prosecution of which Votes, and of these

our just and humble desires, We are resolved to stand by you to the uttermost of our power, against all opposition whatsoever.

Manuscript

City of London Record Office: Journal of Common Council, vol 40, fo. 313v.

Background

The narrative presented to Parliament with this petition explains that the Common Council's members assembled on 13 January 1649 at the appointed time, but waited three hours for the Lord Mayor, Abraham Reynardson, to arrive. Reynardson — a Presbyterian elected the previous September — had protested against Parliament's revision of the oath to be taken by the many new councillors, and the two houses had agreed to a week's suspension of the ceremony. On the morning of 13 January the Commons ordered him to administer the oath, omitting the pledge to defend 'our Sovereign Lord the King' and his successors. Reynardson obeyed, but refused to allow a proposed petition to be read, or even a vote on whether it should be read. 'After the fruitless expense of many hours', the Lord Mayor and two aldermen left, followed by the common sergeant and town clerk when asked to take the chair. The meeting continued, however, and the petition was read three times, debated, and passed by a vote *nemine contradicente* (no one voting against). The Commons approved these proceedings and ordered the narrative to be entered in the Council's journal along with the text above. In February 1649, they ruled that any forty members of the Common Council constituted a quorum, with or without the Lord Mayor and aldermen.

This London constitutional revolution was the culmination of a long struggle against the domination of the city's civic institutions by a narrow oligarchy. Candidates for the mayoralty and other offices were nominated by the Common Hall of the city's craft and trading companies, and chosen by the aldermen. Each alderman was selected by the Lord Mayor from four candidates nominated by their ward meeting, to serve ordinarily for life. The system had frequently been contested over the centuries by appeals to the 1215 charter granting London citizens the right of self-government. From the early 1640s, protests focused on the Lord Mayor and aldermen's veto over Common Council decisions, and the takeover of ward meetings by parish vestry committees. The future Leveller William Walwyn was involved, and several citizens soon to be identified with the Levellers took part in a protest at the mayoral election in 1646; while John Lilburne contributed *London's Liberty in Chains Discovered* and *The Charters of London*. Philip Baker has argued that the Levellers learned their language of freedom partly around these issues in the early 1640s.

In a volatile situation, London's electoral calendar was another problem.

The two sheriffs were chosen in June, the Lord Mayor in September, and Common Councillors in December. The Lord Mayor elected in September 1641 was Sir Richard Gurney, a rich silk merchant who orchestrated the city's display of loyalty to the king on his return from Scotland, and tried to stop a petition for the abolition of bishops. But the Common Council elections in December installed the puritan opposition, and six months later Gurney was impeached by Parliament for attempting to raise troops for the king.

After the first civil war, religious allegiances became aligned with political positions, with some overlap between religious Presbyterians and political Independents. Presbyterianism flourished among London ministers and their parishioners, while the Independents had their own congregations, and separatist sects challenged the whole concept of a single established church. Despite the king's rejection of the Newcastle propositions from the English and Scottish parliaments in July 1646, the Presbyterian faction in the House of Commons tried to push through a peace settlement by disbanding the New Model Army and negotiating directly with the king. Their party triumphed at the Common Council elections of December that year.

London's Presbyterians prepared for counter-revolution, raising alternative military forces to confront Fairfax's army. They signed up disbanded soldiers, the so-called 'reformadoes', recruited 500 cavalry, and stockpiled munitions for a major conflict. Nevertheless, when the trained bands were called out to oppose the New Model Army's approach to London in July 1647, very few of these citizen-soldiers turned up. When a mob invaded the House of Commons on 26 July and forced the reversal of a resolution taking the city's militia committee under Parliament's control, sixty Independent MPs fled to New Model Army headquarters, and the army occupied London peacefully two weeks later. In September a Common Hall surrounded by New Model soldiers chose tobacco merchant John Warner as Lord Mayor. Warner was no army puppet, having been an alderman since 1640. Robert Brenner has identified him as a member of the group of radically-inclined 'new merchants' engaged in colonial trade who were to dominate the revolution of 1649, steering clear of both Presbyterians and Levellers.

On the eve of the second civil war, many of London's civic leaders were ready to ally with the Scots and city royalists for peace on whatever terms the king would accept. Royalist activity was rife in 1648, with street bonfires on 25 March, the anniversary of Charles I's accession. When soldiers stopped the apprentices' sabbath-breaking games in April, there was a serious armed attack on Warner's home, and the Leadenhall arsenal was raided. Royalists recruited men in London for the Kentish rising, sending supplies of ammunition across the Thames. The city militia committee, meanwhile, demanded control over all the forces in the metropolis including the suburbs, but accepted Parliament's nominee, Philip Skippon, as major-general of the trained bands. Skippon had commanded the London militia in 1642-3 before joining Essex's army and later the New Model. Though a Presbyterian in religion, he strongly supported the army's revolt in 1647.

When the New Model regiments were withdrawn in May 1648 to fight in Kent and elsewhere, Skippon managed the defence of London, recruiting reinforcements in the city and suburbs, and was accused by his enemies of arming a rabble of servants against their masters. He was nevertheless able to persuade the citizen guards outside Parliament on 6 December to stand down in favour of Pride's men. According to *Mercurius Pragmaticus*, it was Skippon who moved in the Commons that London's election ban should be extended to all who had signed the petition for a personal treaty in June 1648.

The petition in question was presented to Parliament four days after the Commons decided to consider re-opening negotiations with the king. It did not insist on bringing the king to London, but wished to see 'the Power and Privileges of Parliament maintained, the just Rights and Liberties of the Subjects restored'; also Presbyterian religious uniformity to be established, the 1643 Covenant observed, and 'our brethren of Scotland' invited to the peace talks. The Scottish parliament was already known to be raising an army to invade England for the king; but London Presbyterians also knew that the dominant party in the Kirk bitterly opposed it. In the circumstances, the Londoners' petition could be interpreted as a last-ditch attempt to forestall the invasion by uniting with their Scottish brethren. By December, after the defeat of the Scots, it could be seen as a potentially treasonous invitation to a foreign invader, even if few of those who signed it had thought that was what they were doing; and they were all barred from Common Council elections in December.

In adopting the above petition on 13 January 1649, the Common Council were not tamely submitting to army or parliamentary control. A first text, already signed by 'divers citizens', had been printed in *The Moderate* and presented to the council's meeting on 9 January. There it was referred to a committee including two aldermen and a number of radical merchants, who reported to the next meeting on 13 January. The numbered demands then adopted are very little different from the earlier version, but the preamble had been rewritten, and the welcome for the declaration of the Commons' supremacy moved into the numbered list. Explicit mention of the king's responsibility for the wars was removed, as was a reference to 'other evill-affected persons, in places of Power and Trust in the City, Kingdome, and Navie'. Such choices matter, and we do not know how many other petitions in this collection resulted from a similar process of discussion and amendment, because so few original drafts survive.

Related sources

City of London Record Office: Journal of Common Council, vol 40, fos. 310, 313.
The Moderate, No. 26, 2-9 January 1648[9]. BL/EEBO: E.537[26].

Journal of the House of Commons, vol. 5, 27 June 1648.
Ibid, vol. 6, 23 January 1649, 1 February 1649.
Rushworth, *Historical Collections*, vol. 7, 27 June 1648.
Mercurius Pragmaticus, No. 39, 19-26 December 1648. BL/EEBO: E.477[30].
Valerie Pearl, 'London's Counter-Revolution' in G. E. Aylmer (ed.), *The Interregnum: the Quest for Settlement* (London, Macmillan, 1972).
Ian Gentles, 'The Struggle for London in the Second Civil War', *Historical Journal*, vol. 26 (1983).
Philip Baker, '*London's Liberty in Chains Discovered*: The Levellers, the Civic Past, and Popular Protest in Civil War London' *Huntington Library Quarterly*, vol. 76 (2013).
Robert Ashton, *Counter-Revolution* (Chapter Four).
Robert Brenner, *Merchants and Revolution: Commercial Change, Political Conflict, and London's Overseas Traders* (Cambridge, Cambridge University Press, 1993).
Sean Kelsey, *Inventing a Republic: The Political Culture of the English Commonwealth, 1649-1653* (Stanford CA, Stanford University Press, 1997).
Valerie Pearl, *London and the Outbreak of the Puritan Revolution, City Government and National Politics, 1625-43* (Oxford, Oxford University Press, 1961).
Keith Lindley, *Popular Politics and Religion in Civil War London* (Aldershot, Ashgate, 1997).
Norah Carlin, 'Liberty and Fraternities in the English Revolution: The Politics of London Artisans' Protests, 1635-1659', *International Review of Social History*, vol. 39 (1994).

62: SOUTH COAST AND MALMESBURY
17 January 1649

Context

This petition to Parliament followed shortly after one addressed to Fairfax from the same area (43 above). Subscribers from the ports and garrisons of Weymouth, Poole and Southampton, with Brownsea and Southsea castles, have here joined those at Portsmouth, the Isle of Wight and Hurst; and Malmesbury in Wiltshire, about eighty miles away from Southampton, is also included. The petition claims many thousands of supporters, compared with the figure of 'above 1600 persons' said to have subscribed the first; but the note at the end suggests these may have been counted in a different way.

It was delivered on the day before Charles's trial began, by which time explicit mention of him could hardly be avoided; but it also demands justice against the other 'Grand Delinquents' whose fate seemed to have been put on hold. The act of 4 January set up a High Court of Justice to try the king only, and it was not until March 1649 that a new court with the same name was set up to deal with leading royalists (starting with the Duke of Hamilton). The petitioners also reminded Parliament of the demands in the army's *Remonstrance* concerning the Prince of Wales and other royalist leaders currently abroad. Where the petition to Fairfax from this area endorsed the Large Petition of 11 September and others in general terms, this one recommends specific reforms for the remedy of grievances. John Rees is surely right to take these as evidence of a close relationship with the Levellers and familiarity with their ideas, reinforced by the known history of individual subscribers. The abolition of tithes notably appears here not as a religious issue but as one of several financial measures to relieve the burdens of the common people.

Text

To the Honourable the Commons House of ENGLAND, The humble Petition and Representation of the Officers and Souldiers of the Garrisons of Portsmouth, Southsea Castle, Southton, Hurst Castle, Poole, and Brownsea Castle, Weymouth, The Castles, Forts and Forces in the Isle of Wight, and the Garrison of Malmsbury, together with many thousand publique spirited persons of those places and parts adjacent. BL/EEBO: 669.f.13[71]

SHEWETH, That as we have with all readinesse and chearfulnesse served our Country against the Tyrannical Oppressours thereof; So we doe, at present, conceive our selves in duty obliged to express the deep sense we still retain of the severall weighty, and insupportable burdens, which the oppressed Commonalty for a long time have been, and still are groaning under. For the speedy removall whereof, We apply our selves to this Honourable House, who undoubtedly ought to relieve the Nation herein, you having now opportunity with power in your hands; God making the

Army, and all wel-affected people as Wals and Bulwarks to defend you, whilest you faithfully discharge that Trust committed to you for the benefit of this Nation. And being assured, that it is our undoubted right, as Members of the Common-wealth, to represent the grievances thereof to you by way of Petition, and to offer such sutable remedies as we apprehend to be effectuall for their redresse; We humbly tender these ensuing particulars to your serious and speedy consideration.

Grievance, 1. That Justice is not yet executed upon the Grand Delinquents and Authors of our miseries, bloud-shed and calamities, notwithstanding the many and earnest Petitions of Well-affected People (as that of *Kent*, and other Counties lately presented) earnestly desiring the same.

Remedy. For remedy whereof, we humbly offer, That the King, and all others the Grand Contrivers of, and Actors in the first and second warre, may be brought to speedy Triall; as also those of your own House that have betrayed their Trust; and all other Capitall Offendours, without respect of persons; and that Justice be executed upon them according to their demerits; Likewise that the Prince, Duke, and other Delinquents beyond the Seas, be speedily summoned, and a time fixed for their coming in, that so they may receive a due Triall: And in case they exceed that time, to be proceeded against as enemies to the Common-wealth: And that a day be appointed, within two months, for all Delinquents who are not already discovered, to compound; and if they shall not compound in that time, then their estates to be wholly forfeited and imployed for payment of publique debts.

Grievance, 2. That the intollerable burden of Free Quarter is yet continued upon the people, notwithstanding the Assessments are generally paid, although very unequally laid upon many Counties, Divisions, Hundreds, Cities, Townes and Villages; the great oppression by Tithes continued; Excise most unconscionably exacted from the poore, and no Account publiquely given how the vast summes received have beene spent and imployed.

Remedy. For redresse whereof, we propound, 1. That Free Quarter be immediately taken off. 2. Constant pay, or Assignations; and that the Assessments, whilst continued, be more equally proportioned. 3. That Impropriators being first satisfied, Tithes be taken away. 4. That the Excise be taken off from all, except Imported commodities; that no more engagements be laid upon it; and that clipt money be immediately called in. Further that it be declared, that as soon as the Engagements already charged, *ut supra*, be satisified, it shall be wholly taken away. 5. That all new Taxes be abolished, and an equall way of Subsidies onely continued: And that you may be enabled to take away those Taxes, We further offer, That Forrests Lands, the Whole Revenue formerly belonging to the Crowne, Bishops Lands, Deanes and Chapters Lands, Compositions of Delinquents, and Sequestrations, be speedily improved to the best advantage, for the ends aforesaid; and that all who have beene, or now are publique Treasurers and Collectors of moneys, be forthwith called to an acount, *viz*, Excise men, Sequestrators, Customers, together with all other Receivers whatsoever; And for that end we desire, that able Accomptants, Men of known fidelity to the publique Interest be imployed for the bringing of the fore-mentioned Treasurers, &c. to a speedy Account, that so the Commons of *England* may know how the vast summes of money raised under pretence of paying souldiers, have beene disposed of; by which meanes also discoverie may be made of great summes of money which hitherto hath beene concealed.

Grievance, 3. That by reason of the multitude of Officers who depend for maintenance out of the severall receipts, great summes of money are devoured, and by meanes thereof, Accounts made difficult.

Remedy. For remedy wherof, We offer, That all publique moneys be brought into one common Treasury, which wil much lessen the former charge, that at the end of every six months an exact Accompt be published in print of all those summes of money disbursed by the said Treasurers; which to know, we conceive is of right due to the Commons of England; and that for their further satisfaction, all publique disbursements which are of necessity, may speedily be computed, and the Receipts proportioned thereunto, with some over-plus that may alwaies be in a readinesse for any publique and sudden occasion.

Grievance, 4. That it hath beene, and still is, a great grievance and vexation unto the Officers and Souldiers of the Army, Garrisons and others our fellow Commoners, who have causes extraordinary relating to, and occasioned by the late troubles depending before the Committees of your House, and other Committees of the severall Counties; as also divers disaffected and corrupt Justices of the Peace, by whom their persons have beene slighted, their businesse (though never so just) neglected and protracted, to the great expence of time and money; which hath impoverished some, and almost destroyed others, whilst enemies to the State, whose causes have beene unjust, doe by their friends, Allies, wealth or potency, soone obtaine to be heard and answered.

Redresse. For redresse whereof we desire you will appoint Committees of Indempnity in each County, and that all corrupt Members of Committees, and Justices may be outed, and such onely chosen and impowered in the Common-wealth, as are of impartiall, upright and judiciall spirits, who by their judgements and fidelity, may doe justest to the meanest, and that speedily without the aforesaid charge and trouble to the Common-wealth.

Grievance, 5. That there is by sad experience found, (especially to the poor) a daily decay of Trade (the main pillar of the Common-wealths subsistence) occasioned by the continuation of Monopolizing Charters, and associated Companies, who have power to interrupt and deterre all other Natives from the Exercise of free Trade and Commerce: and of late also in a more speciall manner, the Irish Pirats by their increase and strength, have made themselves almost Lords of the Narrow Seas, robbing and carrying away Ships and Goods from the mouths of our own Harbours, to the great losse and undoing of many.

Remedy. For remedy whereof we humbly desire, That you will declare that all free Dennizons of this Nation, and Friends to the Weale publike, may enjoy their Rights by imploiment and improvement of their Estates and Stocks, without the afore said restrictions in free Traffique and Commerce both Forraign and Domestique; and that all such monopolizing and encroaching Charters, may be abolished; and that for the better suppressing all Pirats; and securing of Trade there may be a speedy and powerfull Guard appointed for the Seas, and entrusted with persons of approved integrity; most part of the Frigots to set forth from Portsmouth, which we humbly offer as the most convenient place upon the Southern Coast, for the furthering and advance of that Service: And that for an encouragement of all Sea-men, there may be established a way of competent subsistence for those that shall lose their limbes or livelihood in any Service for the Defence of their Countrey, as also for the Widdows and Children of such, or any others that shall die in the said Service, whereby they may be preserved from perishing.

Grievance, 6. That the chargeable proceedings in the Common Law, and all Courts of Judicature (a Grievance of long continuance, and universally knowne and felt) are not yet abolished, but the Natives still exposed to great trouble and vast expence, which doe uphold the corrupt interest of a Generation of men, who like Locusts and Caterpillers will (if not timely prevented) devour the Common-wealth.

Red. For prevention whereof, we offer, That twelve able and impartiall men, be chosen by the well-affected of each Hundred or Division, any seven of them to have Power to hear and determine all differences arising within the said Hundred or Division: and that there be every twelve months at the most, a new Election, that so none of them may continue in that Trust unlesse they be elected thereunto. And also that plain and just Rules be laid down for them to act by, from which they may be bound by some Penalty not to recede. And for the better security and maintenance of the Premisses, its humbly desired, that the Lord *FAIRFAX* may be appointed by this House to grant Commissions to such persons as are of approved fidelity to the publike Interest, for the well ordering and disposing of the Militia.

These things we doe with all clearnesse and faithfulnesse offer to your speedy Consideration, as that which we conceive for the substance of it) will tend to a settlement of this Nation, together with the particulars (not here expressed) contained in the late Remonstrance of the Army, and Petition of the 11th of September last, which if insisted on, and vigorously prosecuted (not answered with a formal complement, as hath been usuall, but really accomplished) will be a happy beginning of the establishment of the Peoples Freedoms; but if the present happy opportunity in your hands, shall be neglected, we are like to be (if God prevent it not) compleatly miserable, and shall become the scorn of all Nations, and a shame to posterity, haveing so freely spent our Bloud and Treasure, to purchase Justice and Freedome, and in stead therof be reduced to a worse condition of oppression and slavery then formerly.

Wherefore as a Testimony of that affection and duty we bear to our Native Countrey, we leave these things before you, hoping that God may yet use you as Instruments to ease this oppressed Nation, however we are confident he will open a way for the People, to obtain these and all other their just Rights and Liberties by overthrowing all unrighteous powers whatsoever.

Isle of Wight: Thomas Bowreman, Edm. Rolph, George Elsinore, John Basket, Richard Tonson. Hen. Duck, Richard Colman, John Fox, Henry Harwell, Thomas Borles, Tho. Ward, Steven Burton, Ed. Templer.

Portsmouth & Southsea-Cas.: Ro. Saunders, George Joyce, John Pitson, Rob. Peacock, Tho. Mathews, Jo. Tarant, Edw. Hopgood, Abraham Peters, Tho. Hurst, Ro. Durnford, Ro. Weston, William Bell, Rich. Prat.

South[amp]ton: Peter Murford, George Embry, Io. Durnford, Io. Hubblethorn George Burton, Iohn Barton, Will. Cole jun.

Pool and Hurst: Tho. Ethers, J. Rede, Ed. Snering, Ed. Taylor, Fran, Chick, Lieut. Wansey, Hen. Easman, Hum. Walle.

Weymouth and Malmsbury: Iam. Hayns, William Harden, Nat. Chase, Rich. Clun, Ralph Carde, Tho. Loving, Fran. Stokes.

These our Subscriptions, are in the Name and behalf of those under our Commands, together with our Neighbours and fellow Commoners, being betrusted and impowered to agitate in their behalf, for the Redemption of our Native Rights and Freedoms.

Background

The outstanding feature of this petition is the number of known army activists among the named subscribers and the representative role they claim. Both Lieutenant-Colonel Robert Saunders and Major Edmund Rolph, instrumental in the removal of the king from the Isle of Wight a few weeks earlier (see 43 above), had been involved in the army's resistance to Parliament from its beginnings in 1647. Rolph had spoken at Putney in favour of army unity and electoral reform, and during his service under Hammond on the Isle of Wight had been accused of plotting to kill the king, charged with high treason and imprisoned, but was acquitted at the Hampshire assizes. Saunders had been at the forefront of resistance to the

Irish service in Hammond's regiment, and was examined by the Commons for distributing a Leveller pamphlet among the soldiers. Like Rolph, he was present at Putney and accompanied Hammond to the Isle of Wight. Malcolm Wanklyn's invaluable lists of known New Model Army officers show that Richard Tonson and Henry Duck were officers in Ewer's regiment, previously Hammond's; while Captain George Elsmore (or Elsinore) and Lieutenant Thomas Ward belonged to Rich's. John Rede and Henry Wansey, signing for Poole and Hurst, had both served in Sir William Waller's Southern Association army. Rede was appointed governor of Poole by Fairfax on the last day of the Putney Debates, and was welcomed there by a petition from 150 townspeople. When later ousted from that office, he founded or joined a Baptist church at his native Porton in Wiltshire (see also 8 above). Wansey was the London watchmaker chosen by radical ward meetings as their candidate for Lord Mayor in 1646, in an attempt to overturn the indirect method of election. Wanklyn's lists also identify Nathaniel Chase and Ralphe Carde as respectively a captain and an ensign in Sir Hardress Waller's regiment (see 27 above). James 'Hayns', as printed at the head of the Weymouth list, is identified by John Rees as James Heane, governor of Weymouth, who had served in Colonel Robert Butler's Southern Association regiment and had assisted Batten's naval force against the royalist blockade of Weymouth in 1645. He later appears as Rede's ally against the conservative Presbyterian elite of Poole.

George Joyce, governor of Southsea Castle, had as a junior officer famously removed Charles I from Parliament's custody at Holmby House, replying to the king's demand to see his commission by pointing to the 500 troopers behind him. His visit to Hammond and other friends on the Isle of Wight immediately before the king's removal had been kept secret, 'to take off the scandal of an agitating businesse' (see 43 above). By contrast, this petition claims that the signatories had been empowered by the men they commanded and their civilian supporters to 'agitate' on their behalf.

These men had experience of holding meetings, passing resolutions, and getting mandates. They included a cluster of individuals who were important links in the chain connecting discontented soldiers with Leveller ideas and — crucially, as John Rees has shown — with Leveller printers. Though caution must be exercised in labelling individuals as Levellers, the content of the petition situates it within the concentric circles of activists in touch with Leveller ideas. Meetings may also have been organised among their civilian allies in the places they name, and the 'many thousands' of supporters claimed on the title page (though not in the petition itself) may indicate substantial numbers attending such meetings, rather than a count of individual subscriptions. How Malmesbury was drawn into this petition, and whether the signatories were mainly from the garrison or the town, is unknown. Personal and political contact were most probably behind the invitation to the sympathisers there to join in this petition.

The south coast locations, on the other hand, were bound together by economic, political and defence concerns. While Portsmouth was especially important as a naval base, Southampton, Poole and Weymouth were heavily involved in colonial trade. After decades struggling against the monopolies of the great London trading companies, these outports (as they were known) had begun before the civil wars to enjoy the benefits of free trade with the British colonies in North America. Robert Brenner has identified many London merchants involved in the Atlantic trades, whose politics tended strongly towards the radical wing of the Independents. Further investigation of their connections with the south coast ports could perhaps throw further light on local political allegiances.

These had been parliamentarian in sympathy throughout the civil wars, despite the ebb and flow of military control. In Portsmouth a royalist garrison was expelled in the summer of 1642, while Weymouth's resistance to Goring's army in 1645 became a local legend, and Poole has been described as the headquarters of the parliamentary cause in Dorset. During the second civil war the whole south coast was vulnerable to royalist attack from the sea and the spread of naval revolt (see 39 above). The discovery of a royalist plot to take Weymouth and rumours of a planned royalist rendezvous in Hampshire, together with the possibility of the king's escape from the Isle of Wight, made this once again a front-line area, despite the absence of any actual insurgency. Meanwhile, the Prince of Wales's seizure of the Scilly Isles in September 1648 compounded the problem of piracy from Irish bases that had disrupted the region's trade for years. The cost of maintaining the parliamentary garrisons weighed heavily on the population, but they were recognised as essential for their safety, and as Portsmouth's citizens pointed out (43 above) their demand for necessities contributed to the urban economy while external trade faltered.

Related sources

Commons Journal, 17 January 1649.
Fairfax Correspondence, British Library Additional Ms. 18979 (fo. 262, Portsmouth petition).
ODNB: Keith Roberts, 'Rolph, Edmund (*bap.* 1619, d. 1668), parliamentarian army officer'.
ODNB: G. E. Aylmer, 'Joyce, George (b. 1618), parliamentarian army officer'.
John Rees, *The Leveller Revolution* (London, Verso, 2017).
Wanklyn, *Reconstructing the New Model Army*.
Laurence Spring, *Waller's Army, The Regiments of Sir William Waller's Southern Association Army* (Farnham, Pike and Shot Society, 2007).
Gentles, *New Model Army*.
Tony MacLachlan, *The Civil War in Hampshire* (Salisbury, Rowanvale, 2000)
Clarendon, *History of the Rebellion*, vol. 4, p. 404.

VCH: *Dorset*, vol. 2.
'The Crabchurch Conspiracy — February 1645', thedorsetpage.com.

63: NOTTINGHAMSHIRE

30 January 1649

Context

The *Commons Journal* records that this petition was read on the morning of the king's execution. No printed version is known, but the manuscript is preserved in the House of Lords archives. The covering letter to Colonel Hutchinson apologises for the small number of subscriptions the organisers were able to collect in the time available. The 309 names are not reproduced here, but are discussed in the background section below.

The petitioners' agenda is wide. Like many others they prioritise local concerns, beginning and ending with a plea for relief from the burden of maintaining local forces; but they also approve of the legal proceedings against the king as 'impartial justice', show equal concern for justice against his chief supporters, and urge the present Parliament to dissolve itself after the essential measures — including electoral reforms — have been carried out.

Text

House of Lords record Office: Main Papers, 20 November 1648 – House of Lords Main Papers: 1648 (undated), fo. 229.

To the Right Honourable the Commons of England in Parliament Assembled: The humble Petition of divers well affected People in Nottinghamshire, and in the Towne of Nottingham.

Sheweth: That this County hath from the first begininge of these sad times borne a proportionable share with the deepest sufferers in the kingdome And in some particulars almost unparalleld Burdens have layen upon them, as wittness the vast Charges towards maintaininge the Scotts League against Newarke Etc But besides these remoter grievances, this poore County did upon the breakinge out of these later troubles at their generall Charge raise a Regiment of Horse, under the Command of the Commitee for the Militia here, when other Counties of far greater abillitie raised but one or two Troops, The foresaid Regiment haveinge also receaved large Contributions from your Petitioners for their maintenance since they were formed, doe att present lie upon free Quarter in the County, Noe order being taken for their present pay or orderly disbanding, which together with the Monethly Assessment to the Army, and the late charge of Free Quarter upon their severall marches this way, as also the new levies for the siege of Pontefract, make us (though unwillingly) complaine of insufferable pressures: yet Neither doe the senses of our particular sufferings becalme us into a disregard of the more generall Concernements of the Kingdome, who ever travell [travail] in expectation of what God will give in to be the product of your present Counsells, towards the Settlement of a firme and righteous peace. And in relation thereto we much reioyce to behold your Resolutions now at last aspireing that height of Justice as to be noe respecter of persons, worthily desistinge anie longer to Court your twice conquered faithles Enemy into a Condition to destroy your selves and those who with most faithfulnes assisted you, which we conceave was the designe of the designers and promoters of the late unsafe Treaty, who doubtles were also Confederate with that perfidious rabble of Scotts, who under the Conduct of their traiterous Duke lately invaded this kingdome, which devouringe deluge together with many other raginge floods of mischiefe readie to drowne this poore Land in universall ruine, hath by the power of God in the hands of your ever faithfull & victorious Armie bene hitherto prevented. And they further made happie to us, in promoteing those good thinges contained in their late Remonstrance from St Albans, wherein, as to the Nations generall good much of what we have to desire is bound up, In relation to which together with the premises, we humbly pray,

1. That you would be pleased effectuallie and fullie to proceed in acting impartiall Justice upon the principall Instruments of our troubles, & by a timely performance, asmuch as possibly may be, evade the dangers incident to delaies, least some unlooked for obstructions, which may justly be feared, interposeing your good endeavours may render them fruitles, & be of perillous Consequence to your selves and all the welwishers of Justice & freedome.
2. That likewise all such formerly of your owne Partie, as shalbe found to have Confederated with the Scotts invaders, or anie other rebellious disturbers of the kingdomes peace, in this later Commotion, may be proceeded against as Rebells and Traitors.
3. That so soone as your pressing occasions will permitt itt, all officers of State emploied by you for the receipt & disbursement of publique Money, may be called to a strickt & speedy Account, that soe the Country that paies it may knowe what becomes of their Monies, and in case of wilfull default the offenders severely punished.
4. That haveing effected those good thinges for the kingdome contained in the Armies Remonstrance, And what else in your wisdome seemes necessary for the establishment of a true peace, and soe provided for the succession of future equall Representatives, you will accordinge to the desire of the said Remonstrance prefixe a short period to your owne power, That soe all the world may see, you feare not to have your Actions stand, by soe indifferent a Judicatory as a future Parliament duely elected seemes to be.

And in relation to our particular forementioned grievances we humbly pray, that the Regiment of horse now Quartered upon us (being duely satisfied for their faithfull service) may be speedily disbanded, or if it seeme necessary they be continued, That soe many of them may be brought into the Establishment of the Army as the Lord Generall shall thinke fitt to be entrusted in that service.

And for our partes as we have represented these our desires not out of anie vaine glorious End but in discharge of what God by the dictate of our owne Consciences leads us to: and as the subscription of our hands hereunto testifie our desires to further the publique good, so we hope our heart & hands (if God call us to it) shall wittnes the same in assistinge this honorable House and all the Lovers of Justice truth and freedome in all their good endeavours for your obtaininge thereof,

And ever pray &c.

[Followed by 309 names in one hand.]

Background

The town of Nottingham supported Parliament throughout the first civil war. The majority of the county gentry were royalist, but the parliamentarian minority were able to raise their own forces, including Thornhaugh's horse regiment (31 above). There was constant tension between the town corporation and Colonel Hutchinson, military governor of Nottingham, who considered the town's fortifications untenable, and in 1643 moved their guns into the castle for fear they would be taken at the royalists' next assault. Hutchinson also quarrelled with the parliamentarian County Committee, and attempts by the Committee of Both Kingdoms at Derby House to reconcile them were only superficially successful. The colonel was elected an MP for the shire in 1646, but never really got on with his colleague Gilbert Millington, despite sharing his Independent politics. Both sat on the High Court of Justice that tried the king.

Several reasons for local parliamentarians' hostility to Hutchinson emerge from his widow Lucy's vivid memoirs of his life, written after the Restoration. One is his confidence in his own military responsibility and judgement — surely justified by the major contribution he made to Parliament's defence in the Midlands, despite local attempts to undermine his authority and obstruct his response to orders from above. A second reason is his position as a country gentleman, who according to Lucy prided himself on his fairness towards defeated enemies of the same status, leading to accusations of softness towards royalists and even of readiness to betray Nottingham Castle to his royalist cousins. Glimpses of the social gulf between the urban elite and county gentry appear in Lucy's remark that the mayor of Nottingham, though honest and brave, 'had no more than a burgher's discretion'. She suspected that the godly citizens of Nottingham, in their turn, 'thought it scarce possible for anyone to continue a gentleman and firm to a godly interest'.

Hutchinson's religious radicalism was an additional cause of friction, and one that grew as the town's ministers veered towards Presbyterianism during 1646-8. The governor's toleration of alternative religious gatherings held by the castle's gunners was limited at first. He imprisoned them at the town ministers' request, releasing them on condition that they did not seek converts in the town, though many townswomen still came to hear a visiting preacher of theirs. The Hutchinsons' sympathy increased after they read Baptist pamphlets brought to the castle by soldiers, and decided together not to have their second child baptised in infancy. While most of our information about Nottingham's Baptist congregation comes from the 1650s, it is likely that the ground was prepared in the late 1640s in places such as Nottingham, Kneesall and Skegby. The county was frequently visited by travelling evangelists, and in 1648 the future Quaker leader George Fox found members of a 'shattered' Baptist group in Nottingham. In the following year Fox would be arrested for his intervention in a service at St Mary's parish church, and go on to convert the household of the friendly sheriff of Nottingham, John Reckless, into whose custody he was sent. Reckless himself was inspired to go to the marketplace on a Sunday — in his slippers — to preach. Fox also converted Elizabeth Hooton (or Hooten) in Skegby from her Baptist faith; while James Parnel, who died for his Quaker beliefs at Colchester in 1656, was from East Retford. This Baptist and proto-Quaker circle is evoked by the appearance of John Reckless himself and Elizabeth Hooton's husband Oliver (who did not at first share her Quaker views) among the petitioners.

Local research into the list of 309 names is beyond the scope of this book, but Dr Peter Seddon has kindly allowed me to use the results of research he did some years ago in response to my enquiry. Only two active JPs, Thomas Lindley and Richard Dobson, and one member of Nottingham's town corporation signed the petition, which seems to have been organised from outside the main structures of local power, possibly through networks of parish office-holders and minor gentry. Comparing the list with the very full Nottinghamshire returns for the Protestation of 1642, Dr Seddon found 162 names appearing at both dates. Given the likely impact of natural mortality, war conditions and economic instability on the population over the previous six years, this is a significant proportion. The names of all except 42 individuals — probably those of higher social status — are arranged by parish; and outside Nottingham itself (with 20 names) they came from three distinct clusters. Sixty-nine were from the Mansfield area of Sherwood Forest, with its mainly pastoral economy, widespread poverty and substantial enclosures, whose recent history of riotous disorders is attributed by Martyn Bennet to the instability of its society. Two of its parishes, Kneesall and Skegby, had General Baptist congregations by the 1650s. The family of JP Thomas Lyndley owned the manor of Skegby; and the Huthwaite family (two of whom signed the accompanying letter to Hutchinson) held Sutton-in-Ashfield. From the second cluster, three Sherbrookes appear around Epperstone and Calverton, where their family held land for centuries and a present-day school is named after one of them; and the neighbouring parish of Arnold had a General Baptist congregation in the 1650s. In the cluster of 45 names around Owthorpe, where John and

Lucy Hutchison lived before the wartime damage to their home, six signed up in Owthorpe itself but the highest number (15) came from Upper Broughton.

A surviving letter to Colonel Hutchinson dated 20 January [1649] asks him to present the petition to the House of Commons on behalf of the subscribers, 'who (though not numerous) we are Confident are Cordiall (for the most part)'. Had time allowed, 'it might have beene lengthened with a far larger Trayne of Subscribers', but considering 'the present and most important affaires now in agitation with you' it has been forwarded in haste. The signatories are the two JPs Lyndley and Dobson, Thomas and Robert Huthwaite, one Thomas Lupton, and George Fox's future host John Reckless. The haste with which support was canvassed helps to explain the clustered hotspots. Some doubt may be raised by the letter-writers' confidence that the subscribers are 'Cordiall (for the most part)'. Did they know less about some of them? Were some men's names put down by neighbours, family members or pastors who firmly believed they would have subscribed in person if they had been present? This is not to suggest the whole exercise was a fake: if the promoters were not honest they surely would have listed a much larger number of names. But the procedure was probably less meticulous that the detailed one imposed by the instructions for the Protestation six years earlier. It is not clear why the text was presented to Parliament a full ten days after the letter was written, within hours of the king's execution. Hutchinson, who had participated fully in the king's trial, may have hung on to the letter until it became an endorsement of the action completed; perhaps to protect the petitioners from the perilous consequences of 'unlooked for obstructions' even at what we — with hindsight — may think of as the last minute.

Related sources

Thomas Lindley and others to Colonel John Hutchinson, 20 January [1649], House of Lords Record Office, Main Papers, 1648 [*sic*].
Lucy Hutchinson, *Memoirs of the Life of Colonel Hutchinson*, ed. N. H. Keeble (London, Phoenix Press, 1995).
John L. Nickalls, *The Journal of George Fox, A Revised Edition* (Cambridge University Press, 1952).
Robert Thoroton, *The Antiquities of Nottinghamshire* (republished 1972, E. P. Publishing and Nottinghamshire County Library).
Alfred C. Wood, *Nottinghamshire in the Civil War* (Oxford, Clarendon Press, 1937).
P. R. Seddon, 'Colonel Hutchinson and the Disputes between the Nottinghamshire Parliamentarians, New Evidence Analysed', in *Transactions of the Thoroton Society of Nottinghamshire*, vol. 98 (1990).

Martyn Bennett, 'Nottinghamshire and the High Road to Civil War', in Martyn Bennett (ed.), *Society, Religion and Culture in Seventeenth-Century Nottinghamshire* (New York, Edwin Mellen, 2005).

Stuart B. Jennings, '"When Women Preach and Cobblers Pray", The Religious Experience of Nottinghamshire, 1640-1662', Ibid.

Thomas Pert, 'Colonel John Hutchinson (1615-1664) and Nottingham in the English Civil War, 1643-1646', *East Midlands History and Heritage*, Issue 1 (June 2015). Online at eastmidlandshistory.org.uk/magazine-issue-1.

ODNB: Richard L. Greaves, 'Millington, Gilbert (c. 1598 – 1666), regicide'.

ODNB: Caroline L. Leachman, 'Hooten [Hooton; née Carrier], Elizabeth (d. 1672), Quaker preacher'.

F. M. W. Harrison, 'Nottinghamshire Baptists, Their Rise and Expansion', *Baptist Quarterly*, vol. 25(2), 1973-4.

64: SURREY

1 February 1649

Context

The *Commons Journal* records the presentation of this petition on the day after the king's execution. Unlike the earlier petition from Surrey presented to the Council of Officers almost seven weeks earlier (48 above), which contained constitutional proposals sympathetic to the *Agreement of the People* and was aimed at the Council's debate on that document, this one's demands are principally concerned with securing the new regime. It picks up where the first left off, with the exclusion of the regime's opponents from local offices, and especially from the county militia. The militia was an important issue, because its restructuring, county by county, had begun before Pride's Purge and was still continuing. The exclusion is here extended from known opponents to 'neutrals', which may seem undemocratic, but the comparison given, to the exclusion of many citizens from London's Common Council elections, suggests that it is seen as a temporary measure.

Text

The Moderate, No. 30 (30 January - 6 February 1648-9). BL/EEBO: E.541[15]

To the supream Authority of this Nation, the Commons of England, in Parliament assembled. The humble Petition of divers (in the name of themselves and others) being known well affected to the Publike Interest of this Nation in the County of Surrey.

Sheweth, That having found by sad experience the continuation of the Publike Calamities of this Nation, to have been principally occasioned by the prevalency of a corrupted party, lately within this house, and by dividing the supream Authority thereof, into the hands of such as are not intrusted thereto by the people, which hath daily brought forth cross, delatory, and so distructive proceedings; and blessing God for your so happy deliverance from your entanglements within, and opposition without. We your Petitioners, do hope now, that for the time to come, you will not admit so destructive a distribution of your supream Authority, but proceed of your selves without any other, to take such effectual course for the ease of the Nation, as shall be requisite. In order thereunto, we humbly desire,

1. That the Militia of the County of Surrey, and all other places, may be put into the hands of such, and such only as have expressed a firm and constant affection to the freedoms of their Countrey, lest the power thereof should be exercised against this honorable House, your most renowned Army, and such of the people, as show most affection to your just proceedings; and that all others, whether neutrals, being such as have pollitickly acted on both sides, or may be charged with a probable suspition of evil to their Countrey, may be rendered uncapable of trust,

by an effectual interdiction, upon a penalty, according to the example of your Ordinance for choosing Common Counsel men, &c in the City of London.
2. That all the Magistrates, Officers, and others in Authority in the County of Surrey, may be chosen by the wel-affected thereof; and such as have assisted the King in purse or person, or promoted the late tumultuous engagement for a personal Treaty, or otherwise abetted the same, may upon a penalty be prohibited, at least for a time, from being choosers, or chosen thereunto.
3. That the Ordinance for Tythes upon treble damages maybe speedily revoked; and that hereafter no enforced maintenance be imposed upon the people for the publike ministry. And if you shall think fit to settle a publike ministry for the instruction of the Nation, that a just and more equal way of maintenance may be made for their subsistance.
4. That a Committee may be chosen by the wel-affected Inhabitants of Surrey, to take accompts of such as have had charge of the Counties disbursements.
5. That speedy means may be used for taking off that intolerable burthen of free-quarter, and that it may never be permitted for the future; that so we may see some real fruits and benefits of your supream Authority, and be engaged thereby to maintain the same to you and all future Representatives.

Die Jovis, 1 Febr. 1648.

Background

The impact of Pride's Purge on the composition of Surrey's parliamentarian regime has been discussed in relation to the earlier petition addressed to the Council of Officers (48 above). The shock at that time had allowed Leveller sympathisers, based mainly in the London suburbs south of Thames, to step in and gather the support for the *Agreement of the People*. By the time of this petition, the officers' version of the *Agreement* had been presented to the Commons and laid aside, to be ignored for several years to come. Perhaps the more revolutionary constitutional demands of December were dropped because the main issue of the Commons' supremacy had been settled; or the Levellers active in promoting those demands played less part in this petition, which addresses primarily the regime's security needs. Yet the petition's most radical demand, the abolition and replacement of tithes — without mentioning compensation to private owners — was considered revolutionary enough by those in power to bring down the Barebones Parliament almost five years later. The late John Gurney, in exploring the background to the 1649 Digger settlement at Cobham, found a number of separatist congregations existing in Surrey by the mid-1640s, along with Baptist groups stemming from earlier 'dipping tours' by preachers such as Samuel Oates and William Lambe. The religious radicals behind this demand do not rule out a national church, but 'no enforced maintenance' implies freedom of choice.

Related source

John Gurney, *Brave Community, The Digger Movement in the English Revolution* (Manchester University Press, 2007).

For other related sources, see 48 above.

65: KENT

2 February 1649

Context

The *Commons Journal* records the presentation of this petition on 2 February 1649, the spokesman for the petitioners confirming there that it had been signed and sent before the king's execution. 'What it hath pleased God hath been acted since the Subscribing of this Petition, the Petitioners could not take Notice of in the Petition; but the Petitioners resolve, in what you have lately acted, to stick to you with their Lives and Fortunes,' he said. Two petitions from Kent had already been delivered, to Parliament and the army respectively (51 and 57 above) on 23 December, and the organisers of this one had been busy since then collecting subscriptions to yet another. It is remarkable for coming nearest of any to demanding the king's death, not only welcoming his trial but citing the biblical justification for capital punishment which only one other (28 above) had done. As far as Charles himself is concerned, their use of his surname — unique among these petitions, and echoing the prosecution at his trial — does not deprive him of any of his royal titles, though reducing them to 'King &c'. All this, of course, was safe to say now that the king was dead. If it had indeed been sent as well as signed before the regicide took place, one wonders who had held it back. Three printed and two manuscript copies of the text survive, three of them including a list of 1135 subscribers' names; the printed version below has been selected for the additional information it provides about the presentation of the petition to Parliament, while the lists of subscribers are discussed in the background below.

Text

A Perfect Collection of Exact Passages of Parliament and Other choyce Intelligence... No. 2 (29 Jan. – 3 Feb. 1648/9). BL/EEBO: E.527[15]

A Petition was presented to the Commons, and read as followeth:

To the supreame Authority, the Commons of England assembled in Parliament. The Humble Petition of the well affected in the County of Kent.

Humbly sheweth: That your Petitioners cannot but in all gratitude declare how much their spirits are refreshed, and heightned upon the observation; especially of the late imparalleld actings of this Honourable House, far above all others formerly; insomuch as your Petitioners are incouraged to believe that the yeare of this Nations freedome (through Gods blessings upon your endeavours) is begun: And in order hereunto, we cannot but express our hearty and high acknowledgement of thankes to this honourable House, for their vindicating and preserving the just power of the people in those late Votes that declared, that the legislative power originally was in the people, and derivatively in the House of Commons, as their

Representative: And also for the forwardnesse of this honourable House to favor (Ms satisfie) the earnest and just desires of this, and other Counties, for the bringing of the person of the late* King, together with the rest of the grand Delinquents to a speedy tryall.

And for asmuch as wee are not Ignorant of the plottings and practises of the ill affected, to retarde, and (if possible) to make void the proceedings of this honourable House, and high Court of Justice, and also to foment and raise (asmuch as in them lies) another war: Wee are forced (omitting other great and necessary particulars for present) in all earnestnesse and submission, to propose these two ensuing particulars to your serious and speedy considerations.

1. That (notwithstanding all suggestions to the contrary) the tryall of Charles Stuart late* King, &c. may be vigorously prosecuted, and that no pretences or overtures whatsoever may cause this honourable House, and high Court of Justice to be satisifed with [for, mss] the blood of three States, with lesse then the blood of those persons, who have been the principall Authors of its effusion; for asmuch as God himselfe hath said without distinction of persons, that who so sheddeth mans blood, by man shall his blood be shed.
2. That for the prevention of future insurrections and rebellions, this honourable House would be pleased to commit the Militia of this, and all other Counties to his Excellency the Lord Fairfax Generall, &c. So to be new modellized, as that the commissionating and arming of all forces whatsoever, may by immediate power and authority from him be deputed, and put into the hands of such, and none but such as adhere to the Parliament and Army in their present proceedings.

And your Petitioners (as ready to stand to you herein With their lives and fortunes) shall ever pray, &c.

This Petition was presented by Capt. Scot, Capt. Brown, Capt. Scot junior, Capt. May, Mr. Henry Knight, and Mr. Thomas Paramour, from the Petitioners of the County: And they had the thanks of the House.

The House referred the aforesaid Petition to a Committee; It seemes the Petition was signed, and sent before the King was put to death, but was not brought, and presented to the Parliament untill this day.

Manuscript texts

Bodleian Library, Oxford: Ms Tanner 57(2), fos. 467-87.
Ibid, Ms Rawlinson A298.

---

* The word 'late' does not appear in the two manuscript texts, which have 'Charles Stewart King &c'. It seems to have been inserted by the news editor because, as he notes, the king was dead by the time of printing.

Other editions

The Armies Modest Intelligencer, No. 3, 1-8 February 1648/9. BL/EEBO: E.541[28].

Thomas Hearne, *Liber Niger Saccarii* (London, 1771), vol. 2, pp. 694-714.

Background

Oxford's Bodleian library today contains two manuscript copies of the text, each with a list of 1135 names. The first is among the papers of William Lenthall, Speaker of the House of Commons throughout the Long Parliament, bequeathed to the library by the antiquary Thomas Tanner (1674-1735). The second was acquired in 1756 in Richard Rawlinson's collection, among the papers of another antiquary, Thomas Hearne (1678-1735). Hearne had a transcript of this document printed, with all the names, in his collection of miscellaneous historical sources first published in 1728. The Tanner manuscript seems to have been copied from the sheets of paper on which it was presented to Parliament. Lenthall — or the clerk who copied it for him — made marginal notes on how many names were in the individuals' own handwriting, or (in a handful of cases) consisted of a mark rather than a signature. Approximately 47% of the names were in blocks noted as 'subscribed by the parties owne hands', and the rest 'written by one hand'. This may indicate that Lenthall was suspicious of the petition's authenticity; but many local lists of petitioners may have been presented in fair copies, as they had been for the 1641-2 Protestation. Marginal notes also point to Canterbury, Sandwich, and Hythe, though with no indication of where these sections begin or end. There are a few notes on individuals: Francis Prentis was a minister, and Thomas Foster a jurat (the equivalent of an alderman in the Cinque Ports); while Tenterden's local history website places 'Thomas Plummer Maire' there in 1649.

Thomas Hearne had his copy from Dr John Thorpe of Rochester, who had it from the Rev. Richard Forster, rector of Crondale (Crundal or Crundale) in Kent. Hearne struggled with the handwriting, attributing it to 'no very skillful scribe'; and the surviving copy may be Hearne's own transcript, making it a third generation one. The names are listed in a very different order from those in the Tanner manuscript, presumably because it was copied from sheets differently gathered. Hearne or his printer may have introduced some distortion into the names: was 'Honey' Stephenson originally Henry, for example? Cross-checking all names with the Tanner version would be a laborious task, which has not been undertaken for the present study. The geographically limited survival of the 1642 Protestation returns for Kent also limits any search for names comparable with Dr Seddon's research on the Nottinghamshire petition (63 above), particularly as the whole Wealden area and the Medway ports are missing.

It is hard to identify the gentlemen who presented this petition to the Commons. None of the three members for Kentish seats still sitting after the purge are among them; and several common surnames are given without forenames. Captain Brown may have been the John Brown who held that rank in Fairfax's regiment, but Captains Scot Senior and Junior may have belonged to local forces. Thomas Paramour, however, was probably from a family of minor gentry at Ash and St Nicholas at Wade, and an earlier one of his name had been Mayor of Canterbury in 1607. Another Thomas Paramour, of St Nicholas at Wade in Thanet, sat in Parliament for Lyme Regis from 1625 to 1628; but either he or his son of the same name, who fought for the king in the civil wars, refused the Protestation oath in 1642 so would have been very unlikely to support this petition.

Jacqueline Eales, for her two articles listed below, has examined the whole list of subscribers, identifying town councillors of Canterbury, Sandwich and Hythe, and individual ministers or members of Independent church congregations, but no one from any major gentry family. As well as finding some of the 'new men' who had recently risen in urban hierarchies, she puts the petition in the context of religious diversity in Kent, including strong pockets of nonconformity that could be found in parishes near London and in Maidstone, Ashford, Canterbury, Sandwich and Dover at this time. A conventicle at Cranbrook in the heart of the Weald, whose scattered population and textile industry had a less traditional structure, was attended by believers from Goudhurst, Biddenden and Benenden. The name of one of its early leaders, substantial clothier Richard Robson, is also on Hearne's list, and the Baptist leader Francis Cornwell seems to have signed for other members of his church in Smarden. Some other radical religious leaders of the early 1640s, such as Richard Culmer, did not sign this petition, however. John Durant, a separatist leader in Canterbury at the time who was said after the Restoration to have collected subscriptions for it, did not sign; but in her research Madeline Jones identified ten members of his congregation who did. Though Durant was notorious for having preached in 1646 that the king should be brought in chains to Parliament, by 1648 he was becoming more moderate, with a preacher's position in Canterbury cathedral. A few minor gentlemen among the subscribers may be traceable individually, such as William Kenwrick, who stands at the top of Hearne's list and would be one of Kent's members in the Barebones Parliament (1653): he was the sixth son of Robert Kenwrick, who leased Boughton under Blean from the dean and chapter of Canterbury Cathedral. Eales has found less information about the contribution of radical groups outside these congregations, such as the friends in Dartford, Gravesend and Maidstone claimed by the Levellers a year earlier (see 51 above), though this may mark a split in Kent not only between Presbyterians and Independents, but between Independents and Levellers.

Related sources

Kent Protestation Returns (digital publication by the Institute of Heraldic and Genealogical Studies, Canterbury).

Jacqueline Eales, 'Kent and the English Civil Wars, 1640-1660', in Frederick Lansberry (ed.), *Government and Politics in Kent 1640-1914* (Woodbridge, Boydell, 2001).

Jacqueline Eales, '"So many sects and schisms": religious diversity in revolutionary Kent, 1640-60', in Christopher Durston and Judith Maltby (eds.), *Religion in Revolutionary England* (Manchester, Manchester University Press, 2006).

Norman L. Hopkins, *The Baptists of Smarden and the Weald of Kent, 1640-2000* (Mickle Print, Canterbury, 2000).

ODNB: Theodor Harmsen, 'Hearne, Thomas (*bap.* 1678, d. 1735)'.

historyofparliamentonline.org/volume/1604-1629/member/paramour-thomas-1585-1636.

mytenterden.co.uk/directory/the-bailiffs-and-mayors-of-tenterden-since-1449-article-207.aspx#.W7d8itNKjIV.

66: BUCKINGHAMSHIRE

14 February 1649

Context

Though this petition was presented to the House of Commons two weeks after regicide had become a fact, it shares with many of those above a concern for retribution against the late king's chief supporters, and for radical proposals for constitutional, legal and social reforms that foreshadow later events of 1649. That year saw not only the crest of the revolutionary wave, with the abolition of monarchy and the House of Lords; but also the defeat of a Leveller-inspired rising led by former soldier William Thompson, and the start of the Digger movement taking over common lands. The petitioners' demands for the abolition of the House of Lords and of legal proceedings in languages other than English were soon to be fulfilled by the Rump Parliament; but the burden of tithes for the support of a national church and the centralisation of justice were to last for centuries. The 'Norman Yoke' of feudal land law, insofar as it concerned the lord of the manor's fealty to the king or other superior, was abolished in the 1650s; but for the lords' tenants it did not die out until the nineteenth century.

According to the *Commons Journal*, the Speaker responded to the petition's presenters by assuring them on behalf of the MPs, that 'it is their present care, to settle the Government of this Commonwealth' and that 'this House is resolved to maintain the Liberty of the Subject: and to avoid and prevent whatsoever may tend to Tyranny or Confusion'. The reference to 'confusion', or anarchy, sounds a warning note. The Speaker also thanked the petitioners for their 'good Affections' towards what Parliament had already done; to which the editor of *The Moderate* retorted, 'And why not for their good Petition too? Surely they well deserved it, if I may dare to say so.' *The Moderate*'s version was printed without the heading given in both the version below and the *Commons Journal*.

Text

Perfect Occurrences, No. 111, 9-16 February 1648/9. BL/EEBO: E.527[21]

Wednesday, Febr. 14
This day a paper was presented to the Commons by some Gentlemen entitled thus; To the supreame Authority of this Nation, the Commons assembled in Parliament; The representation of divers Inhabitants of the County of Bucks. The particulars represented were these:

1. That you would proceed to speedy Triall and publique Justice upon all those who shall be found guilty of procuring acting, or abetting the first or second War, or the invasion of the Scots, to the utter ruine of many hundreds (if not thousands) of Families, because Justice is not speedily executed upon evill doers, therefore the hearts of the Sons of men are continually set upon mischiefe.

2. That you would adhere to your late just and honourable Votes concerning the Supreame and Legislative power of the Nation, for we cannot but take notice of the late endeavours of those men called Lords, how they leave no meanes unattempted to thrust themselves againe into power, and we have cause to feare, to no other end but to improve their interests to returne us againe unto our regall and tyrannical bondage.
3. That Tythes, whose beginning in this Nation is known to be superfluous, and found by sad experience to be exceeding oppressive, and vexatious to all sorts of people, especially the poor Husbandman, who is thereby deprived both of the benefit of his stock and labour, and hath been so often petitioned against as a grievance to the Nation may be wholly taken away.
4. That the people of the Nation be made free, by having their lands wholly cleared and discharged from all manner of [F]ealty and Homage, claimed by any Lord, or others as Lords of Mannours, that being a badge and brute of the Normand slavery.
5. That the many great and needlesse Volumes of Statute Lawes be well reversed and such only left in force as are made needfull in the Commonwealth and that all Lawes, Writs, Commissions, Pleadings, Records and Processe be in the English Tongue, and that there be Courts erected in every Hundred by 12 of the same hundred.
6. That you would take some speedy and effectuall course for the payment of the Publique debts.
7. That the present Army under the conduct of the Lord Generall be so provided for, that they may not be necessitated to take free quarter.
8. That effectuall and speedy provision may be made for the reliefe and maintenance of the poore, by improvement of Comuons [*sic*] and other waste Lands or otherwise as your wisdomes shall think fit, for the raising a stock for their imployment, that so many thousands be not suffered to begge, or perish by starving, which is indeed a shame and dishonour to a Nation professing Christianity.

The Gentlemen were called in, and had thanks for their good affections.

Background

The evidence for radicalism in 1640s Buckinghamshire, though substantial, is unfortunately insufficient to identify the authors of this particular petition. Among previous petitions from inhabitants of the shire addressed to Parliament or the army, some had offered explicit support for Leveller or Independent politics. In February 1647, an appeal from Buckinghamshire and Hertfordshire for the release of John Lilburne, Richard Overton and others who had been imprisoned by the House of Lords claimed (somewhat implausibly) 10,000 signatures and was said to have been accompanied to Parliament by 500 gentlemen and yeomen, but was refused a hearing there. Four months later, as the New Model Army took its stand against

Parliament, Buckinghamshire petitioners appealed to its leaders to mediate with Parliament, since their appeal for rights due to them 'both by common birthright and the law of the Kingdom' had been ignored. In March 1648 another Buckinghamshire petition, welcoming the Vote of No Addresses, was presented to the Commons by a member of the County Committee, Christopher Egleton or Eggleston. This was well received and sent to one of the House's regular publishers. In August that year, the Leveller-style broadside, *A New Engagement, or Manifesto* claimed supporters in Buckinghamshire and other counties around London.

Buckinghamshire petitioners sometimes joined with others to protest against the burdens of free quarter and tithes. The Leveller Richard Overton had been writing on this issue since 1645, reaching out to rural anti-tithe feeling especially through the General Baptists, but firm evidence for the presence of the sect in Buckinghamshire dates only from after 1650. The unknown author of *The Husbandman's Plea against Tithes* incorporated in his treatise a petition from Hertfordshire with adjacent parts of Bedfordshire and Buckinghamshire, corresponding to the area of the Chiltern Hills. In September 1647 Buckinghamshire petitioners appealed to Parliament again to end free quarter, from which they got some relief with the support of MPs Edmund West and Simon Mayne; and also to remove 'the intollerable burdens of the distressed Commons on their Conscience and Estates' imposed by the ordinance enforcing the payment of tithes. The petition from Newport Pagnell in Buckinghamshire (53 above) also includes a plea for the complete abolition of tithes. This was perhaps the most radical rural issue before the Surrey Diggers took to the commons in April 1649 and their example was followed at Colnbrook and Iver in this county.

The petition's denunciation of the House of Lords, anti-feudal stance, and plea for the development of commons to benefit the poor, all share the argument of *Light Shining in Buckingham-shire*, first published in early December 1648. The style of the petition is, however, very different from that of the tract, aptly described by Christopher Hill as 'vigorous, rudely boisterous and bellicose'. John Gurney suggested that although no one now accepts that *Light Shining in Buckingham-shire* was written by Winstanley himself, it may have influenced his development at this time, particularly in its broad definition of kingly power and denunciation of the Norman Yoke (see 26, 28 and 44 above). Historians have been unable to suggest alternative candidates for its authorship, however — or for that of its March 1649 sequel, *More Light Shining in Buckingham-shire*.

Opposition to landlords' feudal rights was an urban as well as rural grievance in seventeenth-century Buckinghamshire, when the corporations of Aylesbury, Amersham and Newport Pagnell struggled from time to time to defend their privileges against aggressive local lords. In High Wycombe, however, contemporary protests were directed against the mayor and corporation, accused of taking the income from corn market tolls away from the poor relief funds. These protests, led by one of the overseers of the poor, Samuel Guy, escalated into riots later in 1649, which were said to have been instigated by local Levellers. It seems that High Wycombe (the only Buckinghamshire town whose chief officer was called mayor rather than bailiff) was the birthplace of *Light Shining in Buckinghamshire*, with its heated denunciation of 'a thing called a Major ... a Just-asse of the Peace', parading in archaic effeminate robes and followed by his aldermen 'as so many fools in a Mid-summer Aile'.

In Aylesbury, an iconoclastic riot in 1640 was caused by outsiders, levied as soldiers for Charles I's war with the Scots; but the town itself seems to have been radicalised by the civil wars. Henry Marten, who was to become the Levellers' best friend among politicians, commanded Aylesbury's garrison for a time in 1644, obtaining payment of their arrears and restoring their morale. In 1645 the borough elected two Independents, local gentleman Simon Mayne and London lawyer Thomas Scott, to replace the royalists elected in 1640. The Levellers regarded Scott as a friend, and according to John Lilburne his name was put forward at Windsor for the joint committee to finalise the *Agreement of the People* that would go to the army council in December 1648 (see 47 above) but he never attended. Scott helped to formulate the declaration of the Commons' supremacy, but his support for constitutional revolution stopped short of the proposals in the *Agreement*. Together with Simon Mayne and Buckinghamshire MP George Fleetwood, Scott would sit on the High Court of Justice that tried the king and sign the death warrant, going on to serve the Commonwealth government. These men, and most of their colleagues on the County Committee, were firmly Independent in their politics but unlikely to have initiated the above petition. For them the revolution was over with the king's execution; while for the petitioners above and those who thought like them, it was only beginning. A manifesto in the name of the well affected 'middle sort of men' of the Chiltern hundreds (Stoke, Desborough and Burnham) and part of Aylesbury Hundred, denounced Norman institutions 'whereby we, the lower sort of People, are made slaves to the wills of Tyrants', just as new risings broke out in the army and elsewhere. Their revolution was not to be, but its expectation, as we have seen, was one of the frequent themes of petitioners in the months preceding the king's execution.

Related sources

To the Right Honourable, the betrusted knights, citizens and burgesses in the Commons House of Parliament, Englands Legal Sovereign Power, Assembled, The Humble Petition of the inhabitants of Buckingham-shire, whose names are hereunto subscribed. No printer or publisher named. BL/EEBO: 669.f.10[115].

Four Petitions to His Excellency Sir Thomas Fairfax... Printed for Lawrence Chapman. June 18. 1647. BL/EEBO: E.393[7].

The copie of three petitions as they were presented to the Honourable, the House of Commons assembled in Parliament, September 14th. and 15th. 1647. Printed for William Larnar. BL/EEBO: E.407[29].

The humble petition and representation of many inhabitants of the county of Buckingham, concerning the late votes passed, touching no farther address to the King, presented to the Honorable House of Commons ... Printed for Edward Husband, Printer to the Honorable House of Commons, March 15. 1647 [1648]. BL/EEBO: E.432[12].

The husbandmans plea against tithes. Or, Two petitions presented unto the House of Commons assembled in Parliament ... Published by some of the said petitioners whose names are set down in the latter end of this book ... Printed in the yeer 1647. BL/EEBO: E.389[2]

A New Engagement, or Manifesto ... Printed in the year MDCXLVIII. BL/EEBO: 669.f.12[97].

A Declaration of the Wel-affected in the County of Buckinghamshire, being a Representation of the middle sort of Men within the three Chilterne Hundreds ... Printed in the year 1649. BL/EEBO: E.555[1].

Ian F. W. Beckett, *Wanton Troopers, Buckinghamshire in the Civil Wars, 1640-1660* (Barnsley, Pen & Sword, 2015).

VCH: *Buckinghamshire*, vols 2 (political history), 3 (Amersham, Aylesbury, High Wycombe), 4 (Newport Pagnell).

John Gurney, *Brave Community, The Digger Movement in the English Revolution* (Manchester University Press, 2007).

John Gurney, 'Gerrard Winstanley and the context of place', in *Prose Studies*, vol. 36 (1), 2014.

ODNB: C. H. Firth (revised by Sean Kelsey), 'Scott (Scot), Thomas (d. 1660), politician and regicide'.

Index

Abingdon (Berkshire/Oxfordshire), 58, 121, 246
acquittal, possibility of king's, 27, 30, 70, 71, 110, 114, 115
Act of Oblivion, 13, 19, 23, 37, 58, 227, 284
Adis, John, 298
Adlam, William, 52
Agreement of the People, 2, 20, 30, 31, 76, 89, 101, 112, 120, 141, 152, 192, 211, 233, 234, 242, 245, 248, 250, 254, 266, 273, 303, 323, 324, 334
Allanson, William, 40
Allen, Hanna, 288
Amersham (Buckinghamshire), 333
Anderson, Capt. Robert, 92
Andrews, Thomas, 297
Anglesey, 208-9
Appleby (Westmorland/Cumbria), 46, 48, 73, 197
Assignation, *see* pay, army's
Arnold (Nottinghamshire), 320
Arnold, Robert, 130
arrears, *see* pay, army's
Arundel (Sussex), 153, 162, 163
Ash (Kent), 329
Ashford (Kent), 260. 329
Ashton (Assheton), Col. Ralph, 48, 117, 196-7
Atkin, Malcolm, 277
Atkins, Thomas, MP, 294, 295
Atkinson, Edward, 67
Aubrey, John, 32
Audeley, Maj. Lewis, 250
Axtell, Maj. Daniel, 135, 171, 273
Aylesbury (Buckinghamshire), 333, 334
Aylmer, Gerald, 185, 300

Badger, Edmund, 146
Baker, Philip, 305
Baldwin, Robert, 67
Bamber, Capt., 198
Banbury (Oxfordshire), 24-5, 186, 213
Baptists, 25, 30, 35, 53, 67, 130, 135, 233, 242, 250, 256, 260, 269, 273, 278, 286, 299, 314, 320, 324, 329, 333
Barber, Sarah, 9, 57
Barbour, Gabriel, 273

Barkstead, Col. John, 82, 86, 103, 216, 250
Barnard Castle (Durham/Teesdale), 46, 48, 176
Barnes, Ensign John, 92
Barnstaple (Devon), 69, 151
Bartholomew, Francis, 146
Barton, John, 313
Barton, Nathaniel, 155
Baskerville, Thomas, 297, 300
Basket, John, 313
Bate, Dr George, 72
Batten, Vice-Admiral William, 201-3, 314
Baxter, Richard, 85, 112, 277, 278
Baxter, Thomas, 146
Baynes, Capt. Adam, 182, 233, 234
Baynes, John, 146
Baynton, Sir Edward, 54
Beaumont, Capt. Richard, 269
Bedfordshire, 273, 333
Belcham, Lt Anthony, 92
Bell, William, 313
Bellany, Alastair, 29
Benenden (Kent), 329
Bennet, Martyn, 320
Berkeley Castle, siege of, 92
Berkshire, 24, 56-8, 68, 212, 244-6
Berwick-upon-Tweed, 34, 68, 92-3, 120, 147, 230
Bethel, Rowland, 297
Bewdley (Worcestershire), 278
Bicester (Oxfordshire), 25
Biddenden (Kent), 329
Bifield, Francis, 298
Birch, Col. John, 297, 298, 299-300
Bishops' Wars, 34, 273
Blackerby, Samuel, 29
Blackmore, John, 116
Blakiston, John MP, 35
Blaney, Thomas, 299-300
Blethin, Capt. Francis, 69
'blood and treasure', 8, 42, 51, 76, 115, 165-6, 215, 245, 255, 267, 292, 313
Bond, Dennis MP, 33
Borles, Thomas, 313
Borne, Ensign Richard, 92
Boston (Lincolnshire), 160, 190-1
Boughton under Blean (Kent), 329

337

Bowreman, Thomas, 313
Bradford (Yorkshire), 40-1
Bray, Lt. William, 185, 186, 206
Brayfield, Capt., 188
Brenner, Robert, 306, 315
Bridges, Sir John, 297, 300
Bright, Col. John, 181, 232, 233
Bristol, 35, 68, 89, 120, 121, 254-7, 264, 277, 285, 299, 300
  Broadmead church, 256, 257
  corporation, 257
Broadway (Worcestershire), 278
Bromley, Arthur, 67
Broughton, Andrew, 260
Brown (Browne), Maj.-Gen. Richard MP, 172-3, 174
Brown, William, 297
Browne, Francis, 116
Bucke, Cornet William, 42, 78
Buckingham, George Villiers Duke of, 29, 70
Buckinghamshire, 24, 156, 269, 273, 331-4
Burford, 1649 mutiny at, 135, 186, 286
Burton, George, 313
Burton, Steven, 313
Butler, Col. John, 139, 314
Byfeild, John, 116
Byron, John Lord, 166-7, 208

'C.W.' (publisher), 63, 67, 80
Cadwell, Matthew, 67, 69
Calvert, Giles, 24, 27, 31, 256, 257, 276, 296
Calvert, Hugh, 230
Calvinism, 9, 50, 135
Canon Frome (Herefordshire), 298
Canterbury (Kent), 205, 258, 259, 260, 288, 295, 328, 329
Capel, Arthur Lord, 65
Carde, Ralph, 313, 314
Cardiff (Glamorgan), 264
Careles (Careless), Thomas, 297, 300
Careles (Careless), William, 298
Carisbrooke Castle, 2, 132, 216
Carlisle (Westmorland/Cumbria), 46, 68, 92, 121
Carwardine, Anthony, 297
Cecil, Capt. William, 104
Chambers, Oliver, 297

Chapman, Lawrence, 274, 334
Charles I, king, 1, 2-4, 7-9, 13, 20, 22, 24, 27, 34, 35, 37, 50, 86, 94, 95, 109, 149, 151, 152, 153, 155, 175, 176, 186, 190, 199, 202, 204, 215-16, 232, 244, 250, 258, 264, 284, 306, 314, 315
  as 'Charles Stuart', 3, 8, 234, 327
  responsibility for bloodshed, 7, 8, 29, 30, 33, 63, 95, 112, 118, 128, 135, 137, 141, 157, 288, 326, 327
Charles II, king, 77, 188, 300
  as Prince of Wales, 309, 315
Chase, Nathaniel, 313, 314
Chepstow (Monmouthshire), 68, 156
Chichester (Sussex), 153, 162, 163
Chick, Francis, 313
Chiltern Hills, 24, 273, 333
Cholmeley, Col. Sir Henry, 89
Cholmley, John, 89, 298
Christmas, 40, 205, 259, 290, 295
Church, Thomas, 297
Cinque Ports, 258, 288, 328
Clare, Henry, 72
Clarendon, Edward Hyde Earl of, 201
Clark, James, 67
Clark, Maj. Samuel, 255, 257
Clark, Peter, 260
Clark, William, 63, 297
Clarke, Capt, 64, 149
Clarke, William, 91, 181, 234
Clifton, Lt. Richard, 92
Clotworthy, Sir John MP, 174
Clowes, John, 42, 78
Clun, Richard, 313
Cobb, William, 116
Cobbett, Maj. John, 64, 67
Cobbett, Lt.-Col. Ralph, 86, 216, 244
Cobham (Surrey), 324
Cockerham, Arthur, 297
Cogswell, Thomas, 29
Colchester, siege of, 3, 73, 86, 89
Cole, William Jr., 313
Coleman, Maj. William, 42, 78
Colley, John, 297
Collier, Thomas, 231, 286
Collingwood, Lt Henry, 92
Colman, Richard, 313
Colnbrook (Buckinghamshire), 333

conscience, freedom of, 66, 145, 149, 150, 200, 229, 256, 272, 303
conscription, *see* impressment
Constable, Sir William MP, 40, 43, 66, 67, 68, 104, 135
Constant Warwick, ship, 202
Coquetdale (Northumberland), 147
Corbett, Miles, MP, 294, 295
Cornwall, 151, 274
Cornwell, Francis, 329
Cotton, John, 191
Cotton, Giles, 147
Council of Officers, 2, 3, 5, 20, 56, 69, 75, 79, 80, 87, 91, 93, 94-104, 117, 127, 128, 132, 135, 153, 162, 171-5, 192, 204, 216, 233, 244, 247, 276, 291, 303, 323, 324
Council of State, Commonwealth, 101, 160, 226
Covenant, Scottish National (1638), 34, 257
Covenant, Solemn League and (1643), 22, 36, 39-40, 50, 95, 109, 124, 126, 201, 256, 269, 283-4, 286, 307
Coventry (Warwickshire), 156, 278
Cradock, Walter, 264
Cranbrook (Kent), 260, 329
Crawford, Patricia, 8
Cripps, Henry, 231
Cromwell, Capt. Henry, 198
Cromwell, Oliver Jr., 268-9
Cromwell, Lt-Gen. Oliver, 2, 4, 46, 47, 63, 67, 77, 80, 85, 87, 89, 92, 103-4, 109, 111, 112, 118, 120, 121, 126, 139, 159, 165, 167, 175, 176, 181, 183, 185, 187, 197-8, 209, 230, 242, 246, 257, 268, 269, 271, 273, 283, 294, 295, 296
  regiment of, 6, 114-17, 155-6, 185
  Ironsides, 116
Crowch (Crouch), Richard, 52, 53, 54
Crowland (Lincolnshire), 88, 191
Culmer, Richard, 329
Cumberland, 47, 143, 147, 197

Danet, Thomas, 297
Deal, 188
Deal Castle, 201
Denbigh, Basil Fielding, Earl of, 194
Denbigh, corporation of, 209

Derby House committee, 73, 82, 152, 160, 163, 185, 191, 197, 201, 205, 206, 212, 215, 319
Devon, 149, 151, 152, 174
Diggers, 324, 331, 333
Dobson, Richard, 320, 321
Dodington, Sir Francis, 285
Doncaster, 82, 87, 89, 167
Dover Castle, 187-8
Downs (Kent, anchorage), 199-203
Duck, Henry, 313, 314
Dudley, Col. Dud, 278
Dun, John, 67
Durant, John, 329
Durham, county, 35, 46, 130
  horse regiment of, 147
Durnford, Joseph, 313
Durnford, Ro., 313
Durston, Christopher, 57, 58
Dyer, George, 52, 54

Eales, Jacqueline, 260, 329
Easington (Yorkshire), 230
Easman, Henry, 313
Eastern Association, 159-60, 293, 294
Edgehill, battle of, 68, 159
Edinburgh, 46, 112, 120, 126, 278
Edwards, Thomas, 116
Egleton (Eggleston), Christopher, 333
elections, 35, 73, 75, 76, 85, 226, 260
  corporation of London, 18, 24, 303, 306, 307, 314, 323
  parliamentary, 9, 16, 30, 41, 47, 54, 57, 110, 142, 142, 153, 174, 175, 180, 181, 194, 225, 244, 261, 274, 277, 285, 294-5, 299, 300, 305, 318, 319, 334
Elsinore (Elsmore), George, 313, 314
Elsynge, Henry, 94, 284
Elton, Ambrose Jr., 301
Ely, Isle of (Cambridgeshire), 68, 160, 191
Embleton (Northumberland), 147
Embry, George, 313
Epperstone (Nottinghamshire), 320
Erbery, William, 69, 76, 164
Essex, Robert Devereux Earl of, 76, 120, 155, 159, 306
Ethers, Thomas, 313
Everard, Robert, 30

339

Everitt, Alan, 259, 260
Ewer, Col. Isaac, 76, 82, 104, 116, 214
Exeter (Devon), 35, 152
Eynion, Thomas, 297
Eyre (Ayres), William, 52, 53, 54
Eyre (Ayres), Col. Thomas, 52, 54, 216
Eyres, William, Leveller, 58

Fairfax, Ferdinando Lord, 40
Fairfax, Sir Thomas/Lord, 2, 5, 7, 9, 18, 23, 31, 40, 42, 43-4, 47, 52, 56, 63-93, 95, 104, 109-239, 242, 244, 247, 249, 254, 264, 266, 269, 271, 273-4, 276, 285, 291, 295, 299, 306, 309, 312, 314, 315, 329
Farnham (Surrey), 73
Farrow, William, 146
Fenn, Capt. Matthew, 92
Fenwick, Lt.-Col./Col. George, 68, 93, 147
Feoffees for Impropriations, 194, 222
Field, John, 127, 171
Fielding, W., 126
Fiennes, Nathaniel, 25
Flacket, Robert, 297
Fleetwood, Col. Charles, 271
  regiment of, 42-4, 78, 82, 85, 86, 103, 269, 295
Fleetwood, George (regicide), 44
Fleetwood, George MP, 344
Fletcher, Anthony, 163
Forster, Richard, 328
Fortescue, Col. Richard, 86
Foster, Thomas, 328
Fox, George, 269, 320, 321
Fox, John, 116, 313
free quarter, 9, 24, 43, 44, 78, 80, 82, 84, 92, 110, 115, 119, 121, 133, 138, 143, 149, 150, 154, 156, 157, 158, 217, 250, 273, 293, 297, 324, 332, 333
Freeman, Lt., 242
French, Capt. Thomas, 299
Frippe, Edward, 52

Gainsborough, siege of, 156
Gardiner, Samuel Rawson, 104
garrisons
  Berwick-upon-Tweed, 68, 93, 130, 147
  Boston (Lincolnshire), 160, 190-1
  Denbigh Castle, 207-9
  Dover, 187-8
  Holy Island, 128, 147
  Hull, 5, 218-231, 290-1
  Hurst Castle, 214-17, 309
  Isle of Wight, 214-17, 309
  Ludlow, 192-4
  Newport Pagnell, 266-70
  Portsmouth, 214-17, 309, 315
  Shrewsbury, 192-4
  Tynemouth, 64, 130
Garston, Alexander, 298
Gell, Col. Sir John, 155
General Council of the Army, 2, 20, 63, 69, 75, 86, 112, 185
Gentles, Ian, 127
Gerard, Col. Charles, 264
Gibbons, Maj. Robert, 73
Gibbs, John, 269
Glamorgan(shire), 262-5
Gloucestershire, 121, 256
God, anger of, 19, 23, 95, 110, 111, 114, 245, 292, 295, 296, 304
God, giving victories, 15, 16, 23, 38-9, 42, 57, 75, 76, 82, 83, 91, 95, 102, 116, 118, 137, 138, 142, 143, 154, 157, 166, 177, 188, 192, 193, 194, 196, 199, 200, 204, 205, 208, 211, 214, 229, 232, 233, 241, 247, 249, 262, 267, 284, 292, 296, 309-10, 318, 323, 326
Goodwin, James, 116
Goodwin, Thomas, 68, 136
Goring, George Lord, 65, 216, 285, 315
Goudhurst (Kent), 329
Gough, Capt. William, 92
Gouleney, Adam, 52
Graves, Col. Richard, 155
Gravesend (Kent), 260, 329
Greene, Nicholas, 52, 53, 54
Groby, Thomas Lord Grey of, 30, 31, 35, 36, 156, 242, 271
Grice, John, 146
Griffin, John, 146
Grime (Grimes, Gryme), Mark, 67, 69
Grubb, Edmund, 298
Gurney, John, 324, 333
Gurney, Sir Richard, 306
Guy, Samuel, 334
Gwatkin, Richard, 297

Haddocke, Capt. Richard, 200
Hall, Bishop Joseph, 294
Hall, Henry, 116
Hamilton, James Hamilton Duke of, 8, 65, 138, 178, 259, 309
Hammond, Col. Robert, 2, 80, 109, 126, 132, 187, 215, 216, 283, 313, 314
Harden, William, 313
Hardman, John, 116
Hardres, Sir Richard, 188
Harison, John, 146
Harleys of Brampton Bryan, 299, 300
  Col. Edward, 299, 300
  Brilliana, Lady, 299
  Robert (Robin), Maj. MP, 300
  Robert, Sir MP, 299
Harris, John, 24, 298
Harrison, George, 67
Harrison, Col. Thomas, 112, 135, 186, 247, 249, 271, 301
  regiment of, 6, 68, 109-12, 114, 117, 197
Harrison, Thomas, sailor, 200
Harwell, Henry, 313
Hawnby, Edward, 146
Hayns (Heane), James, 313, 314
Hazzard, Dorothy, 256
Hazzard, Matthew, 257
Heads of a Diarie, 196
Heads of the Proposals, 13, 80, 104
Hearne, Thomas, 328, 329
Heely (Hely), James, 52, 54
Hemel Hempstead (Hertfordshire), 273
Henley (Oxfordshire), 24, 25
Henrietta Maria, Queen, 91
Herbert, Col. William, 92
Herbert, Sir Thomas, 216
Hereford, 68, 69, 276, 296-300
Herefordshire, 6, 276, 296-301
Herring, John, 298
Hesilrige, Sir Arthur MP, 29, 35, 67, 68, 130, 139, 147
Hesilrige, Thomas, 29
Hewet, Thomas, 298
Hewson, Col. John, 132-5, 192, 273
Heytesbury (Wiltshire), 54
Higgins, Robert, 297, 300
Higgins, Thomas, 297, 300
Higgins, Verney, 298, 300
High Wycombe (Buckinghamshire), 333, 334
Hill, Christopher, 8, 277, 333
Hill, Miles, 297, 300
Hobart, Col. Sir Miles, 294
Hobson, Paul, 4, 35, 63, 64, 67, 130, 233, 269
Holdenby (Northamptonshire), 43
Holland, Cornelius, 35, 58, 246
Holland, Hwnry Rich Earl of, 65, 70
Holles, Denzil MP, 174
Holy Island (Northumberland), 128, 147
Hood, Henry, 31
Hooton (Hooten)
  Elizabeth, 518
  Oliver, 518
Hoper, William
Hopgood, Edward
Hopper, Andrew, 394
Horton, Col. Thomas, 137-9, 300
House of Commons, 3, 5, 9, 13-62, 65, 73, 79, 83, 92, 94, 100, 102, 104, 110, 112, 117, 119, 125, 128, 134, 144, 147, 149, 150, 153, 167, 171, 172-3, 174, 175, 178, 190, 192, 198, 200, 204, 211, 212, 225, 232, 233, 240, 241, 242, 254, 255, 256, 260, 262, 271, 272, 273, 274, 278, 283-336
House of Lords, 1, 9, 14, 15, 22, 33, 50, 65, 83, 92, 110, 119, 145, 150, 192, 200, 212, 213, 225, 272, 303, 317, 331, 332, 333
Howell, Roger, 34-5
Hoyle, Thomas MP, 37, 40
Hubblethorn, Joseph, 313
Hull (Kingston upon Hull), 38, 39, 40, 191, 230, 240
  corporation of, 40, 230
  garrison of, 5, 92, 93, 218-31, 290-1
Hunt, Lt Thomas, 92
Huntingdonshire, 159, 295
Huntington, Henry, 116
Hurst Castle, 3, 54, 153, 186, 214-16, 244, 247, 254, 258, 309
Hurst, Thomas, 313, 314
Husband, Edward, 283
Husbandman's Plea against Tithes, The, 269, 333
Hussey, Edward, 298
Hutchinson, Col. John, 6, 166, 167, 317, 319, 320, 321

Hutchinson, Lucy, 156, 167, 320
Huthwaite, Robert, 320, 321
Huthwaite, Thomas, 320, 321
Hyland, Samuel, 250
Hythe (Kent), 328, 329

Ibbotson, Robert, 105
impressment (conscription), 9, 145
'incendiaries', 39, 144, 190, 262
indemnity, 15, 80, 274
Independents, 1
  in religion, 4, 6, 13, 25, 30, 31, 35, 40, 69, 135, 136, 151, 152, 160, 191, 197, 209, 256, 263, 286, 294, 296, 300, 329
  in politics, 21, 23, 25, 33, 35, 40, 41, 46, 54, 68, 90, 123, 126, 139, 164, 191, 194, 205, 209, 212, 213, 218, 230, 239, 244, 245, 246, 260, 264, 273, 274, 277, 278, 284, 285, 294, 295, 300, 301, 306, 315, 319, 329, 332, 334
Ingoldsby, Col. Richard, 76-7, 271
  regiment of, 24, 69, 75-7, 121
Ireland, 1, 2, 3, 28, 50, 62, 83, 86, 92, 111, 120, 124, 128, 129, 133, 135, 157, 158, 185, 186, 192, 193, 197, 198, 206, 219, 222, 226, 230, 299
  rebellion in (1641), 152
Ireton, Commissary-general Henry, 4, 7, 53, 63, 67, 70-3, 79, 80, 82, 94-5, 104, 105, 121, 135, 155, 183, 205, 271
Isle of Wight, 1, 2, 3, 46, 80, 86, 104, 109, 118, 132, 137, 147, 153, 214-16, 254, 288, 309, 313, 314, 315
Iver (Buckinghamshire), 333
Ives, Jeremiah, 53

Jackson, Ensign William, 92
James VI of Scotland, I of England, king, 3, 28, 29, 224, 240
James, Duke of York, 97, 259
James, John, JP, 67, 296, 297
James, John, soldier, 300
Jeake, Samuel, 163
Jefferie, Lt. Jervise (Jarvis, Jervaise), 72,
Jennings (Gennings), James, 72
Jennings, Lt. James, 72
Jessey, Henry, 257

Johnstone (Jhonstone), William, 67
Jones (Jhones), Rhys (Rise), soldier, 67
Jones of Llanfihangel-ar-Elai, Basset, 263, 265
Jones of Llanfihangel-ar-Elai, Richard, 265
Jones, Col. Philip, 264, 265
Jones, Madeline, 329
Joyce, Capt. George, 111, 116, 313, 314
Jubbes, Lt.-Col. John, 135, 294
Justice, High Court of, 33, 41, 44, 77, 86, 112, 121, 135, 152, 155, 160, 188, 211, 232, 242, 271, 278, 286, 309, 319, 334
justice, impartial, 8, 28, 34, 38, 56, 71, 84, 88, 110, 111, 114, 115, 138, 165, 183, 184, 187, 190, 205, 252, 284, 292, 293, 317, 318

Kelsey, Maj., later Lt.-Col., Thomas, 24, 69, 76, 104
Kem, Samuel, 201
Kensworth, 273
Kent, 6, 121, 130, 152, 155, 204, 205, 206, 212, 250, 258-60, 288-9, 293, 307, 310, 326-9
  revolt in, 70, 76, 185, 188, 201-2, 259, 306
Kenwrick, Robert, 329
Kenwrick, William, 329
Kidderminster (Worcestershire), 277
Kiffin, William, 135
King, Col. Edward, 191
King, Dr John, 273
Kingdoms Weekly Intelligencer, The, 72, 77, 198, 292
Knollys (Knowles), Capt. William, 92
Knottingley (Yorkshire), 80, 104, 109, 111
Knox, John, 34

Lambe, Thomas, 53
Lambe, William, 324
Lambert, Col. John, later Maj.-Gen., 40, 68, 69, 80, 112, 117, 176, 181-2, 232, 233-4
Lanark, William Hamilton Earl of, 156
Lancashire, 117, 196-8, 212, 299
Langdale, Sir Marmaduke, 89, 167
Langport, battle of, 89, 112, 121

Large Petition, 11 Sept. 1648, 4, 6, 9, 13-21, 30, 35, 36, 51, 52, 53, 63, 102, 104, 114, 139, 141, 149, 150, 214, 216, 247, 252, 272, 274, 309, 312
Larner (Larnar), William, 239, 273
Laud, William, Archbishop, 69, 194
Laudianism, 34, 40, 151
Laugharne (Laughorne), Maj.-Gen. Rowland, 65, 139, 167
laws in English, 133, 134, 145, 267, 293, 295, 301, 331, 332
Leake, Edward, 146
Leake, Richard, 146
Ledger, Thomas, 34
Leech, John Jr., 297
Leicester, 30, 92, 156, 240
Leicester, Robert Sidney Earl of, 188, 206
Leicestershire, 27-31, 35, 56, 68, 124, 139, 193, 240, 252
Lenitoll, John, 297
Lenthall, William, 25, 328
Levellers, 4, 5, 6, 8, 9, 13-21, 24, 25, 30, 31, 35, 39, 44, 53, 54, 58, 63, 73, 76, 87, 90, 104, 112, 123, 127, 130, 134, 135, 139, 141, 147, 149, 160, 165, 185, 186, 206, 214, 216, 230, 233, 239, 242, 244, 245, 246, 250, 252, 256, 260, 273, 274, 286, 295, 305, 306, 309, 314, 324, 329, 331, 332, 333, 334
Light Shining in Buckingham-shire, 333, 334
Lilburne, Lt.-Col. Henry, 130
Lilburne, John, 6, 20, 35, 47, 68, 104, 130, 147, 160, 191, 245, 246, 260, 273, 274, 305, 332, 334
Lilburne, Col. Robert, 130, 147, 232, 233
  regiment of, 35, 130, 181, 185
Lincoln, 156
Lincoln, President Abraham, 294
Lindley, Thomas, 320
Lingen, Sir Henry, 299
Livesey (Livesay), Col. Sir Michael, 185, 204-6, 259, 271
Llanfaches (Monmouthshire), 69, 263
Lloyd, Col. Walter, 92
Lloyd, Lodowick, 231
Llwyd, Morgan, 209
Lollards, 163

London, 3, 4, 5, 6, 9, 13-21, 22, 23, 24, 28, 31, 35, 36, 37, 40, 47, 50, 54, 65, 66, 68, 76, 83, 84, 86, 88, 90, 92, 96, 102, 104, 111, 112, 116, 117, 118, 119, 120, 121, 124, 126, 130, 135, 138, 139, 142, 151, 153, 155, 156, 157, 167, 171, 172, 174-5, 185, 193, 194, 199, 202, 209, 214, 216, 223, 230, 232, 234, 240, 241, 244, 245, 246, 252, 256, 257, 259, 260, 273, 274, 303-18, 324
  Common Council of, 65, 303-7, 323, 324
Long, John, 51, 52, 53, 54
Long, Lislebone MP, 284
Long, Walter MP, 54, 174
Loving, James, 67
Loving, Thomas, 313
Ludlow, 192, 194
Ludlow, Edmund, 126, 171
Ludlow, William, 52, 53, 54
Lufton, John, 297
Luke, Col. Sir Samuel, 35, 269
Lynn (King's Lynn, Norfolk), 159, 160, 191, 294, 295

Mabbott, Gilbert, 28
Mackworth, Col. Humphrey, 194
Macock, John, 176
Maidstone, battle of, 86, 259
Malmesbury (Wiltshire), 309, 314
'man of blood', 3, 137
Manchester, Edward Montagu Earl of, 159, 160
Mansfield (Nottinghamshire), 320
Margetts, Thomas, 176, 181, 233, 234
Marsh, William, 297
Marston Moor, battle of, 68, 116, 159
Marten, Col. Henry, 4, 39, 57, 58, 68, 212, 245, 246, 249, 271, 334
Martin, Ensign Samuel, 92
Massachusetts, 294, 301
Massey, Col. Edward, 172, 298
Mathews, Thomas, 313
Maynard, Sir John MP, 174
Mayne, Simon MP, 333, 334
Mercurio Volpone, 33
Mercurius Elencticus, 23, 300
Mercurius Militaris, 104
Mercurius Pragmaticus, 21, 33, 37, 67, 94,

104, 135, 212, 285, 307
Merriweather, Christopher, 52, 54
militia, 22, 29, 53, 54, 90, 130, 151-2, 197, 212, 213, 247, 250, 260, 263, 273, 294, 300, 306, 323
Millington, Gilbert MP, 319
Moderate Intelligencer, The, 46, 123, 262, 300
Moderate, The, 22, 33, 34, 35, 36, 38, 39, 40, 54, 66, 73, 87, 91, 126, 137, 149, 185, 187, 190, 207, 211, 247, 254, 258, 263, 271, 307, 323, 331
monopolies, 34, 312, 315
Montagu, Col. Edward, 68, 69
Moores, John, 146
More Light Shining in Buckingham-shire, 333
Morgan, Anthony, 72
Morgan, Capt. Anthony, 72, 73
Morley, Herbert, 164
Morrill, John, 299
Moulton, Robert, 200
Mountjoy, William, 52
Moxon, James and Joseph, 156, 239
Murford, Peter, 313
Mytton, Col. Thomas, 208, 209

Naseby, battle of, 1, 68, 85, 88, 120, 121, 139, 223, 264
navy, 7, 88, 89, 121, 192, 199, 201, 202, 203, 204, 260, 264, 314, 315
Naylier, John, 185
Naylor, Quartermaster James, 181-2
Neate, Thomas, 52
Nedham, Marchamont, 33, 37, 38, 40
Neile, Richard, 34
New Model Army, 1, 2, 3, 7, 10, 20, 24, 42, 43-4, 68-9, 72-3, 76, 82, 86, 88, 90, 112, 116, 120, 121, 126, 127, 128, 130, 134-5, 139, 152, 155-6, 160, 163, 174, 175, 185, 196, 197-8, 201, 205, 216, 233, 250, 262, 264, 271, 273, 277, 278, 294, 299, 306-7, 314, 332-3
Newbury (Berkshire), 58, 116, 236
Newcastle-upon-Tyne, 6, 22, 33-5, 39, 46, 47, 64, 66, 67, 116, 121, 128, 130, 147, 233, 306
Newport (Isle of Wight), 3, 25, 118, 167, 215, 216
Newport Pagnell (Buckinghamshire), 35,
68, 266-9, 333
Newport Treaty, 3, 8-9, 13, 21, 22, 25, 33, 46, 50, 54, 70, 109, 141, 149, 175, 185, 187, 215, 216, 245, 262, 216, 271
newsbooks, 5, 6, 20, 23, 33, 37, 39, 46, 63, 67, 76, 79, 80, 82, 88, 104, 121, 132, 137, 141, 151, 212, 252, 290
Nichols, Ensign Joseph, 92
Norfolk, 1, 116, 160, 292-4
Norman Yoke, 141, 155, 331, 333
Northamptonshire, 24, 30, 116
'Northern Gentlemen', 46, 48
Northumberland, 47, 130
Northumberland Horse regiment, 68, 93, 141-7, 212
Northumberland, Algernon Percy Earl of, 250
Norwich, 242, 292, 293, 294, 295
Nottingham, 87, 156, 317, 319, 320
Nottingham Castle, 156, 165-6
Nottinghamshire, 1, 5, 6, 155, 166, 317-20, 328
Nye, Philip, 68

Oates, Samuel, 30, 242, 324
Okey, Col. John, 117, 278
Oldisworth, Michael, 264
Oliver, Richard, 67
Onslow, Sir Richard MP, 249, 250
Ormond, James Butler Marquis of, 192, 193, 194
Orpin, Capt. Edward, 92
Overton, Richard, 135, 273, 332, 333
Overton, Col. Robert, 7, 68, 91-3, 130, 147, 218, 229-31
Owen, Sir John, 208-9
Owthorpe (Nottinghamshire), 320-1
Oxfordshire, 6, 22-5, 155, 211-13, 273

Packets of Letters, 79, 80
Pain, John, 146
Paramour, Thomas, 327, 329
Parliament, of England and Wales, 1-9, 13, 16, 20, 22, 23, 24, 27, 28, 30, 33, 34, 36-40, 42, 44, 46-8, 50, 52, 54, 56, 63, 64-4, 66, 68, 70-1, 75-7, 78-80, 266
Parliament, of Scotland, 1, 2, 13, 102, 125, 126, 298, 307

INDEX

Parnel, James, 320
Partridge, John, 95, 128, 132, 153, 171, 176
Patshal, Joseph, 298
Paulden, Capt. Thomas, 89
pay, army's, 9, 18, 42-4, 71, 79, 80, 82, 84-5, 88, 110, 112, 115, 121, 124, 125, 127, 139, 143, 144, 153, 155, 156, 158, 182, 197, 202, 212, 217, 220, 221, 223, 229, 246, 250, 267, 272, 293, 297, 298, 299, 310-11, 317, 344
Peaceable Army, 264
Peacey, Jason, 243
Peacock, Robert, 313
Peck, Robert, 294
Pelham, Peregrine, 40
Pelham, Sir Thomas, 164
Pember, Francis, 297, 300
Pember, Francis Jr., 297, 300
Pembridg, John, 298
Pembroke, 139, 156
Pembroke, Philip Herbert Earl of, 264
Pennington, Alderman Isaac MP, 303
Penrose (Penne), Francis, 200
Penshurst (Kent), 206
Perfect Diurnall, A, 29, 75, 192, 214, 232, 290, 292
Perfect Occurrences, 331
Perfect Weekly Account, 52, 252
Peter (Peters), Hugh, 296
Peterborough, 185
Peters, Abraham, 313
Pierrepont, William, 171
Pitson, John, 313
Playford, John, 199, 204, 218
Plummer, Thomas, 328
Plymouth (Devon), 151, 152
Pontefract (Yorkshire), 3, 7, 46, 80, 87, 89, 112, 116, 121, 167, 175, 181, 185, 232-4, 317
Poole (Dorset), 53, 286, 309, 314, 315
Popham, Alexander, 285
Porton (Wiltshire), 53, 314
Portsmouth (Hampshire), 121, 202, 214-6, 309, 312, 313, 315
Potts, Sir John, MP, 293
Poulton, Capt. Thomas, 166-7
Powell, Col. Rhys, 139
Powell, James, 257

Poyer, Col. John, 65, 138, 139, 167
Prat, Richard, 313
Prentis, Francis, 328
Presbyterians,
  in religion, 2, 22, 25, 30, 34, 35, 40, 53, 85, 90, 109, 117, 120, 152, 160, 191, 197, 199, 201, 202, 212, 260, 269, 284, 285, 286, 294, 295, 299, 306, 307, 319
  in politics, 1, 20, 22, 24, 30, 35, 54, 109, 116, 126, 129, 164, 174, 191, 197, 202, 203, 212, 249, 269, 273, 278, 294, 299, 305, 306, 314, 319, 329
Preston, battle of, 3, 112, 116, 120, 121, 135, 155, 156, 181, 197
Pride, Col. Thomas, 3, 30, 109, 118-21, 123-7, 153, 157, 171, 175, 271, 307
Pride's Purge, 3-4, 5, 25 35, 41, 42, 48, 54, 56, 127, 152, 164, 176, 194, 197, 209, 232, 249, 250, 252, 278, 286, 288, 290, 294, 300, 323, 324
Propagation of the Gospel in Wales, Commission for, 209, 264, 296
Prynne, William MP, 285
Putney (Surrey), 2, 20, 43, 53, 69, 79, 86, 89, 112, 121, 130, 135, 152, 201, 250, 313, 314
Putney, Richard, 298
Pyne, John MP, 285, 286

Quakers, 25, 35. 181, 269, 320
Queenborough (Kent), 205

'R.A.' (publisher), 81, 85, 90
'R.W.' (publisher), 73
Radman, John, 76
Raglan (Monmothshire), 264
Rainborowe (Rainsborough), Col. Thomas, 82, 83, 84, 87, 88-90, 104, 116, 121, 144, 150, 167, 176, 201-2, 234, 241, 278
  regiment of, 76, 82, 87-8, 92, 121, 278
Raunce (Rauce), Cornet William, 72
Rawlings, Thomas, 296, 297, 300
Rawlinson, Richard, 328
Reade, Capt. Robert, 92
Reade, Lt.-Col. Thomas, 53, 68
Reckless, John, 320-1
Rede (Reade), John, 52, 53, 54, 313, 314
Reece, Henry, 160, 230

345

Rees, John, 20, 53, 58, 309, 314
'reformadoes', 306
Reformation (Constant Reformation), ship, 201
religion, freedom of, 2, 4, 8, 9, 13, 17, 31, 35, 40, 104, 135, 149, 155, 230, 242, 247, 250, 266, 269
Remonstrance of the Army, 3, 5, 37, 76, 79, 82, 87, 94-108, 111, 117, 118, 123, 128, 132, 153, 155, 162, 165-6, 173, 174, 181, 185, 187, 190, 196, 199, 214, 244, 246, 250, 258, 276, 286, 288, 290, 309, 312, 318
Reynardson, Abraham, 305
Reynolds, Col. John, 25, 183-6, 205-6, 216
Rich, Nathaniel, 76, 82, 104, 188, 263, 313, 314
Roberts, Stephen, 264
Robinson, Richard, 136
Robson, Richard, 329
Rogers, Maj. Wroth, 67, 69, 299, 300, 301
Rolph, Maj. Edmund, 216, 313, 314
Rose, Samuel, 67
Rupert, Prince, 256
Rushworth, John, 94, 103, 171
Russell, Ensign Thomas, 92
Rutland, 31, 239-42
Rye (Sussex), 153, 162, 163

Salisbury (Wiltshire), 53, 54
Saltmarsh, John, 260
Salway, Humphrey, 278
Salway, Richard, 278
Sanders (Saunders), Col. Thomas, 153-6, 157, 162, 165
Sanderson, Maj. John, 147, 181
Sandown Castle, 188
Sandwich (Kent), 328, 329
Sankie, Capt. Richard, 42, 78
Saunders, Maj. Robert, 216, 313
Savage, Thomas, 116
Saye and Sele, William Fiennes Viscount, 25, 212-13
Scilly Isles, 315
Scobel, H. (Henry Scobell), 304
Scotland, Scots, 1, 2, 3, 9, 13, 15, 22, 27, 30, 34, 46-7, 48, 57, 68, 70, 79, 83, 88, 102, 110, 112, 115, 116, 117, 119, 120, 121, 123, 124, 125, 126, 129, 130, 135, 137, 150, 158, 172, 175, 178, 181, 184, 196-7, 202, 208, 212, 218, 222, 234, 252, 253, 257, 259, 273, 278, 292, 296, 297, 298, 300, 303, 306, 307, 317, 318, 331, 334
Scott (Scot), Thomas MP, 334
Scotton, Lt. Edward, 116
Scowen (Scawen), Robert, 43
Scroop (Scrope), Col. Adrian, 104, 153-5, 157, 162, 165
Seaborne, Richard, 300
Seaborne, Thomas, 297, 300
Seddon, Peter, 320, 328
Self-Denying Ordinance, 68, 116, 160, 191, 202, 271
sequestrations, 48, 272, 300
Sevenoaks (Kent), 206
Sheffield, Co. Thomas, 111, 112
Sherbrooke family, 320
Sheward, Francis, 297
Ship Money, 14, 54, 204, 219, 228
Sidney (Sydney), Col. Algernon, 188, 206
Simmonds, John, 297
Simmons, Matthew, 175
Skegby (Nottinghamshire), 320
Skippon, Maj.-Gen. Philip, 130, 171, 271, 306, 307
Smalley, Francis, 29
Smarden (Kent), 329
Smith (Smyth), Capt. Henry, 31, 211, 212
Smith, Thomas, 197
Smith, William, 29, 31
Smithurst, R., 64
Snering, Ed., 313
Somerset, 6, 33, 37, 120, 256, 278, 283-6
South, Walter, 52, 54
Southampton (Hampshire), 309, 313, 315
Southwark, 13, 66, 120, 249, 250
Southwood, Edward, 116
St Albans (Hertfordshire), 63, 75, 76, 79, 80, 82, 85, 86, 87, 91, 93, 94, 95, 103-4, 111, 112, 128, 155, 165, 273-4, 318
St Nicholas at Wade (Kent), 329
St. George, ship, 199, 200

Stafford, William, 116
Stanard, Lt. Robert, 42, 78
stannaries, 149, 151
Sterky, Philip, 298
Stevens, John, 52, 54
Stokes, Edward, 52, 53, 54
Stokes, Francis, 313
Stoyle, Mark, 151
Strickland, Walter, MP, 286
Strode, William, MP, 286
Supreme authority or power, 14-15, 23, 51, 84, 99-100, 241, 225, 232, 323-4, 331-2, 326
Sussex, garrisons, 162-4
Sutton-in-Ashfield (Nottinghamshire), 320
Swaine (Swayne), Bennet, 52, 54
Swallow, Capt. Robert, 294
Swansea (Glamorgan), 264
Syler, Col. Edward, 191

Tanner, Thomas, 328
Tarant, Joseph, 313
Taunton (Somerset), 33, 285, 286
taxation, 2, 9, 17, 24, 44, 52, 54, 71, 84, 88, 119, 124, 143, 152, 153, 177, 193, 212, 219, 222, 264, 274, 278, 293, 298, 299, 300, 310
Taylor, Ed., 313
Taylor, John, 297
Temple, Peter, 30, 31
Templer, Ed., 313
Tenterden (Kent), 328
Thomason, George, 94, 111, 202
Thornhaugh, Col. Francis, 155, 156, 319
Thorpe, John, 328
Thorpe, Lt John, 92
Tichborne, Col. Robert, 89
tithes, 8, 9, 14, 24, 31, 51, 53, 63, 157, 159, 194, 209, 242, 247, 269, 273, 274, 283, 294, 309, 310, 324, 331, 333
Toll, Thomas, MP, 295
Tombes, John, 257, 278, 299
Tomson, Edward, 67
Turner, Sir James, 218
Twogood (Tongood), Lt. Sampson, 72
Tynemouth, 64, 66, 128, 130, 233

Underdown, David, 52, 53, 239, 271, 276, 285, 286
Unicorn, ship, 199, 200
Upper Broughton (Nottinghamshire), 321
Utting, Richard, 295

Vane, Sir Henry Jr, 46, 109
Venn, Col. John MP, 246, 303
Vermuyden, Col. Bartholomew, 116
Vermuyden, Cornelius, 116
Vernal, John, 297
Vote of No Addresses, 2, 3, 27, 29, 112, 114, 135, 173, 175, 271, 272, 283, 333

Waite (Wayte), Thomas, 31
Waite, Col. Thomas, 242
Wakefield (Yorkshire), 111, 112
Wales, 2, 3, 68, 70, 82, 92, 110, 115, 116, 120, 121, 123, 137-8, 155, 157, 163, 167, 190, 202, 204, 207, 208-9, 211, 246, 263, 264, 274, 277, 296, 299
Walker, Clement, 152, 160, 191, 285, 286
Walker, Francis, 297
Wallaston, Walter, 298
Walle, Humphrey, 313
Waller, Col. Sir Hardress, 149-52, 314
Waller, Gen. Sir William, 54, 126, 139, 152, 205, 314
Wallington, Capt. Joseph, 116
Walmer Castle, 188
Walsam, John, 298
Walton (Wauton), Col. Valentine, 44, 153, 157-60, 162, 165, 191, 271, 295
Walwyn, William, 305
Wanklyn, Malcolm, 44, 116, 314
Wansey, Lieut. Henry, 313, 314
Wansey, Thomas, 52
Wapping, 20, 87, 260
Ward, Thomas, 313, 314
Ware (Hertfordshire), 20, 58, 89, 112, 130, 201, 230, 233, 252, 273, 274
Wark, William Lord Grey of, 294, 299
Warmington, Andrew, 40
Warner, John, 306
Warren, Edward, 116
Warwick, Robert Rich Earl of, 199, 200, 201, 202, 203
Watford (Hertfordshire), 274

347

Weald (Kent and Sussex), 163, 260, 329
Weaver, John, 37, 40
'well affected', 6, 13, 19, 20, 22, 33-4, 37, 38, 50, 51, 56, 64-6, 83, 88, 92, 114, 115, 138, 149, 154, 173, 177-80, 181, 193, 207, 214, 215, 216, 232, 234, 239, 241, 244, 247, 248, 250, 252, 258, 266, 268, 271, 273, 276, 283, 284, 286, 288, 289, 292, 293, 301, 310, 312, 317, 323, 324, 326, 334
West, Edmund MP, 333
Westbury (Wiltshire), 52
Westminster Assembly, 50, 269, 286
Westmorland, 47, 48, 147, 197
Weston, Ro., 313
Wetwang, Joshua, 146, 147
Weymouth (Dorset), 309, 313, 314, 315
Whalley, Col. Edward, 44, 82, 85-6, 103, 104, 135, 171
Wheeler, Ensign John, 92
White, Capt. Steven, 42, 78
White, Henry, 52, 54
White, R. (Robert), 256
Whitehall, 1, 76, 79, 93, 104, 112, 135, 149, 153, 155, 192. 247, 254, 258, 266, 268
Whitelocke, Bulstrode, 70, 303
Whiting, Samuel, 116
Whittington, George, 82, 83, 95
Williams, Cornet William, 42, 78

Williams, Henry, 297-8
Williams, Henry, JP, 297
Williams, Roger, 301
Williams, Thomas, (Grand Jury member), 297
Williams, Thomas, (Gentleman), 298
Williams, William (Herefordshire), 298
Williamson, R. (Robert), 112, 126
Wilson, Nehemiah, 134
Windsor (Berkshire), 3, 35, 58, 67, 73, 128, 129, 132, 134, 137, 139, 141, 153, 185, 204, 211, 216, 244, 245-6, 249, 258, 288, 334
Winthrop, Stephen, 301
Wither, George, 249, 250
Wogan, Capt. Edward, 278
Wolfe, John, 298
Woodhouse, James, 298
Worcestershire, 276-8, 300
Wren, Bishop Matthew, 294
Wroth, Sir Thomas, MP, 285
Wroth, William, 69
Wylde, George, 278
Wylde, John, 278, 285
Wymondham (Norfolk), 294

Y Dalar Hir, battle, 208
Yarmouth, Great (Norfolk), 86, 155, 294
Yorkshire, 3, 37-40, 47, 48, 68, 80, 116, 120, 201, 209, 246, 290

Also from
BREVIARY STUFF PUBLICATIONS

Ralph Anstis, WARREN JAMES AND THE DEAN FOREST RIOTS, *The Disturbances of 1831*
£17.00 • 242pp *paperback* • 191x235mm • ISBN 978-0-9564827-7-8

John E. Archer, 'BY A FLASH AND A SCARE', *Arson, Animal Maiming, and Poaching in East Anglia 1815-1870*
£15.00 • 206pp *paperback* • 191x235mm • ISBN 978-0-9564827-1-6

Victor Bailey, CHARLES BOOTH'S POLICEMEN, *Crime, Police and Community in Jack-the-Ripper's London*
£17.00 • 162pp *paperback* • *2 colour and 8 b/w images* • 140x216mm • ISBN 978-0-9564827-6-1

Victor Bailey, ORDER AND DISORDER IN MODERN BRITAIN, *Essays on Riot, Crime, Policing and Punishment*
£15.00 • 214pp *paperback* • *5 b/w images* • 191x235mm • ISBN 978-0-9570005-5-1

Roger Ball, Dave Beckwith, Steve Hunt, Mike Richardson, STRIKERS, HOBBLERS, CONCHIES & REDS, *A Radical History of Bristol, 1880-1939*
£18.50 • 366pp *paperback* • *101 b/w images* • 156x234mm • ISBN 978-0-9929466-0-9

John Belchem, 'ORATOR' HUNT, *Henry Hunt and English Working Class Radicalism*
£17.50 • 248pp *paperback* • 191x235mm • ISBN 978-0-9564827-8-5

Alastair Bonnett & Keith Armstrong (eds.), THOMAS SPENCE: THE POOR MAN'S REVOLUTIONARY
£15.00 • 214pp *paperback* • 156x234mm • ISBN 978-0-9570005-9-9

Bob Bushaway, BY RITE, *Custom, Ceremony and Community in England 1700-1880*
£16.00 • 206pp *paperback* • 191x235mm • ISBN 978-0-9564827-6-1

Malcolm Chase, THE PEOPLE'S FARM, *English Radical Agrarianism 1775-1840*
£12.00 • 212pp *paperback* • 152x229mm • ISBN 978-0-9564827-5-4

Malcolm Chase, EARLY TRADE UNIONISM, Fraternity, *Skill and the Politics of Labour*
£17.00 • 248pp *paperback* • 191x235mm • ISBN 978-0-9570005-2-0

Nigel Costley, WEST COUNTRY REBELS
£20.00 • 220pp *full colour illustrated paperback* • 216x216mm • ISBN 978-0-9570005-4-4

James Epstein, THE LION OF FREEDOM, *Feargus O'Connor and the Chartist Movement, 1832-1842*
£17.00 • 296pp *paperback* • 156x234mm • ISBN 978-0-9929466-1-6

James Epstein, RADICAL EXPRESSION, *Political Language, Ritual, and Symbol in England, 1790-1850*
£15.00 • 220pp *paperback* • 156x234mm • ISBN 978-0-9929466-2-3

Chris Fisher, CUSTOM, WORK & MARKET CAPITALISM, *The Forest of Dean Colliers, 1788-1888*
£14.00 • 198pp *paperback* • 156x234mm • ISBN 978-0-9929466-7-8

Also from
BREVIARY STUFF PUBLICATIONS

Ariel Hessayon (ed.), THE REFINER'S FIRE, *The Collected Works of TheaurauJohn Tany*
£25.00 • 552pp *paperback* • 156x234mm • ISBN 978-0-9570005-7-5

Catherine Howe, HALIFAX 1842, *A Year of Crisis*
£14.50 • 202pp *paperback* • 156x234mm • ISBN 978-0-9570005-8-2

Barry Reay, THE LAST RISING OF THE AGRICULTURAL LABOURERS, *Rural Life and Protest in Nineteenth-Century England*
£15.00 • 192pp *paperback* • 191x235mm • ISBN 978-0-9564827-2-3

Philip Ruff, A TOWERING FLAME, *The Life & Times of the Elusive Latvian Anarchist Peter the Painter*
£17.00 • 284pp *paperback* • 156x234mm • ISBN 978-0-9929466-5-4
£25.00 • 284pp *hardback* • 156x234mm • ISBN 978-0-9929466-8-5

Buchanan Sharp, IN CONTEMPT OF ALL AUTHORITY, *Rural Artisans and Riot in the West of England, 1586-1660*
£15.00 • 204pp *paperback* • 191x235mm • ISBN 978-0-9564827-0-9

Dorothy Thompson, THE CHARTISTS, *Popular Politics in the Industrial Revolution*
£17.00 • 280pp *paperback* • 191x235mm • ISBN 978-0-9570005-3-7

E. P. Thompson, WHIGS AND HUNTERS, *The Origin of the Black Act*
£16.00 • 278pp *paperback* • 156x234mm • ISBN 978-0-9570005-2-0
£30.00 • 278pp *hardback* • 156x234mm • ISBN 978-0-9929466-6-1

David Walsh, MAKING ANGELS IN MARBLE, *The Conservatives, the Early Industrial Working Class and Attempts at Political Incorporation*
£15.00 • 268pp *paperback* • 191x235mm • ISBN 978-0-9570005-0-6

David Walsh, THE SONS OF BELIAL, *Protest and Community Change in the North-West, 1740-1770*
£16.00 • 272pp *paperback* • 156x234mm • ISBN 978-0-9929466-9-2

Roger Wells, INSURRECTION, *The British Experience 1795-1803*
£22.00 • 372pp *paperback* • 191x235mm • ISBN 978-0-9564827-3-0

Roger Wells, WRETCHED FACES, *Famine in Wartime England 1793-1801*
£23.00 • 412pp *paperback* • 191x235mm • ISBN 978-0-9564827-4-7

David Worrall, RADICAL CULTURE, *Discourse, Resistance and Surveillance, 1790-1820*
£15.00 • 186pp *paperback* • 156x234mm • ISBN 978-0-9929466-4-7

www.ingramcontent.com/pod-product-compliance
Lightning Source LLC
Chambersburg PA
CBHW031753220426
43662CB00007B/389